Crime and Networks

One of the more innovative fields that has been steadily on the rise in criminology over the last decade consists of the application of the social network framework to various forms of crime phenomena. *Crime and Networks* combines the most recent empirical research contributions from the top scholars in this area. More than any other past research endeavor, the seventeen chapters in this book transpose to criminology the many conceptual and methodological options from the social network analysis repertoire. *Crime and Networks* pushes the sociology of crime to new levels by introducing the most advanced assessments of the structural and organizational features of crime.

Carlo Morselli is a Professor at the École de criminologie, Université de Montréal and Deputy Director of the International Centre for Comparative Criminology. His research focuses on criminal networks and organized crime, with recent studies aimed specifically at illegal firearm markets, synthetic drug markets, collusion in the construction industry, and denunciation. In 2011, he was awarded the Outstanding Publication Award from the International Association for the Study of Organized Crime (IASOC) for his book *Inside Criminal Networks* (2009). He is also the author of *Contacts, Opportunities, and Criminal Enterprise* (2005) and a series of articles that have been published in *Criminology*; *Journal of Research in Crime and Delinquency*; *Critical Criminology*; *Crime, Law, and Social Change*; and *Social Networks*. Since 2011, he has served as the Editor-in-Chief for the journal *Global Crime*.

CRIMINOLOGY AND JUSTICE STUDIES SERIES

Edited by **Chester Britt, Northeastern University, and Shaun L. Gabbidon,**
        Penn State Harrisburg

Criminology and Justice Studies offers works that make both intellectual and stylistic innovations in the study of crime and criminal justice. The goal of the series is to publish works that model the best scholarship and thinking in the criminology and criminal justice field today, but in a style that connects that scholarship to a wider audience including advanced undergraduates, graduate students, and the general public. The works in this series help fill the gap between academic monographs and encyclopedic textbooks by making innovative scholarship accessible to a large audience without the superficiality of many texts.

Books in the Series:

Published:

Biosocial Criminology: New Directions in Theory and Research edited by Anthony Walsh and Kevin M. Beaver

Community Policing in America by Jeremy M. Wilson

Criminal Justice Theory: Explaining the Nature and Behavior of Criminal Justice edited by David E. Duffee and Edward R. Maguire

Lifers: Seeking Redemption in Prison by John Irwin

Today's White Collar Crime by Hank J. Brightman

White Collar Crime: Opportunity Perspectives by Michael Benson and Sally Simpson

The New Criminal Justice: American Communities and the Changing World of Crime Control by John Klofas, Natalie Hipple, and Edmund McGarrell

The Policing of Terrorism: Organizational and Global Perspectives by Mathieu Deflem

Criminological Perspectives in Race and Crime, 2/e by Shaun Gabbidon

Corrections by Jeanne Stinchcomb

Community Policing by Michael Palmiotto

A Theory of African American Offending by James Unnever and Shaun Gabbidon

When Crime Appears: The Role of Emergence by Jean McGloin, Christopher Sullivan, and Leslie Kennedy

Voices from Criminal Justice edited by Heith Copes and Mark Pogrebin

Crime and the Life Course, 2/e by Michael Benson

Human Trafficking: Interdisciplinary Perspectives edited by Mary C. Burke

Wrongful Convictions and Miscarriages of Justice edited by C. Ronald Huff & Martin Killias

Race, Law and American Society, 2/e: 1607 to Present by Gloria J. Browne-Marshall

Research Methods in Crime and Justice by Brian Withrow

Forthcoming:
Wrongful Conviction and Criminal Justice Reform edited by Marvin Zalman & Julia Carrano

Books of Related Interest
Regression Analysis for the Social Sciences by Rachel A. Gordon

Applied Statistics for the Social and Health Sciences by Rachel A. Gordon

The Connected City by Zachary P. Neal

Ethnography and the City by Richard E. Ocejo

Forthcoming:
Social Statistics: Contemporary Techniques for a Data-Filled World, 2ⁿᵈ Edition by Thomas J. Linneman

GIS and Spatial Analysis, 2nd Edition by Robert Parker Nash and Emily K. Asencio

Crime and Networks

Edited by
Carlo Morselli

Routledge
Taylor & Francis Group

NEW YORK AND LONDON

First published 2014
by Routledge
711 Third Avenue, New York, NY 10017

and by Routledge
2 Park Square, Milton Park, Abingdon, Oxon OX14 4RN

Routledge is an imprint of the Taylor & Francis Group, an informa business

Library of Congress Cataloging in Publication Data
Crime and networks / edited by Carlo Morselli.
    pages cm. — (Criminology and justice studies series)
    Includes bibliographical references and index.
    1. Criminology. 2. Criminals—Social networks. 3. Criminal behavior.
    4. Crime—Sociological aspects. I. Morselli, Carlo.
    HV6025.C696 2014
    364.106—dc23
    2013015127

ISBN: 978–0–415–64453–2 (hbk)
ISBN: 978–0–415–71050–3 (pbk)
ISBN: 978–1–315–88501–8 (ebk)

Typeset in Sabon and Helvetica Neue
by Swales & Willis Ltd, Exeter, Devon

Printed and bound in the United States of America by Sheridan Books, Inc. (a Sheridan Group Company).

CONTENTS

The dynamic and sometimes diffuse nature of membership makes gang boundaries difficult to discern. The current study draws on social network analysis of co-offending data to assess its utility in identifying the "core" membership of a youth gang—the *856 gang* — active in a rural region of British Columbia, Canada. Findings reveal that a total of 60 offenders were potential members of the 856 gang and 13 offenders could be defined as core members.

PART II: ORGANIZED CRIME NETWORKS

Chicago's Prohibition era syndicate represents one of the most studied criminal enterprises. At its core is the mythical Al Capone. This chapter re-examines the Capone era mob using a unique relational dataset created by coding more than 3,000 pages of primary documents. Findings reveal the precise ways in which the criminal networks associated with Al Capone overlapped with political and union networks.

Chinese human smugglers (or snakeheads) are mostly enterprising individuals who use their social networks to provide underground travel services to facilitate the migration of their compatriots to their destination countries. These circles of social contacts resemble a series of cartwheels connected through their central nodes in which a chain-like smuggling process hinges heavily on the successful delivery of required services at each stage. While the enterprise of human smuggling as a whole exhibits much flexibility and resiliency toward market uncertainties and constraints, individual networks nonetheless are highly vulnerable to structural disturbances.

Based on data from police investigations, this chapter examines the network composition of four wholesale cocaine trafficking groups. Analyses focus particularly on the structure of these networks, key participants and roles, and the variety of facilitators from legitimate contexts that also played pivotal parts in the overall drug distribution schemes.

Building off earlier work in which judges' sentencing comments were used to build a network of drug trafficking syndicates that operated in Australia during the 1990s, this chapter evaluates the effectiveness of hypothetical intervention strategies that aim to dismantle the network. Results offer some guidance to intelligence and operational law enforcement when determining which individuals to target and specifically the impact of targeting individuals based on high degree centrality and roles within the networks, as compared with a baseline (random) intervention.

This chapter analyzes network positioning in two mafia-type organizations belonging to the 'Ndrangheta, a mafia-type criminal organization originating from Calabria. The focus is on strategic and vulnerable positioning within the networks. Results show that task and hierarchy are associated with network centrality, but also with accusation, arrest, and conviction. By contrast, high social status within the networks exhibits limited association with network centrality and the outcomes of criminal proceedings.

Transnational drug trafficking requires trade networks that often overlap with legitimate markets; however, countries that are active in the drug trade rarely occupy key positions in the global legitimate economy. Based on data collected by the United Nations Office on Drugs and Crime from 1998 to 2007, this chapter examines separate networks of exchanges between countries involved in the trafficking of cocaine, heroin, and marijuana. Findings demonstrate how, in several ways, transnational drug trafficking is structured inversely to legitimate trade economies.

PART III: CYBERCRIME NETWORKS

Stories of the exploits of computer hackers who have broken into supposedly secure government and corporate information systems appear almost daily on the front pages of newspapers and technology websites. This case study is based on the seized communication logs of 10 confirmed co-offenders and examines how monetization and skills play key roles in profit-oriented malicious hacking and why trust is low in such a network. The need for monetization and social skills as well as the lack of trust between members accounts for why hacker networks are so ephemeral and vulnerable to law enforcement disruption.

This study focuses on how hackers shape their personal communications in order to gather information on potential victims. Using logs of online Internet Chat Relay (IRC), ego networks of hackers that visited hacking chat rooms and talked about hacking with others are examined. Hackers interact with each other in small and dense networks where direct connectivity is more important than indirect connections. The number of contacts in the ego networks is limited in most cases and the number of brokers is fairly poor. Such communications evolve in cliquish networks where everyone knows each other and in which novice hackers are able to hone their skills in a variety of areas.

The availability of internet services has greatly facilitated the production, reproduction, and dissemination of child pornography as well as the creation of communities or support networks to conceal underground activities. Following a description of the newsgroup internet service Usenet, this chapter analyzes how this service is used by cyberpedophiles to share child pornography material as well as ideas and experiences concerning their illicit activities, thus creating a virtual subculture. An analysis of 45 days of text-based communications shows that this community is built through messages that provide moral support, deal with conflicts and disputes, or provide technical information, as well as those that promote pedophile-oriented content.

PART IV: ECONOMIC CRIME NETWORKS

This study examines the network dynamics of a Ponzi scheme. Drawing on survey data, the chapter assesses how investors were drawn into the fraud and the spread of skepticism once it began to unravel to understand the lifecycle of the Eron mortgage fraud. Evidence is provided for a contagious diffusion process and that network relations are instrumental to insulating investors, and thus maintaining their position within the scheme.

The Watergate scandal is used to model the social structure of political conspiracy and to predict which specific conspirators defect from Nixon's cadre. Block modeling the sociomatrices of the Watergate corruption reveals political conspiracies to be organized by decentralized cabals coordinating with a core cadre. Intermediating roles/positions and betweenness centrality predict defection as well as the probability of conviction in court and prison time served. Findings show that brokers benefit individually from their structurally autonomous position, but the autonomy of the individual brokers is a liability for the overall group-level conspiracy as it is at the structural position of the broker where the conspiracy collapses.

PART V: EXTREMIST NETWORKS

In this chapter, a unique longitudinal data set of the Noordin Top terrorist network from 2001–2010 is examined in order to explore how the network's topography (e.g., centralization, density, degree of fragmentation) and effectiveness (e.g., recruitment, number of quality network members) changed over time in light of efforts by Indonesian authorities to disrupt it. This analysis demonstrates how terrorist networks adapt to a hostile environment. While making them more effective, such adaptation can also create new vulnerabilities, particularly when terrorist groups that become too dense or fail to decentralize can become vulnerable to rapid deterioration in the event of a well-connected member's capture.

Conflict-affected environments are prone to housing the "dirty" end of illicit commodity markets, and the protraction of violent conflict where illicit markets proliferate is indeed advantageous to the criminal networks that profit from them. This chapter demonstrates how social network analysis constitutes a vital element toward a better understanding of the transnational organized crime and conflict nexus. While a network mapping of the linkages between trafficking groups and other significant actors highlights "the usual suspects," such as political powerbrokers and militia leaders, the analysis also reveals the importance of actors beyond the immediate conflict environment, and particularly purchasers from the developed "West" that play a critical role in shaping the conflict landscape.

PREFACE

This book is comprised of a collection of studies by the top researchers in the area of crime and network analysis. Recent years have brought us a considerable expansion in innovative studies using various forms of empirical sources that have led to the development and refinement of the social network perspective within criminology. As a community of researchers, we concur that seeking the structure of crime and co-offending is always preferable to assuming such matters. Our principal aim in *Crime and Networks* is to establish more systematic methods and theoretical paths for identifying key patterns in a wide range of crime networks.

The book is divided into five parts. Each part addresses a specific criminal phenomenon: co-offending in Part I; organized crime in Part II; cybercrime in Part III; economic crime in Part IV; and extremist groups in Part V. Each chapter in this book addresses the problem, research tradition, data and methodological background, and empirical underpinnings for a specific analytical object. The chapters that make up this collection are all empirical contributions from the rapidly growing community of experts across a wide range of cultural settings in criminology.

Crime and Networks is the first book of its kind. With its unique focus on social networks across a diversity of crimes and theoretical outlooks, it surpasses the scope and comprehensive outlook of any past study in this field. The book is also designed to relate to newcomers and advanced researchers in this field, from either academic or practical research settings. Indeed, one of the more exciting expectations we have for this book concerns the array of replications and extensions that its various chapters will generate over the years to come. What the community of researchers in this growing field has proven over the past decade is that the challenges of establishing an empirical repertoire and developing an increasingly uniform analytical focus may be overcome. A decade ago, several scholars were promoting the strengths of social network analysis and identifying promising qualitative and quantitative data sources for criminological research. Today, few are simply proposing what should be done. Indeed, such talk has been displaced by actual research, as researchers are increasingly accessing and organizing their empirical sources to demonstrate the many analytical paths and substantive issues that emerge when applying the social network framework to crime. In many ways, this rise is reminiscent of the development of social network analysis as a key sociological paradigm over the past 50 years.

Within the academic teaching community, *Crime and Networks* will be suitable for a variety of methodological and substantive undergraduate or graduate courses. There are a growing number of courses on criminal networks across criminology departments—many of these courses were created and continue to be taught by the authors in this book. While such courses are the ideal fit for this book, the diversity of topics, empirical sources, and methods covered across the chapters also make the book suitable for methodological courses in qualitative, quantitative, or mixed methods. Past experiences using such material for teaching have proven that even the novice researcher can easily grasp notions of matrices, dyads, cliques, or key players and design their first research attempt with this unique method. All it takes to begin is a keen eye for identifying relationships in a group setting, an appreciation for the social basis of crime, and a willingness to learn the basic applications of the many softwares that are available for such analyses. *Crime and Networks* is not simply a methodological reference. As a theoretical and substantive contribution, it would be suitable in any specialized class on the crime phenomena that are the focus in each of the five parts. Finally, and at a more general level, this book also has its place in traditional sociology of crime courses and in any seminar that addresses new and innovative approaches to the study of crime.

Introduction

Carlo Morselli

It is amazing how things change in a few years. During the summer of 2006, Federico Varese and I sent out a call for papers for a special issue on social network analysis and crime for the journal *Global Crime*. We did succeed in preparing a slim issue (five articles plus book reviews), but our concern at the time was with the lack of research in what we believed to be a growing area in criminology and beyond.

Federico and I were probably too precocious in our endeavor. A shift seemed to take place a year or two after our issue was published in 2007. I have been studying in this area since my doctoral work in the mid-1990s. At the time, the few of us who were exploring this area were all aware of Sparrow's (1991) proposal to apply social network analysis to facilitate law enforcement efforts to assess and confront the structural features of various forms of group-level crime. Earlier social network frameworks were also applied in the area of organized crime or criminal enterprise, but most were linked to contesting claims of the presence of a rigid and hierarchical-like Mafia phenomenon. Whether in Italy (Hess, 1973; Blok, 1974), the Netherlands (Klerks, 2001), or the United States (Albini, 1971; Ianni, 1972), the network approach proved effective in demonstrating that what appeared to be formal organizational settings were, on the contrary, loosely structured agglomerations that were shaped for flexibility, a feature that also accounted for much of the more reputed criminal organizations' adaptability, influence, and durability in various contexts.

By the late 1990s, more serious attempts to follow through on Sparrow's call to directly apply the measures and methods of the growing social network analytical field were emerging. Soon after the publication of our *Global Crime* issue, Klaus von Lampe edited a special issue that assembled papers presented at a formidable workshop that took place in Berlin in February 2008. Klaus was somewhat more organized than Federico and I—he had the good idea of creating a workshop event to promote the issue and he also included a mix of criminology researchers and social network specialists. The special issue (with seven articles) was published in 2010 in the journal *Trends in Organized Crime*.

Shadowing the trend representing the rise of social network analysis in the social sciences in general, the application of a social network framework in crime-related research has experienced a sizeable increase over recent years. This rise in criminology has lagged behind the prominent position that the framework has gained in sociology, where the field's main publication outlet, the journal *Social Networks*, has steadily climbed the scholarly rankings and in which the network approach has become amongst the dominant perspectives in a wide range of research areas.

Indications that a change was taking place in crime-related research was first demonstrated by Bergin (2009), who tracked the number of papers applying a social network approach to "dark network" areas that were published annually between 1975 and 2008. The rise takes place in 2001, when the number of papers triples. That year also coincides with Krebs' (2001) seminal analysis of the 9/11 hijacking network, which essentially showed that much can be done and stated with open sources and basic network analysis. By 2006, the publication output doubled once again (Bergin, 2009).

I have not kept track of the annual publication rate of crime-related network studies since, but I have kept pace with the substantial consistency that is reflected by the one or two papers in this area that I review on a monthly basis for scholarly journals. Some of my colleagues who are also studying in this area have shared similar experiences. There is indeed a buzz emerging around this research field.

The relevance of social network analysis for criminology is not new. For many, the field, as we know it today, was born in a crime and deviance environment (see Freeman, 2004; Morselli, 2009; Carrington, 2011). The context was in the Sing Sing Correctional Facility or the Hudson School for Girls, in which Jacob Moreno developed his seminal sociometric research designs for understanding group mechanisms within these settings. Neither Moreno nor most of the researchers that followed over the past seven decades were preoccupied with the deviant element underlying this pioneering research. But crime and deviance settings do shape social networks and the behavior of participants therein. With the rise in past research and publication of the present book, social network analysis has found its way back into the criminological setting once again.

One strong indication of a rising field occurs when scholars begin to appraise an area with elaborate research reviews. Three solid and complete reviews of social network research in criminology have appeared over recent years. The most recent, by Papachristos (2011), argues that we are in the midst of a "networked criminology." His review provides us with the extensive heritage that the network approach has had before entering criminology. From the contemporary cliché of the "connected world" (p. 101) to the rich tradition of research from sociology, political science, anthropology, public health, and physics, Papachristos makes the key point that "social networks matter" and that criminologists have been somewhat late to recognize this. Confirming Bergin's earlier assessment of the rise of the social network approach in crime-related research, he indicates an increase in research in this area around the mid-2000s. Rightfully, Papachristos argues that "[c]riminology is missing an opportunity to test and expand upon some of its most treasured theories and concepts. Indeed, criminological theory oozes with network imagery and jargon" (pp. 102–103). The benefits of the network framework for criminology emerge in two general forms: 1) in its offering of new objects of analysis (or dependent variables); and 2) in the creation of new and important explanations (independent variables) for understanding various forms of criminal phenomena. Such concepts and variables may be designed to account for a wide range of individual and collective behavior.

McGloin and Kirk's (2010) extensive overview of research in social networks and crime provided a similar appraisal. They situated the intellectual tradition of the crime and network approach at the crossroads between Sutherland's differential association theory and Hirschi's social control theory. McGloin and Kirk also highlighted the unique features of the network approach and how it contributes to existing criminological knowledge. First, a new unit of analysis is introduced to the mix, with a direct focus on relationships between actors rather than on the attributes of actors. Second, new assumptions on how social structure influences criminal behavior are added to the criminological repertoire. Such insights lead to the creation of new variables that may be intermingled with the traditional attribute-based concepts that have guided our general field. Advocates of this network framework are also able to cross over into existing criminological frameworks with established concepts, such as rational choice, opportunity, interactionism, situated action, social learning, social contagion, social bonds, social disorganization, and general social support. Third, the relational focus of the network approach allows us to provide a direct operationalization of the "transmission of influence, skills, and norms" (p. 20) that is so central to many criminological theories.

Carrington's (2011) review of past research on social network applications in criminology covers the most ground. He also highlights the capacity of the network perspective to transcend the social support (or control) and differential association traditions in criminology. His review also covers the rising research field on criminal networks, in which this book's 17 chapters are the most recent contributions. Within the criminal network strand, Carrington positions past research along two analytical paths: 1) studies that focus on how "intra and inter-organizational network structures" emerge and respond to the unique crime-related conditions that surround them; and 2) studies that address the performance issues of such network structures. Such research has drawn considerably from the wealth of studies on non-criminal networks, with the most influential insights coming from corporate and career networks, hierarchy and market distinctions, social embeddedness, centrality and key player positioning, homophily, and social capital. He also emphasizes that social network analysis has re-oriented key criminological concepts, particularly on issues such as peer influences and selection, the social organization of crime, social disorganization, gang involvement, and desistance.

One drawback that Carrington, Papachristos, and McGloin and Kirk raise in regard to past research in this area is its exploratory and descriptive nature. Access to a variety of data sources and the creation of new research designs have also been amongst the more serious challenges facing researchers in this area. The studies in the present book not only contribute to the rising research field on crime and networks, but they also carry the field to a new level by exposing new sources, providing more detailed descriptions, and proposing novel explanatory frameworks.

This book is, thus, the most recent piece of evidence that there is a rapid rise of social network analytical applications in crime-related areas. Ironically, it is the product of an idea that began with a scholar who was not a researcher in this area. In 2009, Andrew Goldsmith, at the time the Director of the Centre for Transnational Crime Prevention in Wollongong, Australia, decided to organize a workshop on illicit networks to learn more about this field. He invited a small group of scholars who had already published in this area and asked them to present some of their research over the past decade. Andrew's timing was impeccable, and little did he know that this would become an annual and increasingly expanding event, another irony that reflects the emergent nature of many networks. The Illicit Networks Workshop is now moving toward its fifth edition and shows no signs of slowing down.

The chapters that were selected for publication in this book were first presented at the third (2011) workshop in Montreal, Canada. The most striking feature of this ensemble of studies is in the range of crimes that are addressed. While previous research in this area has contributed significantly to areas more akin to organized crime and terrorism, the chapters in this book address the social organizational and structural features of criminal collectives not only in these traditional criminal contexts, but also in areas such as economic crime, cybercrime, and general co-offending contexts. Each chapter provides an empirical contribution to the crime and network perspective. In doing so, the authors in this book demonstrate the high level of creativity that is required to surpass the main challenges that have confronted researchers in this area in the past. The first challenge begins with accessing relevant data sources that allow us to express our main concepts and propositions in the real world. Whether through official data, survey data, archival data, or various forms of case studies, the empirical sources used in the chapters in this book are amongst the most unique and innovative to date. The second challenge concerns application of social network analytical methods. The studies across this book offer a greater variety than in any previous publication. Ranging from micro to macro outlooks, the chapters are comprised of a repertoire of analyses that range from qualitative assessments of interactions between participants in a common criminal network to the application of cutting-edge statistical techniques that have been recently developed within the field of social network analysis. A third challenge is the relevant application of such a perspective for conceptual purposes. In the past, we have been exposed to some research that has applied tools and methods from the social network field to crime-related settings with little contribution beyond the presentation of an enticing network graph. The authors in this book are not simply applying social network analysis; they are demonstrating how a social network analytical framework allows us to ask new questions about crime, unravel new features of crime, and re-assess what we know about crime. These 17 studies across the five parts in the book place the social network framework amongst the established perspectives in contemporary criminological research.

Part I focuses on co-offending. Each chapter presents the key issues and results from what promises to be a strong contribution to general criminology as scholars access massive datasets of co-offending records across different regions of the world and begin to explore the many patterns that emerge for all forms of crime. In Chapter 1, McGloin and Nguyen lay down the groundwork for research in this area. The chapter covers the basic cooptation processes that have been consistently touched upon in criminological research, but rarely offered any central focus. An additional focus of McGloin and Nguyen's assessment is on the spontaneous or deliberate selection mechanisms that generate co-offending relationships, which ultimately provide the necessary insights for understanding the transition between the making and maintenance of co-offending networks. In Chapter 2, van Mastrigt and Carrington follow through on McGloin and Nguyen's main points by examining the selection processes that are in play within a co-offending (or co-arrest) network in England. Their focus is on how homophily is centered on sex and age variables within this mass network. Such "inbreeding" may be consistent with past research on this concept, but two unique features raised in this chapter concern the variations found between males and females in their same-sex co-offending patterns and the finding that adult offenders are less homophilic than youths. In Chapter 3, Iwanski and Frank shift the co-offending focus to drug crimes in British Columbia and how key network properties in such settings vary across time. In this study, the type of crime is added to the homophily repertoire, with individuals arrested for the same type of crime accounting for one of the main clustering patterns within the network. The development of such clusters and the emergence of gatekeepers and more serious offenders therein were highly dependent on the level of network centralization. Such patterns were ultimately found to be at the root of recruitment processes between established traffickers and incoming young offenders. In Chapter 4, Bouchard and Konarski provide a subset analysis of a co-offending network by examining the boundaries surrounding one of the more reputed gangs in British Columbia. Their concern was not simply on the gang itself, but also on the extensive set of past co-offenders that were linked to the core members that were directly targeted during a police investigation. By expanding the network beyond the core, Bouchard and

Konarski demonstrate that many non-targeted offenders were as central to the network as the targeted core and, inversely, that some within the targeted core were not as central as those who were non-targeted. Recalling past studies, the authors strongly urge law enforcement agencies to integrate the practical applications of social network analysis for intelligence-led investigations.

Bouchard and Konarski's chapter provides the ideal transition toward Part II of the book and the six chapters on organized crime networks. Chapter 5 provides Papachristos and Smith's exhaustive efforts to reconstruct the criminal entrepreneurial network surrounding Al Capone during Chicago's Prohibition era. The strengths of the network framework are indeed in play in this chapter, as the authors assemble mass sets of archival data from the 1920s Chicago Crime Commission and other agencies to retrace the symbiotic networks that embedded organized crime in Chicago during these years. With the multiplexity concept at the forefront, Papachristos and Smith offer a clear-cut demonstration of the organizing crime argument that criminal organizations cannot expand or survive without direct relationships with the legitimate political, economic, and labor elite. In Chapter 6, another important area of organized crime research is addressed as Zhang uses a qualitative approach to examine snakehead networks that orchestrate the smuggling of humans between China and the US. With a cartwheel design as a guiding image for his analysis, Zhang focuses on the brokers in the network and their contribution to maintaining a flexible division of labor. While confirming the strengths of such brokerage positioning that have been found in past research, this chapter also pushes the issue further by demonstrating that the concentration of resources around a small set of actors generates vulnerabilities toward external threats, thus rendering these action-set networks as ephemeral as most groups that form in criminal market settings. In Chapter 7, Giménez-Salinas Framis pursues the key player issue by examining the structure of drug trafficking operations that were targeted by a Spanish police agency in four separate investigations. As with the previous chapters, the author highlights the inherent flexibility across each operation, while also identifying the pivotal actors from legitimate business and community sectors that facilitated drug trafficking activities. Such peripheral participants are generally overlooked in both research and practice, making the facilitator feature one of the more important areas of inquiry to pursue in the crime and network field. Bright, Greenhill, and Levenkova's study in Chapter 8 is arguably the most practice-based study in this book. The research focuses on a methamphetamine trafficking network that was in operation in Australia during the 1990s and generates a series of simulations for intervention strategies that may be applied in police or intelligence settings. The network under analysis is determined to be scale-free (or built around a small set of central actors). Targeting the most connected actors did fragment the network; however, the most effective intervention consisted of a mixed strategy that integrated central positions and roles. The concern with strategic positioning within a crime network is also pursued in Chapter 9, in Calderoni's analysis of two 'Ndrangheta organizations in Calabria, Italy. The study converges on centrality and clustering measures in each of the networks and assesses the specific characteristics of participants' roles, hierarchical positioning, and social status. These features are subsequently related to criminal justice outcomes, such as arrest and conviction. Calderoni's findings lend further support to the argument that, while the reputed leaders of known criminal organizations are likely to have central positions within the wide criminal network surrounding the organization, other high-status participants are less likely to revolve around the center of the network. More importantly, the main difference between the centrally positioned leader and the peripheral high-status player is in the high likelihood of arrest and conviction for the former.

This chapter, while not clearing the matter completely, does add to the increasingly relevant suggestion that the most reputed and publically renowned participants in a crime network are probably not the most important actors. Strategic positioning is taken to a new macro level in Chapter 10, as Boivin offers a unique analysis of international drug trafficking with a country-level unit of analysis. Using a world-systems framework as a guideline for assessing the structure of cocaine, heroin, and marijuana trafficking, Boivin finds an inverted world to the core–periphery organization that has been generally attributed to legitimate global trade, in which the legitimate trade core countries are dependent on the legitimate trade peripheral countries. This is particular to cocaine and heroin trade, for which domestic production is less likely to emerge across a wide range of countries, thus maintaining source countries as staple fixtures of each economy (the cannabis trade would be the exception).

Part III compiles a series of studies on the rapidly growing field of cybercrime research. With more and more researchers gaining knowledge on the various techniques and software that are available for navigating social interactions on the internet, it is quite probable that this particular field will become the most prominent in years to come. Curiously, this part of the book provides some of the more sizeable networks under analysis, while also offering the more extensive qualitative demonstrations for understanding the underlying relational mechanisms at work within these internet-based networks. In Chapter 11, Dupont provides a meticulous analysis of interactions between computer hackers and the development of skills and trust therein. In doing so, he identifies the main challenges facing such offenders, particularly in terms of finding competent co-offenders that may contribute effectively to the time-consuming activities that make up botnet hacking and the heavy constraints facing those seeking the acquisition of monetization skills. Trust is also a fragile feature in such networks, with hackers often falling prey to other hackers for pure diversion. Overall, Dupont's question on how to handle a network that generates harm, but not necessarily for monetary aims, is one that researchers, law enforcement agents, and policy makers will be scratching their heads to for quite some time. Similarly to Dupont, Décary-Hétu examines conversational interactions between hackers in Chapter 12. Using data intercepted from discussion forums, this study examines the clique-like structures in which hackers exchange techniques and skills and through which novice participants may learn from more experienced hackers. While not centering on the challenges that were raised in the previous chapter, Décary-Hétu demonstrates that most participants had a limited number and relatively strong set of contacts. Such a finding on this "learning network" was consistent with research on money-oriented crime networks that are built on more instrumental brokerage points that orient the flow of information. Overall, these tight cliques and pivotal brokers in the network create the focus groups and "mentors" for an effective learning process. In Chapter 13, Fortin carries the cybercrime focus into the world of child pornography by examining Usenet newsgroups that share paraphernalia on such material. Analyses of interactions demonstrate that a firm community is in place to share such content and provide legitimacy for the group as a whole. As with Décary-Hétu's study, Fortin also finds novices learning from established members on how to avoid police detection, increase their activity within the community, and generally find assistance when needed. Such is the strength of networks, even in the less tolerated spheres of society.

Economic crime is the focus in Part IV. Past research in this area has been particularly lacking and the two chapters that make up this part of the book serve as solid models for anyone interested in the social organization of fraud and elite-level crime. In Chapter 14, Malm, Schoepfer, Bichler, and Boyd provide an innovative study of the evolution of the Ponzi scheme that was at the center of a highly publicized mortgage fraud. Based on a survey of investors, the authors retrace the contagion process that began with the initial investors and that extended toward their family members, friends, and acquaintances who also invested in what appeared to be a sound deal. This referral system is crucial for understanding the diffusion of fraud and this study makes the unique proposition that fraudulent systems may expand so rapidly and widely not simply because the principal culprits succeed in gaining the trust of their investors, but because investors serve as trustworthy references for their own contacts that also fall into the fraudulent net. The value of the network framework for reconstructing this scheme was also highlighted by the finding that those investors that were positioned closer to the principal organizers were also quicker to detect the growing problem. This chapter teaches us that the network perspective allows us to understand why and how people fall into a fraudulent scheme, but also why and how some are able to get out while the getting is still relatively good. The structure of elite-level crime is taken to one of the more notorious stages for such activity in Chapter 15, as Faulkner and Cheney revisit the Watergate conspiracy in search of the brokerage points that lead to key defections in such political conspiracies. The authors create the networks of participants that collaborated in the covert activities and those that testified against each other in the subsequent trial. A significant relationship is found between the working network and the defection network. Participants that were positioned as brokers or gatekeepers in the network were the most likely to denounce others during the trial, but were also more likely to succumb to the "broker penalty" as others defected against them. Such participants ultimately faced the highest probability for guilty verdicts and the harshest sentences. Faulkner and Cheney conclude with the general observation that the Watergate conspiracy rose and fell through the inherent brokerage dynamics that were at the base of its social organization. As with crime and network research from the past and in the present book, this chapter provides further evidence that criminal conspiracies are not built around reputed heads and leaders, but on the bridges that keep the overall set of participants together.

Part V of the book covers new research on terrorism and extremist groups. These areas have been amongst the more actively researched topics with the social network framework. The two chapters that comprise this final section of the book offer one of the more in-depth studies on the structure of terrorist groups and novel research on crime networks in conflict settings. In Chapter 16, Everton and Cunningham conduct a temporal analysis of how terrorist networks adapt to a hostile environment and how such adaptations influence their effectiveness. The focus is on the Noordin Top network and the heavy targeting it faced by Indonesian authorities. This case study provides a unique context in that, whereas crime networks tend to decentralize when confronted with heavy targeting, this network became more centralized. This facilitated targeting strategies and led to the eventual demise of the network. In Chapter 17, Lysaght examines the link between illegal markets and conflict-affected settings from a transnational focus. Her analysis centers on the structure of illicit trading networks involved in the extraction and trafficking of minerals within the Democratic Republic of the Congo. While the association between conflict and illegal markets has a rich research tradition, Lysaght demonstrates the pertinence of the network framework for identifying peripheral actors in this nexus. As with many of the other chapters in this book, her analysis fleshes out the more discrete key actors that contributed from well beyond the conflict zone.

Overall, my aim in bringing all these chapters together in a single volume was not simply to promote the social network framework in criminology, although I do believe that the 17 chapters that follow do succeed in doing this. More generally, this book meets Collins' (1992) call for a clear and non-obvious research discipline. Whether through the identification of new structural features of crime, new actors in various forms of criminal collectives, or new explanations generated by this perspective, the social network framework offers a unique angle for research and a vast set of data management and methodological techniques that allow us to express our demonstrations with a strict empirical approach. As each chapter will demonstrate, there is already a well-founded research tradition to build from for each of the areas of crime that are covered in the five parts of the book. This book therefore serves as one collective step in a path that is likely to continue and expand for quite some time.

I must admit that, at first, I was somewhat hesitant to embark on such a project and particularly worried that I would spend more time chasing everyone down for their papers than actually preparing the book. In the end, this project proved to be a learning process for me and confirmed that these researchers that I have come to know to a greater extent over recent years through our common questions and analytical outlooks are true professionals. The completion of this book was clearly facilitated by each of the author's commitment to meeting a series of tasks and deadlines.

Once again, this book began as a workshop endeavor and Andrew Goldsmith should be acknowledged for his brainstorm to initiate such an event in 2009. I thank Fatou Diouf, Sévrine Petit, and Benoit Dupont for their help preparing the 2011 Montreal workshop. Brett Kubicek (Public Safety Canada) and Karen Diepeveen (Canadian Federation for the Humanities and Social Sciences) also contributed with their assistance in locating additional funds for the workshop organization and the book's preparation. I also thank Julie Gaudreault, who took some time off from her graduate research to help me with the more technical areas of the manuscript preparation.

Although not contributing as authors in the book, Michael Levi, Federico Varese, and Samuel Tanner were of considerable help as reviewers of various chapters in this book. The contributing authors were also active in reviewing each other's chapters and providing the necessary suggestions and modifications toward the final product.

My co-members in the Criminal Network Research Team (*ERDR: Équipe de recherché sur la déliquance en reseau*) at the International Centre for Comparative Criminology, Université de Montréal, should also be acknowledged for investing a good portion of the team's funds into this project. This book is the final product that we were expecting when we assembled the team several years ago and the number of researchers that have contributed to this book confirms, once again, that our team is but one small part of a rising community that is coming together in search of similar inquiries.

The book is dedicated to Jean-Paul Brodeur, who saw something enticing in the social network concept, although he was never seduced by the computational features of many of the methods surrounding it. Jean-Paul had the idea to create the Criminal Network Research Team, but did not live to see this final product. Methodological queries aside, I am sure that Jean-Paul would have been impressed with what has been generated and what the future holds for this research tradition.

REFERENCES

Albini, Joseph L. (1971). *The American Mafia: Genesis of a Legend*. New York: Appleton-Century-Crofts.
Bergin, Sean (2009). Social network analysis of "dark networks": Where are we now? Paper presented at the *First Illicit Networks Workshop*, Wollongong, Australia.

Blok, Anton (1974). *The Mafia of a Sicilian Village, 1860–1960: A Study of Violent Peasant Entrepreneurs*. New York: Harper and Row.

Carrington, Peter J. (2011). Crime and social network analysis. In J. Scott & P.J. Carrington (eds.), *Handbook of Social Network Analysis* (pp. 235–255). London: Sage.

Collins, Randall (1992). *Sociological Insight: An Introduction to Non-Obvious Sociology* (2nd ed.). New York: Oxford University Press.

Freeman, Linton C. (2004). *The Development of Social Network Analysis: A Study in the Sociology of Science*. Vancouver: Empirical Press.

Hess, Henner (1973). *Mafia and Mafiosi: The Structure of Power*. Lexington: D.C. Heath.

Ianni, Francis J. (1972). *A Family Business*. New York: Russell Sage Foundation.

Klerks, Peter (2001). The network paradigm applied to criminal organizations. *Connections* 24, 53–65.

Krebs, Valdis (2001). Mapping networks of terrorist cells. *Connections* 24, 43–52.

McGloin, Jean Marie & David S. Kirk (2010). Social network analysis. In A.R. Piquero & D. Weisburd (eds.), *Handbook of Quantitative Criminology* (pp. 209–224). New York: Springer.

Morselli, Carlo (2009). *Inside Criminal Networks*. Springer: New York.

Papachristos, Andrew V. (2011). The coming of a networked criminology? Using social network analysis in the study of crime and deviance. In J. MacDonald (ed.), *Measuring Crime and Criminality: Advances in Criminological Theory*, vol. 13 (pp. 101–140). New Brunswick, NJ: Transaction.

Sparrow, Malcolm K. (1991). The application of network analysis to criminal intelligence: An assessment of the prospects. *Social Networks* 13, 251–274.

PART I

Co-offending Networks

CHAPTER 1

The Importance of Studying Co-offending Networks for Criminological Theory and Policy

Jean Marie McGloin and Holly Nguyen

For nearly a century, criminologists have been well acquainted with the group nature of crime. In the early part of the twentieth century, Shaw and McKay (1942) observed that the vast majority (approximately 80%) of juveniles who were seen in the Cook County Juvenile Court were suspected of committing crimes with accomplices; similar findings have consistently emerged in the decades since with regard to both official records and self-reports, as well as across a wide range of locations (e.g., Carrington, 2002; Sarnecki, 2001; Warr, 2002; cf. Stolzenberg & D'Allesio, 2008). Indeed, Breckinridge and Abbott's (1912) observation that a delinquent who offends alone is a rarity can, at this point, rightly be called a criminological "fact" (McGloin, Sullivan, Piquero, & Bacon, 2008).

It is not surprising then that several core criminological theories either directly root etiological processes in social networks or, at the very least, integrate them into explanations of crime (Akers, 1998; Cloward & Ohlin, 1960; Cohen, 1955; Shaw & McKay, 1942; Short & Strodtbeck, 1965; Sutherland, 1947). Even though so many of our seminal theories use the group nature of crime to buttress their propositions, however, there is minimal research on co-offending patterns, processes, precursors, and consequences. Such a gap leaves answers to even basic questions about why individuals co-offend and the impact that such group behavior can have

on the criminal career under-developed theoretically and in need of empirical guidance. Furthermore, despite some evidence that accomplice networks can be used as a means of social control to reduce crime (Kennedy, 2009) and can enhance prosecutorial strategies (see Natarajan, 2000), policy makers rarely integrate the tendency to offend with accomplices as part of interventions aimed at preventing, ceasing, or punishing criminal activity (Kennedy, 2009).

Perhaps, in part, this void is the result of viewing co-offending simply as a characteristic of the criminal event or as evidence of the power of criminogenic social influence, rather than as holding any unique meaning in and of itself. In recent years, however, researchers have made significant strides in narrowing this empirical gap and, as a consequence, have demonstrated that co-offending is a worthy and important domain of criminological inquiry. There are clear indications that group crime can alter and change offending pathways and that understanding the patterns and processes of co-offending can provide important guidance for law enforcement interventions. For example, Conway and McCord (2002) suggest that co-offending increases the likelihood of persistent criminality, especially when coupled with early onset. On the policy side, Piquero and Blumstein (2007) argue it is important to understand co-offending dynamics because, on one hand, imprisoning one co-offender may not have an effect on the actual crime rate if his/her accomplices continue to offend. On the other hand, imprisoning one co-offender may have a strong deterrent effect for the others, thereby significantly impacting the number of crimes saved.

A significant portion of the insight gained from this research has benefitted from the expanding and deepening parallel literature on criminal networks. Over the previous two decades, there has been a marked growth in discussions and empirical investigations about criminal networks, as scholars embraced the fact that criminal enterprises in general were better described as dynamic networks than as stable, centralized, hierarchical structures (Bunker & Sullivan, 2001; Clarke & Brown, 2003; Coles, 2001; Eck & Gersh, 2000). As a result, there are numerous examples of several scholars translating concepts and methods from the social network analysis tradition to bear on street gangs, organized crime, and other criminogenic networks (e.g., McGloin, 2005; Morselli, 2009; Natarajan, 2006; Papachristos, 2006). Indeed, Morselli's (2009; see also Morselli, 2005) recent book not only offers original analysis that sheds insight on various criminal organizations, but also makes a persuasive case that the integration of network perspectives into criminological research is not simply "fashionable," but benefits theory and offers important guidance for law enforcement.

Though some may view co-offending networks as significantly less complex (or even less compelling) than more traditional criminal networks (see Morselli, 2009), a strong case can be made for viewing co-offending connections as a specific and important form of the criminal network (cf. Felson, 2003). As Waring (2002: 43) declared

> the treatment of co-offending as a network phenomenon is particularly powerful because it has the potential to contribute both to the incorporation of co-offending into models of other

aspects of crime and to the location of social organization of crime within the broader range of forms of social organization.

Even before Waring's conceptual argument, several scholars in Sweden and the Netherlands were using network analysis to study co-offending relationships, offering novel insight for the field. For instance, Sarnecki (1990, 2001) gathered data on individuals aged 20 and younger who were suspected of crime during particular time frames in Sweden (1975–1977, 1991–1995). From these official data, he used information on accomplice ties to create numerous sociograms, which illustrated that even seemingly unconnected crimes could often be tied together in larger offending networks (see also Hakkert, 1998; Pettersson, 2003).

This chapter argues that it is important to firmly place group crime in the larger research agenda on criminal networks and to build on the recent interest and growth in co-offending research. In furthering this argument, we will provide evidence that researching group crime will pay dividends for theory and policy, as well as further general knowledge about offending pathways and processes. Furthermore, we argue that attempts to reduce group crime are important for law enforcement officials and interventions. In the sections to follow, we will first illustrate the importance of investigating group crime. Second, we discuss the applicability of network structure in the investigation of co-offending networks. Third, we examine the salience of particular roles that individuals play within criminal and co-offending networks. Finally, we offer some avenues of future research.

WHY SHOULD WE CARE ABOUT GROUP CRIME?

Although the bulk of research on the detrimental influence of criminogenic groups focuses on deviant peers and street gangs, co-offending networks can also impact criminal careers in meaningful ways. These networks are defined by instances of collective action, rather than other forms of social ties, but group crime nonetheless has the ability to further embed individuals in criminal lifestyles, as well as expand and deepen offending repertoires (Andresen & Felson, 2012). This process can happen through several, often complementary, routes. Group crime provides an opportunity for individuals to learn deviant behavior and attitudes, as well as the ability to recognize a wider range of criminal opportunities. As McAndrew (2000) argues, co-offending connections "can lead to sharing new methods of committing crime, identification of potential targets, information about police activities and opportunities to be part of specific criminal enterprises" (p. 53). In this way, both the criminal repertoire and awareness space can expand (see also Hochstetler, 2001; Mullins & Wright, 2003). Thus, a theoretical case can be made that reducing instances of group crime can limit the extent to which offenders become committed to and embedded in criminal lifestyles.

On some occasions, this learning occurs in the context of a mentorship relationship, which ties nicely with Sutherland's (1947) discussion of tutelage. Several seminal pieces in criminology call attention to the importance of learning from criminal mentors (e.g., Cloward & Ohlin, 1960), though Sutherland is often credited for calling specific attention to this unique and salient relationship within criminal networks. In his work on professional thieves, he observed "any man who hits the big-time in crime, somewhere or other along the road, became associated with a big-timer who picked him up and educated him" (Sutherland, 1937: 23). In short, Sutherland argued that some offenders—notably the "successful" ones—benefitted from the tutelage of more experienced and established offenders, from whom they typically learned while "on the job"—that is, while engaged in criminal action together.

There are several examples of the mentorship process in qualitative, narrative work (for a more detailed review, see Morselli, Tremblay, & McCarthy, 2006). Perhaps the best-known is Shaw's narrative of the delinquent Sidney, whose criminal history has been used frequently to call attention to the importance of co-offending (Shaw, 1931). In discussing his illegal enterprises, Sidney often spoke of learning from older, better-established criminals in his neighborhood. For instance, he spoke of one boy in the following way:

> I would walk behind him and as soon as he would pick up a piece of fruit I was supposed to do likewise. It took lots of practice and he had to set many examples before I could at last gain enough courage to follow suit.
>
> (Shaw, 1931: 58)

McCarthy and Hagan (1995) hypothesized that being embedded in criminal/deviant networks facilitates the establishment of important tutelage relationships. They tested this hypothesis with models of prostitution, theft, and drug selling among a sample of homeless youths and found that exposure to tutelage relationships enhanced the frequency of offending. McCarthy and Hagan suggest that tutelage relationships further embed individuals in criminogenic lifestyles because they enhance criminal skills and attitudes—assets they call "criminal capital."

Morselli et al. (2006) recently renewed interest in mentorship by extending the discussion in important ways through the integration of criminal capital. Social capital, or resources gained from social relationships, is associated with achievement in the legitimate market and individuals with mentors typically have access to additional social networks, which allows them to build and cultivate greater levels of social capital. In this way, mentorship not only can lead to direct tutelage, but can also support success indirectly through social networks. Morselli et al. (2006: 19–20) translated these concepts to the illicit sphere, arguing

> the impact of mentors on achievement may be particularly salient for criminal careers relative to conventional ones. Most offenders earn little money from their crimes . . . [and] there are no schools for crime . . . The inherent secrecy of crime and consistent threat of arrest means that offenders are often outsiders to one another . . . Mentorship addresses the need for security that strong ties offer, while opening doors to the more efficient extensions that emerge from weak ties. In this sense, the criminal mentor is an asset.

Perhaps not surprisingly, when relying on data from over 250 inmates housed in Quebec prisons, Morselli et al. (2006) found that having criminal mentors was associated with greater criminal success, as defined by criminal earnings.

Of course, this mentorship process speaks to a particular sort of co-offending relationship—one that is more stable than the modal connection observed in empirical research. To be clear, the notion and process of mentorship assumes some kind of enduring connection, certainly past the typical duration of most accomplice relationships. As Warr (1996: 33) noted, "delinquent groups are short-lived groups, so short-lived that it may make little sense to even speak of delinquent *groups* at all" [emphasis in original], and that "if groups are defined by the unique combination of individuals that comprise them, the modal life expectancy of offending groups is one event" (p. 23). Of course, Warr's point speaks to the duration of the group as a whole, but even work focusing on single relationships echoes the theme of transience.

Based on official crime data in Sweden, Sarnecki (2001) found that most co-offending relationships last a single event. Furthermore, when focusing on offenders in the Cambridge dataset with at least 10 crime convictions, Reiss and Farrington (1991) found that only 43 out of the 205 identified co-offenders were used more than once (see also Sarnecki, 2001). More recently, McGloin and colleagues developed a measure of co-offender stability, which ranged from 0 to 1, with 0 indicating no stability of co-offenders and 1 indicating that the same co-offenders were used for all instances of group crime. This measure provided an overall sense of the extent to which individuals tended to use the same people in their accomplice network over criminal events. Out of the 218 juvenile offenders in their sample who committed at least two group offenses, 128 had a co-offending stability value of 0, indicating that they did not "re-use" a single accomplice across co-offending incidents (this stands in contrast to the five subjects who showed complete stability of co-offenders).

In light of such "instability" then, should we *only* be concerned about the ability of group crime to embed and expand individuals' offending repertoires in the (relatively) rare situations of mentorship or longer-lasting networks? Unfortunately, the answer is no. Studies have demonstrated that even the typical fleeting and swift co-offending connections are related to more "risky" or serious offending profiles. For instance, returning to the data that informed McGloin et al.'s (2008) co-offender stability findings, Conway and McCord (2002) found that when individuals who had no official record of violent crime offended with accomplices who have a history of violent behavior, they were significantly more likely to "switch" toward violence.

The Importance of Network Structure

At the start of this chapter, the argument was offered that attending to the network structure of co-offending groups lends important insight. Mentor relationships and the offending history of the accomplices to whom subjects are linked can certainly fit within a network view, but there is compelling evidence that more traditional network characteristics can also lend insight. Though the research on co-offending remains a minimal part of that on criminal networks at large—and is an even smaller part of the literature on peer influence—this small literature nonetheless has made strides in recent years by thinking about the role of network structure.

For example, perhaps the most basic network attribute is size. Research has established that most accomplice networks are small, typically dyads, but there is significant variation in the number of people who partake in group offenses. Most work that discusses the size of co-offending networks is simply descriptive (Andresen, Felson, & Frank, 2008; Hakkert, 1998; Suzuki et al., 1994; Reiss, 1988), but a recent piece by McGloin and Piquero (2009) argued that the size of the accomplice network may have criminogenic importance, by embedding it in the literature on collective behavior. Granovetter (1978) argued that some people need minimal situational inducements to engage in deviant behavior (in his discussion, rioting); other people, however, have a much higher threshold and need substantial situational pressures, opportunities, or inducements to partake in deviant behavior. The presence of others who are willing to engage in deviance—that is, the opportunity to be part of collective behavior—can serve as substantial motivation (Granovetter, 1978). Thus, individuals who, under typical conditions, are not prone toward engaging in deviant behavior may be swayed to engage in deviance when in the company of others—and this likelihood increases as the size of the accomplice network grows.

By integrating Granovetter's (1978) work with other literature on how groups can impact social behavior, McGloin and Piquero (2009) offered the hypothesis that, in a large accomplice network, it is easier to feel anonymous and diffuse responsibility, or to "deindividuate," which can reduce the associated risk of engaging in deviance. Furthermore, the associated cost of *not* engaging in the

collective deviance can increase, as fears about nonconformity with the social group rise. They also argued that this connection between the network size and crime would resonate strongly with regard to violence. Using data from juvenile offenders in Philadelphia, McGloin and Piquero (2009: 336) found that: "the odds of an individual's first group offence being violent increases for every additional accomplice present during the event, independent of whether these co-offenders had a history of prior violence." In this way, even something as simple as network size can be one of the deciding factors as to whether a person engages in crime or not.[1]

Though the bulk of the (minimal) work that speaks to the properties of accomplice networks tends to focus on the stability of the ties and the size of the network, scholars have recently made the case that relatively more complicated structural attributes also hold insight on various outcomes that can further embed and attach individuals to a criminal lifestyle. To be clear, personal co-offending networks vary markedly across offenders, not just in terms of their size but also with regard to the pattern and quality of the links. Though some networks are quite simple—perhaps a single dyad or triad—others are quite complex and reflect an impressive culmination of co-offending relationships. For instance, consider Figure 1.1, which provides sociograms for three juvenile offenders who were criminally active in Philadelphia at some point during the late 1970s to the early 1990s (for additional insight on the co-offending networks for the full sample, see McGloin & Piquero, 2010).

In these graphs, links are based on shared criminal events (i.e., group crime) during the offenders' juvenile years (i.e., up to age 18). Because the original researchers also reviewed the criminal records of the subjects' accomplices (see McCord, 2004), the network also accounts for any co-offending relationships among the accomplices in which the subject (or "ego") was not present. In this way, these

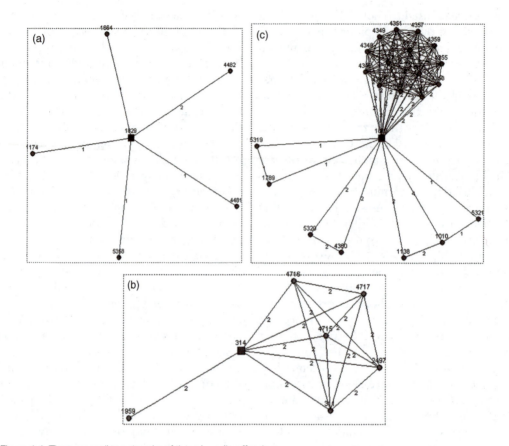

Figure 1.1 The accomplice networks of three juvenile offenders

co-offending networks are ego-centric, with a radius of one. Figure 1.1a is quite simple, reflecting a juvenile who committed five co-offenses, each with a single, different accomplice. Figure 1.1b reflects a somewhat more complicated network structure, portraying a delinquent who committed a co-offense with one accomplice, and also engaged in a group crime with five different co-offenders. Finally, Figure 1.1c reflects a delinquent who, like the subject in Figure 1.1a, engaged in five incidents of group crime. Four of these criminal events involved two accomplices—one of whom was present as a co-offender for two crimes—and one event involved 14 other accomplices. In light of these varied criminal network structures, perhaps it is not surpris-ing that integrating social network concepts into co-offending investigations has proven beneficial. In particular, a handful of schol-ars have translated the concept of "network redundancy" to the criminal sphere, leading to significant intellectual gain.

Redundant social networks are those in which most nodes are directly linked to each other—in other words, they are dense net-works (Wasserman & Faust, 1994). Stem-ming from Granovetter's (1973) discussion of weak ties and building on Burt's (1992) work on structural holes, scholars have argued that networks with many redundant ties limit an actor's exposure to new information and opportunities. In contrast, individuals who are embedded in less redundant networks have greater returns because they are exposed to different populations, knowledge, skills, and opportunities (see also Davern & Hachen, 2006; Lin, 1982; Podolny & Baron, 1997). In this way, non-redundant networks are often tied to economic and occupational success.

Though some scholars have suggested that redundant criminal networks are problematic because they reduce the likelihood of prosocial influence and limit information and exposure almost exclusively to criminal influence (Haynie, 2001; see also Krohn, 1986), others have observed that non-redundant criminal networks can facilitate other problematic criminal outcomes. For instance, Morselli and Tremblay (2004) found that offenders whose co-offending networks were less redundant tended to have greater criminal earnings than their counterparts who reported relatively more redundant accomplice networks.[2] Morselli and Tremblay's work in this area not only provided insight into an outcome that can further embed someone to the illegitimate market, as crime is more attractive and rewarding, but it also demonstrated the potential utility of social network concepts for understanding and studying co-offending.

More recently, McGloin and Piquero (2010) connected non-redundant accomplice networks to another potentially problematic outcome among juvenile offenders: offending versatility. Scholars suggest that youths who engage in a wide range of criminal activity are at added risk for serious and persistent offending later in life, perhaps because they are acquiring a generalized proclivity for offending, rather than a preference for a particular type of deviance (McGloin & Piquero, 2010; see also Loeber, 1988; Loeber & Schmaling, 1985). McGloin and Piquero (2010: 67) argued, "individuals with non-redundant co-offending networks arguably have access to an array of criminal norms, skills and knowledge, models of behavior, and opportunities, which may translate into a versatile offending profile." To some

extent, this view already had empirical backing stemming from Shaw's (1931) aforementioned narrative of the delinquent Sidney. Sidney transitioned through several different accomplice and deviant peer networks during his criminal career, thus creating a non-redundant ego-centric network. As he moved through these different networks, his behavior would often change to be consistent with the group, thereby building a diverse criminal career (see also Warr, 1996).

Using data on juvenile offenders, McGloin and Piquero (2010) directly tested and confirmed this supposed relationship between non-redundant networks and versatile offending, showing that individuals whose ego-centric accomplice networks had lower density scores (i.e., were less redundant) were less likely to commit the same crime across group offenses (i.e., they tended to demonstrate greater offending variety across instances of co-offending). Furthermore, this relationship endured even when accounting for the size of the network, demonstrating that it is not simply how many people a person offends with that facilitates versatility, but the structural properties of the co-offending network.

Roles Within Networks

The larger literature on criminal networks illustrates that networks consist of varied structures and therefore treating all groups as similar is unrealistic. Thus far, research into co-offending networks echoes this finding. In addition to the insight gained from thinking about network structure, recent contributions have considered the different roles which individuals within a network play. Just as the network structure varies, roles are also varied and investigations into the different roles can have important implications for both theory and policy. As Waring (2002: 39–40) urged researchers to consider, "why do arrests of some members (and other interventions) seem to successfully break up some networks and not others?" In adopting a network perspective, and thinking about the growing work of different roles in illicit networks, there are several positions that may be of particular interest if the goal is to dismantle the co-offending network: central individuals and cut points.[3]

Regarding the former, though there are several measures of centrality, the basic essence of this concept is individuals who are the most connected in the network. This can be considered in terms of direct connections (i.e., degree centrality) and indirect connections, in that some people are key mediators or "brokers" through whom other actors in the network must go to connect with each other (i.e., betweenness centrality; see Morselli, 2009). From a law enforcement perspective, central individuals are attractive points of intervention because they may hold more responsibility and their removal may disrupt the functioning of the network (Sparrow, 1991). Though it may be tempting to focus on reputations in structuring interventions, research has shown that network analyses can reveal important positions that otherwise may be missed (McGloin, 2005). As Morselli (2010: 382) demonstrated with an analysis of the Quebec Hells Angels:

> participants with high brokerage level were less likely to be members of the Hells Angels, thus suggesting that targeting strategies must consider the patterns that represent an offender's network at any given time, rather than simply focusing on an offender's status and reputation within a criminal organization.

In addition to central nodes, law enforcement may also derive benefits from focusing on cut points. Cut points are particularly important nodes who serve as a connection between groups that otherwise would be unconnected (Scott, 2000; Wasserman & Faust, 1994; see also McGloin, 2005). In other words, if not for this person, groups (or individuals) would have no linkage among them.

However, given the fleeting nature of most co-offending relationships, does it really make sense to think about interventions that are based on a particular role when accomplice networks tend not to endure? To be clear, with somewhat more stable criminal networks, such as street gangs, organized crime, or drug crews, the focus is on strategically breaking up an existing network. But, from a co-offending perspective, the goal is not so much to dismantle a network but rather to prevent it from occurring in the first place. In other words, by preventing or reducing the likelihood of group crime, one could argue that we reduce the burden on the criminal justice system, and reduce the extent to which individuals are introduced to or become more embedded in criminogenic lifestyles (Andresen & Felson, 2012). In this way, prevention, not intervention, is the goal. With this in mind, what—if any—position in a co-offending network provides leverage to meet this goal? Unlike most other criminogenic networks, there is a position in co-offending networks that has clear and undeniable power and thus nominates itself for focus: the instigator.

Despite the long-known tendency of individuals to offend with accomplices, Reiss' (1986, 1988) work on co-offending was perhaps the first in-depth consideration of this topic. In these pieces, he argued that not all offenders enter into co-offending relationships in the same way; put differently, the decision to co-offend is not necessarily a democratic one based on equal levels of motivation and interest (Warr, 1996). Rather, some people, known as instigators or recruiters, are responsible for the idea and seemingly have the ability to convince others to take part. As Warr (1996) observed in the National Youth Survey (NYS) data, subjects reported that the vast majority of group crimes had a single instigator.

Given the fact that co-offending can embed individuals in criminal networks more deeply, focusing attention on the individuals who tend to instigate these criminal events is a wise investment of resources. Indeed, when a person instigates group crime, s/he is the source of a disproportionate number of cases in the criminal justice system, both in an immediate sense and in the longer-term impact on accomplices (Andresen & Felson, 2012). Yet, despite the clear importance of identifying these individuals, there is scarce research, and that which does exist is limited. Though there are several articles that discuss recruiters, empirical investigations that test the supposed profile of recruiters are rare. There are conceptual reasons to believe that some individuals, who are older than their less-experienced accomplices, are high-rate offenders, and rotate through several accomplice groups, are those who are systematically more prone to instigate group crime (see Reiss & Farrington, 1991; van Mastrigt & Farrington, 2011). Indeed, there are certainly individuals who meet these profiles in various datasets; however, these inquiries did not confirm that these particular individuals were the ones most likely to instigate group crime.

Warr (1996) completed one of the few empirical investigations into patterns of instigation and did find that higher rate offenders were more likely to report instigating group crime. At the same time, however, his work called attention to the situational variation in the tendency to instigate co-offending. Specifically, he noted that individuals tended to be both joiners and followers, suggesting that scholars would benefit from understanding the reasons why people instigate in some circumstances, but not in others. Warr cautioned against the view that certain individuals instigate crime whereas others do not and suggested that the reality was more complicated.

Like many offending characteristics, it appears that both individual-level and situational-level attributes have a role to play in understanding the instigation of group crime. McGloin and Nguyen (2011) recently completed an investigation of the tendency to instigate group offending using data from incarcerated individuals in Colorado. They hypothesized that instigation of group crime is likely to vary across crime types, and that

this variation is tied to the level of expertise that offenders have for that particular crime. At the same time, they tested the premise that more serious, chronic offenders—captured by age of criminal onset and number of felony arrests—would have a greater tendency to instigate. Like Warr (1996), they found evidence of within-individual variation in the tendency to instigate co-offending (along with some stability). Using data at the crime-type level, nested within individuals, their analysis revealed that perceived skill at the crime type in question consistently predicted the tendency to instigate, holding a host of covariates constant.

Though earlier ages of onset generally identified a tendency to instigate, their investigation made it clear that attempts to identify and limit instigation cannot be solely based on offender attributes. Implications of such findings suggest that criminal justice policy might pay dividends by focusing on identifying certain individuals that meet the instigator/recruiter profile, but this would only partially impact the crime rate. Identifying person-based characteristics and situational characteristics of instigators specifically and the mechanisms of co-offending in general are important avenues for future research. The next section considers some additional avenues of future research.

CONCLUSION

In the most general and basic sense, there is a clear need for more data on co-offending. For example, information containing both official records and self-report from people involved in the same event would allow for cross-validation and also provide direct commentary on the way in which co-offending crimes are negotiated and completed. Furthermore, collecting this data over time would offer an important contribution (McGloin et al., 2008). Indeed, such information offers the opportunity to better understand how group crime affects and is effected by criminal pathways (Piquero, Farrington, & Blumstein, 2007). Researchers who study criminal networks are well-acquainted with the difficulty of getting access to necessary data and thinking critically about the validity of this information; co-offending data are no different. Issues such as the fleeting nature of co-offending networks, the flexibility of what defines an "accomplice," and the difficulty of obtaining access are issues with which researchers must creatively contend.

It is also important for future research to study how people find or select co-offenders. Two broad perspectives exist in the treatment of how offenders converge to commit a crime: first, some researchers suggest that co-offending occurs from spontaneous connections forged in common convergence spaces (Stolzenberg & D'Alessio, 2008; Felson, 2003). Contrary to this perspective, other scholars offer an explanation that involves a more deliberate, rational process in the decision to offend with others (Andresen & Felson, 2012; McCarthy, Hagan, & Cohen, 1998; Tremblay, 1993). Scholars who forward this perspective underscore a process whereby individuals choose to offend either alone or with others based on the potential risks and benefits of collaboration. For example, McCarthy et al. (1998) posit that, while there are inherent risks in offending with others, individuals in circumstances of adversity may be more likely to collaborate with others. Weerman (2003) highlights the beneficial aspects of co-offending and posits that offenders come together in a social exchange process, whereby "material and immaterial goods are exchanged" (p. 398). Despite some different commentary on the mechanisms whereby co-offending groups form, few studies have in fact empirically tested these different hypotheses.

Related to this point, the extent to which co-offending networks overlap with or are embedded in larger criminal networks is also unclear. In other words, we need research on how/why individuals decide to co-offend, as well as on who they select as accomplices. Though there is an assumption that offending accomplices are selected from the larger pool of deviant peers or criminal associates (Warr, 2002), this is speculative. As Figure 1.2 demonstrates, there are at least three ways in which the pool of accomplices overlap with the more general criminal network: it may be completely contained within the larger network (Figure 1.2a); it may partially overlap with the criminal/peer network (Figure 1.2b); or accomplices may be individuals who are not connected to the network of deviant peers or criminal associates (Figure 1.2c).

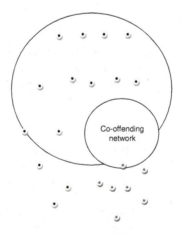

Figure 1.2a The co-offending accomplices are drawn from the pool of individuals in the larger criminal network

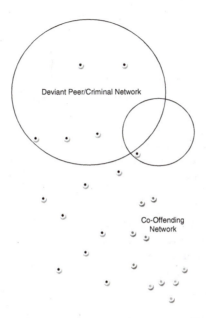

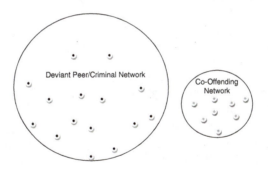

Figure 1.2b Some co-offending accomplices are drawn from the pool of individuals in the larger criminal network, whereas some are not

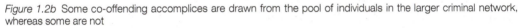

Figure 1.2c The network of co-offending accomplices is distinct and separate from the larger criminal network

If it is the case that the accomplice network is a subgroup of the larger criminal network, then delineating why certain individuals are used as accomplices (while others are not), or at the very least identifying these actors, can lend important insight. As Krohn (1986: S83) argues, "multiplexity in social relationships is likely to constrain individual's behavior." When ties among actors emerge across various social situations and roles, then these links take on added salience and have a greater capacity to shape conformity. In short, individuals who are part of the deviant peer group (or criminal organization) and who are also accomplices in shared criminal behavior may be those who have the greatest priority and power in learning processes (Sutherland, 1947). Thus, in addition to the fact that group offending can broaden an offender's awareness space, in this situation, it can also strengthen the individual's connection to the deviant or criminal network, embedding him even further in a criminal lifestyle.

If it is the case that some accomplices are from the criminal/peer network, whereas others are not, or that an offender uses accomplices who fully exist outside the boundaries of this network, this too could be problematic. After all, this means that the offender is essentially expanding his illicit social network; it also means that law enforcement efforts to dismantle the criminal network nonetheless leaves this individual with a pool of criminal associates who are willing to join him in crime. Future research thus would be well served by being sensitive to the various ties that can define criminal networks (e.g., McGloin, 2005). Obtaining network information across different roles or relationships most certainly makes the data collection process more challenging and is likely to result in more complicated criminal networks, but it would be worth the effort.

In conclusion, though researchers have made significant strides in co-offending research in recent years, the literature remains small and in need of further development. Ideally, scholars interested in group crime will join the momentum of the expanding work on criminal networks and think critically about the way the structure of one's placement in this specific criminal network both impacts and is impacted by the criminal career. Doing so will not only push the development of theory, but will also serve as additional guidance for policy makers and practitioners interested in integrating knowledge about illicit networks into their intervention strategies

NOTES

1. From such arguments, one might assume that co-offending networks have little impact on the pathways of chronic offenders given that they do not need the presence of others to provide sufficient criminal motivation (Moffitt, 1993). But this does not mean that serious chronic offenders do not also derive some benefit from co-offending. Offending with others can make crime easier, by requiring less effort through the division of labor, by using others for their own gain, or by bringing more awareness of criminal opportunities to the table. In short, co-offending oftentimes can be a beneficial instrumental decision (McCarthy et al., 1998; Wright & Decker, 1994). In support of this premise, McGloin and Stickle (2011) recently documented in the Racine cohort data that chronic offenders were less likely than their non-chronic offender counterparts to say that they engaged in offending because of peers, yet they were just as likely to offend with accomplices (i.e., group crime accounted for similar proportions of their offending histories).

2. Please note that this research employed Tremblay's (1993) broad definition of co-offenders, which includes individuals who are instrumental to the crime, not just those individuals who explicitly engage in the crime with the subject.

3. It is important to recognize that there is debate about what positions or roles are the most vulnerable points for intervention in criminal networks (e.g., Carley, Lee, & Krackhardt, 2001; Morselli, 2009; Sparrow, 1991).

REFERENCES

Akers, Ronald L. (1998). *Social Learning and Social Structure: A General Theory of Crime and Deviance.* Boston, MA: Northeastern University Press.

Andresen, Martin & Marcus Felson (2012). Co-offending and the diversification of crime types. *International Journal of Offender Therapy and Comparative Criminology* 56(5), 811–829.

Andresen, Martin A., Marcus Felson, & Richard Frank (2008). *Co-offending by Age of Offenders*, ICURS Fact Sheet Number 8.

Breckinridge, Sophonisba P. & Edith Abbott (1912). *The Delinquent Child and the Home.* New York: Russell Sage Foundation Charities Publication Committee.

Bunker, Robert. J. & John. P. Sullivan (2001). Cartel evolution: Potentials and consequences. *Transnational Organized Crime* 4, 55–74.

Burt, Ronald S. (1992). *Structural Holes: The Social Structure of Competition.* Cambridge, MA: Harvard University Press.

Carley, Kathleen M., Ju-Sung Lee, & David Krackhardt (2001). Destabilizing networks. *Connections* 24(3), 31–44.

Carrington, Peter J. (2002). Group crime in Canada. *Canadian Journal of Criminology* 44, 277–315.

Clarke, Ronald. V. & Rick Brown (2003). International trafficking in stolen vehicles. In M. Tonry (ed.), *Crime and Justice. A Review of Research 30* (pp. 197–227). Chicago: University of Chicago Press.

Cloward, Richard & Lloyd Ohlin (1960). *Delinquency and Opportunity*. New York: Free Press.

Cohen, Albert K. (1955). *Delinquent Boys: The Culture of the Gang*. Glencoe, IL: Free Press.

Coles, Nigel (2001). It's not what you know: It's who you know that counts. Analyzing serious crime groups as social networks. *The British Journal of Criminology* 41, 580–594.

Conway, Kevin P. & Joan McCord (2002). A longitudinal examination of the relation between co-offending with violent accomplices and violent crime. *Aggressive Behavior* 28, 97–108.

Davern, Michael & David S. Hachen (2006). The role of information and influence in social networks: Examining the association between social network structure and job mobility. *American Journal of Economics and Sociology* 65, 269–293.

Eck, John E. & Jeffery S. Gersh (2000). Drug trafficking as a cottage industry. In M. Natarajan & M. Hough (eds.), *Illegal Drug Markets: From Research to Prevention Policy* (pp. 241–271). Monsey, NY: Criminal Justice Press/Willow Tree Press.

Felson, Marcus (2003). The process of co-offending. In Martha J. Smith & Derek B. Cornish (eds.), *Theory for Practice in Situational Crime Prevention*. Crime Prevention Studies, vol. 16 (pp. 149–168). Monsey, NY: Criminal Justice Press.

Granovetter, Mark S. (1973). The strength of weak ties. *The American Journal of Sociology* 78(6), 1360–1380.

Granovetter, Mark (1978). Threshold models of collective behavior. *American Journal of Sociology* 83(6), 1420–1443.

Hakkert, Alfred (1998). Group delinquency in the Netherlands: Some findings from an exploratory study. *International Review of Law, Computers and Technology* 12, 453–474.

Haynie, Dana L. (2001). Delinquent peers revisited: Does network structure matter? *American Journal of Sociology* 106, 1013–1057.

Hochstetler, Andy (2001). Opportunities and decisions: Interactional dynamics in robbery and burglary groups. *Criminology* 39, 737–764.

Kennedy, David (2009). *Deterrence and Crime Prevention: Reconsidering the Prospect of Sanction*. London: Routledge.

Krohn, Marvin D. (1986). The web of conformity: A network approach to the explanation of delinquent behavior. *Social Problems* 3, 601–613.

Lin, Nan (1982). Social resources and instrumental action. In P. Marsden & N. Lin (eds.), *Social Structure and Network Analysis* (pp. 247–271). Beverly Hills, CA: Sage.

Loeber, Rolf (1988). Natural histories of conduct problems, delinquency, and associated substance use: Evidence for developmental progressions. In B. Lahey & A. Kazdin (eds.), *Advances in Clinical Child Psychology* (pp. 73–124). New York: Plenum.

Loeber, Rolf & Karen B. Schmaling (1985). The utility of differentiating between mixed and pure forms of antisocial child behavior. *Journal of Abnormal Child Psychology* 13, 315–335.

McAndrew, David (2000). The structural analysis of criminal networks. In David Canter & Laurence Alison (eds.), *The Social Psychology of Crime: Groups, Teams and Networks—Offender Profiling Series* (pp. 51–94). Aldershot, UK: Ashgate.

McCarthy, Bill & John Hagan (1995). Getting into street crime: The structure and process of criminal embeddedness. *Social Science Research* 24, 63–95.

McCarthy, Bill, John Hagan, & Lawrence E. Cohen (1998). Uncertainty, cooperation and crime: Understanding the decision to co-offend. *Social Forces* 77(1), 155–184.

McCord, Joan (2004). *Patterns of Juvenile Delinquency and Co-offending in Philadelphia, 1976–1994*. Ann Arbor, MI: Interuniversity Consortium for Political and Social Science Research.

McGloin, Jean. M. (2005). Policy and intervention considerations of a network analysis of street gangs. *Criminology and Public Policy* 43, 607–636.

McGloin, Jean M. & Holly Nguyen (2011). "It was my idea": Considering the instigation of co-offending. Unpublished manuscript.

McGloin, Jean M. & Alex R. Piquero (2009). "I wasn't alone": Collective behaviour and violent delinquency. *The Australian and New Zealand Journal of Criminology* 42(3), 336–353.

McGloin, Jean M. & Alex R. Piquero (2010). On

the relationship between co-offending network redundancy and offending versatility. *Journal of Research in Crime and Delinquency* 47, 63–90.

McGloin, Jean M. & Wendy P. Stickle (2011). Influence or convenience? Rethinking the role of peers for chronic offenders. *Journal of Research in Crime and Delinquency*, 48, 419–447.

McGloin, Jean M., Christopher J. Sullivan, Alex R. Piquero, & Sarah Bacon (2008). Investigating the stability of co-offending and co-offenders among a sample of youthful offenders. *Criminology* 46, 155–188.

Moffitt, Terrie E. (1993). Adolescent-limited and life-course persistent anti-social behavior: A developmental taxonomy. *Psychological Review* 100, 674–701.

Morselli, Carlo (2005). *Contacts, Opportunities, and Criminal Enterprise*. Toronto: University of Toronto Press.

Morselli, Carlo (2009). *Inside Criminal Networks*. New York: Springer.

Morselli, Carlo (2010). Assessing vulnerable and strategic positions in a criminal network. *Journal of Contemporary Criminal Justice* 26(4), 382–392.

Morselli, Carlo & Pierre Tremblay (2004). Criminal achievement, offender networks and the benefits of low self-control. *Criminology* 42, 773–804.

Morselli, Carlo, Pierre Tremblay, & Bill McCarthy (2006). Mentors and criminal achievement. *Criminology* 44(1), 17–43.

Mullins, Christopher W. & Richard Wright (2003). Gender, social networks, and residential burglary. *Criminology* 41, 813–839.

Natarajan, Mangai (2000). Understanding the structure of a drug trafficking organization: A conversational analysis. In M. Natarajanand M. Hough (eds.), *Illegal Drug Markets: From Research to Policy, Crime Prevention Studies Volume 11* (pp. 273–298). Monsey, NY: Criminal Justice Press.

Natarajan, Mangai (2006). Understanding the structure of a large heroin distribution network: A quantitative analysis of qualitative data. *Quantitative Journal of Criminology* 22(2), 171–192.

Papachristos, Andrew V. (2006). Social network analysis and gang research: Theory and methods. In James F. Short & Lorine A. Hughes (eds.), *Studying Youth Gangs* (pp. 99–116). Lanham, MD: Alta Mira.

Pettersson, Tove (2003). Ethnicity and violent crime: The ethnic structure of networks of youths suspected of violent offenses in Stockholm. *Journal of Scandinavian Studies in Criminology and Crime Prevention* 4, 143–161.

Piquero, Alex P. & Al Blumstein (2007). Does incapacitation reduce crime? *Journal of Quantitative Criminology* 23, 267–285.

Piquero, Alex R., David P. Farrington, & Al Blumstein (2007). *Key Issues in Criminal Career Research: New Analyses of the Cambridge Study in Delinquent Development*. Cambridge: Cambridge University Press.

Podolny, James. M. & James Baron (1997). Resources and relationships: Social networks and mobility in the workplace. *American Sociological Review* 62, 673–693.

Reiss, Albert J. (1986). Co-offender influences on criminal careers. In Alfred Blumstein, Jaqueline Cohen, Jeffery A. Roth, & Christy A. Visher (eds.), *Criminal Careers and Career Criminals, vol. 2* (pp. 121–160). Washington, DC: National Academy Press.

Reiss, Albert (1988). Co-offending and criminal careers. In Norval Morris & Michael Tonry (eds.), *Crime and Justice, Vol. 10* (pp. 117–170). Chicago: University of Chicago Press.

Reiss, Albert J. & David P. Farrington (1991). Advancing knowledge about co-offending: Results from a prospective longitudinal survey of London males. *Journal of Criminal Law and Criminology* 82, 360–395.

Sarnecki, Jerzy (1990). Delinquent networks in Sweden. *Journal of Quantitative Criminology* 6, 31–50.

Sarnecki, Jerzy (2001). *Delinquent Networks*. Cambridge: Cambridge University Press.

Scott, John P. (2000). *Social Network Analysis: A Handbook* (2nd ed.). London: Sage.

Shaw, Clifford R. (1931). *The Natural History of a Delinquent Career*. Chicago, IL: University of Chicago Press.

Shaw, Clifford R. & Henry D. McKay (1942). *Juvenile Delinquency in Urban Areas*. Chicago, IL: University of Chicago Press.

Short, James F. & Fred L. Strodtbeck (1965). *Group Process and Gang Delinquency*. Chicago, IL: University of Chicago Press.

Sparrow, Malcolm K. (1991). The application of

network analysis to criminal intelligence: An assessment of the prospects. *Social Networks* 13, 251–274.

Stolzenberg, Lisa & Stewart J. D'Alessio (2008). Co-offending and the age-crime curve. *Journal of Research in Crime and Delinquency* 45(1), 65–86.

Sutherland, Edwin H. (1937). *The Professional Thief*. Chicago, IL: University of Chicago Press.

Sutherland, Edwin H. (1947). *Principles of Criminology* (4th ed.). Philadelphia, PA.: Lippincott.

Suzuki, Shingo, Yumiko Inokuchi, Kazumi Takakuwa, Juichi Kobayashi, Seijun Okeda, & Yoshiaki Takahashi (1994). A study of juvenile co-offending: An analysis of group traits by offense type and group size. *Reports of the National Research Institute of Police Science* 35, 1–11.

Tremblay, Pierre (1993). Searching for suitable co-offenders. In Ronald V. Clarke & Marcus Felson (eds.), *Routine Activity and Rational Choice: Advances in Criminological Theory* (pp. 17–36). New Brunswick, NJ: Transaction.

van Mastrigt, Sarah B. & David P. Farrington (2011). Prevalence and characteristics of co-offending recruiters. *Justice Quarterly* 28(2), 325–359.

Waring, Elin J. (2002). Conceptualizing co-offending: A network form of organization. In Elin Waring & David Weisburd (eds.), *Crime and Social Organization: Advances in Criminological Theory Volume 10* (pp. 40–63). Rutgers, NJ: Transaction Publishers.

Warr, Mark (1996). Organization and instigation in delinquent groups. *Criminology* 34, 11–37.

Warr, Mark (2002). *Companions in Crime: The Social Aspects of Criminal Conduct*. Cambridge: Cambridge University Press.

Wasserman, Stanley & Katherine Faust (1994). *Social Network Analysis: Methods and Applications*. Cambridge: Cambridge University Press.

Weerman, Frank (2003). Co-offending as social exchange: Explaining characteristics of co-offending. *British Journal of Criminology* 43, 398–416.

Wright, Richard & Scott Decker (1994). *Burglars on the Job: Streetlife and Residential Break-ins*. Boston, MA: Northeastern University Press.

CHAPTER 2

Sex and Age Homophily in Co-offending Networks

Opportunity or Preference?

Sarah B. van Mastrigt and Peter J. Carrington[1]

Interest in examining the structures and characteristics of social networks has gained considerable popularity over the past few decades, also in criminology (Bouchard & Nuygen, 2010; Carrington, 2011; Haynie, 2002; McGloin & Kirk, 2010; Morselli, 2009; Mullins & Wright, 2003; Sarnecki, 2001). Although criminological attention to the network paradigm has increased recently, there are several areas of inquiry that are particularly well suited to network-type analyses which have yet to be fully explored. One of these is the study of joint criminal action, or co-offending.

It is well known that many offenders commit their crimes with others, yet focused studies of co-offending are relatively rare (Andresen & Felson, 2010; Carrington 2002a, 2009; McGloin, Sullivan, Piquero, & Bacon, 2008; Reiss & Farrington, 1991; van Mastrigt & Farrington, 2009, 2011; Warr, 1996) and data constraints have limited most of the existing investigations to outlining its basic prevalence and correlates, particularly among juveniles (Conway & McCord, 2002; McCord & Conway, 2002, 2005; Reiss, 1988; Sarnecki, 1986, 1990, 2001). Theories of co-offending are also rare (Felson, 2003; McCarthy, Hagan, & Cohen, 1998; Tremblay, 1993; Weerman, 2003). More than two decades ago, Reiss (1988: 117) argued that "understanding co-offending is central to understanding the etiology of crime and the effects of intervention strategies," but even

today key aspects of co-offending, such as the selection of accomplices, are somewhat of a mystery.

Applying network concepts and techniques to the study of group crime has considerable potential with respect to elucidating the formation, composition, and functioning of co-offending groups: information that is central to a better understanding of their impacts. To date, however, only a handful of studies have done so, and most applications have been purely descriptive: either using the concept "network" itself to identify the nature of the associations among co-offenders (Chattoe & Hamill, 2005; Waring, 2002) or constructing sociograms to portray ties within and between co-offending groups (e.g., Sarnecki, 1986, 1990, 2001). Although increases in the availability of network data and related methodological improvements have evidenced more complex modeling attempts in recent years (e.g., Frank & Carrington, 2007; McGloin & Piquero, 2010; Smangs, 2010; Schaefer, 2012), studies that apply network concepts and probability models to test hypotheses about co-offending are still far and few between.

The goal of the present study is to contribute to this burgeoning literature by applying the social network concept of "homophily," the tendency to associate with similar others, to explore alternative theories of the selection of co-offenders. The fact that co-offending networks typically display high levels of homophily, especially for age and sex, is well known (Reiss, 1988; Weerman, 2003). Often, this finding is taken as evidence that offenders exercise a conscious choice when selecting co-offenders and, in doing so, exhibit a clear *preference* for accomplices who share these social attributes (Reiss & Farrington, 1991; Warr, 2002). However, it is also possible that the observed homogeneity of co-offending groups is determined not by preference, but by *structural opportunity* and, specifically, the underlying demography of the offender pool (Carrington, 2002b).

In order to explore these possibilities, we first outline the descriptive and theoretical literature on homophily and introduce a key distinction between homophily resulting from baseline demography and that which reflects a social inbreeding bias. We then apply this distinction to construct probability models of sex and age homophily using data on more than 10,000 co-offending groups detected by police in a large metropolitan area of England.[2] We conclude with a discussion of our key finding that, although inbreeding does appear to drive the selection of co-offenders overall, it does so differentially across age, gender, and co-offending group size.

HOMOPHILY IN CONVENTIONAL AND CRIMINAL NETWORKS

The term homophily, from "homo" = self and "philia" = love, refers to the well-demonstrated tendency for human actors to form relational ties with similar others (Blau, 1977; Lazarsfeld & Merton, 1954; Marsden, 1988; McPherson, Smith-Lovin, & Cook, 2001). Popular references to this principle are pervasive, illustrated by Plato's observation that "similarity begets friendship" and the Gluecks' frequently cited adage that "birds of a feather flock together" (1950: 164). These proverbs have been supported empirically time and again throughout a long history of research in anthropology, social psychology, and sociology aimed at examining the patterning of human relationships: the field now formally known as social network analysis. The robust finding that voluntary contact between similar people occurs at a higher rate than among dissimilar people has been demonstrated across a wide range of demographic and social dimensions and in both face-to-face and online communities. Conventional network ties including friendship (Moody, 2001), marriage (Kalmijn, 1998), confiding relationships (Marsden, 1988), business associations (Ruef, 2002), and leisure activities (Huang, Shen, Williams, & Contractor, 2009) all display high levels of homophily on ascriptive characteristics (such as age, sex, and race/ethnicity), attained characteristics (like income, education, professional experience) and psychological characteristics (including attitudes and values). For a review of this extensive literature, see McPherson et al. (2001).

Homophily for the highly visible characteristics of age and sex, the focal points of the current chapter, has received particularly widespread research attention. Considerable evidence suggests that even young children recognize the social significance of these attributes as organizational features of society, and tend to form their associations accordingly (Maccoby, 1998; Hagestad & Uhlenberg, 2006). Research on conventional networks consistently shows that sex segregation is most pronounced for non-kin emotional ties like friendship, particularly at younger ages (McPherson et al., 2001). As individuals begin to form romantic relationships and friendships with members of the opposite sex in late adolescence and early adulthood, sex segregation diminishes considerably, but classic studies still demonstrate marked gender homophily for close ties amongst both males and females in adulthood; Marsden (1988) found that ties between adults who "discuss important matters" were only 70% as heterogeneous as expected given the relatively balanced sex distribution of the general population. In comparison to close ties, however, ties that are instrumental in nature appear to be less gender homogeneous, especially in populations with skewed gender distributions. In these contexts, both sexes have been shown to commonly use men as "network routes to accomplish tasks" (McPherson et al., 2001: 424).

Patterns of age homogeneity in conventional social networks are more consistent. Many studies show that marriage ties are almost exclusively age homogeneous, and that non-kin ties ranging from friendship to general associations are also overwhelmingly made with alters in the same general age range. In Marsden's (1988) study of confiding networks mentioned above, age heterogeneity was less than half that expected for non-kin relations, a finding that many subsequent studies have replicated (see Burt, 1991; Hagestad & Uhlenberg, 2006).

Although the research on homophily in illicit networks is not nearly as well developed as that for conventional networks, there is growing evidence that similarity on a range of attributes predicts tie formation in criminal and delinquent networks as well.[3] Strong tendencies toward homophily have been demonstrated in the literature on co-offending in particular (Daly, 2005; Malm, Bichler, & Nash, 2011; Reiss & Farrington, 1991; Sarnecki, 2001; Schaefer, 2012; van Mastrigt & Farrington, 2011; Warr, 2002). The descriptive finding that co-offending groups are typically homogeneous with respect to key attributes like age, sex, ethnicity, residence, and criminal experience is so consistent that group homogeneity was recently named as one of eight key characteristics of co-offending identified by Weerman (2003: 400).

Patterns of sex and age homogeneity are especially pronounced. Warr (1996) reported that, based on National Survey of Youth data, between 62% and 90% of delinquent group events involved same-sex co-offenders. Similar figures emerged from the UK Crime and Justice survey, in which more than 70% of co-offending incidents committed across

a wide range of ages implicated same-sex groups (Budd, Sharp, & Mayhew, 2005). In general, whilst both males and females appear to choose co-offenders of the same sex in the majority of cases, "females are more often found in the company of males than vice versa" (Warr, 2002: 79). Stated differently, the sex homogeneity observed in most co-offending groups is driven primarily by all-male co-offending (Pettersson, 2005; Reiss, 1988; Reiss & Farrington, 1991; Sarnecki, 2001; Warr, 2002).

Even at the youngest ages, females are less likely than males to offend with same-sex accomplices. In their analysis of Philadelphia juvenile court records, for example, Conway and McCord (2002) reported that, whereas 95.5% of males had male co-offenders in their first recorded co-offense, only 80.6% of females had female co-offenders. In older samples, even more striking differences are evident. In Carrington's (2002a, 2002b) Canadian analyses, 87% of co-offending males compared to only 50% of co-offending females were involved in same-sex incidents. Similar figures emerged using self-report methods in the UK Crime and Justice Survey (Budd et al., 2005: 61); whereas males reported offending almost exclusively with other males, females reported that they had female co-offenders only half of the time (48%). Finally, in his analysis of Crown Court conviction data, Tarling (1993) reported that, across age and crime type, a small *majority* of females' co-defendants were male (57%), whereas a small *minority* (10%) of males had female co-defendants. Such findings are often interpreted as evidence that males have a greater preference for same-sex accomplices as compared to females (Carrington, 2002b), a point we return to later.

Similar homogeneity patterns have been demonstrated by age. A number of studies have shown that age differences between co-offenders are typically small—one to two years on average—and that there is little overlap between youth and adult criminal networks. Reiss and Farrington (1991: 390) found that, in the Cambridge Study, 54% of offenders were within one year younger or older than their co-offenders and that only 16% of co-offending pairs had an age difference of five or more years. Warr (1996: 24) reported similar findings based on juvenile self-report data, citing an average age difference of less than one year for all co-offenses captured in the National Survey of Youth. Recent evidence from the UK Crime and Justice Survey replicates these findings. Across age, more than 75% of incidents involved co-offenders in the same general age range (Budd et al., 2005: 61). These findings consistently suggest that co-offenders are typically selected from amongst one's same-age peers. Indeed, in her British self-report study, Shapland (1978: 262) reported that very few boys aged 13–14 reported committing offenses with a parent or other adult, a finding that led her to conclude that delinquents had "little contact with any adult criminal culture." Of course, there are exceptions to this general rule. In their legendary case study of Sidney's criminal career, Shaw and McKay (1931) observed that "delinquent boys . . . have contact not only with other delinquents who are their contemporaries but also with older offenders," and more recent evidence illustrates that youths and much older adults do, occasionally, offend together (van Mastrigt & Farrington, 2011).

Although co-offending tends to take place in relatively age-homogeneous groups overall, there is some evidence to suggest that this tendency decreases with age. Recent findings from the UK Crime and Justice survey (Budd et al., 2005: 61) showed that in 83% of incidents reported by 10–15 year olds, all co-offenders were in the same general age range, but that this was the case in only 75% of incidents committed by 16–25 year olds. Sarnecki's Swedish study and Reiss and Farrington's research similarly revealed a "slight tendency for the age difference between actors and their co-offenders. . .to increase as actors

became older" (Sarnecki, 2001: 53), findings which are typically explained with reference to the changing constellations of personal networks across the life course (Reiss & Farrington, 1991; Warr, 1993).

Opportunity Versus Preference

As the above review shows, it is clear that both conventional and illicit networks display marked patterns of homophily across both age and sex. What is less clear is what accounts for these patterns and their variation across attributes. Theoretical explanations generally fall into two competing camps: choice-based explanations and opportunity-based explanations (Franz, Marsili, & Pin, 2010; McPherson & Smith-Lovin, 1987; McPherson et al., 2001).[4]

Choice-based explanations posit that individuals have a social preference for forming relationships with similar alters because these ties are more psychologically rewarding and/or less energy-intensive than those formed with dissimilar alters. Social psychologists have long argued that attraction is strongly influenced by perceived similarity. This idea, formalized as the "similarity-attraction hypothesis," has been supported by a large number of both correlational and experimental studies (Huston & Levinger, 1978; Monge & Contractor, 2003; Byrne, 1971; Turner, Hogg, Oakes, Reicher, & Wetherell, 1987).

According to some theorists, the powerful draw to associate with others like us reflects fundamental processes of social categorization and social comparison, ultimately geared toward the reward of validating one's own social status and identity (Festinger, 1954; Tajfel & Turner, 1986). Others frame their explanations not in terms of maximization of rewards, but in terms of minimization of costs, as sharing a social status is argued to ease understanding and cooperation (Ruef, 2002). According to Mayhew and colleagues (1995: 19–21) differences in social position (e.g., age, race, sex) can act as "energy barriers" to communication and coordinated action. Because humans encode more information about their own social categories' expected behaviors as compared to others', they argue, more time and energy must be expended in heterogeneous groups checking for social signals and action, a requirement that makes these types of associations less attractive.

Irrespective of the specific mechanisms identified, choice-based explanations share the common feature of framing the selection of alters as a conscious process which employs socio-cognitive heuristics that maximize the rewards and minimize the costs of social interaction. Such explanations are consistent with theoretical accounts of co-offender selection that argue that the search for co-offenders is purposeful and reflects a process of (bounded) rationality in which the attractiveness of potential co-offenders is weighed (Tremblay, 1993; Weerman, 2003). A number of studies have shown that criminal cooperation is recognized by many offenders as inherently risky; accomplices may be incompetent, dishonest, or quick to save themselves at others' expense if caught (McCarthy et al., 1998). To the extent that shared social status may ease cooperation and maximize trust, as outlined above (see also, von Lampe & Johansen, 2004), offenders might be expected to limit the risks of co-offending by actively seeking out similar accomplices, a process that could explain the high levels of homogeneity observed in co-offending groups.[5]

In contrast to choice-based explanations, opportunity-based explanations of homophily argue that affiliations are governed not by unconstrained choice, but by underlying structural opportunities (Blau, 1977; Franz et al., 2010). According to these theories, it is the baseline distribution of social characteristics in the selection pool that drive tie formation (McPherson et al., 2001). A strict interpretation of the opportunity paradigm would suggest that individuals select at random from the full population in which they are embedded, and that observed patterns of homophily reflect nothing more than the unequal distribution of social characteristics in that population.

Consider, for example, a population in which the gender distribution is highly skewed in favor of males (as is the case in the offending population). Even in the absence of a psychological preference for same-sex ties, males would, as members of the larger subgroup, have a greater probability of coming into contact and forming ties with one another simply by chance. Thus, an observed tendency for males to differentially associate with other males could simply reflect the baseline structural opportunities that bring males into contact with one another more often than with females. Similarly, low levels of female-to-female contact and correspondingly high levels of female-to-male contact could be explained by the relative scarcity of females in the selection pool (see Carrington, 2002b). Another important consideration for opportunity models is the size of the social unit under observation, as larger groupings of individuals would be expected to be more heterogeneous by chance, for the same reasons outlined above (Mayhew et al., 1995).

Critics of strict opportunity explanations like that provided above argue that, in large populations, an individual is rarely free to choose alters from the entire pool of potential contacts (Feld, 1981). More tempered versions of the opportunity approach thus propose that structural opportunities have a more local character and that one's choice set is constrained to those individuals within the larger population which whom one comes into regular contact via shared spaces and social foci, such as neighborhoods, schools, and workplaces (e.g., Reskin, McBrier, & Kmec, 1999). As the demography of these local selection pools may differ from that of the larger pool of potential contacts, proponents of these more tempered models argue that baseline demography measured at the population level tells only part of the story.[6] Even according to these more lenient theorists, however, structural opportunity, rather than psychological preference, is seen as the key mechanism driving tie formation.

Opportunity theories thus support an alternative view of co-offender selection; namely, that ties between accomplices are formed relatively spontaneously and involve considerably less forethought and planning than choice-based, rational choice models would suggest. Here, co-offending ties might be expected to form more inadvertently between the offenders present when criminal opportunities arise. According to this hypothesis, homophily should simply reflect the demography of the potential co-offender pool, as outlined above.

Felson (2003) argues that routine activities provide frequent opportunities for would-be co-offenders to come together via informal and recurrent meetings at "offender convergence settings." Seen from a structural opportunity perspective, these criminogenic social foci would be expected to determine both the possibilities for co-offending to occur and the selection of potential accomplices.

To recap, two different theoretical explanations have been advanced to explain homophily in conventional social networks: choice and opportunity. Broadly speaking, these two approaches are also evidenced, to a greater or lesser degree, in existing hypotheses regarding the search for co-offenders. Although most scholars, including those cited above, would likely agree that it is a combination of choice and opportunity that governs the selection of co-offenders in practice, current theoretical explanations nonetheless tend to prioritize either structural opportunities or rational choice.

With the exception of one earlier investigation (Carrington 2002b, discussed below), we are not aware of any studies that have empirically pitted these theories against one another in the co-offending context. It is our view that insights regarding the relative import of these factors in the selection of co-offenders would be of considerable theoretical and practical value.

BASIC, BASELINE, AND INBREEDING HOMOPHILY

Any attempt to empirically disentangle the effects of structural opportunity and social preference requires a conceptual distinction between three different, but related, measures of homophily: basic homophily, baseline homophily, and inbreeding homophily (Currarini, Jackson, & Pin, 2009; McPherson et al., 2001).

Basic homophily is a simple descriptive measure, indicating the fraction of same-type (homogeneous) ties in a network. This basic measure of homophily is the one most commonly reported in the studies of co-offending reviewed above. Whilst informative in relation to constructing a descriptive profile of co-offending networks, measures of basic homophily are of limited value for theory evaluation as they fail to take account of the baseline distribution of social characteristics in the offending population and the size of offending groups—factors that are crucial to opportunity models.

Measures of baseline (also called induced) homophily incorporate this important information to provide probability estimates regarding the degree of clustering expected by chance, given the demography of the potential contact pool and the size of the social group (typically expressed as the frequency or proportion of expected same-type ties). Because this measure of homophily assumes random mixing and no social preference for similar others, it provides a straightforward gauge of the baseline constraints on which structural opportunity theories are built; for if opportunity alone governed the selection of alters, the observed and expected number of homogeneous ties would be equal.

In the co-offending context, estimates of baseline homophily are particularly important because of the known age and gender skew in offending populations. A comparison of observed and expected figures is therefore crucial to any meaningful interpretation of the homogeneity of co-offending groups. This was the point made by Carrington (2002b) in the only study of which we are aware that has attempted to compute baseline homophily figures for co-offending groups. Based on his analysis of sex homogeneity using Canadian Uniform Crime Reporting Survey (UCR2) data, Carrington found that the observed frequency of both all-male and all-female co-offending groups exceeded baseline expectation. Moreover, despite the fact that all-male co-offending groups were the norm in descriptive terms, it was all-female groups that displayed the largest differences between observed and expected homogeneity, a finding that led Carrington to conclude that "both males and females prefer to co-offend with members of the same sex, but [contrary to conventional wisdom] the tendency is relatively weak in males and much stronger in females" (2002b: 115). By comparing basic and induced homophily measures, Carrington's earlier analysis was able to show that the selection of co-offenders could not be explained by baseline opportunities alone. What his analysis lacked, however, was specificity. In particular, a standardized measure of deviation from expectation that could be meaningfully compared for males and females, and across group size. Inbreeding coefficients offer one such measure (Coleman, 1958; Currarini et al., 2009; McPherson et al., 2001).

Inbreeding homophily refers to the degree of clustering that *cannot* be explained by baseline opportunity structures. Put another way, it is a measure of the difference between the observed probability of same-type ties and the probability expected by a simple model of random assortment, standardized to "capture . . . how biased a group is compared to how biased it potentially could be" (see Coleman, 1958: 36; Currarini et al., 2009: 1008).

Inbreeding coefficients range between −1 and 1, where 0 = no deviation from baseline. If the observed deviation is in favor of same-type ties, a population is said to exhibit inbreeding bias (1 = total inbreeding), whereas a greater than expected number of out-group ties indicates the opposite (−1 = total outbreeding). Although a handful of studies have recently used inbreeding coefficients to explore racial homophily in friendship ties (Currarini et al., 2009; Currarini, Jackson, & Pin, 2010; Franz et al., 2010), this simple and informative measure of social bias has never, to our knowledge, been applied to criminal networks.

Our use of the term "social bias" instead of "choice" or "preference" is important to note here. Whereas at first glance, inbreeding coefficients appear to provide a direct measure of choice-based homophily in the same way that baseline homophily figures provide a measure of population-based structural opportunity, it is important to recognize that inbreeding patterns can also result from bias in *local* meeting opportunities, or by social structures below the population level, which effectively constrain one's choices to a subset of the population selection pool. Because the demography of local socio-organizational structures may differ from that of the full population pool, inbreeding bias does not necessarily capture "choice or agency purified of [all] structural factors" (McPherson et al., 2001: 419). Instead, it measures the combined social bias for associating with similar others that is produced by preference *and/or* local socio-organizational constraints.[7] In this sense, measures of inbreeding homophily can be used to refute strict structural opportunity theories but not to support choice-based theories or the more local opportunity-based models independently.

Even so, information on inbreeding bias has the potential to advance knowledge of the formation and composition of co-offending networks considerably, not least because it elevates the discussion of homophily beyond the basic descriptive level typically provided in the extant literature. Tests for inbreeding are also of theoretical value, as even refuting strict opportunity theories can go some way toward a better understanding of accomplice selection processes. Furthermore, if standardized inbreeding measures are computed separately for different offender subgroups (males/females; youths/adults), variations in levels of social bias like those noted by Carrington (2002b) can be explored in more detail. In conventional networks, this information has proven useful in exploring segregation, gatekeeping, and inequality in diverse social systems (Moody, 2001), issues that may be of potential interest for criminal networks as well (e.g., see Steffensmeier, 1983).

THE CURRENT STUDY

For all of the reasons outlined above, meaningful discussion regarding the selection of accomplices and the homogeneity of co-offending groups must take as its starting point deviation from baseline expectations. Although information on observed (basic) homophily in co-offending networks is widespread, the baseline and inbreeding measures that are required to interpret these basic findings are lacking. In this study, we extend Carrington's (2002b) earlier work by using all three measures of homophily to explore patterns of both age and sex homogeneity in a large collection of UK police data, and performing statistical tests of the significance of any apparent deviations from baseline homophily. In doing so, we attempt a preliminary test of competing opportunity vs. choice-based hypotheses regarding the selection of co-offenders.

Specifically, we test the following research questions: (1) to what extent are co-offending groups homogeneous with respect to sex and age?; (2) to what extent is their homogeneity an indication of inbreeding homophily?; and (3) does the magnitude of inbreeding homophily vary across age, sex, or group size?

Hypotheses

In relation to the first research question, given the high levels of observed (basic) homophily reported in the existing co-offending literature, we have good reason to expect that the co-offending groups captured in our data will also demonstrate considerable age and sex homogeneity (Hypothesis 1). Moreover, both Carrington's (2002b) earlier analyses and insights from choice-based theories lend support to the hypothesis that these observed patterns of homogeneity are likely to reflect clustering above and beyond what a baseline model would predict. In other words, that co-offending groups will evidence a general tendency toward inbreeding (Hypothesis 2).

Even so, some variations by age, sex, and group size might be expected on both empirical and theoretical grounds. If Mayhew et al.'s (1995: 22) "energy distribution principle" transfers to illicit networks, then inbreeding homophily for both sex and age should increase with increasing group size, as "any increase in heterogeneity with size, or even the same level of heterogeneity at larger sizes, would compound the difficulties in communication and coordination of action" within co-offending groups (Hypothesis 3).

With respect to sex, from a choice-based theoretical standpoint, one would expect that males, rather than females, would exhibit greater inbreeding. A number of scholars have noted that male offenders often see females as less reliable or competent crime partners (Decker, Wright, Redfern, & Smith, 1993; Pettiway, 1987; Steffensmeier & Terry, 1986). In fact, Steffensmeier (1983: 1025) has argued that "institutional sexism is so consistent and pervasive in the underworld that female access is likely to be limited to those circumstances in which male members of the underworld find females to be useful." On these grounds, a higher degree of male inbreeding would be expected (Hypothesis 4).

Finally, we hypothesize that youths will display greater inbreeding homophily as compared to adults (*Hypothesis 5*). This expectation is driven by research which shows that, because of their relatively limited mobility, the "activity spaces" of youths are typically concentrated around local social foci like schools and neighborhoods (Cohen & Felson, 1979; Reiss & Farrington, 1991), whereas adults cast more diverse social and spatial nets. Because the offender convergence settings available to youths are likely to be more homogeneous than those available to adults, similar co-offenders should be more accessible than those who are dissimilar (Felson, 2003; Weerman, 2003). According to this reasoning, local-level opportunities, in addition to choice, could drive youthful inbreeding.

DATA AND ANALYTIC METHODS

The co-offending data analyzed in this study is taken from a large official dataset detailing the full population of notifiable criminal events detected by a large UK police force between March 1, 2002 and February 28, 2005. In total, this data includes information on 105,348 crimes implicating 61,646 different individuals aged 10–74 (for further details, see van Mastrigt & Farrington, 2009). Overall, 30% of offenders were linked to at least one known accomplice during the study period and 10% of offenses involved more than one perpetrator. In the current study, we focus on this subpopulation of joint offenses and adopt the co-offending group as the main unit of analysis (N = 10,997).

Variables

Co-offending Group Size

The co-offending groups captured in our data ranged in size from 2 to 20 members, with 2.37 on average (SD = 0.87). The current analyses are limited to the 10,946 groups with between two and six members,

as the observed and expected numbers for larger groups were too small for meaningful analysis. This restriction is unlikely to have a substantive impact on our conclusions as less than 1% of all groups (N = 51) comprised more than six members.

Sex Composition

Complete information on the sex of all members was available for 10,942 co-offending groups. These groups were coded using a simple tripartite variable indicating whether the group was all-male, all-female, or mixed-sex. Overall, 68.3% of the co-offending groups comprised exclusively males, 11.5% exclusively females, and 20.2% a mix of both sexes.

Age Composition

As Burt (1991) has argued, there is no consensus about the most appropriate coding scheme to capture the social meaning of age. The approach adopted here was to code each co-offending group member's age in relation to the important life stages of youth (<18) and adulthood (≤18), yielding a group composition variable with three levels: all-youth, all-adult, or mixed-age. In total, 10,387 co-offending groups had valid information for this variable: 53.1% of all these groups were all-adult, 29.6% all-youth, and 17.2% mixed-age.

The choice to code age in this manner was taken, in part, to allow a uniform analytic approach to exploring homophily across both age and sex using binomial probability models (see below). This dichotomization also seemed appropriate given the common suggestion in previous research that youth and adult co-offending networks rarely overlap (Reiss & Farrington, 1991; Shapland, 1978). By coding our co-offending groups as all-youth, all-adult, or mixed-age, we are able explore this issue directly by comparing the inbreeding coefficients for each.

Homophily

We use all three homophily measures outlined earlier in our analyses, calculated separately for each subgroup (males, females, youths, adults), and each co-offending-group size. Although formal homophily measures are most often used in the context of dyad-based interactions in populations, they can, with minor modification, also be usefully applied to measure homophily in small interaction cliques such as co-offending groups. The measures developed below are modified versions of those presented by Coleman (1958: 36; see Equations 17 and 18) and re-stated by Currarini et al. (2009: 1007–1008).

There are two sexes and two age groups in the population; let a_{in}, $i = 1, 2$ denote the number of homogeneous co-offending groups of size n composed of individuals of type i, and let a_{3n} denote the number of heterogeneous co-offending groups of size n. Let A_n denote the total number of co-offending groups of size n. Then A_n is $\Sigma a_{in} = a_{1n} + a_{2n} + a_{3n}$.

- **Basic (observed) homophily (H)** is the proportion of homogeneous co-offending groups of a given type of individual and a given size:

$$H_{in} = \frac{a_{in}}{A_n} \qquad (1)$$

For example, of the 8,381 co-offending groups of size 2, 5,649 were all-male; thus basic male 2-group homophily is 0.674.

- In contrast to basic, or observed, homophily, **baseline (expected) homophily (EH)** is computed based on the assumption of random assortment and thus yields *expected* homophily figures. As Coleman (1958) and others (Mayhew et al., 1995; Carrington, 2002b) have pointed out, expected distributions cannot be calculated from simple marginal proportions, as in a contingency table; rather they are based on combinatorics. Because both sex and age were measured as binary variables, the binomial distribution is used to provide the number of co-offending groups of size n and type i that would be expected to form by chance.

Using sex homogeneity as an example, we first determine the proportions p of males and q of females (defined as $1 - p$) in the full offender dataset.[8] These proportions represent the baseline, or random, probability of encountering a male ($p = 0.784$) or a female ($q = 0.216$) in the offending population (for age, p (adult) = 0.767 and q (youth) = 0.233). Using these proportions, binomial expansions are then applied to compute the baseline probabilities, denoted by w_{in}, of observing co-offending groups of different compositions i (e.g., all-male, all-female, and mixed-sex groups) under chance expectation for each size n. Specifically, for groups of size n, $w_{1n} = p^n$ is the expected proportion of all-male groups, $w_{2n} = q^n$ is the expected proportion for all-female groups, and $w_{3n} = 1 - (p^n + q^n)$ is the residual proportion of mixed-sex groups.

For example, for 2-groups (co-offending groups of size 2), baseline (expected) male homophily w_{12} is $0.784^2 = 0.615$, baseline female homophily is $0.216^2 = 0.047$, and baseline heterophily is $1 - (0.615 + 0.047) = 0.338$. Thus, for 2-groups, the observed male and female homophilies of 0.674 and 0.131 considerably exceed baseline homophily, and, concomitantly, the observed heterophily of 0.195 is considerably less than baseline. The difference between observed and baseline homophily can be tested using the usual χ^2 test, with 1 degree of freedom.[9]

- The difference between observed homophily and that expected by chance is defined as *inbreeding homophily (IH)*. The raw difference is normalized by dividing by the maximum possible difference, denoted by m_{in}, so that the result ranges between +1 and −1, with a value of 0 when observed and expected homophily are equal (Coleman, 1958: 36, Equations 17 and 18).

However, the maximum possible value in this case is not simply 1 (cf. Currarini et al., 2009: 1008, Definition 6); its calculation is complicated by limitations due to the numbers of male and female participations in co-offending groups of size *n*. For example, there were 8,381 2-groups, of which 5,649 were all-male, 1,100 all-female, and 1,632 mixed-sex. The maximum possible number of all-male groups is not 8,381, or a proportion of 1.0. There were only 12,930 male participations in 2-groups; thus the maximum number of all-male 2-groups is 12,930/2 = 6,465, or a proportion of $m_{12}= 0.771$ (not 1.0). Similarly, as there were only 3,832 female participations in 2-groups, the maximum possible number of all-female 2-groups is 3,832/2 = 1,916, or a proportion of $m_{22}= 0.229$. (Note that if all male participations are sex-segregated into all-male groups, then the number of mixed groups is 0, and all female participations must be in all-female groups, so the proportion of all-female *n*-groups m_{2n} is $1 - m_{1n}$.)

In cases where observed homophily is *greater* than expected homophily, the inbreeding coefficient is calculated as:

$$IH_{in} = \frac{H_{in} - w_{in}}{m_n - w_{in}} \qquad (2a)$$

In cases where the observed homophily is less than the expected homophily, so that their difference is negative, the maximum value (i.e., of the absolute value) of the difference is simply the expected value itself, so the inbreeding coefficient is:

$$IH_{in} = \frac{H_{in} - w_{in}}{w_{in}} \qquad (2b)$$

RESULTS

Sex Homogeneity

Table 2.1 shows values of basic (observed), baseline (expected), and inbreeding homophily, with chi-square tests of the differences, for male and female co-offending groups, by co-offending group size. Consistent with Hypothesis 1, high levels of basic sex homophily are observed overall: only 20% of co-offending groups are mixed-sex. However, while observed overall male homophily is substantial (68% of all co-offending groups are all-male), observed female homophily is much lower (12% of all co-offending groups).

Hypothesis 2 posits a general tendency toward inbreeding homophily in co-offending groups. Overall, this hypothesis is supported. Observed homophily exceeds baseline homophily for both sexes, observed heterophily is less than expected, and the differences are statistically significant at $p < 0.001$. The values of the inbreeding coefficient are substantial: 0.51 for males and 0.44 for females. The value of *IH* for mixed (heterophilous) groups indicates the normalized extent to which observed heterophily exceeds that expected by chance, and thus serves as a (reverse) indicator of non-sex-specific inbreeding homophily: it is also substantial, at −0.48.

The results for Hypothesis 3 are mixed. Consistent with the hypothesis, inbreeding male homophily increases with co-offending group size, from 0.38 for 2-groups to 0.74 for 5-groups—but it decreases to 0.61 for groups of six co-offenders. Also consistent with Hypothesis 3, outbreeding heterophily decreases with group size, from −0.42 for 2-groups to −0.65 for 5-groups—although it increases slightly to −0.63 for groups of

Table 2.1 Basic, baseline, and inbreeding homophily for males and females, by offending group size

	Number of Offending Groups					Homophily			
Offending Group Size	Observed	Expected	χ^2	p^a	Max^b	Basic (observed) H	Baseline (expected) w	Maximum M	Inbreeding IH
2									
All Male	5649	5154	47.54	0.000	6465	0.674	0.615	0.771	0.378
All Female	1100	394	1265.07	0.000	1916	0.131	0.047	0.229	0.464
Mixed	1632	2833	509.14	0.000	3832	0.195	0.338	0.457	-0.424
Total	8381	8381							
Number of male participations			12930						
Number of female participations			3832						
3									
All Male	1303	874	210.57	0.000	1520	0.719	0.482	0.838	0.664
All Female	125	18	636.06	0.000	292	0.069	0.010	0.161	0.391
Mixed	385	921	311.94	0.000	877	0.212	0.508	0.484	-0.582
Total	1813	1813							
Number of male participations			4562						
Number of female participations			877						
4									
All Male	372	202	143.07	0.000	447	0.698	0.379	0.839	0.694
All Female	32	1^c	961.00	0.000	85	0.060	0.002	0.159	0.369
Mixed	129	330	122.43	0.000	343	0.242	0.619	0.644	-0.609
Total	533	533							
Number of male participations			1789						
Number of female participations			343						
5									
All Male	126	49.5	118.23	0.000	153	0.741	0.296	0.900	0.736
All Female	2	1^c	1.00	0.317	16	0.012	0.000	0.094	0.128
Mixed	42	119.5	50.26	0.000	82	0.247	0.704	0.482	-0.649
Total	170	170							
Number of male participations			768						
Number of female participations			82						

Table 2.1 Continued

Offending Group Size	Number of Offending Groups						Homophily		
	Observed	Expected	χ^2	p^a	Max^b	Basic (observed) H	Baseline (expected) w	Maximum M	Inbreeding IH
6									
All Male	27	9.5	32.24	0.000	37	0.600	0.232	0.822	0.612
All Female	0	1^c	1.00	0.317	7	0.000	0.000	0.156	0.000
Mixed	18	34.5	7.89	0.005	43	0.400	0.768	0.956	−0.628
Total	45	45							
Number of male participations			227						
Number of female participations			43						
All 2–6									
All Male	7477	6289	224.41	0.000	8622	0.683	0.575	0.788	0.509
All Female	1259	415	1716.47	0.000	2316	0.115	0.038	0.212	0.444
Mixed	2206	4238	974.29	0.000	5177	0.202	0.387	0.473	−0.479
Total	10942	10942							
Number of male participations			20276						
Number of female participations			5177						

Notes

Values in highlighted cells may be unreliable due to low expected numbers.

a Statistical significance, $df = 1$

b Maximum possible number of groups

c Expected value rounded to 1 to permit chi-square calculation six co-offenders. Contrary to Hypothesis 3, however, female inbreeding homophily does not increase with group size: it decreases from 0.46 for 2-groups to 0.13 for 5-groups and 0 for 6-groups (however, the values for female homophily for 4-groups and greater may be unreliable due to small numbers).

Finally, there is weak overall support for Hypothesis 4, which posits that male inbreeding homophily will be higher than that of females. The overall value for male inbreeding is 0.51, compared with 0.44 for females, and greater inbreeding for males is also evidenced for 3-groups and larger. However, for groups of two co-offenders, female inbreeding homophily is higher: 0.46 compared with 0.38 for males.

Age Homogeneity

The results for age are shown in Table 2.2. As was the case for sex, considerable observed (basic) age homophily is evidenced overall: 53% of all co-offending groups are all-adult, 30% are all-youth, and only 17% are age-heterogeneous. These findings lend further support to Hypothesis 1: co-offending groups tend toward observed homogeneity overall. For the mixed youth/adult groups, however, considerable age variability was observed. Within these groups there was an average age difference of 6.28 years between members, and less than half of these groups exhibited an age difference of three or fewer years. This indicates that only a minority of the age-heterogeneous groups comprised older youths and younger adults (e.g., 17 and 18 year olds) offending together.

Like the findings for sex, there is also evidence for a general inbreeding tendency by age (Hypothesis 2). The overall value of IH for mixed-age co-offending groups is negative and substantial (-0.58, $p < 0.001$), as are its values for co-offending groups of each size, implying substantially less heterophily than would be expected by chance. However, almost all of the inbreeding homophily

is due to homophily of young offenders, not of adults. Whereas youths' overall inbreeding coefficient is high ($IH = 0.75$), and observed homophily exceeds baseline for youthful co-offending groups of each size ($p < 0.001$), adults exhibit a slight and barely significant tendency toward outbreeding overall ($IH = -0.03$, $p < 0.05$), and for co-offending groups of sizes 2, 3, and 4. This outbreeding pattern is weak, however, and only significant for 3-groups. Further, for adult 5- and 6-groups, the pattern is reversed and there is evidence of inbreeding, although it is significant only for 5-groups ($p < 0.01$). The results for Hypothesis 2 are therefore mixed.

Support for Hypothesis 3—that inbreeding will increase with co-offending group size—is thus also mixed. Consistent with this hypothesis, adult inbreeding does, in fact, increase from -0.02 for 2-groups to a high of 0.40 for 5-groups, although it is lower for both 3- and 4-groups. In contrast, youth inbreeding decreases rather than increases with co-offending group size, from 0.77 for 2-groups to 0.57 for 5-groups—with a slight rise to 0.68 for groups of six co-offenders (although here, too, the values for 4-groups and greater should be interpreted with caution due to small numbers). Outbreeding heterophily exhibits similar variability, increasing with offending group size, from -0.62 for 2-groups to -0.45 for 4-groups—but decreasing again for larger co-offending groups, to a value of -0.63 for 6-groups.

Support for Hypothesis 5 is much more consistent: inbreeding homophily is much greater for youths than adults overall ($IH = 0.75$ vs. -0.03), and for co-offending groups of all sizes. For groups with between two and four co-offenders, youths' IH values are all positive and large, indicating a high degree of inbreeding homophily, whereas adults' coefficients are all negative and small, indicating a weak tendency toward outbreeding. Moreover, even in 5- and 6-groups, where both youths and adults exhibit inbreeding, youths' values are considerably higher.

Table 2.2 Basic, baseline, and inbreeding homophily for youths and adults, by offending group size

Co-offending Group Size	Number of Co-offending Groups					Basic (observed) H	Homophily		
	Observed	Expected	χ^2	p^a	Max^b		Baseline (expected) w	Maximum M	Inbreeding IH
2									
All Youth	2277	434	7826.38	0.000	2825	0.286	0.054	0.355	0.771
All Adult	4593	4685	1.81	0.179	5141	0.577	0.588	0.645	-0.020
Mixed	1097	2848	1076.55	0.000	5651	0.138	0.357	0.709	-0.615
Total	7967	7967			5651				
Number of youth participations	5651								
Number of adult participations	10283								
3									
All Youth	600	19	17766.37	0.000	815	0.348	0.011	0.473	0.730
All Adult	683	778	11.60	0.001	908	0.396	0.451	0.527	-0.122
Mixed	441	927	254.80	0.000	2447	0.256	0.538	1.419	-0.524
Total	1724	1724							
Number of youth participations	2477								
Number of adult participations	2725								
4									
All Youth	147	1^c	21316.00	0.000	233	0.298	0.003	0.473	0.628
All Adult	168	171	0.05	0.819	260	0.341	0.346	0.527	-0.028
Mixed	178	321	63.70	0.000	932	0.361	0.651	1.890	-0.445
Total	493	493							
Number of youth participations	932								
Number of adult participations	1040								
5									
All Youth	40	1^c	1521.00	0.000	70	0.250	0.001	0.438	0.570
All Adult	61	41.5	9.16	0.002	89	0.381	0.265	0.556	0.399
Mixed	59	117.5	29.13	0.000	354	0.369	0.734	2.213	-0.498
Total	160	160							
Number of youth participations	354								
Number of adult participations	446								
6									
All Youth	15	1^c	196.00	0.000	22	0.349	0.000	0.512	0.682
All Adult	12	8.5	1.44	0.230	20	0.279	0.204	0.465	0.287

Mixed	16	43	33.5	43	9.14	0.002	121	0.372	0.796	2.814	−0.628
Total											
Number of youth participations			137								
Number of adult participations			121								

All 2–6

All Youth	3079	456	15088.00	0.000	3965	0.296	0.044	0.382	0.748
All Adult	5517	5684	4.91	0.027	6418	0.531	0.547	0.618	−0.029
Mixed	1791	4247	1420.28	0.000	9505	0.172	0.409	0.915	−0.578
Total	10387	10387							
Number of youth participations	9521								
Number of adult participations	14615								

Notes

Values in highlighted cells may be unreliable due to low expected numbers.

a Statistical significance, $df = 1$

b Maximum possible number of groups

c Expected value rounded to 1 to permit chi-square calculation

DISCUSSION

Students of co-offending have repeatedly observed sex and age homogeneity in co-offending groups, particularly amongst males and youths (Carrington, 2011: 245). These observations have generally been taken as evidence of a preference for accomplices who are similar to oneself; that is, as evidence of choice-based accomplice selection. However, this conclusion is typically drawn in the absence of information regarding baseline opportunities for homophilous co-offending groups to form, given the demographic distribution of the offending population. The objective of this chapter was to explore competing hypotheses regarding the selection of co-offenders by comparing basic, baseline, and inbreeding homophily for different offender subgroups and co-offending group sizes. Specifically, using police data from a large UK metropolitan area, we compared observed age and sex homophily with expectations from a simple probability model in order to compute standardized inbreeding coefficients for males, females, youths, and adults.

We found strong evidence of age and sex inbreeding in co-offending groups. Overall, and for each co-offending group size, the observed number of mixed (heterophilous) groups was substantially and significantly lower than the number expected by chance. This is consistent with the findings of other co-offending research (Carrington, 2011: 245). However, our conclusions concerning sex-specific homophily differ markedly from those of most other research. Although—consistent with other research—there is far more observed homophily among male than female co-offenders in this population, the difference between male and female homophily is very small, once it is normalized to account for the highly skewed sex ratio in the offending population: 0.51 for males and 0.44 for females. Furthermore, for co-offending groups of size 2—which account for 77% of all co-offending groups in this population—normalized female inbreeding homophily *exceeds* that of males (0.46 versus 0.38), even though the basic observed homophily of females in 2-groups is far lower than that of males. These findings provide support for Carrington's (2002b) argument that the high observed frequency of all-male co-offending groups and low observed frequency of all-female co-offending groups is largely accounted for by the sex ratio of the offending population: that is, by sex-specific opportunity. This calls into question the supposed preference of females to co-offend with males (Sarnecki, 2001; Steffensmeier & Terry, 1986), and explanations of female co-offending that highlight the influence of, or coercion by, male associates, especially romantic partners (Fleisher & Krienert, 2004; Haynie, Giordano, Manning, & Longmore, 2005; Vandiver, 2006; Warr, 1996). The finding that both males and females were disproportionately involved with same-sex accomplices is more consistent with the idea that criminal networks are highly segregated by gender and that this segregation, whether a result of choice or exclusion, plays an important role in the selection of co-offenders for both sexes (Alarid, Marquat, Burton, Cullen, & Cuvelier, 1996; Decker et al., 1993).

Whereas males and females demonstrated similarly high levels of inbreeding in this study, the findings for age-specific homophily indicate considerable inbreeding differences between youths and adults. Basic observed homophily is much higher for adults than youths (0.53 versus 0.30), but normalized (inbreeding) homophily is far lower for adults than for youths: in fact, for adults, it is *negative* (–0.03): that is, less than expected by chance; whereas for youths it is strongly positive (0.75). Similarly, at each co-offending group size (except groups of size 6, of which there are few), basic observed homophily is greater among adults, but normalized (inbreeding) homophily is far greater among youths. These findings illustrate the importance of using a normalized index of homophily, rather than basic observed proportions, when making comparisons. The high rates of youthful inbreeding observed in this study are consistent with suggestions made in previous research that there is "substantial separation of juvenile from adult networks in the selection of co-offenders" (Reiss & Farrington, 1991: 390; Sarnecki, 2001; Shapland, 1978), perhaps due to the restricted activity spaces within which young people operate. However, the finding that adults tend *not* to inbreed was unexpected, and warrants future attention. Investigations based on more fine-grained age categorizations could be useful in shedding light on this result.

The variable relationship between homophily and co-offending group size observed in this study also deserves mention. Although we found some support for Mayhew and colleagues' (1995) energy distribution principle for male co-offending groups and, to a lesser extent, adult groups, the findings for females and youths contradict the proposition that larger groupings should evidence greater inbreeding homophily. While it is possible that the "energy barriers" discussed by Mayhew et al. operate differently for female and youth co-offending groups, it is likely that these inconsistent results are due, at least in part, to the very small number of female and youthful co-offending groups of larger sizes.

The strong inbreeding tendency observed in this study confirms the fact that "pure availability . . . does not by itself fully determine or exhaust the search for co-offenders" (Tremblay, 1993: 25). Our findings thus refute strict opportunity-based theories of co-offender selection. However, in the absence of information on the socio-organizational features of offenders' daily lives (e.g., routine activities, convergence settings, and social foci), our police data do not permit a clear test of local opportunity vs. choice-based theories. The homophily patterns observed here could thus reflect psychological biases that render similar accomplices more "attractive," structural factors below the population level that make them more readily "available," or a combination of both (Weerman, 2003). Conventional network studies that include information on local meeting opportunities suggest that "both [structure and choice] play an important but partial role, where each reinforces the other" (Kossinets & Watts, 2009: 409; Currarini et al., 2009; Moody, 2001). The key task for future co-offending research will be to determine how these factors interact to produce inbreeding biases in co-offender selection. Answering this question will require data not typically available in official records.[10]

Supplementing the basic analyses presented here with research using other types of data is important for a number of reasons. First, the homophily findings outlined in this study reflect detected co-offending patterns only, and it is possible that the composition of non-detected co-offending groups may differ. If, for whatever reason, heterogeneous groups are more successful in avoiding capture, inbreeding could be overestimated in this data. Although the high levels of co-offending homogeneity typically observed in self-report studies (e.g., Warr, 1996) suggest that any official bias is likely to be small, it would be useful to verify the present inbreeding findings with non-official data.

Second, and more importantly, in addition to lacking details about local mixing opportunities, official data do not include information on many other offender and offense attributes that are likely to be important for accomplice selection. The current study was focused on the two durable, ascriptive characteristics of age and sex (variables readily available in official records). A focus on these traits is valuable in the sense that these characteristics, by virtue of their visibility, are central to one's social identity, and provide easy markers for similarity/dissimilarity in the search for co-offenders. The focus on these characteristics also avoids questions regarding the selection versus influence debate that typically plagues attempts to explore value homophily (Ruef, 2002). Still, there is good reason to believe that less visible traits also play a role in the selection of co-offenders, and perhaps interact with sex and age. In these analyses, age and sex have been considered separately. In reality, however, it is likely that individuals consider multiple factors simultaneously when forming social ties (Kalmijn & Vermunt, 2007). It would thus be desirable if data were collected on a wide range of additional individual traits not typically found in official records (for example, criminal capital, reputation, attitudes). Multivariate analyses could then be used to establish whether homogeneity on age and sex are selected for directly or whether they are, in fact, by-products of selection on other, related, traits. A latent-class approach to random-effects modeling could prove useful in this regard.

It would also be informative if future analyses controlled for characteristics of the criminal incident (e.g., crime type, difficulty) as it is likely that different types of crimes will call for different types of accomplices (Reiss, 1988: 34; Sarnecki, 2004: 43). To the extent that some offenses may benefit from a division of labor or specialized skills, heterophily, rather than homophily, might optimize the offending groups' performance as is the case in some conventional innovation and information networks (Granovetter, 1973; Ruef, 2002). Investigating whether age and sex homophily maintain independent significance in the prediction of co-offending, net of other factors, will require multivariate methods designed for network data (Scott & Carrington, 2011). Although the structure of the data used in the current study was not suitable for exponential random graph p^* modeling, this method has been usefully applied to study homophily in other contexts (e.g., Kirke, 2009; Lubbers, 2003) and could be used to advance the study of co-offending in future studies (e.g., Schaefer, 2012).

A third benefit of collecting more in-depth data on co-offending networks is that it would allow for analyses of multiplexity. Some research suggests that co-offenders are often selected from amongst the friends, romantic partners, and acquaintances with which one regularly associates (see Budd et al., 2005). As West (1978: 178) eloquently stated, "most teens do not need to befriend somebody to find a 'partner in crime': they already have one." If accomplices are indeed chosen from within one's immediate (conventional) social network, the inbreeding results observed here could simply reflect underlying friendship homophily. With the proper data, it would be straightforward to explore whether individuals' co-offending ties are more or less homophilous than their friendship ties, and thereby determine whether inbreeding homophily in co-offending is a distinct phenomenon.

Finally, an important avenue for future research concerns the practical significance of co-offending homophily. The analyses presented here have focused on the cross-sectional formation of co-offending ties, but another important question is whether homophily encourages the maintenance of co-offending relationships over time. Research on conventional networks suggests that homophily is a strong predictor of relational durability (McPherson et al., 2001; Suitor & Keeton, 1997). From an intervention perspective, it would be of value to identify whether the same is true for co-offending ties. Longitudinal network data are exceptionally rare, particularly in criminology but, if collected, they could provide great insight into the "meaning" of homophily for the selection and stability of co-offenders across the criminal career (Giordano, Cernkovich, & Holland, 2003; Piquero, Farrington, & Blumstein, 2007).

CONCLUSION

In this study, we have demonstrated that deviations from random mixing by age and sex are substantial in co-offending groups of all sizes, but that these deviations are not uniform. Furthermore, we have shown that patterns of normalized inbreeding homophily differ markedly from patterns of basic observed homophily. These findings highlight the importance of exploring null expectations when studying the composition of co-offending groups. Having refuted strict opportunity-based theories of co-offender selection, future research should focus on elucidating the psychological, sociological, and local-structural forces that produce inbreeding homophily in co-offending networks. A number of theoretical possibilities have been proposed above, but the true character of co-offender selection remains an empirical question. Our hope is that this study will provide an impetus for additional research aimed at identifying specific accomplice selection mechanisms and exploring their implications for co-offending networks.

NOTES

1. Preparation of this chapter was supported by a Danish Council for Independent Research grant awarded to the first author and a Social Sciences and Humanities Research Council Standard Research Grant awarded to the second author. The authors are grateful to Professor David Farrington and Dr. Pat Altham of the University of Cambridge for their comments on earlier versions of this work.
2. Our use of the term "group" refers to collectives of two or more individuals who are directly linked through simultaneous joint criminal action. Although some social psychological interpretations of the term "group" assume a shared identity and some degree of role differentiation (Aronson, Wilson, & Akert, 2005), no such assumptions are made in the current study.
3. Although rarely identified as such explicitly, (delinquent) peer behavioral and value homophily have received the most widespread criminological attention. The fact that friends of juvenile delinquents are themselves much more likely to be delinquent than friends of non-delinquents is one of the most robust findings in criminology. The question of whether this association reflects selection or influence effects is still hotly debated, but there is little disagreement about the existence of the association itself (Cairns & Cairns, 1994; Carrington, 2011; Glueck & Glueck, 1950; Haynie, 2002; Matsueda & Anderson, 1998; Smangs, 2010; Warr, 2002). The literature on this topic is vast, but we do not address it here as our interest is in co-offending rather than peer networks, and because social influence effects are not relevant for the stable ascriptive characteristics of age and sex examined in this chapter.
4. In the case of behavioral homophily and similarity for psychological characteristics like attitudes and values, a third theoretical camp proposes that social influence leads to convergence. Because the current chapter is focused on the demographic characteristics of age and sex, which are not subject to change, we limit our attention to theoretical explanations that assume selection.
5. It is worth noting that, although choice-based explanations are typically applied to explain high levels of homophily, they could also be used to account for instances in which a weighing of costs and benefits leads to the choice of dissimilar alters (heterophily).
6. Given that these foci are likely to attract socially similar individuals, even greater structural homophily would be expected to emerge through chance meetings at the local level as compared to the population level.
7. Of course, if detailed information on the demography of localized contact pools were available, this information could be used to compute baseline probabilities instead of using overall population information. In these cases, the presence of inbreeding effects would provide stronger support for choice-based explanations. Unfortunately, this data is difficult to come by, especially for offender populations.
8. A number of alternative baseline proportions were also considered (e.g., the gender and age breakdown of the general population or that of the co-offending population only). These possibilities were ultimately rejected on the grounds that they represented selection pools that were either too broad or too restrictive to be considered realistic.
9. In some cases, the expected number of homogeneous all-female or all-youth groups was less than 1, violating a key assumption of the chi-square test. In these situations, a correction was made in order to permit calculation of the chi-square statistic. This involved increasing the expected count to 1 for that group, while subtracting 0.5 from the counts for each of the other groups. This was done for all-female 5- and 6-groups and all-youth 5- and 6-groups. The results for these co-offending group sizes should be interpreted with caution.
10. Our reliance on official data means that we were not able to explore the cognitive, emotional, or instrumental motivations underlying the selection of co-offenders. As a result, our analysis provides a somewhat superficial view of co-offender selection. A proper evaluation of rational-choice vs. opportunity explanations will require more textured information on offenders' motives and methods of accomplice selection.

REFERENCES

Alarid, L.F., J.W. Marquart, V.S. Burton, F.T. Cullen, & S.J. Cuvelier (1996). Women's roles in serious offenses: A study of adult felons. *Justice Quarterly* 13, 431–454.

Andresen, M.A. & M. Felson (2010). The impact of co-offending. *British Journal of Criminology* 50, 66–81.

Aronson, E., T.D. Wilson, & R.M. Akert (2005). *Social Psychology* (5th ed.). Upper Saddle River, NJ: Pearson Education Inc.

Blau, P.M. (1977). *Inequality and Heterogeneity: A Primitive Theory of Social Structure*. New York: Free Press.

Bouchard, M. & H. Nguyen (2010). Is it who you know, or how many that counts? Criminal networks and cost avoidance in a sample of young offenders. *Justice Quarterly* 27, 130–158.

Budd, T., C. Sharp, & P. Mayhew (2005). *Offending in England and Wales: First Results from the 2003 Crime and Justice Survey*. Home Office Research Study 275. London: Home Office.

Burt, R.S. (1991). Measuring age as a structural concept. *Social Networks* 13, 1–34.

Byrne, D. (1971). *The Attraction Paradigm*. New York: Academic Press.

Cairns, R.B. & B.D. Cairns (1994). *Lifelines and Risks: Pathways of Youth in Our Time*. Cambridge: Cambridge University Press.

Carrington, P.J. (2002a). Group crime in Canada. *Canadian Journal of Criminology* 44, 277–315.

Carrington, P.J. (2002b). Sex homogeneity in co-offending groups. In J. Hagberg (ed.), *Contributions to Social Network Analysis, Information Theory, and Other Topics in Statistics. A Festschrift in Honor of Ove Frank* (pp. 101–116). Stockholm: Stockholm University Press.

Carrington, P.J. (2009). Co-offending and the development of the delinquent career. *Criminology* 47, 1295–1329.

Carrington, P.J. (2011). Crime and social network analysis. In J. Scott & P.J. Carrington (eds.), *SAGE Handbook of Social Network Analysis* (pp. 236–255). London: Sage.

Chattoe, E. & H. Hamill (2005). It's not who you know—it's what you know about people you don't know that counts: Exploring the analysis of crime groups as social networks. *British Journal of Criminology* 45, 860–876.

Cohen, L.E. & M. Felson (1979). Social change and crime rate trends: A routine activity approach. *American Sociological Review* 44, 588–608.

Coleman, J. (1958). Relational analysis: The study of social organizations with survey methods. *Human Organization* 17, 28–36.

Conway, K.P. & J. McCord (2002). A longitudinal examination of the relation between co-offending with violent accomplices and violent crime. *Aggressive Behavior* 28(2), 97–108.

Currarini, S., M.O. Jackson, & P. Pin (2009). An economic model of friendship: Homophily, minorities and segregation. *Econometrica* 77, 1003–1045.

Currarini, S., M.O. Jackson, & P. Pin (2010). Identifying sources of racial homophily in high school friendship networks. *Proceedings of the National Academy of Science of the USA (PNAS)* 107, 4857–4861.

Daly, R. (2005). *Delinquent Networks in Philadelphia: The Structure of Co-offending Among Juveniles*. Unpublished Ph.D. thesis. Philadelphia: University of Pennsylvania.

Decker, S., R. Wright, A. Redfern, & D. Smith (1993). A woman's place is in the home: Females and residential burglary. *Justice Quarterly* 10, 143–162.

Feld, S.L. (1981). The focused organization of social ties. *The American Journal of Sociology* 86, 1015–1035.

Felson, M. (2003). The process of co-offending. In M. Smith & D.B. Cornish (eds.), *Theory for Practice in Situational Crime Prevention* (pp. 149–167). New York: Criminal Justice Press.

Festinger, L. (1954). A theory of social comparison processes. *Human Relations* 7(2), 117–140.

Fleisher, M.S. & Jessie L. Krienert (2004). Life-course events, social networks, and the emergence of violence among female gang members. *Journal of Community Psychology* 32, 607–622.

Frank, O. & P. Carrington (2007). Estimation of offending and co-offending using available data with model support. *The Journal of Mathematical Sociology* 31, 1–46.

Franz, S., M. Marsili, & P. Pin (2010). Observed choices and underlying opportunities. *Science and Culture* 76, 471–476.

Giordano, P.C., S.A. Cernkovich, & D. Holland (2003). Changes in friendship relations over the life course: Implications for desistance from crime. *Criminology* 41(2), 293–327.

Glueck, S. & E. Glueck (1950). *Unraveling Juvenile Delinquency*. Cambridge, MA: Harvard University Press.

Granovetter, Mark S. (1973). The strength of weak ties. *The American Journal of Sociology* 78(6), 1360–1380.

Hagestad, G.O. & P. Uhlenberg (2006). Should we be concerned about age segregation? Some theoretical and empirical explorations. *Research on Aging* 28, 638–653.

Haynie, D.L. (2002) Friendship networks and delinquency: The relative nature of peer delinquency. *Journal of Quantitative Criminology* 18(2), 99–134.

Haynie, D., P. Giordano, W.D. Manning, & M.A. Longmore (2005). Adolescent romantic relationships and delinquency involvement. *Criminology* 43(1), 177–210.

Huang, Y., C. Shen, D. Williams, & N. Contractor (2009). Virtually there: Exploring proximity and homophily in a virtual world. *Computational Science and Engineering* 4, 354–359.

Huston, T.L. & G. Levinger (1978). Interpersonal attraction and relationships. In M.R. Rosenzweig & L.W. Porter (eds.), *Annual Review of Psychology*, Vol. 29 (pp. 115–156). Palo Alto, CA: Annual Reviews.

Kalmijn, M. (1998). Intermarriage and homogamy: Causes patterns and trends. *Annual Review of Sociology* 24, 395–421.

Kalmijn, M. & J.K. Vermunt (2007). Homogeneity of social networks by age and marital status: A multilevel analysis of ego-centered networks. *Social Networks* 29, 25–43.

Kirke, D. (2009). Gender clustering in friendship networks: Some sociological implications. *Methodological Innovations Online* 4, 23–36.

Kossinets, G. & D.J. Watts (2009). Origins of homophily in an evolving social network. *American Journal of Sociology* 115, 405–450.

Lazarsfeld, P.F. & R.K. Merton (1954). Friendship as a social process: A substantive and methodological analysis. In M. Berger (ed.), *Freedom and Control in Modern Society* (pp. 18–66). New York: Van Nostrand.

Lubbers, M.J. (2003). Group composition and network structure in school classes: A multilevel application of the p* model. *Social Networks* 25, 309–332.

Maccoby, E. (1998). *The Two Sexes: Growing up Apart. Coming Together*. Cambridge, MA: Harvard University Press.

Malm, A., G. Bichler, & R. Nash (2011). Co-offending between criminal enterprise groups. *Global Crime* 12(2), 112–128.

Marsden, P.V. (1988). Homogeneity in confiding relations. *Social Networks* 10, 57–76.

Matsueda, R.L. & K. Anderson (1998). The dynamics of delinquent peers and delinquent behavior. *Criminology* 36, 269–308.

Mayhew, B.H., J.M. McPherson, T. Rotolo, & L. Smith-Lovin (1995). Sex and race homogeneity in naturally occurring groups. *Social Forces* 74, 15–52.

McCarthy, B., J. Hagan, & L.E. Cohen (1998). Uncertainty, cooperation, and crime: Understanding the decision to co-offend. *Social Forces* 77(1), 155–184.

McCord, J. & K.P. Conway (2002). Patterns of juvenile delinquency and co-offending. In R. Waring & D. Weisburd (eds.), *Crime and Social Organization* (pp. 15–30). New Brunswick, NJ: Transaction Publishers.

McCord, J. & K.P. Conway (2005). *Co-offending and Patterns of Juvenile Crime*. Research in Brief. NCJ 210360. Washington, DC: National Institute of Justice.

McGloin, J.M. & D.S. Kirk (2010). An overview of social network analysis. *Journal of Criminal Justice Education* 21, 169–181.

McGloin, J.M. & A.R. Piquero (2010). On the relationship between co-offending network redundancy and offending versatility. *Journal of Research in Crime and Delinquency* 47, 63–90.

McGloin, J.M., C.J. Sullivan, A. Piquero, & S. Bacon (2008). Investigating the stability of co-offending and co-offenders among a sample of youthful offenders. *Criminology* 46(1), 155–188.

McPherson, M. & L. Smith-Lovin (1987). Homophily in voluntary organizations: Status distance and the composition of face-to-face groups. *American Sociological Review* 52, 370–379.

McPherson, M., L. Smith-Lovin, & J.M. Cook (2001). Birds of a feather: Homophily in social networks. *Annual Review of Sociology* 27, 415–444.

Monge, P.R. & N.S. Contractor (2003). *Theories of Communication Networks*. New York: Oxford University Press.

Moody, J. (2001). Race, school integration and friendship segregation in America. *American Journal of Sociology* 107, 679–716.

Morselli, C. (2009). *Inside Criminal Networks*. New York: Springer.

Mullins, C.W. & R. Wright (2003). Gender, social networks, and residential burglary. *Criminology* 41(3): 813–839.

Pettersson, T. (2005). Gendering delinquent networks: A gendered analysis of violent crimes and the structure of boys' and girls' co-offending networks. *Young Nordic Journal of Youth Research* 13(3), 247–267.

Pettiway, L. (1987). Participation in crime partnerships by female drug users: The effects of domestic arrangements, drug use, and criminal involvement. *Criminology* 25(3), 741–766.

Piquero, A., D.P. Farrington, & A. Blumstein (2007). *Key Issues in Criminal Career Research*. Cambridge: Cambridge University Press.

Reiss, A.J. (1988). Co-offending and criminal careers. In M. Tonry & N. Morris (eds.), *Crime and Justice: A Review of Research* (Vol. 10, pp. 117–170). Chicago: University of Chicago Press.

Reiss, A.J. & D.P. Farrington (1991). Advancing knowledge about co-offending: Results from a prospective longitudinal survey of London males. *Journal of Criminal Law & Criminology* 82(2), 360–395.

Reskin, B.F., D.B. McBrier, & J.A. Kmec (1999). The determinants and consequences of workplace sex and race composition. *Annual Review of Sociology* 25, 335–336.

Ruef, M. (2002). A structural event approach to the analysis of group composition. *Social Networks* 24, 135–160.

Sarnecki, J. (1986). *Delinquent Networks*. Stockholm: The National Swedish Council for Crime Prevention.

Sarnecki, J. (1990). Delinquent networks in Sweden. *Journal of Quantitative Criminology* 6(1), 31–50.

Sarnecki, J. (2001). *Delinquent Networks: Youth Co-offending in Stockholm*. Cambridge: Cambridge University Press.

Sarnecki, J. (2004). Girls and boys in delinquent networks. *International Annals of Criminology* 42, 29–57.

Schaefer, D.R. (2012). Youth co-offending networks: An investigation of social and spatial effects. *Social Networks* 34(1), 141–149.

Scott, J. & P.J. Carrington (eds.). (2011). *SAGE Handbook of Social Network Analysis*. London: Sage.

Shapland, J.M. (1978). Self-reported delinquency in boys aged 11 to 14. *British Journal of Criminology* 18(3), 255–266.

Shaw, C.R. & H.D. McKay (1931). *Report on the Causes of Crime*. Washington, DC: US Government Printing Office.

Smangs, M. (2010). Delinquency, social skills and the structure of peer relations: Assessing criminological theories by social network theory. *Social Forces* 89, 609–632.

Steffensmeier, D. (1983). Organizational properties and sex segregation in the underworld: Building a sociological theory of sex differences in crime. *Social Forces* 61, 1010–1032.

Steffensmeier, D. & R.M. Terry (1986). Institutional sexism in the underworld: A view from the inside. *Sociological Inquiry* 56(3), 304–323.

Suitor, J. & S. Keeton (1997). Once a friend, always a friend? Effects of homophily on women's support networks across a decade. *Social Networks* 19, 51–62.

Tajfel, H. & J.C. Turner (1986). The social identity theory of inter-group behavior. In S. Worchel & L.W. Austin (eds.), *Psychology of Intergroup Relations* (pp. 7–24). Chicago: Nelson-Hall.

Tarling, R. (1993). *Analysing Offending: Data, Methods and Interpretations*. London: HMSO.

Tremblay, P. (1993). Searching for suitable co-offenders. In R.V. Clarke & M. Felson (eds.), *Routine Activity and Rational Choice* (Vol. 5, pp. 17–36). New Brunswick, NJ: Transaction Publishers.

Turner, J.C., M.A. Hogg, P.J. Oakes, S.D. Reicher, & M.S. Wetherell (1987). *Rediscovering the Social Group: A Self-categorization Theory*. Oxford: Blackwell.

van Mastrigt, S.B. & D.P. Farrington (2009). Age, gender and crime type: Implications for criminal justice policy. *British Journal of Criminology* 49, 552–572.

van Mastrigt, S.B. & D.P. Farrington (2011). Prevalence and characteristics of co-offending recruiters. *Justice Quarterly* 2, 325–359.

Vandiver, Donna M. (2006). Female sex offenders: A comparison of solo offenders and co-offenders. *Violence and Victims* 21, 339–354.

von Lampe, K. & P.O. Johansen (2004). Organized crime and trust: On the conceptualization and empirical relevance of trust in the context of criminal networks. *Global Crime* 6, 159–184.

Waring, E.J. (2002). Co-offending as a network form of social organization. In Elin J. Waring & David Weisburd (eds.), *Crime and Social Organization*, Vol. 10 (pp. 31–47). New Brunswick, NJ: Transaction.

Warr, M. (1993). Age, peers, and delinquency. *Criminology* 31(1), 17–40.

Warr, M. (1996). Organization and instigation in delinquent groups. *Criminology* 34(1), 11–37.

Warr, M. (2002). *Companions in Crime: The Social Aspects of Criminal Conduct*. Cambridge: Cambridge University Press.

Weerman, F.M. (2003). Co-offending as social exchange: Explaining characteristics of co-offending. *British Journal of Criminology* 43(2), 398–416.

West, W.G. (1978). The short term careers of serious thieves. *Canadian Journal of Criminology* 20, 169–190.

CHAPTER 3

The Evolution of a Drug Co-arrest Network

Natalia Iwanski and Richard Frank

The continual increase of drug trafficking in Canada has spurred law enforcement organizations to find improved strategies to decrease supply for illicit substances and target offenders more effectively. In 2007, there were over 100,000 police-reported drug offenses in Canada, marking the highest drug crime rate in 30 years (Dauvergne, 2009). One of the main provinces driving this rate is British Columbia, with the two cities of Vancouver and Victoria consistently having among the highest rates in the country over the last 15 years. In particular, the amount of Canadian youth (aged 12 to 17) participating in drug crime has more than doubled in this time. As a result of such dramatic increases, a National Anti-Drug Strategy was launched in 2007 by government and community organizations to improve drug legislation and to aid in prevention programs (Dauvergne, 2009). Police efforts have largely utilized surveillance and undercover operations to detect and disrupt drug trafficking rings; however, they operate largely on a case-by-case basis (Desroches, 2005). Often those arrested are more visible drug offenders, like those dealing or possessing illegal substances (Dauvergne, 2009). Although cannabis-related crimes account for approximately 60% of all police-reported crimes, cocaine and especially synthetic drugs, like MDMA or ecstasy, are quickly increasing in demand, showing no sign of slowing down (Dauvergne, 2009; Glenny, 2009; RCMP, 2007). This increase in the trafficking of synthetic drugs has the potential to overwhelm law enforcement agencies, which are already using a vast amount of their resources to combat current drug market activities.

Shifting the paradigm of law enforcement strategies from an individual approach to a network approach may provide insight into how to target drug offenders more effectively. It has been shown that drug offenders often work in co-offending groups and at the very least have a loose organizational structure (Brantingham, Ester, Frank, Glässer, & Tayebi, 2011; Desroches, 2005; Heber, 2009; Malm & Bichler, 2011; Xu & Chen, 2003, 2008). To be successful, offenders need to have contacts along various points of the drug commodity chain, starting from the production of illegal substances to their import and export, and finally to their street-level sale. Visualizing offenders as part of networks can help authorities understand their structure and help them identify key figures that are highly embedded in the network. Targeting these types of key offenders can lead to a high degree of disruption in a network, which can potentially decrease drug crime rates (Joffres, Bouchard, Frank, & Westlake, 2011; Malm & Bichler, 2011). Examining drug trafficking rings over time can also help identify patterns in how offenders form and maintain their relationships. Drug offenders are known to have high rates of recidivism and often become entrenched in the drug trade.

They can often change their behavior after arrest in an attempt to decrease their risk of becoming caught by law enforcement (Gallupe, Bouchard, & Caulkins, 2011). As a result, studying the evolution of networks over time is crucial to understanding how offenders form relationships in the drug trade and how they work together. Processes of recruitment can be studied and key events that trigger the growth of these networks can be determined.

Previous studies on drug co-offending networks have contributed a great deal of information in terms of describing their structure (Brantingham et al., 2011; Malm & Bichler, 2011; Xu & Chen, 2003, 2008). Since drug markets manage themselves along a commodity chain, each link along the chain can be characterized by a different pattern of organization. As Malm and Bichler (2011) found, those at the far ends of the commodity chain, such as production and street-level retail activity, are comprised of small groups of loosely connected entrepreneurs, while those toward the middle of the chain, like smugglers and suppliers, are more highly connected and are very difficult to replace if removed.

Desroches (2005) affirms these findings by showing the marked differences between lower-level and higher-level drug dealers. Lower-level dealers are offenders who sell drugs directly to individual consumers. Just as Malm and Bichler (2011) found, they are largely comprised of independent entrepreneurs and are loosely organized. Most often an individual dealer is found to be connected with a large number of independent buyers rather than other dealers (Desroches, 2005; Heber, 2009; Malm & Bichler, 2011; Xu & Chen, 2003, 2008). Street-level sales are largely conducted by males who sell small quantities of drugs to supplement their own income and to support their own drug use (Desroches, 2005; Heber, 2009).

Higher-level drug traffickers, on the other hand, are comprised of importers, manufac-turers, and wholesalers of illicit substances who generate large amounts of profit for themselves and have a high degree of status in the drug market. These types of drug offenders are typically white, middle-class males who operate in very small, tightly knit cliques (Desroches, 2005). Working in such small, tightly connected groups leads to greater success since it decreases the risk of detection. In this context, organized crime usually tends to consist of several small groups temporarily working together for a particular purpose. Since higher-level drug dealing is much more lucrative than lower-level dealing, it is important that higher-level niches of the commodity chain be studied and understood. Targeting individuals in these niches would lead to a great deal more disruption in illicit drug rings. Identifying those offenders with more serious crime offenses within a network, like production or import and export, could help identify how these higher-level offenders interact with other drug offenders in the drug market. For example, a methamphetamine drug network in Arizona, United States, was found to have several high-level individuals connected to a large number of lower-level drug dealers, who were in turn connected to a large number of individual buyers (Xu & Chen, 2008). These higher-level individuals can be identified not only by their connectedness within the network but also by their position in relation to other individuals and by the types of crimes they commit.

In terms of the stability of drug networks over time, some studies have found that co-offending networks in general are unstable and short-lived. Most co-offenders only work with each other once before moving on to different individuals (Brantingham et al., 2011; Heber, 2009; Reiss, 1988). This has been found to be true for lower-level offenders; however, for increasingly serious offenses or higher-level drug crimes, a more stable organization was found to be necessary for success (Desroches, 2005). Examining the evolution of a drug network over time may give some more information about the longitudinal co-offending patterns of higher-level versus lower-level offenders.

Most research about drug networks using social network analysis techniques uses several key statistics that explain certain network dynamics, including average degree, clustering coefficient, and average path length. The average degree of a node, or drug offender in this case, is the number of offenders that they are connected with, or have co-offended with (Nooy, Mrvar, & Batagelj, 2005; Scott, 2000). In the case where the degree distribution follows a power-law distribution, or where the probability of having links is equal to, the network is said to be scale-free. The variable is called the power-law distribution exponent, and the variable c is a constant which controls the curvature of the distribution. In scale-free networks, a large percentage of nodes have only a few links, and a small percentage of nodes have many links (Nooy et al., 2005; Xu & Chen, 2008). These types of networks are said to evolve following preferential attachment, whereby the more links a node has the more new links it will attract. The clustering coefficient is a measure which examines the likelihood that if two nodes are linked to one offender, they are also linked to each other (Hanneman & Riddle, 2005; Nooy et al., 2005). Taking each node's neighbors, it examines the number of links that are present versus the number of possible links between them. A small clustering coefficient indicates that clusters or groups are unlikely to occur, whereas a higher clustering coefficient implies that network actors have close collaboration and efficient communication. In terms of drug networks, the higher the clustering coefficient, the better communication links are between offenders and the easier it becomes to plan and execute a crime (Brantingham et al., 2011; Xu & Chen, 2008). Lastly, the average path length of a network is the average length of all the shortest paths between all pairs of nodes in a network. A small average path length indicates each node can reach any other node within only a few steps, implying a high level of communication efficiency (Hanneman & Riddle, 2005; Nooy et al., 2005; Scott, 2000).

When a network has both a high clustering coefficient and a short average path length, it is said to be small world. In networks of this type, criminals are able to communicate or co-offend with another offender through only a few intermediate connections (Hanneman & Riddle, 2005). Drug networks created from a variety of data sources like arrest data, court documents, or offender interviews have all been found to be both scale-free and small world (Brantingham et al., 2011; Malm & Bichler, 2011; Xu & Chen, 2008). This implies that they are highly resilient against random attacks, and also have very efficient communication. In a small-world network, a leader of a drug-trafficking ring can easily contact those below him to coordinate a criminal event. Moreover, Xu and Chen (2008) have noted that the growth of these networks and their scale-free properties rely not only on preferential attachment but also on the large recruitment process present within drug trafficking rings. By examining drug networks over time, the present study aims to find more evidence of how recruitment takes place and how these types of networks grow.

Despite the large number of studies that have examined drug networks, very few have looked at their evolution over time. Most simply take a snapshot at a certain time and analyze the properties of the static network. However, the few criminological studies that have looked at network evolution usually examine how network statistics change over time (Morselli & Petit, 2007). Studies in other fields, such as news networks, online student communities, email contacts within a university, and scientific co-authorship networks, have also used a similar approach

(Barabási et al., 2002; Falkowski, Bartelheimer, & Siliopoulou, 2006a, 2006b; Kossinets & Watts, 2006). Most choose daily or monthly time intervals, usually depending on the nature of their data. The most common statistics examined are average degree, clustering coefficient, density, centralization, and cluster or group size. For scale-free networks, looking at networks cumulatively over time can also highlight their preferential attachment characteristics. Sometimes, rather than focusing on the entire network, the focus is on how subgroups within a network change over time. Falkowski et al. (2006b) identify six transition types that a subgroup can undergo: it can stay the same, grow, decline, disappear, merge with another group, or split. When these transitional features are identified over time, it is then possible to investigate the underlying causes that led to such a shift.

The present study will apply some of these network evolution techniques to a drug network generated from arrest data. First, a general description of all the networks generated from the dataset will be provided, including an analysis of their composition, size, and the attributes of offenders contained in them. Second, a network will be taken from the pool of networks generated and will be analyzed over monthly time intervals. Several network statistics will be measured at monthly time steps to investigate how the network grows and changes. In addition, central nodes in the network will also be identified and any sharp change in the network statistics will be investigated to identify the offenders and events that triggered the increase or decrease. Lastly, the severity of each offender's crime will be investigated to determine if more severe crimes correspond to more highly connected offenders within the network.

METHODS

The drug networks used in this study were created with data from a collection of databases at the Institute of Canadian Urban Research Studies (ICURS) at Simon Fraser University. These databases contain five years of real-world crime data for the province of British Columbia from the Royal Canadian Mounted Police (RCMP), Canada's federal police force. Information about calls for service from August 1, 2001 to August 1, 2006 is provided, including details of all subjects, vehicles, and businesses involved in a crime event.

For the purposes of this study, only crime events and the subjects who perpetrated drug crime were focused on. In this dataset, each offender has an encrypted name associated with them that is also associated with the crime event they were involved in. Since it is possible for spelling mistakes to occur in police records and for fields such as first name or middle name to be empty, repeat offenders pose a challenge on how to determine whether two records imply the same person. The same offender could be mistakenly listed as two separate individuals or vice versa. After analyzing offenders' full names and correlating them with their date of birth and other personal information, the effect of the above-described problem was found to be negligible. Although offenders do give false information to law enforcement, for a person to be marked as an offender it is assumed that police have fairly reliable information. Repeat offenders become well known to police and the relatively serious cases they are charged with require complete and correct information. Thus multiple records in the database with the same full name were deemed to belong to the same person.

To create the networks, information about offenders committing drug crimes was then extracted from the database resulting in a set, S, of offenders. A random drug offender, D, was then selected from S. All events tied to offender D were then explored, and if a particular event was also associated with another offender, a link was created between them. Links were continually created in this way until all offenders in the network had been explored and all existing links established between them. Once all individuals within a connected network had been found, offenders within that network were removed from S, then another random offender was selected from the remaining set S, and the network-building process was repeated to build up another network. This iterative process was repeated until S was empty. Networks having less than two offenders were discarded, resulting in a set of 4,123 co-offending networks. This set contained a total of 20,653 nodes, representing drug offenders, and 75,925 links, representing events that two or more offenders were arrested for together. Most networks were quite small, with 90 of them having only two offenders. There were only five networks which contained more than 100 offenders, the largest of which had 729 nodes and 14,470 links. This is consistent with previous studies since most drug networks have been found to contain one very large component and a large number of very small groups (Xu & Chen, 2008; Heber, 2009).

As links between offenders were created, a time stamp was also tied to each link in order to identify when the event had taken place. Since the database contains information about drug crimes over five years, or 61 months, each event was assigned a time stamp from 1 to 61(with month 61 representing the complete and full network after five years), indicating which month, with respect to the start of the data (August 1, 2001), it had occurred in. This link and time stamp information was then input into Pajek, a program for the analysis and visualization of large networks. With time stamp information, Pajek is capable of generating a network over time, allowing a network's evolution to be clearly visualized (Batagelj & Mrvar, 2003).

When working with arrest data, there are several limitations that numerous studies have noted (Brantingham et al., 2011; Heber, 2009; Malm & Bichler, 2011; Xu & Chen, 2008). Since drug offenders only become part of the network if they are caught by police, there may be a great deal of missing links in the networks generated. Associations which exist between members in reality may not be reflected in the network (due to co-offenders never having been caught together by police) and networks could be much bigger and denser. Arrest data may also create false links between offenders if they happened to be caught committing the same crime when there is no real relationship between them. For example, two traffickers dealing in the same area may be caught by police at the same time even though no associations between them may exist. This may create the impression that these networks are more connected and efficient than they really are. To test the degree to which missing and fake links distort the structure of a network, Xu and Chen (2008) first randomly removed 10% of an illicit network's nodes and then added 10% additional nodes. Additional nodes were given a higher probability of attaching to higher-degree nodes in order to follow the principle of preferential attachment. In both cases, the network structure and statistics were not significantly affected. This indicates that, although networks generated from arrest data may not be completely accurate, they do offer a rich source of information about illicit networks nonetheless.

Attributes of each network generated from the database were collected to understand their composition, including the gender, age, and region of residence of each offender. Again, there were missing fields in the data; however, the majority of records were filled in correctly and, of the 20,653 offenders, 1,301 were missing an entry for age and 6,981 were missing an address. If a valid age could be determined for an offender from a record within the five years spanned by the database, it was assigned as the offender's age. Hence an offender's true age at a particular point in time can be under- or overestimated by at most five years. To determine a region of residence, the province of British Columbia (BC) was divided into eight regions, corresponding to Northwestern BC, Northeastern BC, the Cariboo, the Thompson Okanagan, the Kootenays, Vancouver Island, Greater Vancouver, and Whistler/Squamish (Figure 3.1). If an offender's place of residence associated with their first criminal event was within one of these regions, then it was assigned as their region of residence.

The majority of offenders were found to be males between the ages of 18 and 23. Most offenders were from Greater Vancouver and Vancouver Island, which is not surpris-

ing since these two regions contain the cities of Vancouver and Victoria, which have extremely high drug crime rates (Dauvergne, 2009). Greater Vancouver is a densely populated metropolitan region that is very close to the US border, so having a large number of offenders in this area is expected. The Thompson Okanagan region ranked third in the number of offenders it contains, with 10.4%. Located to the east of the Greater Vancouver region, it contains a few larger cities and also provides access to the US border. Border guards in this region have reported many marijuana and cocaine seizures, as well

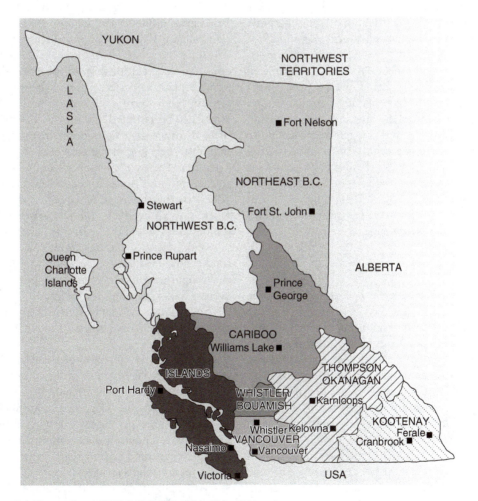

Figure 3.1 The province of British Columbia divided into eight regions

as an increasing amount of synthetic drugs (Glenny, 2009).

In addition to gender, age, and region of residence, all drug-related crimes committed by an offender were listed. A drug crime was classified based on its crime type and drug type. Crime type included the categories import/export, production, trafficking, and possession. Each of these categories was given a code based on its severity, with import/export being the highest (and assigned a value of four) and possession being the lowest (with a value of one). On average, each offender committed 3.6 crimes, with almost half of all crime events being possession charges, and approximately 36% being related to trafficking or retail activity. Production of illicit substances accounted for approximately 15% of crimes and import/export was significantly smaller, making up only 1.7% of reported events. The lower amounts of production and smuggling crimes could be related to the fact that tracking down producers and smugglers is much more difficult for police and the proportion of drug offenders involved in these types of crimes is usually much less than in trafficking or possession (RCMP, 2007). Drug type was coded in two categories—one for cannabis and two for all other hard drugs.

Network Evolution

A single network with a relatively large amount of nodes was chosen for further detailed analysis. This network, the second[1] largest network from the dataset, was taken from the pool of networks generated and was analyzed over monthly time intervals. Two types of temporal analyses are possible. First, the network could be analyzed by breaking it down into 61 independent snapshots (with snapshot #1 being the beginning of month 1, and snapshot #61 being the end of month 60), with each snapshot containing only the nodes that actually were arrested that month, with the links shown between the nodes

representing their corresponding event. Alternatively, the 61 time periods could be analyzed cumulatively, with a specific snapshot including all nodes (and their corresponding links) for all crimes that have occurred up to that point in time.

The second alternative, looking at the networks cumulatively, was selected for two specific reasons. First, stepping through each month highlighted only those nodes that were arrested during that month, and hence the resulting "network" for each month was very sparse, with many disconnected components. The global picture of a single network could not be seen and repeat offenders were very difficult to highlight. Second, human behavior is influenced by memories and experiences, and if an offender is arrested with someone else it was expected that they would continue that relationship. In other words, if two people are co-arrested, and the assumption that they know each other is made, then it can also be assumed that they will be aware of each other at a later point in time, and maintain their link in the network.

Thus the network was built cumulatively so each month's nodes and connections were added to the previous snapshot of the network. This allowed for the analysis of a growing network, while the reason for changes in network statistics moving from one month to the next was investigated by looking at the properties of the offenders (nodes) and events (links) causing the change.

For each month, a set of statistics was gathered to analyze its structure. These include:

- *Network size*: The number of nodes and links were recorded in order to examine the rate at which the network grows.
- *Average degree*: The average number of connections per node, allowing one to see if offenders are becoming more or less connected within the network with respect to the average.
- *Average shortest path*: Average shortest path indicates how far apart any two

given nodes within the network are. It specifies the number of intermediate nodes a particular offender needs to go through in order to communicate with another offender in the network.

- *Clustering coefficient*: The clustering coefficient indicates the likelihood that clusters or groups are present within the network. An increase or decrease in the coefficient indicates whether more or less efficient communication is occurring between offenders.

- *Centrality*: Centrality measures identify key nodes based on their connections and position in a network (Hanneman & Riddle, 2005; Nooy et al., 2005; Scott, 2000).

    a) *Degree centrality*: Degree centrality identifies the nodes with the most direct links in the network. It is theorized that the more direct links a node has the more it can directly influence other nodes, access many resources, and remain well connected, even if some of its links are broken. Nodes with a high degree are commonly identified as leaders; however, in drug networks this is not always true since drug offenders tend to work through others to plan a crime (Xu & Chen, 2003).

    b) *Closeness centrality*: This measure computes the shortest distance between a particular node and all other nodes in the network. The node with the lowest total distance is said to be the most central since it is closer to all other nodes in the network.

    c) *Betweenness centrality*: Betweenness centrality counts the number of times a node lies on a geodesic, or shortest path, between two other nodes. If a node lies along a large number of shortest paths, it is said to be high in betweenness centrality and is said to

be a gatekeeper or broker since it can control access to resources or who communicates with a group. In disconnected networks, only paths between reachable nodes are calculated. If a node does not lie on a shortest path, then it is given a betweenness centrality value of 0.

    d) *Degree and betweenness centralization*: These two measures determine how centralized a network is by measuring the amount of variation in degree or betweenness scores of nodes in the network. If a network contains nodes with very high and very low centrality scores, it is said to be centralized since resources and power seem to pool around key nodes. Star networks have been found to be highly centralized; however, most drug networks have been found to be very decentralized and take the form of a chain network to avoid detection (Brantingham et al., 2011; Xu & Chen, 2003, 2008).

Once these measures were collected over the 60 months, they were analyzed for trends in network development. Any major increases or decreases were investigated to find particular offenders and crime events that influenced the change. Once key offenders and events were identified, they were visualized according to the attributes generated in the composition analysis to further understand the network dynamics that led to particular network statistics. In addition, the networks were examined visually to study how offenders were joining it and if there was an underlying process of recruitment occurring.

Crime Severity and Centrality

The centrality measures defined in the previous section are often used in network studies to identify prolific offenders. Since central nodes are so highly embedded in a network, targeting them usually leads to a high degree of disruption. However, this has had mixed success in drug networks since many higher-level drug offenders tend to work through lower-level criminals in order to avoid detection by police (Xu & Chen, 2003, 2008). Consequently, taking into consideration the severity of an offender's crime, as well as their position, may lead to more effective targeting techniques (Westlake, Bouchard, & Frank, 2011). Hence, the key players found in the centrality analyses for each monthly network were analyzed in depth to see if they were also committing the most severe crimes in the network. Those offenders committing severe crimes were also identified separately and their network connection scores were calculated to examine how embedded they were in the network.

These offenders were also studied to see if increasing or decreasing their crime severity over time led them to be more or less connected in the network with respect to the average node's connectedness. By visualizing the crime types of offenders over 60 months, we hoped to identify if changes in crime severity led to changes in an offender's position in the network.

RESULTS

Network Evolution

After examining the 4,123 networks generated, a network with a relatively large number of nodes was chosen for further detailed analysis. This network was comprised of 393 nodes and 1,071 links, with approximately 80% of offenders committing crimes related to hard drugs, thus this network is referred to as a Hard Drug Network throughout this analysis. Since crimes related to hard drugs are generally regarded as more severe, this network was expected to show a greater degree of clustering and have more group dynamics occurring over time. Thirty-three percent of offenders were female, which

is a slightly larger proportion than that found in the entire set of 4,123 networks. Offenders were also older, with 40% being between the ages of 24 and 35. This could indicate that the offenders within this network are more experienced than the average offender in the 4,123 networks as a whole. Over 60% were from Greater Vancouver with Vancouver Island and the Thompson Okanagan contributing only 6% and 2%, respectively. Of the 678 reported crime events in this network, 60% of them were related to possession, which is 10% higher than the percentage found for the networks as a whole. Trafficking accounted for 38.2% of crime events, while 2% of crime events were related to production and only 0.2% to import/export. The network's composition is summarized in Table 3.1.

When examining how the composition of the networks changed over time, several interesting features were found (Figures 3.2–3.7). At each monthly time step, the average age of all offenders present at that particular time was measured. Since networks were cumulative, each monthly time point also included all offenders that were previously present in the network as well. This average age remained fairly constant, with a value of 31 years, indicating that offenders could be leaving the network as they got older, while new, younger offenders joined. Older, more experienced offenders may be recruiting younger members into the network on a continual basis as well.

The percentage of females was initially quite low, around 20%, but quickly increased to around 34% and remained relatively stable at that value. Visually studying the network confirmed that initial spikes were due to small groups of females joining the network, after which point they recruited more males or they merged with other groups largely containing males.

More than 80% of offenders were found to be from the Greater Vancouver region; however, as the network developed, this

Table 3.1 The composition of all 4,123 networks and the hard drug network chosen for further analysis

	All 4,123 Networks		Hard Drug Network	
Number of Nodes	20,653		393	
Number of Links	75,925		1,071	
Gender				
Male	15,800	76.5%	263	66.9%
Female	4,853	23.5%	130	33.1%
Age				
Null entries	1,301	6.3%	9	2.3%
11 and under	207	1.0%	0	0%
12–17	2,768	13.4%	58	2.1%
18–23	5,989	29.0%	96	24.4%
24–35	5,452	26.4%	156	39.7%
36–50	4,007	19.4%	117	29.7%
51 and over	929	4.5%	7	1.8%
Region				
Null Entries	6,981	33.8%	123	31.3%
Outside BC	21	0.01 %	0	0%
Northwestern BC	496	2.4%	98	0.25%
Northeastern BC	454	2.2%	0	0%
Cariboo	682	3.3%	0	0%
Thompson Okanagan	2,148	10.4%	6	1.55%
Kootenay	204	0.99%	0	0%
Vancouver Island	4,689	22.7%	23	5.8%
Greater Vancouver	4,957	24.0%	240	61.1%
Whistler/Squamish	41	0.2%	0	0%
Drug Crime Events **Crime Type**	11,077 events		678 events	
Possession	5,339	48.2%	406	60.0%
Trafficking	3,943	35.6%	259	38.2%
Production	1,606	14.5%	11	1.6%
Import/Export	189	1.7%	2	0.2%
Drug Type				
Cannabis	6,646	60.0%	142	21.0%
Hard Drugs	4,431	40.0%	536	79.0%

proportion gradually decreased to about 60%. As offenders developed more connections within the network, it was found that a small group of producers from Vancouver Island joined the network and other individuals from Vancouver Island and the Thompson Okanagan linked up to established clusters. This implies that once drug-trafficking groups establish themselves, making connec-

tions with individuals from different regions becomes important, especially in opening new markets and providing resources.

The percentage of offenders involved in trafficking and involved with hard drugs was also monitored and similar patterns were found for both. Trafficking hard drugs was consistently found to be one of the most common offenses over the 60 months, with a large

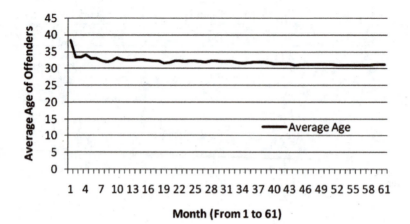

Figure 3.2 Average age of offenders within each monthly network

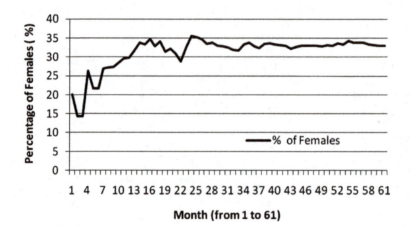

Figure 3.3 Percentage of female offenders within each monthly network

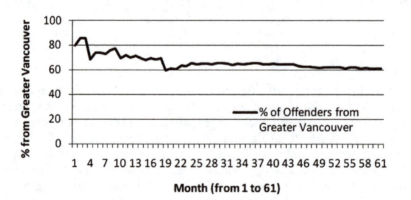

Figure 3.4 Percentage of offenders from Greater Vancouver for each monthly network

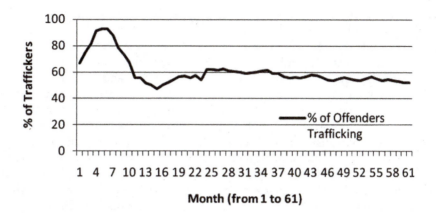

Figure 3.5 Percentage of offenders committing trafficking crimes within each monthly network

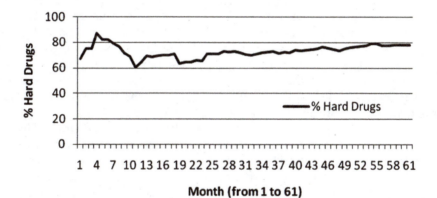

Figure 3.6 Percentage of offenders associated with hard drugs for each monthly network

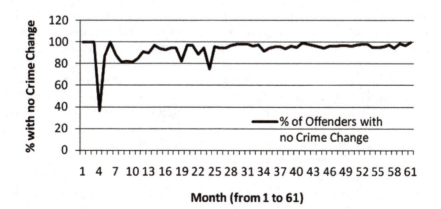

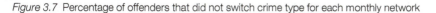

Figure 3.7 Percentage of offenders that did not switch crime type for each monthly network

spike occurring within the first 10 months. This large spike is due to several cliques of traffickers entering the network. However, as the network grew, many offenders initially arrested for trafficking were re-arrested for possession and many new offenders were also charged with possession. This, combined with a small proportion of producers entering the network, causes the percentage of trafficking activity to decrease and quickly stabilize around 50%. However, the percentage of crimes associated with hard drugs remains high, around 80%. The proportion of offenders changing crime types was also examined and corresponds to the patterns found in crime type. Decreases in trafficking coincide with points at which relatively large proportions of offenders switch crime types.

Once the composition of the networks was understood, statistics relating to the structure of the network were collected for each monthly time interval and the results are presented in Figures 3.8–3.13. The general trends of each measure are described below:

- *Network size*: The number of vertices increases linearly from month 1 to month 60, with a small jump at month 24 due to a large new clique entering the network. On average, about six new offenders are added to the network during each month.
- *Average degree*: The average degree sharply increases at months 4, 11, 19, and 24, after which point it gradually decreases and eventually steadies out with a value of 5.5. The sharp jumps detected are related to cliques of offenders entering the network as well as several individual groups merging together. Cliques of offenders usually arise when a group of offenders related to a single event are caught by police and each offender is connected to every other person in the group as a result. Most cliques are comprised of 5–7 offenders; however, at month 24 two cliques of size 11

and 16 join the network, explaining the sharp increase in network size as well.
- *Average shortest path*: The average path length increases fairly quickly between month 1 and month 11, going from a value of 1 to 2.5. There are relatively sharp increases occurring at months 4 and 11, after which point the measure steadies. The two small cliques entering the network at month 4, which caused a spike in the average degree, also increase the path length since they are connected through a single offender. Thus, to go from one clique to another requires an offender to go through this node. At month 11, several groups merge, extending the length between two nodes at opposite edges of the group. Another sharp increase is seen between months 33 and 45, when many groups at the outer edge of the graph become connected. From month 46 and onwards, however, path length decreases due to the merging of groups closer to the center of the graph.
- *Clustering coefficient*: The clustering coefficient steadily decreases over time, going from a value of 1 to approximately 0.75. Due to its high value, there is a high degree of clustering throughout the network's evolution. Up until month 46, most individual groups are highly connected and after month 46, when these groups start to merge, links are created between them, maintaining a high degree of communication efficiency. However, since most individual groups are initially highly connected and connections between groups are looser, merging clusters or groups become gradually less tight-knit, producing a gradual negative linear trend.
- *Centrality*:

a) *Degree centralization*: Degree centralization quickly peaks around month 11 and sharply decreases, reaching a value of less than 0.1 by month 60. The high centralization toward the beginning is due to a group which forms that is highly connected to a single offender, creating a high degree of variation in degree scores. As more groups and cliques enter the network with a similar structure, the variation in centrality scores decreases, explaining the decrease in centralization. Most of these new cliques enter as independent groups, and are not connected to other pre-existing groups. As older people are leaving the network and younger people are joining, newer nodes are continually increasing in degree, decreasing the variation in the network. Also, as offenders are added to the network, there is a natural process of decentralization as they form clusters that are less and less connected with the standing core (Morselli & Petit, 2007).

b) *Betweenness centralization*: Betweenness centralization peaks at month 4, with a value of 0.38562, then drops down to a value of 0.07004 at month 10. The peak at month 4 occurs because there are two cliques that enter the network connected by a single node, which acts as a gatekeeper to both groups. After this point, only smaller dyads and triads join the network and they are largely isolated, so there is not a great deal of variation in betweenness scores. A smaller peak occurs at month 11, which is due to another clique joining the network through an intermediate node. Another increase occurs at month 38 when an important link is created between the largest component in the network and several cliques, introducing several nodes with high betweenness centrality scores. The increase at month 54 is due to a similar situation.

After the 60 months, the network that evolved was highly connected with an average degree of 5.45, and it was also scale-free and small world. Offenders could contact each other within a relatively small amount of steps with an average path length of around 6. The clustering coefficient was 0.74495, indicating a high degree of communication efficiency, and it was significantly larger when compared to a clustering coefficient of a random network of the same size (0.01714). Examining the network from a global, high-level view,

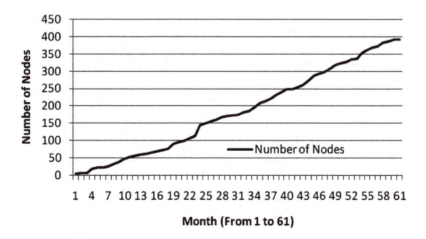

Figure 3.8 Number of nodes in each monthly network

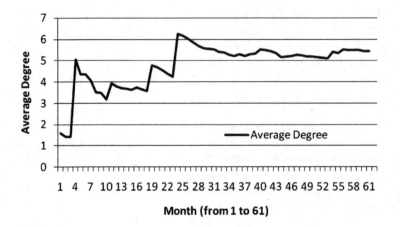

Figure 3.9 Average degree of all nodes in each monthly network

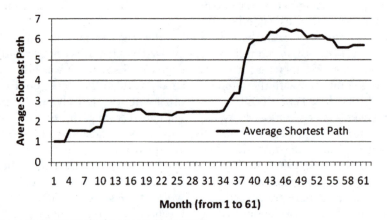

Figure 3.10 Average shortest path of each monthly network

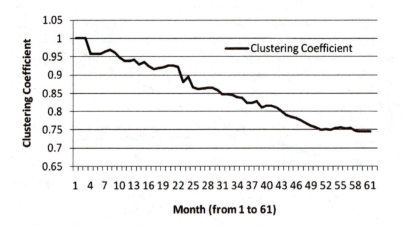

Figure 3.11 Clustering coefficient of each monthly network

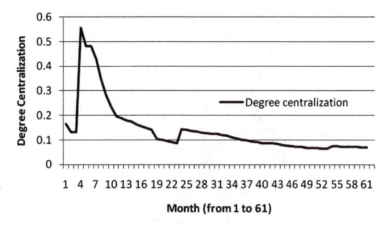

Figure 3.12 Degree centralization of each monthly network

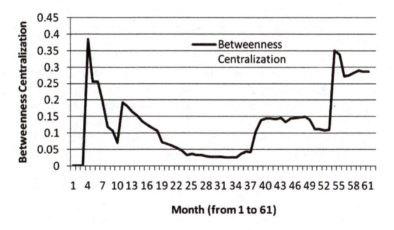

Figure 3.13 Betweenness centralization of each monthly network

the center appears to have a star structure; however, there is also a chain of high degree nodes present and several chains leading out from the star as well (Figure 3.14).

From these measures, several key months that contribute to the development of the network can be identified, specifically months 4, 11, 19, 24, 38, and 54. As has been mentioned above, month 4 shows a significant development since two cliques (of size 6 and 8) join the network and are connected through a single node which has very high centrality scores throughout the network's evolution (Figure 3.15a). These two cliques, which contain 13 offenders in total, are trafficking hard drugs and they are not connected to any offenders charged with possession. They range in age from 19 to 47 and contain four females in total. They are the first of many trafficking groups which arise in the network and, since they are so well connected, they may be higher-level wholesalers rather than individual street dealers. This group is the largest component in the network at month 4 and, as the network grows, it remains the largest throughout the entire evolution of the network.

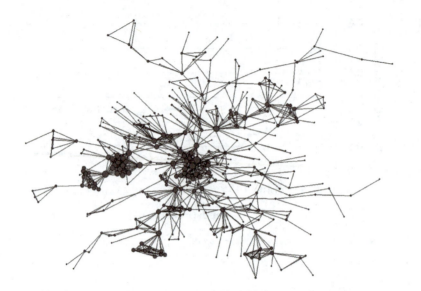

Figure 3.14 The complete network at month 60. Node sizes are drawn based on their degree. Both star and chain structures are present in the network

Another clique, involved in the production of cannabis, joins the group from month 4 (Figure 3.15b). All of its members are from Greater Vancouver, and they are fairly young, ranging from age 19 to 34, and are mostly male. Their link with the hard drug-trafficking group is interesting, indicating that the trafficking group may be involved with more than one type of drug, which is a situation that consistently occurs in later months as well. This production group is linked not only to the trafficking clique from month 4, but also to a smaller group of four offenders and an isolated trafficker. In later months, some members of the large clique switch to production and others switch to trafficking in turn.

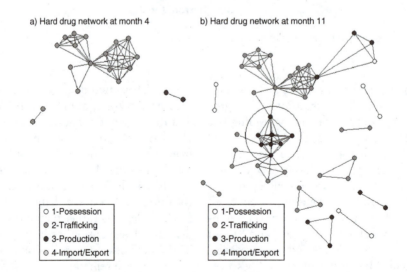

Figure 3.15 Hard drug network at months 4 and 11. Both months have new cliques entering the network

During month 19, as a result of a single arrest event, a major trafficking clique with 14 offenders emerges, which eventually forms the star structure at the center of the complete network (Figure 3.16a). There are two females aged 18 and 19, who are the youngest of the group. Most of these offenders are from Greater Vancouver. A single offender from Vancouver Island is part of the group and almost everyone is trafficking cannabis. Two more cliques join the network in month 24 and are connected by a single node at month 60. At month 38 (Figure 3.17), a key connection is made to an offender, possibly acting as a gatekeeper (Figure 3.16b). These two cliques are trafficking hard drugs within Greater Vancouver, but they are also connected with a small chain of offenders from Vancouver Island who are trafficking cannabis. Hence months 19 and 24 show two highly connected groups: one that concentrates its activities on cannabis, and one that deals with hard drugs. However, as these groups evolve, many members switch drug types and are also charged with possession.

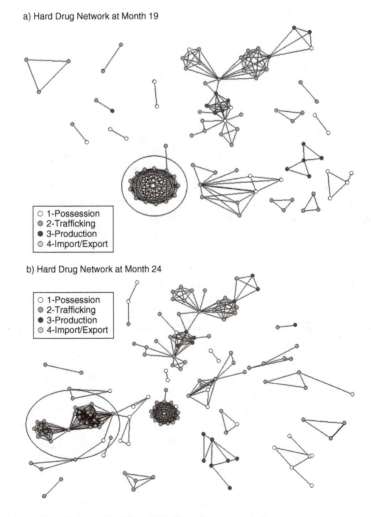

Figure 3.16 Hard drug network at months 19 and 24. New cliques are circled

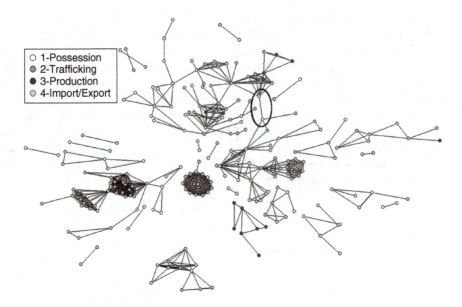

Figure 3.17 Hard drug network at month 38. The new link is circled

Beginning from around month 36, individual groups within the network merge and eventually come together in a large component. At month 38, a key connection is made between a node in the large component (node 107) and a node which is connected to several key groups. This connection gives node 107 the highest closeness centrality score within the network and also causes the size of the large component to grow significantly. Node 107 is indirectly connected to producers within the large component and, with this new link, it connects clusters trafficking cannabis and hard drugs to the large component. In spite of the fact that the link between 107 is a cause of a less serious crime, possession of hard drugs, it is a key factor in the development of the network. Consequently, both network structure and crime seriousness need to be taken into account when studying network evolution.

Lastly, at month 53 (Figure 3.18a), there are two major connected components in the network, and in the next time period (Figure 3.18b) a key cluster emerges that connects the two together. This cluster of five people, mostly in their early forties, is involved in hard drug-trafficking. One individual is from Vancouver Island, while the rest are from an unknown origin, or are from Greater Vancouver. They are connected to clusters that are also trafficking hard drugs and that are largely tied to possession of cannabis or hard drugs. This cluster also indirectly connects several high degree nodes from different clusters, including the cluster from month 19 which forms the center of the star structure of the network.

These key time points highlight the role of clusters in the growth of the network, especially the emerging trafficking clusters which cause the network to become more highly connected. As these groups form connections with producers, with other groups, and with individuals from different regions, they cause the network to become more cohesive. However, there is also a large amount of isolates and small dyads and triads that get recruited into these clusters. Studying these isolates may lend some insight into the preferential attachment properties of the network, which may show how offenders are attracted to

a) Hard Drug Network at Month 53

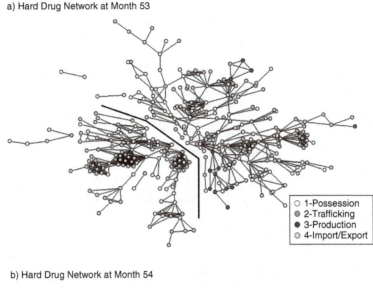

b) Hard Drug Network at Month 54

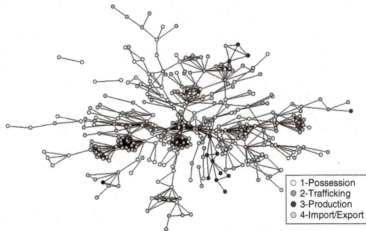

Figure 3.18 The hard drug network at months 53 and 54. Comparing the two, we see that there is a cluster of offenders that emerges in month 53 that connects the two major components of month 54 together

drug trafficking groups. Since there is one large component throughout the 60 months that all other groups end up merging with, the growth of this component was documented over time to investigate its development. Since it was the largest component, it was also deemed to be the most likely cluster that new nodes would be attracted to. Figure 3.19 shows how its size grows over the 60 months.

Up until month 36, the size of the component gradually increases, during which time many isolates or small dyads link up to it. Some of the dyads or triads produce cannabis and are mainly comprised of males. Most isolates at this point are males or females in their twenties and are charged with either trafficking or possession. This supports the idea that younger offenders are joining the network, and that they are forming

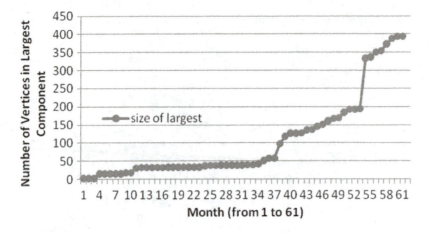

Figure 3.19 Size of largest component over time

connections with more experienced offenders. After month 36, there are mostly small groups or clusters linking up to the component, which contribute to its quick increase in size. Most of these are clusters committing the same types of crimes, like trafficking or possession. Since it remains the largest component throughout the 60 months and because of its rapid growth, the development of this component does show preferential attachment.

Crime Severity and Centrality

Most of the major groups identified in the network evolution analysis were caught for either possession or trafficking. Although these types of activities are important to disrupt, there are more severe crimes, such as production and import/export, which have a greater impact along the drug commodity chain. Since possession and trafficking crimes rely on the successful production and import of illicit substances, disrupting these parts of the chain can make the retail sale of drugs more difficult, and may reduce the size of trafficking clusters in the long term. Table 3.2 shows the key players found during the network evolution analysis and the types of crimes they commit. Only 2 offenders out of

the 12 listed (offenders 235 and 138) were associated with production and were identified by the closeness and betweenness centrality measures. Offender 235 is present in the network from month 1 and is also part of the first clique at month 4, which later evolves into the large component. Hence, he is highly connected in the network and detected by centrality scores. Offender 138 is similarly embedded since he joins the large component during month 11.

However, there are 32 more offenders committing crimes associated with production and one more committing an import/export crime that were not detected. Their centrality scores are displayed in Table 3.3 in order to investigate how central they are to the network and where they are positioned. Of particular interest is node 128, which is the only node in the network involved in import/export, the most serious crime type. Its degree of 3 is lower than the average of 5.42 and its closeness centrality score of 0.132092 is half of the network maximum. It has a value of zero for betweenness centrality, meaning that it does not lie on any shortest paths within the network. It is connected to a relatively small hard drug-trafficking group and is positioned toward the edge of the network. Due to its low centrality scores, and its

Table 3.2 Key players detected by the network evolution analysis (highest scores in degree, closeness, and betweenness centrality)

Offender ID	Drug Crimes	Age	Gender	Region
Degree, Closeness, and Betweenness				
124	Trafficking – hard drugs Possession – hard drugs	44	Male	Greater Vancouver
Degree and Closeness				
8	Trafficking – hard drugs	50	Female	—
Closeness and Betweenness				
211	Trafficking – hard drugs Possession – hard drugs	47	Male	—
55	Trafficking – hard drugs Possession – hard drugs and cannabis	33	Female	Greater Vancouver
Degree				
19	Trafficking – hard drugs and cannabis Possession – hard drugs	32	Male	Greater Vancouver
Closeness				
235	Production – cannabis Trafficking – hard drugs Possession – cannabis	19	Male	Greater Vancouver
107	Trafficking – hard drugs Possession – hard drugs	26	Female	—
216	Trafficking – hard drugs Possession – hard drugs and cannabis	47	Female	—
29	Trafficking – hard drugs	44	Male	Greater Vancouver
50	Trafficking – hard drugs Possession – hard drugs	48	Male	Greater Vancouver
Betweenness				
138	Production – cannabis Trafficking – hard drugs Possession – hard drugs and cannabis	30	Male	Greater Vancouver
23	Trafficking – hard drugs Possession – hard drugs and cannabis	30	Male	Greater Vancouver

low connectedness, node 128 is somewhat of an outlier. This may indicate that offenders committing more serious offenses may in fact be less connected and be less visible in the network, as they may work through others to avoid detection.

For the offenders involved in production, those that commit several different crimes over time tend to have higher degrees and higher betweenness scores. However, this is more a result of the number of crimes they commit rather than the seriousness of their crimes. For the most part, offenders producing cannabis typically have a high closeness centrality score that, in most cases, is very close to the maximum closeness score. Out

Table 3.3 The centrality scores of offenders committing production and import/export crimes within the hard drug network

Offender ID	Time of Offence	Drug Crime	Degree	Closeness	Betweenness	Highest Monthly Closeness Score
15	54	Trafficking – hard drugs	12	0.24468	0	0.2700
	56	Production – cannabis	20	**0.26804***	0.103646	0.2881
17	56	Production – cannabis	8	0.216926*	0	0.2881
18	55	Trafficking – hard drugs	3	0.011019	0	0.2666
	56	Production – cannabis	11	**0.217354***	0.015371	0.2881
21	15	Possession – hard drugs	3	0.060606	0	0.2733
	51	Production – cannabis	6	**0.111243***	0.027299	0.1220
22	10	Production – cannabis	2	0.061224	0	0.3122
	13	Production – cannabis	4	0.080645	0.002186	0.2909
	23	Production – cannabis	5	0.052632	0.001738	0.1570
	51	Production – cannabis	7	0.094462	0.015729	0.1220
62	48	Trafficking – cannabis	5	0.067872	0	0.1099
	49	Trafficking – hard drugs	9	0.078487	0.010725	0.1082
	55	Possession – hard drugs	9	0.155578	0.040159	0.2666
	56	Production – cannabis	15	**0.224884***	0.032493	0.2881
	58	Trafficking – hard drugs	16	0.239459	0.046559	0.2945
63	48	Trafficking – cannabis	5	0.067872	0	0.1099
	56	Production – cannabis	12	**0.224123***	0.018017	0.2881
77	14	Production – cannabis	2	0.053763	0	0.2909
	51	Production – cannabis	4	**0.094143***	0.001725	0.1220
104	51	Production – cannabis	3	**0.094063***	0	0.1220
108	4	Trafficking – hard drugs	7	0.526316	0	0.7895
	9	Production – cannabis	10	**0.31875***	0.05668	0.3825
128	47	Trafficking – hard drugs	1	0.006689	0	0.1123
	49	Trafficking – hard drugs	3	0.050103	0	0.1082
	54	Import/export – hard drugs	3	0.132092	0	0.2700
141	11	Production – cannabis	10	**0.242567***	0	0.3312
142	11	Production – cannabis	10	**0.242567***	0	0.3312
153	32	Trafficking – hard drugs	1	0.065431	0	0.1405
	53	Trafficking – hard drugs	3	0.083921	0.006747	0.1194
166	9	Production – cannabis	3	**0.201316***	0	0.3825
167	9	Production – cannabis	3	**0.201316***	0	0.3825
170	49	Trafficking – hard drugs	5	0.061162	0.002918	0.1082
	55	Possession – hard drugs	5	0.13382	0.010223	0.2666
	56	Production – cannabis	12	**0.217926***	0.021051	0.2881
171	56	Production – cannabis	8	**0.216926***	0	0.2881
174	14	Production – cannabis	2	0.053763	0	0.2909
201	10	Production – cannabis	2	0.061224	0	0.3122
	23	Production – cannabis	3	0.040936	0.00079	0.1570
205	5	Trafficking – cannabis	1	0.086957	0	0.6522
	11	Production – cannabis	8	**0.246032***	0.021045	0.3312
	32	Trafficking – hard drugs	9	0.092166	0.004604	0.1405
209	56	Production – cannabis	8	**0.216926***	0	0.2881
210	10	Production – cannabis	2	0.061224	0	0.3122
213	56	Production – cannabis	8	**0.216926***	0	0.2881
	58	Possession – hard drugs	12	0.244979	0.053114	0.2945
236	58	Production – cannabis	4	0.171987	0	0.2945
237	1	Production – cannabis	1	**0.4***	0	0.6
	31	Trafficking – hard drugs	2	0.017143	0.000066	0.1461
	36	Trafficking – hard drugs	4	0.023148	0.000217	0.1204
249	11	Production – cannabis	7	**0.242567***	0	0.3312

Table 3.3 Conitnued

Offender ID	Time of Offence	Drug Crime	Degree	Closeness	Betweenness	Highest Monthly Closeness Score
269	11	Production – cannabis	7	**0.242567***	0	0.3312
	24	Possession – hard drugs	8	0.101884	0.003161	0.1721
	34	Trafficking – cannabis	9	0.087848	0.004092	0.1313
	54	Trafficking – hard drugs	10	0.184773	0.016026	0.2700
276	11	Production – cannabis	7	**0.242567***	0	0.3312
277	9	Production – cannabis	3	**0.201316***	0	0.3825
326	1	Production – cannabis	1	**0.4***	0	0.6
350	23	Production – cannabis	1	0.030702	0	0.1570
377	23	Production – cannabis	1	0.026316	0	0.1570

Note
The asterisk marks the producers who have high closeness centrality scores in relation to the maximum closeness centrality score for the month.

of the 35 production offenses committed by offenders, 24 (or 69%) had high closeness centrality scores. Since the process of production requires that illicit substances be distributed to drug traffickers, being close to as many nodes as possible in the network is a great benefit to these types of offenders. Once offenders switch to less severe crimes, their closeness centrality scores drop because it is no longer an important factor for success in other types of drug crimes.

In terms of examining whether offenders tend to switch from more severe to less severe crimes, or vice versa, no clear pattern seems to be present. Many producers move to trafficking or possession in a fairly random order, implying that a large proportion of offenders in this network commit multiple types of drug crimes, especially trafficking and possession. In addition, it can be hypothesized that, if an offender is known to police for a crime like production or trafficking, then if they happen to be caught possessing illicit substances they are more likely to be arrested and charged (and hence be in the arrest data used for this chapter).

DISCUSSION

The results of the evolution analysis point to some key dynamics of an arrest-based developing drug network, especially in terms of how offenders form groups and how groups connect with each other. Most apparent is the tendency for offenders to initially form tight-knit groups with those being arrested for the same type of crime. These clusters tend to arise when groups of offenders associated with the same crime event have been caught by law enforcement. Although it could be argued that this is an artifact of the police data used to create the networks, it still highlights the fact that offenders being arrested for similar crime types work together. The continual presence of such groups in the network contributes to the high clustering coefficient seen throughout its development. This also confirms Desroches' (2005) statement that organized crime groups are often a result of tightly knit groups coming together for a particular purpose.

Unlike previous studies which have found that traffickers are loosely connected with other traffickers and highly connected to buyers, this study has found that traffickers seem to form tight-knit groups with each other. Most links between traffickers and buyers occur when members of the group switch to possession, or when small isolates or dyads are recruited into the group. These isolates and dyads later switch to trafficking and usually become more embedded in the group over time. The large degree of switching between possession and trafficking, as well as between hard and soft drugs, could be a result of offenders changing their behavior post-arrest, which confirms that offenders are engaging in active deterrence (Gallupe et al., 2011). It could also indicate that offenders are often engaged in more than one type of drug crime and that they are not only traffickers but also users. Just as Malm and Bichler (2011) found, retailers engaging in more than one type of crime were found to have high small-world properties, meaning that they were closely linked with high clustering coefficients.

When groups of producers make connections with other groups, usually a single producer in the group becomes linked to a single trafficker that is part of a clique. This results in a high betweenness score for the trafficker, who could represent a gatekeeper or broker who handles resources between the two groups, confirming findings from previous studies about offenders with high betweenness scores (Xu & Chen, 2003). By observing these offenders as part of a larger network, as opposed to individuals, several generalizations can be drawn. First, producers were found to initially form smaller and looser groups toward the edges of the network, while traffickers mainly formed cliques (Figures 3.15b, 3.16, and 3.18). These are consistent with the social network structures that have the greatest benefits to these roles. Producers need to get the drugs to the consumers, and this can be done in two different ways: by having many connections to consumers or by having a few connections to traffickers. The prior exposes the producer to more risk, while the latter carries less risk for the producer but requires (a few) connections to traffickers, who themselves have to be embedded in networks of consumers. As expected, in this chapter, the latter was observed in the network structure of drug offenders.

Examining average degree scores for each monthly network was found to be highly effective at detecting when clusters enter the graph. Since these groups are highly connected to each other, they have a high degree and contribute to the quick increase of this measure. Sharp increases over time can indicate when these groups become active and the size of the jump can also indicate how large a group is.

Once groups of offenders establish themselves, they then start to make connections with other groups. Most often links are formed between one or two offenders from each group, causing different clusters to come together. When these clusters join together, the number of nodes that have high betweenness centrality scores rises, and increases in betweenness centralization also occur. Betweenness centralization then becomes a good measure for investigating when groups are joining and when there are key communication links established between gatekeepers and co-offending clusters. If there are any large jumps in the metric, such as at month 4 for this network, then an offender acting as a gatekeeper has entered the network, which could be a good target for law enforcement to monitor more closely.

Examining the number of nodes within the largest component in each monthly network proved to be useful when looking at the process of recruitment and preferential attachment. Since the largest component remained the same in each monthly network, examining its size was a good way to see how many nodes it was attracting. Within the first three years of the network's development, the component was attracting mostly small groups, dyads, triads, and isolates. One small group was involved in production, and the remaining isolates and dyads were largely younger offenders committing possession or trafficking crimes. When combining these results with the proportion of offenders from Greater Vancouver over time, it can be hypothesized that groups are also recruiting individuals from different regions. As they become successful and start to become involved with producers and buyers, they also create ties with other regions in order to expand their market and resources. Hence preferential attachment seems to play a role in recruitment and it may have a factor in the way that smaller groups merge with the large component over time. Thus identifying and removing offenders who have a large number of connections would allow law enforcement to hinder the recruitment process within networks of drug offenders, because new offenders, due to preferential attachment, are likely to make connections to them instead of offenders with a low number of links.

When working with networks built from arrest data, repeat offenders are automatically more embedded in the network because of the increased number of crimes they have been charged with. However, it is important to distinguish between a repeat offender who has been charged with the less severe crime of possession multiple times and a producer or importer/exporter charged only once. The key players found in the network were most often repeat offenders committing trafficking and possession crimes. Many were present in the network very early on and they were also part of cliques. Those with high betweenness centrality scores were often clique members who formed a connection with another group, so gatekeepers were successfully identified. However, hardly any were committing serious crimes, such as production or smuggling. Consequently, examining centrality alone will often not identify offenders committing more severe crimes, meaning that other factors need to be taken into account. When looking at the only offender committing an import/export crime in the network, it was found that he was somewhat of an outlier with respect to the network statistics. Hence detecting individuals within this drug niche may involve identifying those with lower centrality scores, but also those that are still part of small groups. This further adds to the same hypothesis suggested by Xu and Chen (2003), who speculated that offenders with

low centrality scores, or outliers, may in reality be leaders working through lower-level co-offenders.

Producers exhibited some different patterns. Most were committing trafficking and possession crimes in addition to production, and at these times all of their centrality scores were quite low. However, when they were actively involved in production, their closeness centrality scores often rose and were quite close to the maximum score in the network. Since producers need to work closely with traffickers in order to make a profit, being close to many nodes in the network increases their chances of success. Thus, to detect producers, a good strategy for law enforcement could be to monitor the closeness centrality scores of offenders and focus on those offenders who have the highest centrality score.

Most repeat offenders committed different types of crimes involving both hard and soft drugs, and they often switched from more serious to less serious crimes, and vice versa. However, looking at the relationship between changes in crime severity and connectedness revealed no significant patterns. The offenders trafficking were often the most connected, but they often remained well connected in their groups even when switching to possession. The same pattern was found for producers. In most cases, the number of offenses committed by an offender played a larger role in their connectedness rather than their crime severity.

These mixed results are largely due to the limitations associated with the arrest data used to build the networks. Once an offender committing drug crimes becomes known to police, their activities become more closely monitored and even committing a less serious crime is likely to lead to a re-arrest. Thus any crime that an offender commits after their first arrest will likely lead them to be more embedded in the network. The offenders studied are also those that have been caught by law enforcement, so in a sense they can be regarded as unsuccessful. Those offenders that have managed to avoid detection may present different evolution and co-offending patterns than those known to police. The way in which crimes are reported in arrest data also has an impact on the amount of clusters found in the network. When an event occurs and offenders associated with the event are arrested, they are all linked to each other, forming a clique in the network. This may create the impression that these offenders collaborate closely when, in reality, only a few may know each other really well. But regardless of this, all of the offenders were caught for the same crime event and hence must know each other to a certain extent. Hence, arrest data still presents a valuable resource with which to monitor repeat offenders and still gives a general sense of how groups form.

Although social network analysis (SNA) allowed for the identification of those offenders who are the most important in the network, or have the most impact on the evolvement of the network structure, many patterns in this network were discovered only after manually following up the results provided by SNA. Thus, some important developments may have been overlooked. Creating computer algorithms or software specifically designed to look at a network's evolution in terms of subgroup development, or statistical changes, may be a better approach since observations can be gathered in a more systematic way. The community detection algorithms from SNA studies in other fields can be taken and adapted to drug networks to provide a more in depth quantitative analysis (Falkowski et al., 2006a, 2006b). With an automated approach, more networks out of the 4,123 detected could also be analyzed. However, a visual analysis is still a good starting point for determining general trends in co-arrest patterns, and has led to many key insights into both the macro- and the micro-level dynamics occurring within drug networks.

CONCLUSION

This study aimed to uncover key trends in the evolvement of drug networks generated from co-arrest data and to identify prolific offenders actively engaged in higher-level crimes. Understanding how illicit networks grow and change over time may lead to improved knowledge about disruption strategies for law enforcement, especially in terms of the best positions in the network to target. Since the first half of the network's evolution involved the growth of groups, early detection of such groups may in fact prevent further growth. If production or trafficking groups are disrupted before they have a chance to form connections, or before they have a chance to recruit offenders from different regions, a large amount of drug activity may be reduced. In addition, key measures such as average degree and betweenness centralization were found to be useful in detecting significant developments in the network over time, especially in the increase of clusters and gatekeepers. The evolution analysis also confirmed that co-offending groups, especially trafficking cliques, are actively engaged in the processes of recruitment. These groups tend to attract producers and also attract younger offenders by selling them drugs and eventually leading them into trafficking.

Centrality measures were found to mostly detect repeat offenders, not necessarily those who commit more severe crimes. Crimes such as import/export were found to be performed by offenders on the edges of the network, and producers were found to have low degree and betweenness centrality scores. However, a relationship between closeness centrality and production was found in that producers often had high scores close to the maximum score for each month. Consequently, monitoring jumps in an offender's closeness scores may help identify the presence of producers in a network.

In the future, measures like network capital, which examines both an offender's connectedness and their ability to share resources within a network, can be used to identify higher-level offenders (Schwartz & Rouselle, 2009). Also, different data sources, such as court records or police surveillance observations, can be incorporated into arrest data to investigate if similar patterns still emerge. With key developments in the network identified, different disruption techniques can then be tested at different time points to study how the network's evolution changes. This can provide an opportunity to model the results of disruption techniques before applying them in practice.

These findings highlight the need for further research in the evolution of drug networks. With improved knowledge about how illicit networks develop, both predicting and disrupting the activities of drug offenders can become more effective. Using statistical techniques from social network analysis has shown to draw attention to important events in the growth of drug trafficking rings, and has also identified the positions that higher-level offenders occupy over time. Introducing a time element into social network analysis can prove to be highly beneficial in the attempts to combat rising drug crimes not only within British Columbia but in other regions as well.

NOTE

1. The first largest network contained 729 nodes and 14,470 links, and had a very large clique, significantly influencing all network statistics. Because of this clique, the decision was made to use the second largest network from the dataset.

REFERENCES

Barabási, A.L., H. Jeong, Z. Néda, E. Ravasz, A. Schubert, & T. Vicsek (2002). Evolution of the social network of scientific collaborations. *Physica A: Statistical Mechanics and its Applications* 311(3–4), 590–614.

Brantingham, P.L., M. Ester, R. Frank, U. Glässer, & M.A. Tayebi (2011). Co-offending network mining. In U.K. Wiil (ed.), *Counterterrorism*

and Open Source Intelligence (pp. 73–102). Vienna: Springer.

Dauvergne, M. (2009). Trends in police-reported drug offences in Canada. *Juristat: Canadian Centre for Justice Statistics* 29(2), 1C–25C.

Desroches, F.J. (2005). *The Crime that Pays: Drug Trafficking and Organized Crime in Canada.* Toronto: Canadian Scholars' Press.

Falkowski, T., J. Bartelheimer, & M. Siliopoulou (2006a). Community dynamics mining. *Proceedings of 14th European Conference on Information Systems*, Paper 173.

Falkowski, T., J. Bartelheimer, & M. Spiliopoulou (2006b). *Mining and Visualizing the Evolution of Subgroups in Social Networks.* Washington, DC: IEEE Computer Society.

Gallupe, O., M. Bouchard, & J.P. Caulkins (2011). No change is a good change? Restrictive deterrence in illegal drug markets. *Journal of Criminal Justice* 39(1), 81–89.

Glenny, M. (2009). Canada: The new global drug lord. *Maclean's* 122(32), 16–18.

Hanneman, R.A. & M. Riddle (2005). *Introduction to Social Network Methods.* Riverside, CA: University of California, Riverside.

Heber, A. (2009). The networks of drug offenders. *Trends in Organized Crime* 12(1), 1–20.

Joffres, K., M. Bouchard, R. Frank, & B. Westlake (2011). Strategies to disrupt online child pornography networks. *Proceedings of the 2011 European Intelligence and Security Informatics Conference (EISIC)*, pp. 163–170. Athens, Greece.

Kossinets, G. & D.J. Watts (2006). Empirical analysis of an evolving social network. *Science* 311(5757), 88–90.

Malm, A. & G. Bichler (2011). Networks of collaborating criminals: Assessing the structural vulnerability of drug markets. *Journal of Research in Crime and Delinquency* 48, 271–297.

Morselli, C. & K. Petit (2007). Law enforcement disruption of a drug importation network. *Global Crime* 8(2), 109–130.

Nooy, W.D., A. Mrvar, & V. Batagelj (eds.). (2005). *Exploratory Social Network Analysis with Pajek.* New York: Cambridge University Press.

Reiss, A.J. (1988). Co-offending and criminal careers. *Crime and Justice* 10, 117–170.

Royal Canadian Mounted Police (RCMP). (2007). *Drug Situation in Canada.* Ottawa: RCMP.

Available at: www.rcmp-grc.gc.ca/drugs-drogues/ pdf/drug-drogue-situation-2007-eng.pdf.

Schwartz, D. & T.D.A. Rouselle (2009). Using social network analysis to target criminal networks. *Trends in Organized Crime* 12(2), 188–207.

Scott, J. (2000). *Social Network Analysis: A Handbook* (2nd ed.). London: Sage.

Westlake, B.G., M. Bouchard, & R. Frank (2011). Finding the key players in online child exploitation networks. *Policy & Internet* 3(2), Article 6.

Xu, J. & H. Chen (2003). Untangling criminal networks: A case study. In H. Chen, R. Miranda, D. Zeng, C. Demchak, J. Schroeder, & T. Madhusudan (eds.), *Intelligence and Security Informatics* (p. 958). Berlin, Heidelberg: Springer.

Xu, J. & H. Chen (2008). The topology of dark networks. *Communications of the ACM* 51(10), 58–65.

CHAPTER 4

Assessing the Core Membership of a Youth Gang from its Co-offending Network

Martin Bouchard and Richard Konarski

The dynamic and sometimes diffuse nature of membership makes gang boundaries difficult to discern for law enforcement officials or researchers, and even for members themselves. Yet, the temptation to classify gangs and their members into orderly, mutually exclusive groupings is high. Street observations of gang behavior, language, and symbolism generally fit an ideal type of a bounded and cohesive social group (Fleisher, 2005), especially during times of conflicts (Decker, 1996). Gang intervention programs are most efficient when they are able to differentiate between "core" and "fringe" members (Maxson, 2011), or between the minority of "organized" and the majority of disorganized gangs (Spindler & Bouchard, 2011; see also Esbensen, Winfree, He, & Taylor, 2001). Police interventions are often designed to crack down on a specific gang that should be easily discernible from others.

An increasing amount of gang research, however, started to show that this idea of a bounded social group may in fact hide a much more complex set of interactions among a larger social (or criminal) scene that has consequences on gang behavior. Key to this shift is the use of social network analysis (SNA) in gang studies (McGloin, 2005; Papachristos, 2006; Morselli, 2009; Sarnecki, 2001). SNA allowed researchers: 1) to realize that gang members were interacting with a larger social scene that included many non-members, yet, criminally involved actors; 2) to not take gang boundaries for granted, but to let them emerge from relational data.

At least two studies provided clear demonstrations of those two points. Combining the ego-centric networks of two female members of the Vice Lords in Champaign, Illinois, Fleisher (2005) illustrated how such specific gang affiliation did not preclude friendship interactions with members of two other gangs:

> North-end gang women identified themselves as members of Vice Lords, Gangster Disciples, and Black P-Stones, but gang affiliation had no necessary criminal or social obligations; there were no gang meetings, no script to memorize, no need to participate in gang fights or sell drugs, and no need to hang out with or feel personal closeness to fellow gang members. There were no fights supporting gang pride. Violence was personal and usually instigated by love relations gone awry. Most important, a gang affiliation did not impede social, economic, or personal relationships among north-end gang women.
>
> (Fleisher, 2005: 126)

Fleisher's (2005) study is important in demonstrating how different research designs may lead to different conclusions about gang boundaries: street observations seem to fit the cohesive, territorial gang perspective, while an analysis of social interactions suggest much more blurry boundaries between groupings. The fact that some gang studies rely on co-offending data and others on participant observation or conversations extracted from wiretap data should not be lost on researchers who interpret their results in light of prior studies.

This particular point is well illustrated in Morselli's (2009) reliance on wiretap data to examine the role of a major gang in a drug distribution trade network in Montreal. In launching three successive investigations targeting one gang (the Bo-Gars), the objective of the Montreal Police Department was clear: eliminate this gang which was thought to control drug distribution in the north part of Montreal. The Bo-Gars proved to be a rather elusive group. Of the 70 individuals identified as participants in the drug distribution trade over the course of these three investigations, only 23 were gang members, including 11 Bo-Gars members. Interestingly, gang members were not the most central players in this network: of the five individuals identified as the backbone of the distribution chain (highest betweenness centrality scores), only one was a gang member. The relatively minor role played by the Bo-Gars in the network may be interpreted either as an illustration of their peripheral role in the distribution trade uncovered by the investigations, or as a prime example of strategic positioning by key players (or leaders) who are able to remain at a secure distance[1] from the main distribution activities (Morselli leans toward the latter interpretation). This reminds us of the limitations of social network analysis, if used alone, in providing a clear picture of who the key players are in a network. Complementary information on the nature of interactions among network participants, as well as data on the functions and roles of network members, is necessary for an accurate representation of individuals' significance in criminal and other networks.

Studies relying on official data have limitations that other sources do not have, but may still reveal important information on a specific type of gang interaction (official co-offending) not covered by other data sources. Co-offending data are likely to point toward less stable relationships than studies relying on observational or wiretap data. The high turnover rate from one arrest to another is a typical result of co-offending studies (Sarnecki, 2001; Warr, 2002; see McGloin & Nguyen, 2011 for a recent review). For the purpose of determining gang boundaries, such variations pose a challenge as co-offenders may or may not be actual "members" of the gang, and it is impossible to determine without complementary data. At the same time, gang members will have a tendency not to stray too far from their immediate pool of associates (Decker & Curry, 2000) and to choose co-offenders within their own gang. "Core members" will generally be found among the most criminally active members and will generate the largest number of different co-offenders (McGloin, 2005; Sarnecki, 2001). These core members will, in other words, occupy central positions in official co-offending networks. Not only does the identification of this core have implications for gang intervention strategies (McGloin, 2005), but it suits our needs for a strategy to identify core gang membership. In this chapter, we argue that where those boundaries start and where they end is something that is most suitably determined within a social network perspective.

THE CURRENT STUDY

The lessons learned from the above studies directly inform the problem at the core of the current case study. In 2007, the neighboring cities of Aldergrove and Langley, British Columbia, were facing a gang problem of their own. The "856 gang" became a significant concern to the police and local population after criminal actions attributed to the group included two attempted murders, and the public attempted assassination at gunpoint of the father of one of the alleged 856 members (Kieltyka, 2007; The Vancouver

Province, 2007). As the police were planning an intervention on the gang, a group of investigators set out to conduct a review of all police files with reference to this gang in order to develop a strategy to disassemble the group. Through this review, a "core" group of members were identified. Files were included for consideration if there was a reference to the 856 gang. Beyond those criteria, there were no specifics in relation to the selection and identification process that was followed leading to the identification of the core six. The investigators were keen, however, to understand the scope of those involved in the 856 gang, as it was evident that many individuals were associated to the 856 gang through rumor (Kieltyka, 2007). The core group was identified largely through confirmation of overt self-identification by those in question, combined with corroboration from credible witnesses or other members of the gang. In short, the process was more intuitive than systematic.

This process led to the identification of six 856 members who were arrested and charged in the summer of 2007. When they settled on targeting six adolescents, the Langley Royal Canadian Mounted Police (RCMP) did not assume they had the "full" 856 gang. Instead, they figured they identified the "core" members, actors important enough to destroy what held the 856 gang together as a recognizable entity.

In this study, we assess the validity of the decision to target those six individuals as representing the core of the 856 gang (henceforth the "targeted six").[2] We do so by providing a systematic analysis of the larger network of co-offenders who gravitated around the targeted members in the five years prior to police intervention. Given our two-mode research design, which relies solely on the co-offending associations of the six targeted 856 members, we are not in a position to offer a purely independent alternative method of identification that can be compared and contrasted. However, the additional, complementary information offered by a social network analysis of co-offending associations can help answer the following questions:

- Are the "core six" 856 gang members as identified by investigators reproduced in the co-offending network? Is there a clear boundary between these six and other potential members once co-offending data is considered? More generally: were the proper six members targeted?
- Was "six" an adequate number of members to target, or does a different number of offenders emerge as the core members in the co-offending network?

DATA AND METHODS

The targeted six 856 members were all Caucasian males between 16 and 19 years old at the time of arrest (mean: 17.3 years old). Their co-offending associations were retrieved in October 2010 by searching out all the police files related to each member. The time frame allowed to retrieve the data was extremely limited—in practical terms, the data collection was unpaid overtime work for a crime analyst already working around the clock on time-sensitive cases. Thus, little information on the characteristics of the individuals retrieved as members of the co-offending network could be collected—an unfortunate limitation of this study. The files for consideration mirrored the time frame utilized by the police investigators, spanning January 2003 to June 2007.[3] In addition to the inclusion of co-offending associations when two or more offenders were being officially charged together, it was deemed appropriate to include those categories where an offender was suspected of committing an offense, but for a variety of reasons insufficient evidence existed to proceed with charges. The broader focus provided more information on the co-offending associations of the targeted six 856 members (after all, co-suspects were found in some form of interaction, whether it was actual offending or otherwise) and is consistent with the research question which aims to assess the gang's core members. While the police intervention was concerned with youth offenders, co-offenders were included for consideration regardless of age in order to obtain the most complete understanding of the co-offending network.

The process of constructing a gang network from co-offending data requires a meaningful starting point in order to decide around whom one should collect the data. Those six starting points are meaningful here because they were identified as "members" in police files, and more informally through corroboration with witnesses or other members of the gang. The strategy chosen to construct the network resembles the one used by Sarnecki (2001) for the Angen gang. In that case, seven individuals had been identified through various sources as known members of the Angen gang and were the starting points for creating the network, drawing from five years of data (1991 to 1995). An important difference is that Sarnecki was able to extract the networks of the identified co-offenders as well. The final co-offending network effectively reached offenders two steps removed from the seven egos (egos, their co-offenders, and the co-offenders of those co-offenders).

Our design does not allow such a level of precision, as we were limited to the co-offending patterns of each of the six targeted members, and no one else. In addition, in the limited time frame allowed to collect the data, it was not possible to assess the co-offending association of those new offenders identified as connected to the targeted six. For these reasons, the data was coded directly as an affiliation network (Borgatti & Everett, 1997; Borgatti & Halgin, 2011; Faust, 1997); that is, offenders were included in the network to the extent that they were connected (i.e., affiliated) to at least one of the six targeted 856 members. In other words, co-offending ties between co-offenders were not coded if they did not involve one of the six members initially targeted. The data was thus treated and analyzed as a two-mode network, with one mode representing the six targeted members and the other representing their co-offenders. This design is effectively the same as classical two-mode representations of individuals and events where it is not possible to know whether two individuals are directly connected—only if they attended the same event. In those cases, the individuals are deemed to have a higher likelihood of being connected through their mutual connection to one or more events (Borgatti & Halgin, 2011). In our case, offenders (mode 1) are connected to the extent that they have a common co-offending association to a member of the targeted six (mode 2). Note that each member of the targeted six was allowed to co-offend with one or more of the other five.[4] In those instances, both targeted members were included as co-offenders in mode 1 (e.g., n8 and B_1), with an affiliation link to one another through mode 2 (n8 to B_2; B_1 to A_2—for two total co-offending entries).

Multiple counts of co-offending with a member of the targeted six were coded to create a valued, two-mode co-offending network. More frequent co-offending associations with members of the targeted six were thus taken into account to determine the core of the 856 gang. Co-offending associations for a single individual ranged between 1 and 18, with a mean of 3.07 total associations with the targeted six members for the full sample.

Centrality Measures

The design of this study implies that we calculate centrality scores adapted to the logic of two-mode networks. In such cases, an actor is central relative to the events it connects to (here the targeted six). Conversely, events are central relative to the size or nature of their memberships (Borgatti & Everett, 1997; Faust, 1997). Two measures of centrality are used in this study—*degree* and *eigenvector*.

From the point of view of individuals, degree centrality refers to a binary, normalized measure of the number of ties offenders have with members of the targeted six. The maximum number of possible ties is six (or five for members of the targeted six in mode 1). For members of the targeted six in mode 2, degree centrality refers to the normalized number of ties they have with the full set of co-offenders in the network. Normalization is important to the extent that we wish to directly compare the degree centrality of both actors and events (Borgatti & Halgin, 2011).

In eigenvector centrality, the centrality of an entity's connections is also taken into account. This might be important for our purposes given our objective to find "core" members, as opposed to just any type of affiliation to the 856 gang. In two-mode networks, an actor scores higher in eigenvector centrality to the extent that it is connected to central events (Borgatti & Everett, 1997; Faust, 1997). In our case, an offender's eigenvector centrality score is proportional to the sum of centralities of the targeted six members he/she is connected to (and vice versa for eigenvector centrality scores of the targeted six members). All network measures are calculated using UCINET 6.352 (Borgatti, Everett, & Freeman, 2002); mathematical details can be found in Borgatti and Everett (1997), as well as Faust (1997).

Co-affiliation

Affiliation data may also be transformed into a one-mode matrix where a tie exists between two individuals if both are connected to the same member of the targeted six. In such cases, these actors are said to be co-affiliated, and the new person-by-person matrix may be analyzed using standard one-mode tools (Borgatti & Halgin, 2011). The more affiliations in common to members of the targeted six, the stronger the connection between two offenders. As will be detailed below, both the affiliation and the co-affiliation matrices will

be used to determine whether the network exhibits a core–periphery structure (Borgatti & Everett, 1999). Should such a structure be found, the size and content of the list of core members derived from those analyses will be compared to the list of six core members targeted by the RCMP intervention.

RESULTS

The analysis of co-offending data reveals that 54 previously unidentified offenders were arrested with one of the targeted six members identified by investigators between 2003 and 2007. If we consider that members of the targeted six were also "allowed" to co-offend with the other five (that is, they were allowed to act as co-offender in mode 1 as well), we have a network of 60 offenders (mode 1) who co-offended with at least one member of the targeted six (mode 2). A total of 185 bidirectional links were found between the targeted six and the other offenders, for a mean of just over three links per offender for the network as a whole. The two-mode density of 0.311 indicates a relatively dense network of 60 young offenders, where the targeted six members were involved on average with close to one-third of all possible connections.

A graph representation of the 856 co-offending network between 2003 and 2007 is presented in Figure 4.1.[5] The targeted six members can easily be identified through darker node colors: n1, n2, n3, n4, n5, n6. The black squares represent the targeted six members in mode 2, and the circles are the co-offenders (mode 1). The targeted six as co-offenders in mode 1 are represented by gray circles, and line thickness reflects frequency of co-offending incidents.[6] Figure 4.1 first shows that not all targeted six members have similar patterns of connections. N5, for example, is the center of a star network involving as many as 18 actors with no connections to the rest of the targeted six. His unique pattern of contacts has him standing on the left side of the graph, yet relatively close to n6, with whom he shares nine connections—most found in the middle of the graph (n4, n1, n15, n14, n8, n3, n22, n9, n13). N5 is the most connected member of the targeted six, and his network position gives him the highest degree centrality score among his peers (see Table 4.1). Yet n5 only ranks third in eigenvector centrality because the majority of his connections are not connected to any other members of the targeted six. The eigenvector scores of n4 and n6 reveal that their connections are more central to the overall network. The oldest (n1) and youngest (n2) members of the targeted six are found at the top of the graph, with a similar pattern of connections that involves three of the targeted six (including each other). Both have a small number of co-offending connections, suggesting a more peripheral role in the 856 gang, or at least

in its criminal activities most exposed to law enforcement interventions.

Not all members of the targeted six co-offended with all of the other five (Table 4.2). N5 and n6 are the only ones to have done so, including five times together. All four others co-offended with three out of the five others, putting everyone as relatively central players in the network (see Figure 4.1). Yet, they have done so at different rates. N1, n3, and n4 had, respectively, 8, 9, and 14 co-offending occurrences with other members of the targeted six. N2, on the other hand, only has three. These variations could be: 1) a sign of the targeted six not being as cohesive as the investigators projected them to be; 2) an indication of different subgroups among the core; or 3) an artifact of the research design relying on official data.

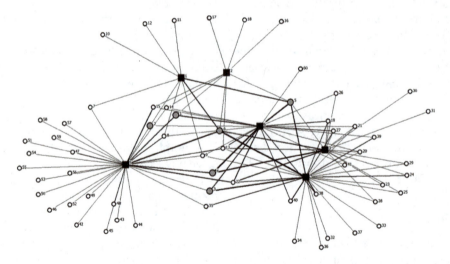

Figure 4.1 Two-mode co-offending network of the targeted six 856 gang members, 2003–2007

Table 4.1 Two-mode degree and eigenvector centrality scores of the targeted six 856 members

Node	Age	Degree	Eigenvector
n5	17	0.517	0.497
n4	17	0.417	0.535
n6	18	0.350	0.510
n3	17	0.283	0.386
n1	19	0.150	0.160
n2	16	0.150	0.179

Table 4.2 Number of co-offending associations within the targeted six 856 members

	n1	n2	n3	n4	n5	n6	total
n1	—	1	0	0	4	3	8
n2	1	—	0	0	1	1	3
n3	0	0	—	5	1	3	9
n4	0	0	5	—	3	6	14
n5	4	1	1	3	—	5	14
n6	3	1	3	6	5	—	18

What is intriguing is that other co-offenders emerged as much more central to the targeted six. A total of 22 other offenders had at least two connections with the targeted six, and as many as 10 of those had connections with three different members of the targeted six. N22, for example, was arrested multiple times with each of n3, n4, n5, and n6 (12 total connections). This leads to obvious questions: should n22 have been part of the targeted six, and should n2 be excluded? From a strict degree centrality perspective, and should we only have to choose six offenders to target, the answer would be yes. Table 4.3 presents the top 16 degree and eigenvector centrality rankings[7] for the two-mode 856 co-offending network. As we can see, five offenders stand out as being highly connected with the targeted 856 members (four or five connections): n5, n6, n13, n22, and n9. Only the first two are members of the targeted six; the other three are not. The last 11 offenders completing the top 16, all with three co-offending associations with the targeted six, include the last four offenders targeted, but also seven others. Based on this information alone, the decision to target those six offenders is not unreasonable. Should only six be chosen, a case could be made for n13, n22, and n9 to be included in lieu of three of the original targets. Based on his eigenvector score (0.210), one of the original six (n3) would complete the top six. This means that n1, n4, or n2 would not have made it. And while the eigenvector scores present more variations among nodes,

Table 4.3 Two-mode degree and eigenvector centrality for top 15 offenders

	Degree	Rank (degree)	Eigenvector	Rank (eigen)
n5	0.833	1	0.245	3
n6	0.833	1	0.240	4
n13	0.833	1	0.289	1
n9	0.667	4	0.230	5
n22	0.667	4	0.264	2
n1	0.500	6	0.159	12
n3	0.500	6	0.210	6
n4	0.500	6	0.189	11
n8	0.500	6	0.155	16
n14	0.500	6	0.159	12
n15	0.500	6	0.159	12
n19	0.500	6	0.200	7
n20	0.500	6	0.200	7
n21	0.500	6	0.200	7
n27	0.500	6	0.200	7
n2	0.500	6	0.158	15

Note
Targeted six in bold.

the absolute differences between the top and bottom nodes are not important enough to base a targeting decision on them. Given the small differences between centrality scores in the top 16, however, the real question is whether the "core" 856 gang should actually be reduced to only six offenders, an issue to which we turn below.

Core/Periphery Analyses

Some SNA tools examine the data to find out whether they exhibit a core/periphery structure. That is, whether a densely connected subset of actors can be observed and significantly differentiated from a more sparse peripheral set of actors (Borgatti & Everett, 1999). Those methods are intuitively appealing for our purposes, which consists in finding out whether a closer analysis of the co-offending network matches what the investigators identified as the core of the 856 gang.

In UCINET 6.352, core–periphery analyses are available for data structured as two-mode networks, and also for the same data after transformation into a one-mode, co-affiliation network. Both types of analyses provide complementary information. The two-mode analysis aims to identify a core of co-offenders that is more densely connected to a core of the initial six gang members. In addition to preserving the logic of data collection, the two-mode analysis has the advantage of identifying important players in both modes, including among those who were initially targeted (i.e., "a core among the core"). Conversely, this particularity also acts as a disadvantage. The algorithm forces a separation among the initial six members that may or may not be fruitful. The one-mode analysis has the advantage of not forcing this separation, treating connections to any of the initial six members equally. An added advantage is that the one-mode analysis handles a categorical analysis as well as a continuous core/periphery analysis. In other words, instead of treating actors as members of either the core

or the periphery, the continuous analysis calculates a "coreness" score, and then aims to find a breaking point in the score distribution to suggest a "core" and a "periphery" (Borgatti & Everett, 1999).

Table 4.4 presents the results of two types of categorical core/periphery analyses (two-mode and one-mode), as well as a one-mode continuous core/periphery analysis. Starting with the two-mode analysis, a core of nine members is suggested, identified through their affiliation to three core actors: n4, n5, and n6. The 0.66 score obtained for this solution suggests a moderately good fit to the data, meaning that the data can reasonably be represented as exhibiting a core/periphery structure. This "core nine" includes four of the original six targeted members, only excluding n2 and n3. Seven of the nine core members were part of the top 16 nodes in degree centrality (Table 4.3), leaving only n38 and n40 as less connected yet "core" members. Their presence may be explained in that both have multiple connections to the same two core members of the targeted six, n4 and n6.

The one-mode categorical and continuous analyses each provide the exact same solution, a slightly different one than that which we found in the two-mode analysis. The one-mode analysis suggests a core of 13 members, including 7 who were also identified in the two-mode analysis (n5, n6, n22, n1, n4, n38, and n40). The two others were n8 and n14, both of whom had also been identified as key actors from their degree centrality scores (Table 4.3). The continuous core/periphery analysis is shown in the last two columns of Table 4.4. This analysis calculates a "coreness" score for each node instead of simply breaking the sample into two components, making it the most attractive solution for our purposes. The suggested number of nodes to be included in the core (13) is based on a fit criterion that chooses the solution with the highest correlation between the coreness scores and an ideal score of 1 for every core

Table 4.4 Two-mode and one-mode core/periphery analyses of the 856 co-offending network

Two-mode Categorical N = 9	One-mode Categorical N = 13	One-mode Continuous N = 13[b]	One-mode Continuous Score (rank)
n6	n6	n6	0.304 (3)
—	n13	n13	0.291 (4)
—	n9	n9	0.159 (12)
n22	n22	n22	0.373 (1)
—	n3	n3	0.267 (6)
n4	n4	n4	0.272 (5)
n1	n1	n1	0.210 (9)
—	n15	n15	0.151 (13)
n5	n5	n5	0.306 (2)
—	n27	n27	0.215 (7)
—	n19	n19	0.213 (8)
n38	n38	n38	0.184 (11)
n40	n40	n40	0.185 (10)
n8	—	—	—
n14	—	—	—
Fit[a]: 0.66 Core – mode 2 n4, n5, n6	Fit: 0.78	Fit: 0.84 Gini: 0.50	

Notes

a Best fit chosen after 20 separate runs

b n2 is ranked twenty-first (0.100)

member and 0 for actors in the periphery (Borgatti & Everett, 1999). The fit score of 0.84 is relatively high, giving us some confidence in interpreting the results.

This coreness analysis reveals that the targeted six in fact represented 38.5% (5/13) of what the co-offending network analysis suggests is the core 856 gang. Four of the targeted six are included in the top six coreness scores: n5, n6, n4, and n3. On the other hand, n22, who ranks number one on this measure, was excluded from the police intervention. The same thing can be said of n13, who completes the top six. This analysis takes the frequency of associations into account, putting at a disadvantage highly central n9, whose pattern of connections includes a single association with four different members of the targeted six. N9 would nonetheless be included in the network-based identification of the core 13 members of the 856 gang. It

is important to note that the coreness score is not a mere reproduction of the results of centrality analyses. Six actors found in the top 16 centrality scores (Table 4.3) were not found to be "core members": n27, n21, n20, n14, and n8, as well as targeted six member n2. These actors had a smaller total number of associations with the targeted six, something that is not taken into account in tradinial (binary) centrality analyses.[8]

CONCLUSION

The objective of this chapter was to examine if the decision made by the Langley RCMP to target six of their young local offenders as representing the core of the 856 gang based on manual file reviews was supported by an analysis of the co-offending network surrounding those targeted offenders. The results show that:

- The targeted six members were central in the network, but no more than at least 10 other, non-targeted offenders;
- Core/periphery analyses of the co-offending network suggest that the data does exhibit such a structure; 13 offenders would be part of the core, with 47 in the periphery. Five of those 13 (38.5%) were identified and targeted by the Langley RCMP, but not the offender ranked number one on this measure;
- If forced to choose a top six to represent the core, two of the initial targets would not make the cut.

In the absence of interviews with the 856 gang members themselves, little information is available to assess the size of the "core" or the gang itself. Media articles that followed the summer 2007 shooting provide some hints in regards to the perception of the RCMP and of the population. An article based on an interview with a RCMP officer mentioned numbers in the vicinity of what we found here: "The group of about 10 to 15 men in their late teens and early 20s began in Aldergrove" (The Vancouver Province, 2007). Another interviewed students at the school that some of the 856 members attended, shedding light on the reputation that the 856 had gained prior to the events that led to the police intervention:

"A lot of the students have been talking about it, everyone knows who the 856 are," said one student, who did not want to be named. The student said fewer than a dozen teens began calling themselves 856, the first three digits of most Aldergrove phone numbers. They've since graduated but the gang still has ties to the school through younger relatives and recruits, and the name comes with some notoriety. "I don't know how many people at school are in it, but there are a lot of them claim they're in 856," the student said. "It's like if you're with them it makes you cool."

(Kieltyka, 2007)

This extract from a media article hints at the possibility of younger recruits associated to an older "core," a sign that the gang had some traction at the time of the public shooting that led to the police intervention. It also provides additional context to the difficulty of identifying gang boundaries from only one source of data. Self-nomination techniques conducted at that school may have been useful in identifying a few 856 members. At the same time, it may have led to some over-identification (the "cool" factor) and some under-representation (older members who had already graduated). Co-offending data have limits of their own, especially in regards to understanding non-criminal, social interactions among members and non-members. However, it has the advantage of focusing associations on actual (official) criminal activity between two or more alleged members of a gang, which is often considered as a key criterion for discriminating street gangs from other sorts of youth groups (Klein & Maxson, 2006; Bouchard & Spindler, 2010).

Identification of the "core" members of a gang may, or may not, be an exercise worth undertaking. This exogenously determined core may change daily, may vary greatly based on the type of data used to establish it, may not correspond to what gang members perceive as the core, or may be artificial—in fact, it may not exist at all. The question of the utility of classifying gang members into "core" and "peripheral/fringe" members is not likely to have an absolute answer. Fortunately, the question does not have to be resolved subjectively. Social network data, when available, are naturally compatible with those types of questions (Borgatti & Everett, 1999). The results of core/periphery analyses may point to networks where no core is easily identifiable. Alternatively, it may lead to the identification of a core so large that it lacks practical intervention utility (if 80% of the members form a core, why bother choosing?). The bottom line, of course, is the importance of drawing from data to establish a probability, and avoid guesswork. In the case of the 856 gang, our results reveal a core that represents 22% of all offenders (13 of the 60) identified in the co-offending data.

This is not to suggest that the manual file reviews conducted by the Langley RCMP to identify the core 856 members were not useful. On the contrary, we want to suggest that neither SNA nor manual file reviews, alone, are likely to provide a fully satisfactory solution to the gang boundaries problem. This can be illustrated by the seemingly surprising inclusion, by the Langley RCMP, of n2 in the targeted six members. Although the co-offending network labels him as a peripheral member, it may very well be that n2 is simply more successful than others at avoiding detection—much like Morselli`s (2009) Bo-Gars in Montreal. Or, much more probable, his younger age (16) did not expose him as much as others to police detection between 2003 and 2007. Controlling for police exposure or age is thus important. Network data alone, without the benefit of context or node attributes, result in conclusions that are helpful, but sometimes tentative. Network visibility as measured by centrality need not be automatically associated to a position of leadership or high social status in the network (Morselli, 2009; Sarnecki, 2001; Fleisher, 2005; Papachristos, 2006). This is especially the case for official data. Note, however, that all six targeted 856 members were found to be in the most central actors in the co-offending network. Clearly, co-offending data is suitable for the purposes of understanding the social environment of street gangs.

A limitation of our study emerges from the two-mode research design that we adopted. The lack of information on co-offending outside of the targeted six makes our study dependent on those six, failing to provide a truly alternative method to assess the core of the 856 gang. At the same time, part of this dependence by design was necessary: a starting point was needed to construct the network (see also Sarnecki, 2001), and the targeted six was a reasonable one. Analyzing any co-offending network near or far of those six offenders could have led to the emergence of different key players or a different core, but there would be little to connect those central actors to the actual 856 gang problem that Aldergrove and Langley were facing. Although not perfect, reliance on the targeted six 856 members for network construction allowed us to stay on target given the data available.

Other limitations of this study and their implications have been discussed earlier, including the lack of attribute data on offenders in this co-offending network. We approached this analysis with little information on the characteristics of the offenders in the sample. While this "blind approach" may have helped avoid certain biases, this is certainly not an ideal situation. In addition, our reliance on official co-offending records only presented a missing data issue that is common in social network studies. Missing, in this case, is the majority of co-offending associations for which members were not suspected or charged with a crime. What we have is a sample of co-offending associations that were subject to police detection. As such, the crimes for which we considered co-offending patterns may have been more serious and/or more risky than those for which they were not caught. This potential bias may somehow work in our favor given the focus of this study on "core" gang members.

Future work should pursue Sarnecki's (2001), Fleisher's (2005), and Morselli's (2009) efforts in providing systematic comparisons of the results of social network analyses conducted from two or more sets of alternative data (e.g., wiretap vs. co-offending data). Criminology historically devoted much research to determining precisely the implications of relying on different sets of data (official records, self-reported delinquency, and victimization surveys). No one is surprised, for example, to find that violent crimes are over-represented in official data given their visibility and importance for police priorities, or that offenders are officially charged with fewer accomplices than they had in reality (and would self-report). The pool of SNA-based criminology studies is growing and the data sources are varied, but the implications for interpretation have yet to be made explicit.

NOTES

1. In the end, only 36% of the Bo-Gars were arrested, compared to 92% of other gang members and 62% of the non-gang members.
2. The six offenders targeted by the police in 2007 will be referred to as the "targeted six" to differentiate them from the "core" members identified through a social network analysis of co-offending data.
3. A change in the electronic records management system occurred on December 12, 2006, when the Langley RCMP switched from the Police Information Retrieval System (PIRS) to the Police Records Information Management Environment (PRIME). There was an unknown amount of attrition in the data from the PIRS. In that electronic system, files were automatically purged from the system once the retention period elapsed. For example, property crime offenses may have a retention period ranging from two to five years. In reflecting on the range of files examined by the investigative team dating back to January 2003, it should be expected that a small number of these files were purged at the time of this study.
4. In theory, the targeted six are treated as equals to other potential 856 members in mode 1. In practice, each member of the targeted six did not have an equivalent chance of inclusion because they could co-offend with a maximum of only five, as opposed to six, offenders. Because self-associations were excluded, no member of the targeted six has the possibility of obtaining the maximum centrality scores. However, note that additional analyses allowing for the self-associations did not substantively change the results of the study.
5. Using NETDRAW 2.113 (Borgatti, 2002).
6. We used spring embedding with equal mode length bias for the graph layout.
7. Sixteen being the total number of offenders with at least three co-offending associations with the targeted six.
8. An additional two-mode categorical core/periphery analysis was conducted using a sample in which the targeted six members were only included in mode 2 and could not be considered in their roles as co-offenders (i.e., a matrix of 54 × 6 instead of 60 × 6). Little novel information was found. The results suggest a core of 10 offenders by 3—the same three targeted six that were identified as such in the previous analysis: n4, n5, and n6. The majority of the core members were found in the previous analyses, with only n35 and n39 not being mentioned before as central or core members.

REFERENCES

Borgatti, S.P. & D. Halgin (2011). Analyzing affiliation networks. In P. Carrington & J. Scott (eds.) *The Sage Handbook of Social Network Analysis* (pp. 417–433). Thousand Oaks, CA: Sage Publications.

Borgatti, S.P. & M.G. Everett (1997). Network analysis of 2-mode data. *Social Networks* 19, 243–269.

Borgatti, S.P. & M.G. Everett (1999). Models of core/periphery structures. *Social Networks* 21, 375–395.

Borgatti, S.P., M.G. Everett, & L.C. Freeman (2002). *UCINET for Windows: Software for Social Network Analysis*. Harvard, MA: Analytic Technologies.

Borgatti, S.P. (2002). *NetDraw: Graph Visualization Software*. Harvard, MA: Analytic Technologies.

Bouchard, M. & A. Spindler (2010). Gangs, groups, and delinquency: Does organization matter? *Journal of Criminal Justice* 38, 921–933.

Decker, S.H. (1996). Collective and normative features of gang violence. *Justice Quarterly 13*, 243–264.

Decker, S.H. & G.D. Curry (2000). Addressing key features of gang membership: Measuring the involvement of young members. *Journal of Criminal Justice 28*, 473–482.

Esbensen, F., L.T. Winfree, N. He, & T.J. Taylor (2001). Youth gangs and definitional issues: When is a gang a gang and why does it matter? *Crime and Delinquency 47*, 105–130.

Faust, K. (1997). Centrality in affiliation networks. *Social Networks 19*, 157–191.

Fleisher, M.S. (2005). Fieldwork research and social network analysis. Different methods creating complementary perspectives. *Journal of Contemporary Criminal Justice 21*, 120–134.

Kieltyka, M. (2007). 856 gang in the spotlight. *24 Hours—Vancouver*, September 13.

Klein, M.W. & C.L. Maxson (2006). *Street Gang Patterns and Policies*. New York: Oxford University Press.

Maxson, C. (2011). Street gangs. In J.Q. Wilson & J. Petersilia (eds.), *Crime and Public Policy* (pp. 158–182). New York: Oxford University Press.

McGloin, J. (2005). Policy and intervention considerations of a network analysis of street gangs. *Criminology & Public Policy* 4, 607–635.

McGloin, J. & H. Nguyen (2011). The importance of studying co-offending networks for criminological theory and policy. Paper presented at the 3rd international Illicit Networks conference, Montreal, October.

Morselli, C. (2009). *Inside Criminal Networks.* New York: Springer.

Papachristos, A.V. (2006). Social network analysis and gang research: Theory and methods. In J.F. Short & L.A. Hughes (eds.), *Studying Youth Gangs* (pp. 99–116). New York: Alta Mira Press.

Sarnecki, J. (2001). *Delinquent Networks: Youth Co-offending in Stockholm.* Cambridge: Cambridge University Press.

Spindler, A. & M. Bouchard (2011). Structure or behaviour? Revisiting gang typologies. *International Criminal Justice Review* 21, 263–282.

The Vancouver Province (2007). Mounties became aware of Eight Five Six gang one year ago. *The Vancouver Province*, September 12.

Warr, M. (2002). *Companions in Crime.* Cambridge: Cambridge University Press.

PART II

Organized Crime Networks

CHAPTER 5

The Embedded and Multiplex Nature of Al Capone[1]

Andrew V. Papachristos and Chris M. Smith

One of the distinguishing characteristics of organized crime is the extent to which it intermingles with non-criminal domains of society. In some instances, such as the case of labor racketeering in the 1950s and 1960s (Jacobs, 2006), this infusion of organized crime into legitimate institutions is *in toto*. But, more typically, the daily grind and schemes of organized crime require some basic level of integration into the non-criminal world, if only to pay a cop to look the other way, to find legitimate businesses to flip stolen goods, or to partner with wire services for bookmaking operations. In short, organized crime's existence is contingent on its embeddedness within larger political, cultural, and economic networks.

This intermingling of social worlds that defines organized crime relates to two key sociological concepts: embeddedness and multiplexity. *Embeddedness* refers to the nesting of individuals and groups within larger networks, structures, and cultural frames (Baker & Faulkner, 2009; Feld, 1997; Granovetter, 1985; Moody & White, 2003; Uzzi, 1996). Individuals live and act in social circles that nest within each other, overlap, interconnect, and are almost always reflections of larger social and cultural contexts. Moreover, individuals are often tied to each other through multiple types of relationships, a property known as *multiplexity*—e.g., two people can be both neighbors and co-workers (Kadushin, 2012; Verbrugge, 1979). Often researchers simplify complex webs of social relationships

into parsimonious categories but, in so doing, overlook the nuances and interdependences of social networks that truly shape social life (see Emirbayer, 1997). And, although theories readily acknowledge the embedded and multiplex nature of organized crime, most empirical studies forsake such complexities due to data limitations or methodological traditions.

This study directly considers the embedded and multiplex nature of organized crime by combining a social network methodology with a unique set of relational data between nearly 2,000 individuals connected to Al Capone's Syndicate. Our main objective is to explore how these concepts can elucidate our understanding of the reach, depth, and contours of organized crime. More specifically, we argue that, while exploring segments of organized crime networks may provide some insight into specific activities or organizational characteristics, considering the ways in which crime spills into and intersects with legitimate social institutions provides a more nuanced view of organized crime. It is the amalgamation of the underworld and the legitimate world that truly shapes organized crime.

In the sections that follow, we consider how the research on organized crime and social networks intersect, paying particular attention to the concepts of embeddedness and multiplexity. Then, we introduce our "Capone database," describing its relational nature and content. The analysis proceeds in a piecewise fashion that builds up the large social network of organized crime during Prohibition in Chicago. Our findings reveal that, when considering only illegal activities and relationships between members of organized crime groups, Al Capone's Syndicate can be described as a social network with a highly cohesive and embedded core. However, the social structure of organized crime gets increasingly complex if one considers the multiplex nature of social relationships. The end result is a social network that spans multiple spheres and is what we understand to be organized crime in early 1900s Chicago.

ORGANIZED CRIME

Empirical research often views organized crime as a social system shaped by sets of overlapping relationships based on kinship; neighborhood and village ties; shared cultural values; and, more importantly, the exchange of resources, power, and favors (Abadinsky, 2010; Albini, 1971; Haller, 1970, 1990; Ianni & Reuss-Ianni, 1976). Albini (1971), for instance, conceives of organized crime as a series of patron–client relationships in which individuals who rise to positions of prominence are those who cultivate and maintain more advantaged sets of clients and patrons. Such a system folds into itself in that individuals can be a patron in one set of relations and a client in another. Adding yet another level of complexity, kinship, friendship, and marriage ties often crosscut, bolster, or undermine patron–client ties (Ianni & Reuss-Ianni, 1972, 1976). Regardless of the exact structure of such networks, organized crime is not a hierarchical secret bureaucracy of Italian blood oaths and garlic bullets, but rather a series of intertwining social circles held together by sets of obligations and patterns of exchange.

One of the hallmarks of organized crime is the extent to which it bleeds into legitimate social institutions. Such an intermingling of the criminal and legitimate worlds happens in at least three ways. First and foremost, organized crime is part of larger society, rather than

a network distinct from it. Unlike extremist groups that withdraw from society, organized crime groups intermingle with legitimate social institutions. Moreover, organized crime is often an attempt by disenfranchised populations to further integrate into mainstream society.[2] As Daniel Bell (1953) put it, organized crime is part of the American dream: illicit activities are means to achieve financial success and social status within the larger non-criminal community.[3]

Second, the activities and actions of organized crime require individuals outside of the bounded criminal group. In many cases, organized crime groups market their services and products to the non-criminal public. For example, although ordinary citizens may shun some organized criminal activity (e.g., violence), they are still willing to buy a household appliance that "fell off of a truck," procure a loan in the grey economy when one is unavailable from a bank, or consume black-market entertainment, such as gambling and prostitution. Prohibition is perhaps the most striking example of citizens from all walks of life who saw bootleggers as public servants and willingly participated in the "crime" of consuming alcohol. Al Capone once quipped, "I've been spending the best years of my life as a public benefactor. I've given people the light pleasures, shown them a good time" (*Chicago Tribune*, 1927: 1).

By gaining entrance into mainstream society and marketing their wares to the non-criminal public, organized crime groups expose themselves to surveillance and prosecution by legal institutions. This exposure necessitates relationships with authorities that can ensure the continuation of criminal enterprises. As such, the third way in which organized crime integrates into legitimate society is through relationships with authorities whose influence might minimize the effects of visibility. Tactics to avoid apprehension and prosecution range from simple bribes, extortion, and bomb tossing to large-scale political corruption, such as vote fixing or jury tampering. However, corruption need not be dramatic, nor does being on a politician's friendly side always require illegality. Organized crime groups can encourage their devoted neighbors to vote for preferred candidates, donate cash to campaigns, and attend political campaign galas.

To summarize our argument thus far, the nature of organized crime is not a hierarchical or bureaucratic entity but rather a set of overlapping social networks based on exchange and power. Furthermore, such overlapping networks link to legitimate social institutions in that: 1) they exist and operate within mainstream society; 2) they market their criminal enterprises to a non-criminal public; and 3) they require connections to authority in order to avoid exposure, detection, and prosecution. We maintain that these elements of organized crime can be explored theoretically and empirically through the concepts of embeddedness and multiplexity.

EMBEDDEDNESS AND MULTIPLEXITY

The concepts of embeddedness and multiplexity have come to mean many things in sociological discourse, but these concepts broadly assume that individuals exist and act in overlapping social worlds. We use the term *embeddedness* to refer to the significance of social networks for social action—i.e., people are situated in particular constellations of social relationships and these structures influence behaviors, opinions, and attitudes (see also Moody & White, 2003). As developed by Granovetter (1985), the idea of

structural embeddedness posits that individuals do not act as under-socialized economic automatons, but rather individuals act as contextualized and culturalized social beings. In our network usage of the term, *structural embeddedness* occurs insofar as individuals sit within or between social circles that nest or overlap, creating situations in which they process information and act on constraints from multiple and, at times, competing sets of obligations and relationships.

Multiplexity refers to the idea that the same individuals can be connected in multiple ways or through multiple types of relationships. This can mean either: a) role multiplexity— two individuals occupy positions that intersect, such as two people who are co-workers and also friends; or b) content multiplexity— the different flows of resources, information, and influence between two individuals (Boorman & White, 1976; see Kadushin, 2012, for a summary). Multiplex ties are strong ties in that the social relationship has multiple bases and, therefore, can foster deeper levels of trust or greater sets of opportunities. For example, Roger Gould (1991) finds that mobilization during the Paris Commune would not have been possible without the multiplex ties created by both party affiliation *and* neighborhood attachments. For Gould, it was not one type of tie or the other that was responsible for collective action, but rather the interaction of informal neighborhood ties *and* insurgency ties that made mobilization possible.

Figure 5.1 depicts a hypothetical network that illustrates embeddedness and multiplexity. This network comprises 11 actors

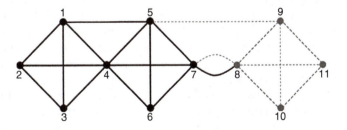

Figure 5.1 Hypothetical network

(nodes) and two different types of ties that are depicted by different lines (black solid and grey dashed). Formally, structural embeddedness describes the extent to which actors or sets of actors exist in overlapping sets of cliques. Consider the network cluster of black solid ties on the left side of Figure 5.1. All of the actors in this part of the network (nodes 1 through 7) are tied to each other either directly or indirectly. We can deconstruct this part of the network to identify smaller sets of overlapping cliques. In fact, there are nine cliques of three on the left side of this network, and all nine cliques share members with other cliques. Take, for example, the cliques among nodes 1, 2, and 3; nodes 1, 4, and 3; and nodes 1, 4, and 5. Each of these triangles is unique, but there is considerable overlap in clique membership. Like a set of *matryoshka* dolls, it is the stacking of these overlapping cliques that creates the larger embedded network.

To understand the idea of multiplexity, consider both sets of ties that make up the entirety of the hypothetical network in Figure 5.1. Assume that the different line types represent different types of social relationships. A multiplex relationship exists when two actors have more than one type of relationship. In this network, one multiplex relationship exists between nodes 7 and 8. While one other actor (node 5) has both a black solid tie and a grey dashed tie, only the node 7 and 8 dyad is multiplex.

We maintain that organized crime requires *both* structural embeddedness *and* multiplexity. If Figure 5.1 were an actual instance of organized crime, one would need to understand both the nested sets of relationships between members *and* the presence of multiple types of ties. Examining organized crime networks otherwise risks missing the important structural subtleties that distinguish organized crime. Say, for instance, that the black solid ties are criminal relationships and the grey dashed ties are political relationships. Examining only the black solid ties would

reveal the embedded nature of the criminal group and the presence of an important actor (node 4), but this limited view would fail to see the structural importance of nodes 5, 7, 8, and 9. Likewise, considering only the political ties might demonstrate political alliances or clusters but would fail to see the criminal action of nodes 7 and 8 who link the two domains. The individuals that occupy multiple clusters and the multiplex ties between them give organized crime its unique sociological form. The goal of our empirical analysis is to unpack these two concepts in order to understand not simply the structure of criminal ties, but also the ways in which different sets of social relationships converge to organize crime.

ORGANIZED CRIME NETWORKS

Prima facie evidence exists supporting this line of reasoning as several noteworthy studies have documented embeddedness and multiplexity in organized crime—though not using those terms. John Landesco ([1929] 1968) offered the most prominent example of organized crime networks extending beyond gangsters and bootleggers.[4] Conducting and writing his research during Prohibition, Landesco ([1929] 1968) spotlighted the social ties between gangsters, politicians, law enforcement, and unions in his *Organized Crime in Chicago* report. For example, the funeral of gang boss Big Jim Colosimo contained all the ceremony and opulence typically reserved for royalty. Newspapers reported more than 5,000 mourners at the funeral and extravagant floral arrangements lining the gravesite, casket, and funeral vehicles. Funeral attendees chanted prayers led by a local politician and listened to hymns sung by members of the Chicago Opera Company. The list of funeral attendees and pallbearers included judges, aldermen, local politicians, a state representative, and a member of Congress right alongside gangsters, gamblers, and brothel owners (*Chicago Tribune*, 1920;

Landesco, [1929] 1968). Landesco's chapter on gangsters' funerals reveals one of the most significant aspects of organized crime: its relationship to politics and the legitimate social world. Like a magician revealing a not-so-well-kept secret, the funeral of Colosimo exposed the blatant intermixing of Chicago's legitimate and criminal worlds that made vice both possible and profitable for politicians and criminals alike.

Picking up where Landesco left off, urban historian Mark Haller developed a theory that situated organized crime precisely in its connections to the legitimate world (Haller, 1970, 1971, 1990; see also Yeager, 2012). According to Haller, organized crime as a social phenomenon is distinguished not by the attributes of its members or particular organizational structure, but rather by the beneficial relationships between illegal enterprises and legitimate society (Haller, 1990). Such relationships develop locally, often originating in neighborhoods, through the mutual exchange of friendship and favors (Blok, 1974; Boissevain, 1974; Haller, 1970, 1971). This foregrounding research has contributed important insights required for studying organized crime, especially in Chicago.

Our study follows the theoretical tradition of Landesco and Haller, but we make a distinct theoretical and methodological advancement by situating our analysis in the growing field of social network analysis. To greatly simplify this area of scientific inquiry, the main premise of social network analysis maintains that the ways in which people, groups, and institutions are connected play an important role in shaping opinions, behaviors, and beliefs (Wasserman and Faust, 1994). For our present case, social network analysis theoretically treats embeddedness and multiplexity as central to human social behavior and methodologically models these interdependencies.

Although arriving a little late to this network turn in the social sciences, criminology is currently experiencing its own surge of network-related scholarship (see Papachristos, 2011). The application of social network analysis to the study of criminal groups and organizations is one area showing notable growth. To date, criminologists have employed formal social network analysis to describe the structure of street and motorcycle gangs (Fleisher, 2006; McGloin, 2005; Morselli, 2009; Nakamura, Tita, & Krackhardt, 2011; Papachristos, 2009), organized crime syndicates (Klerks, 2001; Malm, Bichler, & Van De Walle, 2010; McIllwain, 1999; Morselli, 2003), narcotics distribution (Natarajan, 2006), terrorist organizations (Pedahzur & Perliger, 2006; Xu & Chen, 2003), and white-collar conspiracies (Baker & Faulkner, 1993, 2003). For the most part, empirical research tends to analyze the network structure of a bounded criminal group in order to identify key individuals (McGloin, 2005) or to compare topologies across criminal networks (Morselli, Giguère, & Petit, 2007; Xu & Chen, 2008). Often this strategy requires limiting a network to those who have been labeled as targets and examining the ties among those targets. However, consistent with our approach, a small body of research demonstrates that the study of criminal networks should move beyond the focus of members of a bounded criminal group. For example, analyses of wiretap data have revealed that many individuals who are not law enforcement targets or even known criminals make up substantial portions of the criminal communication networks (Morselli & Giguère, 2006; Natarajan, 2006), and in some cases these non-targets hold important structural positions of reciprocity and brokerage in the network (Morselli & Giguère, 2006). Malm and colleagues' (2010) study of Canadian organized crime analyzes four different types of ties (family, arrest, crime group associate, and legitimate/business associate) across targets to compare cohesiveness across the different networks. This work by Malm et al. (2010), especially, serves as an example of the multiplexity of ties within a bounded criminal group, and we would expand this argument by suggesting that this multiplexity of ties extends beyond the crime group into the legitimate sphere where the potential to organize crime resides.

Our study advances prior social network and crime research in three ways. First and foremost, we explicitly link the theoretical concepts and methodological instruments of embeddedness and multiplexity to organized crime. Similar to work by Baker and Faulkner (1993), we believe that rich theoretical constructs often used in studies of legitimate organizations also apply to criminal settings. The idea is not simply to cut and paste a concept from one line of research to another. Rather, we seek to open a dialogue between network theory and research on organized crime. Second, and related to the first, we add to the growing body of research using social network analysis to examine organized crime, but extend this work by more fully considering the links between organized crime and the legitimate world. Finally, our study contributes empirically to the large body of work on organized crime during America's Prohibition era. While a great deal of historical research and cultural analyses exist of this time period—and of Al Capone in particular—our study is one of the first to apply formal network models to this historical moment and, in so doing, is poised to see how the concepts of embeddedness and multiplexity might alter our understanding of Al Capone and his criminal syndicate.

THE CAPONE DATABASE

Prohibition legislation introduced an invasion of home and leisure that was so culturally divisive that even some politicians adopted anti-Prohibition platforms. Cops, politicians, and judges kept drinking; housewives continued brewing home batches of hooch; and street gang youth found their time more valuable when delivering beer. The federal government allocated a minimal amount of resources for the enforcement of Prohibition. Successful bootlegging, then, required knowing when and where raids would occur, ensuring that the top guys of the crime organization were not present during those raids, knowing which agents would take a bribe, and guaranteeing that public attorneys never had enough evidence to prosecute. For bootlegging entrepreneurs like Al Capone, this meant having friends in high places and generously granting favors.

Prohibition offers an exceptional case for social scientific analysis in that it truly was the failed noble experiment. Prohibition remains the only amendment in the US Constitution that was repealed by a later constitutional amendment. Like marijuana and gambling today, there was cultural enthusiasm or, at the very least, tolerance for criminalized alcohol; but unlike marijuana and gambling, the period of criminalization for alcohol was a short 13 years (1920–1933). These two points—the public contempt for the law and the short period of criminalization—suggest an unprecedented level of integration of crime into the legitimate spheres to the extent that even supporters of Prohibition saw the law as a complete failure. Researching this unique historical moment has the advantage of a clear temporal beginning and end; publicly known relationships between criminal and non-criminal elements that no one bothered to conceal; and a continued present-day fascination with the gangster era, which has pressured archives to make their sources publicly available and easily accessible.

In short, we analyze Prohibition-era organized crime in Chicago, and Al Capone specifically, because of the large historical record of this period as well as the integration of organized crime into the legitimate world. Prohibition is a prominent and well-studied example of organized crime, but more important for our purposes are the patterns of embeddedness and multiplexity found in this case of organized crime.

Data Sources

Since June 2008, we have collected, digitized, and coded documents from several archival sources, including: the Chicago Crime Commission, the Internal Revenue Service, the Federal Bureau of Investigation, the National Archives Great Lakes Region, Northwestern's History of Homicide in Chicago 1870–1930 database, and Proquest Newspapers. We supplemented these archival documents with secondary sources in order to triangulate historical records and contemporary accounts. The types of documents in these archives vary greatly, ranging from newspaper clippings and obituaries to details of police investigations, personal letters, bail-bond cards, tax documents, and court testimony. To date, we have coded more than 4,000 pages of primary and secondary sources. Each entry in the database links directly to a source, thus permitting cross-referencing and data filtering.

Sampling

Unlike some historical projects with a defined archive or defined focus on a particular set of events, ours is an attempt to compile a database of early twentieth-century organized crime in Chicago. This presents various challenges: the most problematic is boundary specification, namely who is "in" the data and who is "out." Certain individuals and events are much more prominent in the historical record than others; and crime reporting often includes contradictions, typos, allegations, and bias. To address some of these challenges, we took a two-fold sampling approach. First, we attempted a random seeding method to identify as many individuals as possible in the archival materials by sampling specific documents and files. This entailed locating "consolidation" files of the Chicago Crime Commission (CCC) that summarized key figures and events during and before Prohibition.[5] CCC members wrote these executive summaries contemporaneously and retrospectively on various corruption and criminal cases, relying on their own primary investigations as well as legal documents and newspapers. Our main goal with this sampling step was to generate a list of individuals from all available sources who were somehow mentioned in connection with organized crime.

Second, we adopted an informant-based sampling strategy familiar in qualitative research. Fortunately for our research purposes, the national and international public had a fascination with Al Capone and left behind a massive record. We have collected and coded a population of archival documents generated from searching the informant, Al Capone. Additionally, we have searched and coded for individuals connected to Capone, individuals listed as "public enemies" by the CCC, court indictments and legal documents, the Illinois Crime Survey of 1929 (Landesco, [1929] 1968), and significant events and individuals referenced in secondary sources, such as Asbury (1940). Documents associated with our informant include: Internal Revenue Service (IRS) documents, court testimony and transcripts, police and arrest records, newspaper articles, and more.

The resulting database—which we call simply "The Capone Data"—currently contains 2,892 unique individuals whose names appeared in records from years 1882 to 1949. Although our sampling strategy is neither exhaustive nor completely random, we believe that it accurately captures a range of observable individuals and activities. Even the cleverest criminal minds would be hard-pressed to generate a list of 3,000 individuals with whom they associate.

Relational Coding Strategy

We coded all documents to identify relationships between unique individuals. Relational coding includes events, allegations, descriptions, and associations. Every time two or more names appeared together in a record, we coded a relational tie. Each tie pulls two names from the individual-level database, one individual as a sender and one individual as a receiver.[6]

In the process of coding relationships, we have identified 11 top-level ties: business, criminal, family/personal, financial, funeral, legal, political, rival/informant, union, violence/crime, and other. A second-level of coding includes 102 "tie descriptors," which contain more precise details of the specific relationship. For example, the criminal code contains more specific ties, such as arrests, corruption, racketeering, criminal associates, and illegitimate business ventures. Likewise, the family/personal code includes relationships such as family members, friends, mistresses, neighbors, acquaintances, etc. We have coded 14,130 ties to date.

ANALYTICAL APPROACH

Our analysis proceeds in three stages. First, we examine the bounded group of individuals that constitutes what most people would refer to as Al Capone's "Syndicate." Specifically, we analyze the patterns of criminal ties within this group during the Prohibition era. To the extent that an organized criminal syndicate exists, it should be evident in the patterns of relationships among these group members and through their links of criminal activity. The second stage of analysis highlights the multiplex nature of organized crime by zooming in on one specific enterprise—the investment of Capone and his associates in the Hawthorne Kennel Club. This enterprise has been the subject of previous criminological analysis (Haller, 1990), but our data allow us to plot the multiplexity of relationships entwined in this enterprise. The third stage expands the focus of multiplexity by considering not a single event, but rather the full extent of criminal, legitimate, and personal ties in the data. Here, the analysis focuses on the contours of several sets of social ties among one set of individuals and, more importantly, the extent to which these

ties overlap. Throughout the analyses, we employ a range of statistical measures and techniques, the descriptions of which occur as they are employed.

CAPONE'S CRIMINAL SYNDICATE: A GROUP-BOUNDED ANALYSIS

Al Capone is often cited as a rags-to-riches illegal robber baron, a self-made gangster who started as muscle and a doorman but later assembled a vast criminal empire. Al Capone arrived in Chicago around 1919 as a protégé and assistant to Johnny "The Fox" Torrio. These two entrepreneurs were well connected to Chicago's underworld through "Big Jim" Colosimo. Colosimo was quite possibly Chicago's original Italian gangster, who oversaw the Levee district vice ring. Prohibition afforded a new criminal enterprise that would eventually catapult gangsters like Capone into the national spotlight. Capone and Torrio—after the unsolved but suspiciously timed murder of their boss, Colosimo—dove headfirst into bootlegging and quickly carved out a large distribution territory among dozens of other Chicago gangs. In January of 1925, Torrio was shot while walking home with his wife. He survived the injuries but shortly thereafter retired to New York, leaving Al Capone as boss of their Chicago crime organization—often referred to by the moniker "The Syndicate." In the years to follow, Al Capone's charismatic personality, economic success, and facial scar led him to be known internationally as Chicago's most notorious gangster.

The Syndicate focused mainly on bootlegging and alcohol distribution, but Capone's operations also expanded to unions, racetracks, and elections. It is important to keep in mind that *all* of these operations involved both a) some level of monitoring and management and b) some connection to the legitimate world. Bootlegging in particular required complex networks and division of labor that included brew masters, truck drivers, speakeasy operators, importers, and crooked cops. While later stages of our analysis will focus on the intersection of the underworld and the legitimate world, we turn now to an examination of the criminal ties and illegitimate enterprises among individuals in the Syndicate. Typically, individuals in these types of organizations are labeled gangsters or mobsters and, therefore, often become the target of law enforcement investigation or popular culture. If there is a structure to organized criminal groups, it might very well be apparent among this group of individuals.

We identified 178 individuals in our archival materials that were noted as members or associates of Capone's Syndicate. To recreate the social structure of the Syndicate, we extracted all criminal ties between these individuals. The resulting network is displayed in Figure 5.2, where each node represents a unique individual and each line represents a criminal tie between individuals. The criminal ties between these Syndicate men include arrests, illegitimate businesses, co-offending,

and general criminal associations. Each of the ties—and there are 1,628 edges in the network, many of which are redundant—represents a unique association between two individuals.[7] On average, individuals have approximately 18.3 ties. However, the distribution of ties (degree distribution) is highly skewed, with a minimum of one tie and a maximum of 567 ties, the latter belonging to none other than Al Capone.[8]

Visually, this network looks like starburst, with a dominant center and densely connected pockets of ties. These various clusters throughout the network represent small co-offending groups or crews that were involved in specific enterprises or activities. For example, one such cluster is the Italian Importing and Manufacturing Company, a business front for a group of 22 Sicilian bootleggers who were accused of being Communists. Another offshoot is bridged by John Scalise and Albert Anselmi, who were gunmen for the Syndicate and suspects in the Valentine's Day Massacre. The Syndicate members in

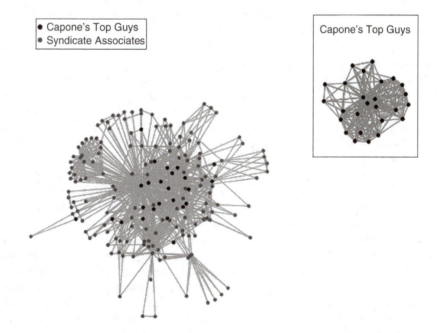

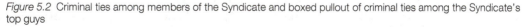

Figure 5.2 Criminal ties among members of the Syndicate and boxed pullout of criminal ties among the Syndicate's top guys

this offshoot collected cash for Scalise and Anselmi's legal defense fund and allegedly murdered individuals who refused to donate. Clusters such as these are connected to the center of the network by one or two ties—a property reminiscent of a patron–client network (Gould, 1996; Montgomery, 2007)—whereby a patron ("connector") brokers relationships between his crew and the larger Syndicate. Perhaps the greatest patron, Al Capone, is at the middle of this network.

As expected, Al Capone rests at the center of this graph surrounded by his "Top Guys," by which we mean individuals who were identified in the archives as members of Capone's inner council or Capone's board of directors. The boxed pullout in Figure 5.2 displays all criminal ties among these top guys (N = 26). Relative to the larger Syndicate, this inner circle is a fairly dense network (density = 0.55) with fewer offshoot clusters.

Consistent with our argument, we see that the top guys network at the core of the Syndicate is not a simple hierarchy but rather overlapping cliques or an embedded set of social circles. Using Moody and White's (2003) measure of *k-connectivity*, we find that this top guys network displays considerable structural cohesion. In fact, this small network of 26 individuals contains eight nested components (subgraphs). The k-connectivity of the top guys network is five, meaning it would require the removal of five individuals to break this network apart. Yet, as one considers the various and overlapping clusters in this network, the k-connectivity level reaches a maximum of 11—i.e., it would take the removal of 11 individuals (42% of the total nodes) to fundamentally alter the density of the network.[9] In other words, the cohesion and structure of this top guys network rests on the embedded nature of these clusters, and not on the centrality of a single person—even if that single person is Al Capone.

What also becomes clear in the top guys network is that Capone is not alone as the center of the Syndicate. There are actually *four* nodes at the center of this graph: Al Capone, his successor Frank "the Enforcer" Nitti, Syndicate accountant Jack "Greasy Thumb" Guzik, and Al's older brother, Ralph "Bottles" Capone. Thus, whereas Al Capone is sometimes credited as being the "boss of bosses" of the Chicago Syndicate, he shares considerable structural power and overlap with these other three men.[10] Haller (1990) describes these four as the "senior partners" who together oversaw all of the smaller enterprises that the Capone gang had infiltrated, including cleaning and dying unions, gambling, racetracks, brothels, and beer distribution. In many ways, Capone was the figurehead—and lightening rod—of the Syndicate, while much of the daily operations, decisions, and oversight fell to these other three men. This was especially the case when Capone was serving a gun-carrying sentence in Philadelphia and later when he spent most of his time at his Miami beachhouse, escaping the Chicago scrutiny. Nitti, Guzik, and Ralph frequently visited Capone's Miami estate and, upon Capone's lengthy incarceration for tax fraud, these three took over the Chicago operations and developed them into what came to be known as "the Outfit."

Stopping the analysis at this point would already shed some light on the complexity of organized crime networks. Al Capone's Syndicate—and likely syndicates from other eras or countries—was created by overlapping sets of dense network clusters. However, the embeddedness we observe in the Syndicate is underestimated because we have considered only criminal ties. If, as we argue, organized crime is contingent on links between the underworld and the legitimate world, then the true structure of organized crime should grow increasingly more complex when one considers additional types of social relationships. However, before adding levels of complexity onto this Syndicate network, we first illustrate the role of multiplex relationships in organized crime by zooming in on a single criminal enterprise: the Hawthorne Kennel Club.

NETWORK MULTIPLEXITY AND THE HAWTHORNE CLUB

Al Capone loved dog racing. Capone, his brother Ralph, and some of the other top guys opened the Hawthorne Kennel Club along with Edward O'Hare, a lawyer and dog-racing entrepreneur.[11] O'Hare served as President of the Hawthorne Kennel Club for his business partners Al and Ralph Capone, the Guzik brothers, Nitti, Levine, and Patton. Patton served as a manager of operations at the tracks.

Unlike horse races, betting on dog races was not—nor had ever been—legal in Illinois, but the dog racetrack investors found a loophole through a certificate payment system. On June 12, 1928, Judge Harry Fisher granted a temporary injunction protecting the operation of dog races while the legality of the certificate betting system was being contested in the courts.[12] The state's attorney's office was furious because Judge Fisher's injunction kept legal battles and court proceeding tied up for years. In both the 1927 and 1930 elections, the Hawthorne Kennel Club mobilized incredible political support and money for politicians who favored the legalization of dog racing. Capone reached out to political allies through substantial campaign contributions, taking them to Cubs games, and even chartering trips to Havana. Ultimately, Capone and company lost this legal battle, though O'Hare's racing investments grew to include dog tracks in Massachusetts and Florida and a thoroughbred horse racetrack in Chicago, Sportsman's Park, which stands to this day. Figure 5.3 plots the various relationships of the Hawthorne Kennel Club.[13]

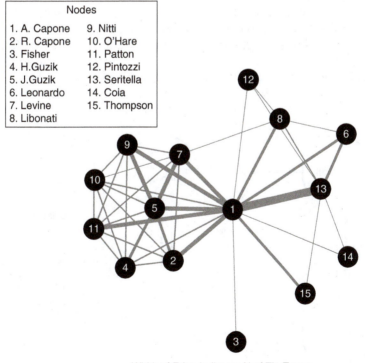

Nodes

1. A. Capone	9. Nitti
2. R. Capone	10. O'Hare
3. Fisher	11. Patton
4. H.Guzik	12. Pintozzi
5. J.Guzik	13. Seritella
6. Leonardo	14. Coia
7. Levine	15. Thompson
8. Libonati	

Width of Edge indicates N of Tie Types

Figure 5.3 Embedded and multiplex ties of the Hawthorne Kennel Club

The network in Figure 5.3 contains 15 individuals involved with the Hawthorne Kennel Club. The network depicts 57 ties with the varying thickness representing the level of multiplexity; only nine of these ties represent a single relationship. These 57 ties aggregate different types of relationships: 29 Hawthorne Kennel Club business associations, 47 criminal associations, two family ties, 13 friend ties, two attorney/client ties, one judge tie, five political associations, seven political supporters/contributors ties, and five political corruption associations. For visual clarity, the width of the lines in Figure 5.3 indicates the number of tie *types* between any two individuals (minimum = 1, maximum = 4). For example, there is only one type of tie between Al Capone and Pintozzi (a political contribution), while there are three different tie types between Nitti and J. Guzik (business, criminal, and friend).

Al Capone is at the center of this network because he was responsible for making the campaign contributions to politicians opposed to strict gambling legislation. The individuals in the cluster on the left side of the graph are all connected to each other both through the criminal ties of the Syndicate as well as through the business ties of the Hawthorne Kennel Club. This network also contains two sets of brothers (the Capone brothers and the Guzik brothers) and several dyads of longtime friends and golf buddies. While the types of ties and ways in which people are connected are quite complex, Figure 5.3 demonstrates that the Hawthorne Kennel Club converged business, criminal, legal, and political spheres.

Even in the small network in Figure 5.3, the extent of multiplexity can be dizzying. To focus more clearly on the ways in which the same sets of individuals can be connected, Figure 5.4 displays a network of three of the Hawthorne Kennel Club's operators (Al Capone, Jack Guzik, and Hymie Levine) and a lawyer turned politician (Roland Libonati). Figure 5.4 is extracted directly from the larger disaggregated Hawthorne edgelist and contains 13 ties of five tie types. In all but one relationship (between Libonati and Levine), everyone is connected by no less than three types of social relationships. Between Capone and Guzik is the Hawthorne Kennel Club business tie, but as long-time Syndicate associates they worked together in multiple enterprises, including gambling, brothels,

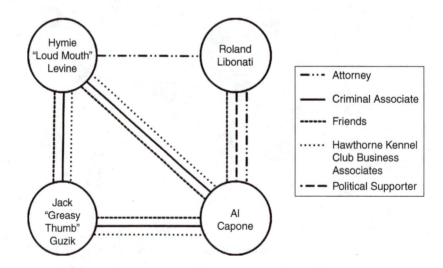

Figure 5.4 A tetrad extracted from the Hawthorne network

and directing the Sanitary Cleaning Shops. Guzik wired money to Miami for Capone and visited the Miami estate regularly. Guzik and Capone were closely linked in Figure 5.2; yet, Figure 5.4 shows that more than just crime binds these two. Likewise, Levine is tied in multiple ways to both Capone and Guzik through the Hawthorne Kennel Club and as a member of the Syndicate. Levine collected Syndicate dues and payments in the Loop district and was a golf buddy of Capone and Guzik's. Libonati, a lawyer who later became a politician, only has a professional legal relationship with Levine—the only non-multiplex relationship in Figure 5.4. Libonati also acted as Capone's lawyer, later received political contributions on behalf of the Hawthorne Club, and accompanied Capone to a Cubs game.[14]

The Hawthorne Kennel Club was just one of many illicit enterprises operated by the Capone Syndicate. But even this single example illustrates the extent to which multiple relationships define organized crime. In the case of the Hawthorne Kennel Club, pockets of criminals (the cluster on the left side of Figure 5.3) are connected to other parts of the network through intermediaries. Some of these relationships are multiplex, as in the deep ties between Capone and Libonati, while others are singular, like the tie between Levine and Libonati. Thus, both multiplex and singular relationships are necessary in such networks, but it is the interaction between the two that generates the observed organized crime networks and patterns of behavior.

THE OVERLAPPING SPHERES ORGANIZING CRIME

To this point we have examined 1) the embedded nature of criminal ties among the members of the Syndicate, and 2) the extent to which multiplex ties situate shady enterprises such as the Hawthorne Kennel Club. Yet, our larger argument is that the form of organized crime cannot be understood by analyzing enterprises in isolation; instead we must understand that such activities, enterprises, and relationships build larger social systems and structures. The final stages of analysis expand this thinking by considering the embedded and multiplex network structures of all the individuals from our database relevant to the organized crime network of Chicago. Specifically, we consider *three* sets of relationships at the heart of organized crime: criminal ties, personal (family and friends) ties, and legitimate (non-criminal) ties. One could, as we did in the first part of our analysis, consider each of these types of relationships as distinct social networks: a criminal network, a personal network, and legitimate network. To this end, the right side of Figure 5.5 depicts the largest component from each of these relationships; Table 5.1 lists the basic network properties of these isolated networks.

Given our focus on organized crime, it should be of no surprise that the criminal network is the largest of these three isolated networks. There are 104 unique components in the criminal network, and the largest component (Figure 5.5b) contains 1,015 unique individuals and 3,287 ties. On average, individuals in the largest component have approximately 6.5 ties to others in the network. In contrast to Figure 5.2, this criminal network moves way beyond Syndicate membership to include arrests, co-offending, and criminal associations between members and non-members of the Syndicate. A point of interest is that gangs *rival* to the Syndicate show up in this crime network through co-arrests, individuals leaving one gang for Capone's Syndicate, individuals leaving the Syndicate for a rival gang, and attempts at a citywide truce. In other words, gangs that might be considered distinct organizational entities—indeed, even competitors—are only a handshake or two removed from each other.[15]

The personal network contains 128 unique components, and the largest component (Figure 5.5c) consists of 410 individuals and

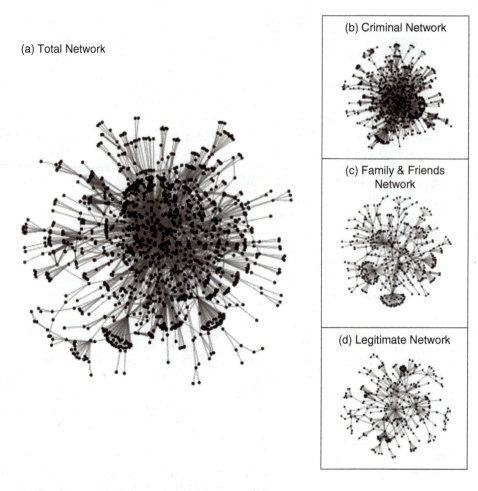

(a) Total Network

(b) Criminal Network

(c) Family & Friends Network

(d) Legitimate Network

Figure 5.5 The total organized crime network and components

Table 5.1 Descriptive properties compared across networks

	The Syndicate	*Criminal Network*	*Family/Friend Network*	*Legitimate Network*	*Total Network*
Total Network					
N of Nodes	182	1339	738	435	1883
N of Edges	1631	5592	1020	1120	7732
Mean Degree	17.92	8.35	2.76	4.94	8.21
Capone's Degree	567	787	107	91	985
N of Components	3	104	128	56	143
Largest Component					
N of Nodes	178	1015	410	285	1469
N of Edges	1628	3287	587	674	4396
Mean Degree	18.29	6.48	2.86	4.73	5.99

587 ties. On average, individuals in the largest component have 2.9 ties in this network. Ties include known familial relations as well as life-long and short-term friendships. This network is a conservative estimate in that we did not impute ties (a friend of a friend is a friend, or a relative of a relative is a relative), and, instead, we only coded ties that appeared in the archives.

The legitimate network has 56 components. The largest component (Figure 5.5d) has fewer individuals (285 nodes) than the other two isolated networks, but it has more ties (674 edges) and a greater average number of ties per person (degree = 4.7) than the personal network. Legitimate ties include legitimate business associations, union associations, organizational associations, and political associations.

While parsing out these networks allows us to examine the different properties across tie types, our argument is that it is the convergence and overlap of these networks that make organized crime possible. Figure 5.5a displays the largest component when one layers all three types of relationships onto a single network. Doing so has two important structural implications. First, the size of the largest component increases, thereby linking a greater number of individuals. In this case, the large component in the total network contains 78% of all individuals in the data. The largest component of the total network has 45% more nodes and 34% more edges than just the criminal network. Second, such an expansion of the size of the largest component begins to indirectly link people from the various subnetworks (criminal, personal, and legitimate) that would otherwise be disconnected. That is, these different tie types are a set of multiplex relationships rather than distinct social realms. Not only are some people directly connected in multiple ways, but people who would otherwise be disconnected become linked indirectly through people in the middle of these multiplex relationships.

It is this last point that truly captures the embeddedness issue described in this study. Individuals can be nested into clusters within each of these separate spheres of relationships, and in some cases people can be tied in multiple ways. More than that, though, some individuals can be nested in clusters in multiple types of relationships, or else they can have ties that link together clusters from different domains. Figure 5.6 illustrates this point with a Venn diagram of the overlapping ties among the 1,883 individuals in the largest component of the total network (Figure 5.5a). Figure 5.6 shows that 46% of individuals in this sample have *only* criminal ties. Conversely, less than 6% of individuals have ties that span all three domains, an additional 6% occupy the criminal and legitimate networks, 13% occupy the criminal and personal networks, and 4% occupy the legitimate and personal networks—taken together, 29% of this sample occupies more than one sphere.

This Venn diagram supports one of the main cruxes of our argument. Organized crime is not simply the sets of illegal ties among gangsters, but the coming together of various types of relationships that facilitate various criminal enterprises like the Hawthorne Kennel Club. The total network in

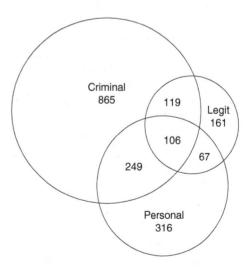

Figure 5.5 Venn diagram of ties in criminal, personal, and legitimate spheres

Figure 5.5a and the Venn diagram in Figure 5.6 represent the merging of these worlds that made Capone's Syndicate possible. To be clear, we are not arguing that all individuals in these figures were criminals (i.e., individuals who committed a criminal act); instead, our argument is that it is these embedded and multiplex relationships between gangsters, small-time criminals, and legitimate folks that organize crime.

CONCLUSION

Organized crime is not easily bounded. Organized crime groups may or may not have some criteria for membership, but organized criminal activities seep into the legitimate spheres of society. Indeed, as we have maintained here, it is at the boundaries of the underworld and the upper world where crime gets organized. In this study, we make two propositions about the nature of organized crime. First, organized crime is *embedded*, meaning that the social networks of interpersonal relationships (be they criminal or non-criminal) overlap and intersect with one another so that individuals exist and act simultaneously in multiple social circles. Second, this embeddedness is compounded when ties cross multiple social relationships, a property referred to as *multiplexity*. In particular, the hallmark of organized crime occurs when underworld networks integrate with legitimate networks.

Our analysis of Prohibition-era Chicago supposes these two claims. Our findings show that the network structure of Al Capone's Syndicate displays properties of a complex patron–client network but with considerable overlap and nesting. While Al Capone is at the center of this network, he is not alone nor is he structurally distinct from his closest associates. In fact, Capone, just like other members of the Syndicate, sits in the middle of a highly embedded social network of overlapping cliques and clusters. Zooming out from the criminal ties of the Syndi-

cate, our results reveal the highly multiplex nature of organized crime. Our network data span three social worlds—the criminal, the legitimate, and the personal—and contain 1,883 individuals. Most of these individuals (approximately 70%) exist in a single social world. But roughly 30% of the individuals in this network have ties in more than one sphere.

Our study is not without limitations, three of which we mention here. First, even though the links between the legitimate world and organized crime were apparent during Prohibition, we no doubt underestimate the size and scope of this overlap because of the nature of our archival data. We are beholden to the work of Prohibition-era journalists, researchers, and law enforcement for their uncovering of friendships and favors between gangsters and politicians. Relationships that have remained concealed throughout history remain concealed from our analysis. Second, selectivity into networks varies by the type of network ties. In particular, the judges and politicians in the network may be of a different type and character than the judges and prosecutors who pursued the gangsters of the day. Even in Chicago, one hopes that the politician who takes a bribe is the exception rather than the rule, but without exhaustive data it is difficult to test how these claims might affect our measurement. Finally, this study taps into but a handful of network properties and measures that might be used to explain and explore the issues of embeddedness and multiplexity. Other types of network properties and positions might differently explain the structure and nature of organized crime. We in no way suggest that other network characteristics are unimportant, but we do suggest that the theories and instruments of embeddedness and multiplexity are valuable to the study of organized crime.

These caveats notwithstanding, this study offers important insights for future research. First, though this study points out the presence of distinct clusters and events, it does not distinguish among them. Future research would do well to consider how different types of network clustering and positions might influence specific organized crime enterprises. Second, in addition to offering a unique perspective on organized crime, these data and our approach point to the resilience or vulnerability of social networks. Prohibition has a clear temporal end, and organized crime networks were subjected to severe exogenous shocks in the form of federal law enforcement and the repeal of the Eighteenth Amendment. We know that organized crime and even Capone's Syndicate survived such shocks, and some of the answers about this resilience may rest in the structure of these social networks.

NOTES

1. A Faculty Research Grant from the University of Massachusetts Amherst funded the original data collection for this project. Direct all correspondence to Andrew Papachristos.
2. Simmel argued that secret societies craft themselves into a "counter-image" of mainstream society through the incorporation of hierarchy and formalism (Simmel, 1950: 360). In essence, secret societies are ersatz institutions distinct from the pro-social realm. Our argument, however, is that organized crime attempts to socially integrate rather than separate. In this way, we are borrowing from Simmel's (1955) other work on "webs of group affiliations" that conceptualizes individuals and groups as products of the overlap of various social realms and forms of action.
3. This mirrors Robert Merton's argument of "innovation" for which he uses Al Capone as an illustration in his famous essay "Social Structure and Anomie" (1938).
4. Landesco was a student of Ernest Burgess. Landesco never completed his dissertation and, instead, went to work for the Illinois Parole Board not long after completing the *Survey of Organized Crime*. His other work included research on Chicago's 42 Gang and the criminal history of pickpocket Eddie Jackson (see Haller, 1968).
5. Chicago's business elites began the Chicago Crime Commission in 1919. Its purpose was to pick up after Chicago's failed police department by uncovering corruption and tracking notorious figures (Ruth, 1996). The civilian-based organization continues today.
6. Though the direction of the tie is irrelevant for most tie types.

7. For the sake of visual clarity, we ignore the number of ties, or tie strength, in the present analysis and assume a simple binary relationship.
8. We dropped all nodes with a degree of one for plotting Figure 5.2.
9. As a point of comparison, the k-connectivity of the hypothetical network in Figure 5.1 is three.
10. Interestingly, all four of these men were separately found guilty of tax evasion and served federal sentences. Guzik and Ralph's takedowns occurred before Al's, and Nitti's was roughly the same time as Al's. Though only Al Capone makes the list of IRS historical highlights (IRS, 2011).
11. O'Hare had been a lawyer in St. Louis, moved into the dog-racing business with the patent for the mechanical rabbit, and made big (legal and illegal) money in dog racing. In spite of Hawthorne's success, O'Hare became an informant in the IRS' case against Capone and was gunned down nine years later while driving from his office. O'Hare's surname has been memorialized at the Chicago O'Hare airport via his progeny, Butch O'Hare, a World War II hero (Eig, 2010).
12. Neither friend nor foe, Judge Fisher had reservations about racetracks in general and threatened to end the temporary protected status when he visited the dog tracks and saw children there.
13. For illustrative purposes, we bounded this network by pulling the business ties of the Hawthorne Kennel Club, the political contribution ties made on behalf of the Hawthorne Kennel Club, and the legal tie that ruled for the injunction to maintain operations of the Hawthorne Kennel Club. That generated the list of 15 individuals and then we returned to the database and pulled other ties that existed between this bounded set of individuals.
14. This moment was captured in the famous *Chicago Tribune* photo of Libonati sitting next to Capone and his son at the Cubs versus White Sox charity game of 1931 (Vaughan, 1931).
15. A similar observation can be found in network studies of contemporary street gangs (Fleisher, 2006; McGloin, 2005; Papachristos, Braga, & Hureau, 2012).

REFERENCES

Abadinsky, Howard (2010). *Organized Crime* (9th ed.). Belmont, CA: Wadsworth.

Albini, Joseph L. (1971). *American Mafia: Genesis of a Legend*. New York: Appleton-Century-Crofts, Inc.

Asbury, Herbert (1940). *Gem of the Prairie: An Informal History of the Chicago Underworld*. New York: Alfred A. Knoff, Inc.

Baker, Wayne E. & Robert R. Faulkner (1993). The social organization of conspiracy: Illegal networks in the heavy electric equipment industry. *American Sociological Review* 58(6), 837–860.

Baker, Wayne E. & Robert R. Faulkner (2003). Diffusion of fraud: Intermediate economic crime and investor dynamics. *Criminology* 41(4), 1173–1206.

Baker, Wayne E. & Robert R. Faulkner (2009). Social capital, double embeddedness, and mechanisms of stability and change. *American Behavioral Scientist* 52(11), 1531–1555.

Bell, Daniel (1953). Crime as an American way of life. *The Antioch Review* 13(2), 131–154.

Blok, Anton (1974). *The Mafia in a Sicilian Village, 1860-1960: A Study of Violent Peasant Entrepreneurs*. New York: Harper and Row.

Boissevain, Jeremy (1974). *Friends of Friends: Networks, Manipulators, and Coalitions*. Oxford: Basil Blackwell.

Boorman, Scott A. & Harrison C. White (1976). Social structure from multiple networks. II. Role structures. *American Journal of Sociology* 81(6), 1384–1446.

Chicago Tribune (1920). Courts, opera, underworld to bury Colosimo. May 14, p. 2.

Chicago Tribune (1927). "You Can All Go Thirsty" Is Al Capone's Adieu. December 6, pp. 1, 6.

Eig, Jonathan (2010). *Get Capone: The Secret Plot That Captured America's Most Wanted Gangster*. New York: Simon & Schuster.

Emirbayer, Mustafa (1997). Manifesto for a relational sociology. *American Journal of Sociology* 103(2), 281–317.

Feld, Scott L. (1997). Structural embeddedness and stability of interpersonal relations. *Social Networks* 19(1), 91–95.

Fleisher, Mark S. (2006). Youth gang social dynamics and social network analysis: Applying degree centrality measures to assess the nature of gang boundaries. In J.F. Short & L.A. Hughes (eds.), *Studying Youth Gangs* (pp. 85–98). Lanham, MD: Alta Mira Press.

Gould, Roger V. (1991). Multiple networks and mobilization in the Paris Commune, 1871. *American Sociological Review* 56(6), 716–729.

Gould, Roger V. (1996). Patron-Client Ties, State Centralization, and the Whiskey Rebellion. *American Journal of Sociology* 102(2), 400–429.

Granovetter, Mark (1985). Economic action and social structure: The problem of embeddedness. *American Journal of Sociology* 91(3), 481–510.

Haller, Mark H. (1968). Introduction. In John Landesco, *Organized Crime in Chicago* (pp. vii–xviii). Chicago, IL: University of Chicago Press.

Haller, Mark H. (1970). Urban crime and criminal justice: The Chicago case. *Journal of American History* 57 (3), 619–635.

Haller, Mark H. (1971). Organized crime in urban history: Chicago in the twentieth century. *Journal of Social History* 5(2), 210–234.

Haller, Mark H. (1990). Illegal enterprise: A theoretical and historical interpretation. *Criminology* 28(2), 207–235.

Ianni, Francis A.J. & Elizabeth Reuss-Ianni (1972). *A Family Business: Kinship and Social Control in Organized Crime*. New York: Russell Sage Foundation.

Ianni, Francis A.J. & Elizabeth Reuss-Ianni (1976). *The Crime Society: Organized Crime and Corruption in America*. New York: Plume.

Internal Revenue Service (2011). *Historical Highlights of the IRS*. Retrieved February 23, 2012 from www.irs.gov/uac/Historical-Highlights-of-the-IRS

Jacobs, James B. (2006). *Mobsters, Unions, and Feds: The Mafia and the American Labor Movement*. New York: New York University Press.

Kadushin, Charles (2012). *Understanding Social Networks: Theories, Concepts, and Findings*. New York: Oxford University Press.

Klerks, Peter (2001). The network paradigm applied to criminal organisations: Theoretical nitpicking or a relevant doctrine for investigators? Recent developments in the Netherlands. *Connections* 24(3), 53–65.

Landesco, John ([1929] 1968). *Organized Crime in Chicago*. Chicago, IL: University of Chicago Press.

Malm, Aili, Gisela Bichler, & Stephanie Van De Walle (2010). Comparing the ties that bind criminal networks: Is blood thicker than water? *Security Journal* 23, 52–74.

McGloin, Jean Marie (2005). Policy and intervention considerations of a network analysis of street gangs. *Criminology & Public Policy* 4(3), 607–636.

McIllwain, Jeffrey Scott (1999). Organized crime: A social network approach. *Crime, Law & Social Change* 32(4), 301–323.

Merton, Robert K. (1938). Social structure and anomie. *American Sociological Review* 3(5), 672–682.

Montgomery, James D. (2007). The structure of norms and relations in patronage systems. *Social Networks* 29(4), 565–584.

Moody, James & Douglas R. White (2003). Structural cohesion and embeddedness: A hierarchical concept of social groups. *American Sociological Review* 68(1), 103–127.

Morselli, Carlo (2003). Career opportunities and network-based privileges in the Cosa Nostra. *Crime, Law and Social Change* 39(4), 383–418.

Morselli, Carlo (2009). Hells Angels in springtime. *Trends in Organized Crime* 12(2), 145–158.

Morselli, Carlo & Cynthia Giguère (2006). Legitimate strengths in criminal networks. *Crime, Law, and Social Change* 45, 185–200.

Morselli, Carlo, Cynthia Giguère, & Katia Petit (2007). The efficiency/security trade-off in criminal networks. *Social Networks* 29(1), 143–153.

Nakamura, Kiminori, George Tita, & David Krackhardt (2011). Violence in the "balance": A structural analysis of how rivals, allies, and third-parties shape inter-gang violence. University of Maryland, College Park, MD.

Natarajan, Mangai (2006). Understanding the structure of a large heroin distribution network: A quantitative analysis of qualitative data. *Journal of Quantitative Criminology* 22(2), 171–192.

Papachristos, Andrew V. (2009). Murder by structure: Dominance relations and the social structure of gang homicide. *American Journal of Sociology* 115(1), 74–128.

Papachristos, Andrew V. (2011). The coming of a networked criminology? In J. MacDonald (ed.), *Measuring Crime and Criminality: Advances in Criminological Theory*, Vol. 17 (pp. 101–140). New Brunswick, NJ: Transaction Publishers.

Papachristos, Andrew V., Anthony A. Braga, & David M. Hureau (2012). Social networks and the risk of gunshot injury. *Journal of Urban Health* 89(6), 992–1003.

Pedahzur, Ami & Arie Perliger (2006). The changing nature of suicide attacks: A social network perspective. *Social Forces* 84(4), 1987–2008.

Ruth, David E. (1996). *Inventing the Public Enemy: The Gangster in American Culture, 1918–1934*. Chicago, IL: University of Chicago Press.

Simmel, Georg (1950). *The Sociology of Georg Simmel*. Edited and translated by K.H. Wolff. New York: The Free Press.

Simmel, Georg (1955). *Conflict & the Web of Group Affiliations*. Translated by K.H. Wolff & R. Bendix. New York: The Free Press.

Uzzi, Brian (1996). The sources and consequences of embeddedness for the economic performances of organizations: The network effect. *American Sociological Review* 16(4), 674–698.

Vaughan, Irving (1931). Cubs beat White Sox, 3–0, before 34,865. *Chicago Tribune*, September 10, pp. 21–23.

Verbrugge, Lois M. (1979). Multiplexity in adult friendships. *Social Forces* 57(4), 1286–1309.

Wasserman, Stanley & Katherine Faust (1994). *Social Network Analysis: Methods and Applications*. New York: Cambridge University Press.

Xu, Jennifer & Hsinchun Chen (2003). Untangling criminal networks: A case study. In H. Chen, R. Miranda, D. Zeng, C. Demchak, J. Schroeder, & T. Madhusudan (eds.), *Proceedings of the First NSF/NIJ Symposium on Intelligence and Security Informatics* (pp. 232–248). Berlin: Springer.

Xu, Jennifer & Hsinchun Chen (2008). The topology of dark networks. *Communications of the ACM* 51(10), 58–65.

Yeager, Matthew G. (2012). "Fifty years of research on illegal enterprise: An interview with Mark Haller. *Trends in Organized Crime* 15(1), 1–12.

CHAPTER 6

Snakeheads and the Cartwheel Network

Functional Fluidity as Opposed to Structural Flexibility

Sheldon Zhang

Chinese human smuggling has emerged and prospered in the past few decades because of the increased demand for transnational migration in China. The restrictive immigration procedures imposed by most western countries, the US in particular, have only fueled the demand for services provided by human smugglers (Zhang, 2007). This has been coupled with a reformulated conceptualization of emigration in China: no longer considered a traitorous act, it is now encouraged as a means of bringing foreign revenue into the country (Landolt & Da, 2005).

Research by Zhang (2008) and Chin (1999) suggests that Chinese human smuggling activities mostly consist of serial transactions in which one snakehead brings forth the desired goods or service to the next, who in turn sells to yet another. The process goes on and on until the migrant reaches his/her final destination. Compared to traditional criminal organizations, such as the Hong Kong triads or Italian mafia, empirical research thus far indicates that Chinese smuggling organizations are made up of loosely affiliated individuals who, through fortuitous opportunities and social connections, pool their resources to provide underground travel services. One special feature of these smuggling organizations is their adaptability and flexibility in a hostile business environment. Zhang and Chin (2002) argued that there are many structural advantages in favor of these loosely structured

organizations, in contrast to the traditional criminal organizations. However, much more conceptual development and elaboration are needed to explain what makes the Chinese human smuggling organizations flexible and adaptive.

BROKERS IN CRIME

An influential article by Morselli and Roy (2008), who studied automobile theft and exportation businesses (or the ringing operations), found that individuals occupying brokering positions inside criminal networks were most responsible for smoothing or lubricating otherwise disjointed facets of the illicit enterprise—from stealing and pawning the stolen vehicles to arranging for their exportation. The work by Morselli and Roy was informed by Burt (2005), who posited that brokers are advantageous in a competitive environment because of their ability to connect otherwise disjointed partners for business transactions. Brokers occupy a position that separates participants from access to their desired services or goods; as long as the asymmetries of information and access remain, the broker will benefit from this competitive edge (Burt, 1992).

Morselli and Roy (2008) observed similar functions in criminal enterprises because disconnected participants must rely on brokers to complete their transactions. By analyzing both the crime process and social networks,

Morselli and Roy (2008) found that the simple removal of a few brokers would cause major disruptions to the ringing operations and significantly reduce the options for others involved in the enterprise. In other words, the criminal network would simply fall apart without the hinges provided by these brokers. The flexibility often found in illicit enterprises is therefore a product of such brokerage functions.

This study re-examines previously collected data on Chinese human smugglers (also known as snakeheads) and attempts to understand how snakeheads provide flexibility to the illicit enterprise. Recent law enforcement intelligence suggests that Chinese human smuggling into the US is not only alive and well but also remains adaptable to law enforcement efforts. For instance, maritime-based smuggling operations directly to US shores have largely vanished. Instead, Chinese human smugglers are now using Latin American countries to off-load their cargoes. For more than a century, Chinese human smugglers have used the porous borders between the US and Mexico to transport their clients (Chao, 2005; Zhang, 2008), but rarely were they found to mix with local migrants. In a recent case, more than 500 migrants were found in two trailers crossing from Guatemala into Chiapas, Mexico, among whom were scores of Chinese nationals mixed with Guatemalans, Nepalese, and Indians (Corcoran, 2011). While Chinese human smuggling has received much news coverage and some academic attention, the flexibility and adaptability observed among the smuggling organizations are not well understood.

METHOD

The data in this chapter were based on interviews with 129 human smugglers who were directly involved in organizing and transporting Chinese nationals to the US. Interviews were conducted in three primary sites: New York City, Los Angeles, and Fuzhou (China). Purposive sampling was used to recruit participants through personal networks of the project staff. Two types of interviews were conducted in both countries—formal and informal. Formal interviews used an instrument with semi-structured questions. Informal interviews often took place over tea or dinner tables, where formal inquiries were neither feasible nor socially acceptable. Interviewers therefore had to jot down the details immediately after these informal meetings. All interviews were conducted in the subjects' native language.

Several strategies were used to improve the validity and reliability of the data collected in this study. As with all field research involving face-to-face interactions with study participants, the primary goal is to build rapport and trust. Research staff in this study spent a significant amount of time in the field meeting and talking to their social contacts who were in the smuggling business. Moreover, several interviewers hired by the project were themselves at one time illegal immigrants smuggled into the US. As a result, this study was able to reach a much larger smuggler population through their direct connections in the communities.

Internal validity was further strengthened by crosschecking different data sources as well as field observations. All formal interviews were conducted individually with no one else knowing when, where, or whether the conversation would take place. The informal interviews were either conducted spontaneously or scheduled, depending on the availability of the participants, without the knowledge of their referrals. Therefore, it would be all but impossible for study participants to conspire to mislead the interviewers. Although deficient in many aspects, the methods employed in this study were probably the only viable way to gain entrance into the secret world of human smuggling.

SMUGGLERS AND THEIR BROKERING ROLES

Multiple tasks are involved in a smuggling operation. Depending on the complexity of the transportation plan, some smuggling operations involve more specialized tasks than others. The complexity in business arrangements and corresponding tasks often make it difficult to separate snakeheads into meaningful categories. For instance, one respondent in Fuzhou acted as a recruiter, but he also provided transportation for his clients to meet with his partner. When the parties reached an agreement, he collected the down-payments.

At the end of a smuggling operation, he was also responsible for collecting the remaining balance from the relatives in China. Therefore, this snakehead played multiple roles—a recruiter, a payment collector, and a transporter. Although some snakeheads can play multiple roles, others are responsible for only one task, such as procuring travel documents or bribing security personnel at an exit checkpoint. To avoid glossing over crucial details of the many specific tasks snakeheads undertake, respondents in this study were grouped by their primary responsibilities, as shown in Table 6.1.

Table 6.1 Specific roles among Chinese human smugglers (N = 129)

	Frequency	*Percent (rounded)*
Primary Roles in Smuggling Business		
Recruiter	29	22.5
Document vendor	16	12.4
Payment collector	15	11.6
Coordinator	11	8.5
Transporter	8	6.2
Arrange fraudulent business delegation	5	3.9
Secure deposit	5	3.9
Escort	4	3.1
Fraudulent marriage matchmaker	4	3.1
Guard	3	2.3
Arrange travel	2	1.6
Guarantor	2	1.6
Lease boat	2	1.6
Receive clients	2	1.6
Corrupt official	1	0.8
Arrange stowaways	1	0.8
Student visa fraud	1	0.8
Unable to determine	18	14.0
Total	129	100
Role Changes Over Time		
Yes	47	36.6
No	45	34.9
No longer in business	13	10.1
Unable to determine	24	18.6
Total	129	100
Role Complexity		
Single role	83	64.3
Multiple roles	28	21.7
Unable to determine	18	14.0
Total	129	100

The largest three categories were recruiters, document vendors, and payment collectors, and these roles can be further divided into more specific groups of tasks. One cannot assume that all recruiters are the same, as they tend to target different clients and use variant methods of recruitment. Some only approach would-be clients, while others recruit US passport or green card holders in order to procure their legal documents. Still others look only for eligible bachelors willing to enter into fraudulent marriages. For the document vendors, some specialize in preparing documents for business delegations or securing certificates for fraudulent marriages. Others produce paperwork for various student or trainee visa applications or arrange for photo substitutions. Irrespective of their specific tasks, recruiters generally perform either of two functions in the smuggling business—enlisting fee-paying clients or acquiring legal papers that enable clients to travel.

Document vendors also fall into different specializations, depending on their connections and the type of legal papers required for each smuggling operation. Because many government agencies and commercial entities can produce legal documents that facilitate smuggling activities (i.e., passports, birth certificates, marriage licenses, business letters, and financial affidavits), document vendors are of a mixed bunch. Some are only tangentially involved because the value of their documents is limited (such as providing business letters and company descriptions), but others play influential roles in smuggling operations by supplying birth certificates and passports. Then there are counterfeit artists, who either alter authentic legal documents or produce entirely bogus ones. Document vendors command essential positions in the smuggling business and are also the most diverse in their composition.

Payment collectors also fall under different categories. Some collect down-payments when clients sign up with their smugglers, and others collect the remaining fees at the end of an operation. In sum, not all snakeheads engage in identical activities. Most carry out activities determined by the resources at their disposal. The specific players needed for a smuggling operation vary, depending on its complexity and the transportation method. These roles usually play out in successive stages according to the sequence of a smuggling operation.

A Broker-Dominated Business Environment

In the course of the data collection, a common finding quickly emerged. Transactions among snakeheads typically terminate at the next contact point. Snakeheads were found to deal with each other mostly one on one, or on a dyadic basis. This style of transaction becomes the tell-tale sign of a business environment where brokers are playing the dominant role. The question of resource sharing (such as "do you have a backup plan?" or "who is your partner dealing with?") was repeatedly put forth to the respondents; but snakeheads simply looked incredulous—why would anyone give up their advantageous position? As explained in later sections, this practice of one-on-one relationships is dictated by two essential requisites for survival in the business—profit protection and risk management.

It should be noted that this broker-dominant environment does not mean that snakeheads are stuck in one role forever. As they expand their social networks and become established in the smuggling business, their tasks and responsibilities also seem to multiply. Most of the changes appear to evolve from low-level activities like making referrals and recruiting clients to more complex tasks, such as coordinating several partners and making arrangements for transportation and payment guarantee tasks. The gradual accumulation in experiences and social contacts in the smuggling business appear to be the main impetus behind the shift in roles. A

36-year-old snakehead in Lianjian County, who also owned and operated a brick factory, described how his roles in the smuggling business have changed over time:

> At first I was merely looking for would-be clients for other snakeheads. I don't recruit any more. Instead, I gather information in my village or neighboring villages about those villagers who have already obtained US citizenship, and find out if any of them are about to come home for a visit from the US. As soon as they return, I approach them and try to buy their passports. Once I obtain a passport, I inform my recruiters, who will in turn look for a client whose appearance and age will best match those in the passport.

Another indicator of this broker-controlled market is that almost no respondents in this study were working for a "godfather" who dictated their schedule or assignment. Although there were a few "big" snakeheads in this study, none considered themselves the boss. Most respondents would describe others in their network as their friends or business partners. Because of the specialized tasks, there were multiple layers of operatives, each revolving around an inner core—the broker. Because transnational human smuggling involves several stages—recruitment, travel preparation, departure, transit, arrival, and payment collection—each is coordinated by snakeheads supported by additional networks of friends and partners.

A third indicator that Chinese smuggling organizations are dominated by brokers is the snakeheads' self-identity with regard to their group affiliation. As Table 6.2 shows, all respondents claimed to be working within a group of varying size. More than one-third claimed that they worked closely with two to five partners. Another 17% claimed that their core members numbered six or more. Surprisingly, 40% of the respondents did not acknowledge the concept of group in any way; they were simply working with friends or business associates. These respondents truly believed that the casual and sporadic nature of their business activities, and their get-togethers in restaurants or teahouses, were nothing more than routine social activities. These were the same activities that they would have done with their friends anyway, with or without any business prospect. One female snakehead in Fuzhou stated:

> Most of us in this business do not deal with each other like a formal business. When I get together with my friends (other snakeheads), we typically eat out and we take turns to treat one another. When I am with my friends [female snakeheads], we sometimes go to the sauna, take a hot bath, get a massage, and then we play cards or drink tea and chat. It is very relaxing that way. We don't always do business. If we have business, we will take care of it.

MARKET CONSTRAINTS IN A TRANSNATIONAL ENVIRONMENT

Smith (1980) argued that the study of organized crime should focus on the activities (i.e., the enterprise) rather than the group or groups of individuals undertaking the enterprise. Along the same lines, the best way to understand the organizational and operational attributes of Chinese human smuggling is perhaps to examine the nature of the smuggling business and its market environment. Oliver Williamson (1975), in his analysis of entrepreneurships and organizational hierarchies, argued that a business entity takes the structural form most conducive to facilitating optimal exchange relations under existing market conditions. Similarly, transnational human smuggling as an illicit business has its own market conditions, which dictate the organizational as well as operational characteristics of the smuggling organizations. Successful transactions, therefore, require snakeheads to overcome these obstacles in order to reach the eventual profit.

Table 6.2 Characteristics of smuggling organizations

	Frequency*	Percent (rounded)
Number of Core Members		
Denied any group identity	45	40.9
2–3 core members	30	27.3
4–5 core members	18	16.4
6–7 core members	6	5.5
8–10 core members	4	3.6
11–20 core members	3	2.7
More than 20 core members	4	3.6
Total	110	100.0
Decision Makers		
Independent decision	18	16.5
Collective decision	21	19.3
Snakehead in charge	50	45.9
Follow boss instruction	10	9.2
Depends on contribution/ability	3	2.8
No idea	7	6.4
Total	109	100.0
Clarity in Division of Labor		
Clear division of labor	76	72.4
Somewhat clear division of labor	5	4.8
Unclear division of labor	14	13.3
Difficult to describe	2	1.9
No idea	8	7.6
Total	105	100.0
Collaboration with Other Smuggling Groups		
Yes	30	28.8
No	74	71.2
Total	104	100.0
Partners		
Stable partners	70	63.6
Unstable partners	40	36.4
Total	110	100.0

Note
* Effective sample size. Refusals and non-responses were excluded.

Law Enforcement Interference

Fear of law enforcement crackdowns is pervasive among all snakeheads, both in China and in the US. For instance, the US Congress passed the Violent Crime Control and Law Enforcement Act of 1994, which stipulates that illegal migrant smuggling faces a possible imprisonment term of 10 years (and/or fines), and the penalty is increased to 20 years per illegal immigrant if bodily injury occurs or life is placed in jeopardy in connection with the smuggling offense (US Commission on Immigration Reform, 1994: 48). To raise the financial stakes further, the US Senate in 1995 allowed law enforcement agencies to use the tools authorized under the RICO (Racketeering-Influenced and Corrupt Organizations) legislation to combat human smuggling.[1] The RICO legislation has for decades been reserved for fighting the most notorious organized crime groups in cities such as New York and Chicago. As a result, smugglers strive to keep their transactions clandestine, thus restricting most activities to those of immediate social networks.

Limited Clientele

Human smuggling as a business offers poor prospects for growth because of its limited clientele. Although this assertion appears counterintuitive because one expects that millions in China would be eager to come to America, the reality is that only a handful may be considered worthy of being smuggled. A prospective client must have the financial wherewithal to even begin looking for a snakehead. Snakeheads have also developed elaborate procedures to verify whether prospective clients can pay. The most common way to prove one's financial means is to provide evidence that one has family members or close relatives in America with enough savings. Otherwise, a prospective client must find a relative or friend of significant social standing in the community to convince the snakehead that enough money can be raised from friends and relatives.

Financial screening is only one aspect of this unstable business. A snakehead must first identify "worthy" clients, a different task, because there are no open markets for smugglers and would-be migrants to meet one another. As a result, most illegal Chinese immigrants come from a limited number of regions in China. The fact that Chinese human smuggling activities are not widespread phenomena in China is in line with existing literature on international migration. As Massey, Durand, and Malone (2002: 143) point out, wage differentials do not necessarily cause international migration and the poorest countries "do not yield significant migration streams, even in the absence of formal barriers." International migration relies on the infrastructure that is often built through kinship networks and friendship. A relative or a member from the same home village becomes a contact as well as a source of social capital for others to migrate. The volume of the migration is limited to the capacity of the existing social networks already overseas. For instance, Chin and Kelly (1997) found, in their survey of illegal Chinese immigrants in New York City, that almost 90% of the respondents were from regions within 50 kilometers of Fuzhou, the capital city of Fujian province. The clandestine nature of the business, the need to screen prospective clients, and the small regions where eligible clients may be found combine to restrict the scope of the smuggling business and service territories.

Operational Complexity

The movement of undocumented immigrants across borders faces many logistical challenges. To launch an operation, snakeheads must plan their trips, acquire proper documents, and coordinate schedules with partners at transit points. This process does not take into account possible interferences by law enforcement activities, which often disrupt or delay smuggling activities. Although most would-be migrants would prefer direct flights to the United States (typically through the use of identity substitution), this smuggling method is rarely available and finding snakeheads capable of arranging such trips is difficult. Chin and Kelly (1997), after interviewing 300 smuggled Chinese immigrants in New York, found that only seven flew directly from China to America. The rest had to go through multiple and often treacherous transits.

One of the few findings that news media accounts, government reports, and academic studies all seem to agree on is that snakeheads use elaborate transportation routes to exploit international border control inadequacies and avoid detection. These routes extend around the world, often involving ethnic Chinese enclaves in various nations that provide shelter, cultural and culinary comfort, and technical know-how to facilitate the movement of their countrymen to their destination. Ethnic enclaves overseas provide the most important infrastructure required to sustain international migration, legal or illegal (Massey & Zenteno, 1999).

Operational Hazards

Inherent in all cross-border smuggling activities is the danger of accidents and mishaps. Although all snakeheads strive to safeguard their "cargoes," the clandestine nature of the business almost makes accidents unavoidable. In 1999, 58 illegal Chinese immigrants, all from Fujian Province, were found asphyxiated to death inside a refrigerator truck in Dover, England; the shipment was traced back to the Netherlands and Belgium (Woods, 2000). McCarthy (2000) reported that, when illegal immigrants fell ill and died during a long sea journey to the United States, their bodies were simply pushed off board. Stories like these appear from time to time in the news, although they most likely represent a small number of actual accidents. During this study, there have been many stories about people whose whereabouts remain unknown after having left the villages years ago. A smuggler in China told this story:

A guy from my village crossed the border into Vietnam with the help of a snakehead and stayed there for weeks, waiting to start the next leg of the journey. The group he was traveling with walked for many days in thick wooded areas. Many of them fell ill, throwing up and having fevers. One man in the group later died, supposedly bitten to death by a swarm of mosquitoes in the jungle. People back at home couldn't believe what they heard. Have you ever heard of anyone being eaten alive by mosquitoes?

Small but non-fatal incidents happen even more frequently. A simple glitch (e.g., failing to pick up clients at a pre-arranged location, or staff changes at a border checkpoint) can cause the entire operation to fall apart. For instance, in August 1999, 82 Chinese nationals were taken into custody by Mexican authorities in Ensenada, Baja California after the police found them wandering near a highway (Lau & Dibble, 1999). The group had arrived by boat five days earlier but the local collaborator failed to show up. After four days without food, these immigrants had to leave their hideout and venture out on their own.

Sporadic Smuggling Opportunities

Human smuggling is a business of opportunities. Eligible clients are not always available, even when a snakehead has the proper contacts to launch a smuggling operation. The snakehead needs to verify the financial wherewithal of prospective clients. Preparations such as acquiring travel documents and notifying transit coordinators all take time. Long waiting periods exist between operations, thus making the business protracted in operation as well as unpredictable in outcome. Such an unstable business environment helps explain why most of the respondents in this study had other jobs or ran other businesses. It also explains why most smuggling organizations are nothing more than temporary alliances oriented toward one operation at a time, and snakeheads usually focus on carrying out one operation or one set of related tasks at a time.

RISK MANAGEMENT AND STRUCTURAL VULNERABILITY

As described earlier, transnational human smuggling is replete with uncertainties and risks. Chin (1999: 33) once quoted a snakehead who characterized Chinese smuggling process as a dragon: "although it's a lengthy creature, various organic parts (of the body) are tightly linked." If any joint of this lengthy creature becomes disconnected, the entire operation will be paralyzed, stranding clients in transit countries. Therefore, it is important to understand how snakeheads manage the risks and protect their profits.

A criminal organization, whether composed of complex command structures or simple peer groups, must reduce uncertainties and risk-bearing factors in the marketplace in order to achieve successful transactions. Accordingly, snakeheads almost always choose to interact with their partners on a one-on-one basis and share as little information as possible about their smuggling resources. This is for insurance purposes, because such arrangements guarantee a buffer for unanticipated events and provide contingency plans during a smuggling operation. One recruitment coordinator in China, who specialized in sea-based smuggling operations, explained how he managed the risk of detection by law enforcement agencies:

> What I am most afraid of are two things—one, when some of my clients change their minds and don't want to go anymore, in which case they can expose my action plan; and two, probably the worst, there might be informants among my clients working for the border patrol police. Therefore I never tell my clients in advance when they will leave or where to meet. I always make last-minute announcements to get them to the gathering location, and I do not allow them to contact anyone, not even their families. I usually give out only my pager numbers and use payphones to give instructions.

Because of the illicit nature of the business, the absence of formal legal protection, and the fear of law enforcement activities, people involved in the smuggling business must stay inconspicuous and seek as little attention as possible. Risk management becomes the defining factor in their group structure and operational style. It begins at the very front of an operation (i.e., client recruitment and screening) and continues until the very end, when the smuggling fees are collected. Once an opportunity arises, risk management by all snakeheads participating in the operation becomes the focal point in every stage of the smuggling process. To a great extent, this mediates not only the organizational structure but also individual behavior within the organization. Snakeheads use several protective strategies for risk management purposes.

Protective Strategies

Snakeheads have developed strategies to increase safety and reduce uncertainties inherent in the business. These include ethnic exclusivity (i.e., hometown dialects, ancestral linage, and familial relationships), one-on-one business relations, underground banking, frequent change of cell phone and pager numbers, and spontaneous meeting locations. Many of these strategies are innovative as well as unique.

An example is the way large sums of money are exchanged. In addition to direct cash transactions, which remain the predominant payment method in the smuggling business, there are two common methods involving legitimate entities to handle payment issues. Both methods reportedly have emerged in response to occasional fraud or fraudulent representation in the smuggling business—a con-artist may portray himself as a snakehead and request a down-payment from his or her clients, then disappear. In one method, to ensure service provision and payment receipt, the client and the snakehead will go to a bank to open a joint account requiring both signatures to withdraw money. When the smuggling operation is completed or the agreed-upon tasks fulfilled, both parties return to the bank to settle the payment. In the second method, the client (usually a relative of the smuggled client) opens a bank account and deposits the agreed-upon sum of money, then gives the passbook—but not the password—to the snakehead. Without the password, the snakehead cannot make a withdrawal, but neither can the client without the passbook. When the smuggling operation is completed, the client will supply the password to the snakehead, who can then withdraw the money. Because of the expanding economy in China, such financial transactions rarely arouse suspicion from the authorities.

Furthermore, because most smuggling operations take months, if not years (e.g., fraudulent marriages) to complete, these bank deposits are usually long term and hence even less visible to any official scrutiny.

Despite huge profit potential, most subjects in this study remained extremely cautious and conservative in their business approach. Many seemed to have developed certain profiles to scrutinize prospective clients; others preferred a particular style in carrying out smuggling activities. As one smuggler in Fuzhou described:

> I only do a small-scale smuggling business because I am not greedy. Some people, after they've succeeded in a few cases, become so carried away that they drastically increase the number of clients in subsequent operations. That's how they get into trouble. These aggressive snakeheads are mostly young guys. I am more conservative. I don't get involved if I am not 100% sure, nor do I do business with strangers. That's why I've been able to stay in this business for such a long time.

Secrecy in this business is an absolute necessity. The snakeheads in this study mostly used mobile phones and pagers to communicate with their clients and partners. Some snakeheads even avoided dealing with clients in the townships where they lived. They would arrange to meet in a public place first, such as a restaurant or hotel lobby, and then proceed to a mutually comfortable location to discuss details. Since there are no venues for public announcement or open advertising in this business, snakeheads' networking and self-promotion takes place only under circumstances in which trust can be easily built—among members of a family clan or people from the same village. Secrecy is also ensured when snakeheads deal only with their partners or clients on a one-on-one basis, for self-protection and to avoid being cut out of a deal. As one document vendor in Fuzhou described an interaction with his higher-up partner:

> Whenever I want to see my "big brother," I always call his cell phone. He never tells me where he is except right before he wants to meet me. He calls me and tells me where to meet him and at what time. When I deliver my documents (photo-substituted passports) to him, he usually drops them into his briefcase where I often see dozens of other different passports bundled together. There have been a few times when I asked about his other contacts, and he would snap at me, "Why are you asking? It is none of your business." In this business, as long as you can provide the service as promised, no one will ask about how things come about.

Such one-on-one interactions, although conducive to protecting individual smugglers, also seem to make the smuggling organization vulnerable to structural disturbances. Few snakeheads know anyone above or below their direct contacts. Smuggling networks generally consist of a tight inner circle that few are able to infiltrate. Smugglers who are well known in one village are usually strangers in neighboring townships. They operate mostly within their own circles of contacts and seldom know what other snakeheads are doing. One's reputation as a snakehead typically goes only as far as his or her social networks.

Another defensive measure for snakeheads and their operatives is to temporarily suspend all activities, a typical response to crackdowns by Chinese or US authorities on human smuggling activities. It reduces their visibility in the community and deflects attention from their social networks. For example, soon after the Dover incident, a massive manhunt was launched in China to catch those responsible for the smuggling operation. The word of the crackdown immediately spread to the smuggling communities and sent most, if not all, snakeheads into hiding. Almost all of the community contacts in this study in China as well as in the United States disappeared. Attempts to reach these people went nowhere. Their cell phones were canceled and pagers turned off. Previously scheduled interviews and meetings were canceled without notice. The impact was also evident on many would-be migrants who were in the middle of their smuggling preparation, as one such client in Fuzhou complained:

> I am really disappointed after [name of a snakehead] told me today what has happened in Dover, England. I mean my plan to go to the US is in limbo now. I have called my snakehead several times today and I have not been able to get through to him. His wife answered the phone when I called his home and she said: "I am not his wife. The family has already moved and I've just moved in. I don't know where they are." I knew that it was his wife, but she would not acknowledge it. I tried his mobile phone but it's been turned off. You see, he has my passport, but I can't find him.

Finally, being a member of a unique cultural group provides one of the best assurances and protection for people as to who can be trusted within an illicit business (Smith, 1980), although some scholars question the notion of ethnic ties as a key component of organized crime (Potter, 1994). In the context of Chinese human smuggling, having a common ancestral linage or hometown carries considerable influence among snakeheads in determining whose clients are trustworthy. Speaking the same dialect and knowing each other's social circles can greatly strengthen the expectations of mutual interest in and commitment to the illicit activities. It is also the best way to prevent the infiltration of outsiders.

The Cartwheel and Circle of Social Networks

The market conditions described above illustrate the kind of challenges and obstacles snakeheads must overcome to complete their transactions. Human smuggling operations are mostly task-oriented, which helps those involved focus their energy and resources on their immediate jobs. In accordance with Williamson's analysis of peer groups in economic activities (1975), human smuggling operations can be perceived as exchanges among peers. Activities among these peers require minimal organizational structure and a limited hierarchy. However, unlike peer groups in legal and normal economic activities, members of a smuggling organization rarely engage in teamwork (i.e., collective engagement in similar tasks and resource sharing). Their relations with each other are usually secretive and involve dyadic transactions. Each individual snakehead develops and maintains additional contacts and resources that are also clandestine in nature and dyadic in format. Figure 6.1 illustrates the *dyadic cartwheel network perspective* on the multi-levels of one-on-one relationships characteristic of Chinese human smuggling organizations.

Such an organizational structure, containing members of one's close social network and oriented toward specific tasks, appears to have many advantages. First of all, in a business environment in which contractual relationships consist of mere spoken agreements (and are thus without formal legal protection), interactions within a small group of one's friends and relatives serve to increase shared understanding of the tasks that need to be completed. Two parties must reach an agreement that spells out service and financial requirements or the dyadic transaction will not occur. The dyadic cartwheel network effectively minimizes interpersonal tension and increases personal accountability. A favorable trading atmosphere, therefore, is easy to achieve and maintain because only individuals who can perform and deliver agreed-upon services can join and stay in the network. Those who cannot perform will be excluded because there will not any meaningful roles for them to play. Shared expectations are easily promoted in these small groups. The resultant mutual understanding reduces uncertainty, increases collective commitment, and produces smooth transactions.

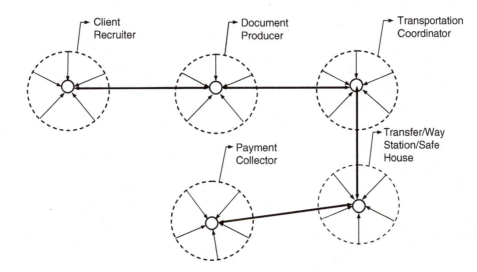

Figure 6.1 The cartwheel network—the Chinese human smuggling process

This is particularly true when the core members of a smuggling organization speak the same dialect and grew up in the same ancestral township.

Second, small group interactions expedite information gathering and forwarding, improve communication, and facilitate decision making, particularly when most transactions take place on a dyadic basis—i.e., through brokers. The one-on-one transactions common to most smuggling operations, by definition, prevent any large complex organizations from emerging.

Because of their deliberate efforts to evade law enforcement activities, snakeheads often plan complex transportation routes and rendezvous points. Completion of each stage of a smuggling operation relies solely on successfully getting through the previous stage. Small-group interactions can therefore reduce sequential complexity in smuggling operations. Each cluster of individuals (or task force) focuses on completing one phase or one set of tasks, such as obtaining fraudulent documents, arranging transportation, or securing cooperation from corrupt officials at border checkpoints. Timely adaptation in decision making is therefore possible when

there are only a small number of brokers involved in a limited number of tasks. Maximum efficiency is possible with a minimal number of players because any transaction or exchange occurs over the shortest distance—between two individuals.

Third, the dyadic cartwheel network can achieve maximum security with minimal exposure to law enforcement personnel or other operational hazards. Because of the restricted flow of information and limited contact with other members along the smuggling chain, individuals or clusters of individuals in a smuggling ring are insulated from one another. When one snakehead is arrested or one stage falls apart, the remaining members of the smuggling group will not likely face any imminent danger.

Additionally, the dyadic cartwheel network increases transactional security against unscrupulous snakeheads. When any pair of snakeheads engages in a transaction, one expresses what service she needs and the other indicates whether he and only he can supply the service. Even if he cannot provide the requested service himself, the information about where the needed service can be obtained is deliberately withheld. Instead, the broker will find and acquire the needed service from someone else. Services or goods vital to smuggling activities are exclusively held and carefully guarded by these brokers. As long as the asymmetries of information and access are maintained by the brokers, both safety and profit can be maximized.

Structural Venerability and Need for Additional Conceptual Clarification

As described earlier, the success of a human smuggling operation relies on the success of each and every stage along the process. The dyadic cartwheel network is made up of snakehead brokers with their own networks and resources. There is minimal redundancy, and one-on-one transactions ensure maximum profits for all parties involved. Because of the illicit nature of the business, there are few opportunities to shop around, although over time a snakehead may expand his or her network of resources. Protection of one's profit therefore relies solely on one's ability to keep his or her resources inaccessible to others. However, such a business arrangement is highly vulnerable to external threats and structural disturbances. The many stories on failed operations uncovered in this study and reported in the news were mostly due to a failed linkage in this dragon-like smuggling process. An entire operation collapses if one broker fails to deliver the needed service.

One must then ask what about the flexibility and adaptability touted earlier. Brokers seem only able to facilitate business transactions among those of their own social networks. Therefore, any flexibility observed is restricted to specific networks. If the cartwheel network holds any truth, smuggling organizations are not flexible as individuals but highly vulnerable.

Perhaps one may argue that the survival of human smuggling as a business in general does not hinge upon the success of any specific organization, but rather on the collective entrepreneurial efforts of the many groups of individuals involved. In circumstances where contingent transactions are the norm and sequential operations are unpredictable and vulnerable to disruption, small groups as a whole are capable of expanding and contracting in response to market demands. Small groups of entrepreneurs (as opposed to any specific smuggling organization) can emerge to take advantage of new opportunities and adjust to different client demands and transportation strategies. Most snakeheads operate other legitimate or illicit businesses and only gather for a viable opportunity. After the smuggling operation is complete, the group of snakeheads will disband or remain social friends and go about their daily business as usual. Therefore, small exchange relations (with minimal organizational structure and simple hierarchies) can withstand the few opportunities in an uncertain market.

CONCLUSION

Chinese human smuggling organizations are made up of peer-group entrepreneurs. However, unlike peer groups in legitimate businesses, smugglers rarely engage in teamwork (i.e., collective engagement in similar tasks or resource sharing); their relations with each other involve mostly one-on-one (i.e., dyadic) transactions. Each human smuggler has additional circles of contacts and resources that are also clandestine in nature and dyadic in format. Many specialized roles have emerged in response to specific tasks in smuggling operations, such as those who acquire fraudulent documents, recruit prospective migrants, serve as border crossing guides, drive smuggling vehicles, and guard safe houses. Some smuggling operations involve more specialized tasks than others. These roles are usually played out in successive stages following the sequence of a smuggling operation, with the recruiter working in the front and the debt collector coming at the end. In re-analyzing the data previously collected from interviews with Chinese human smugglers, this chapter confirms the findings of Morselli and Roy (2008) that brokers are vital in connecting otherwise disjointed players in the criminal enterprise. The removal of any broker at any stage can lead to the collapse of an entire smuggling operation.

This chapter, however, attempts to expand the work by Morselli and Roy and argues that, as far as Chinese human smuggling is concerned, the snakehead networks are neither flexible nor adaptable in and of themselves in response to external threats and socio-legal obstacles inherent in the marketplace. In fact, smuggling organizations are precariously assembled by brokers who happen to have the right connections at the right time.

Since dyadic relationships prevent resource sharing, a smuggling operation can only be carried out by individuals who fulfill specific roles. Their secrecy and self-preservation thus make individual smuggling rings vulnerable to changes in external conditions. Because transnational human smuggling takes place over vast distances and through mostly one-on-one transactions, the loss of a key player or any mishap during any of the stages will severely weaken or even cause the demise of the entire smuggling group. Unlike legitimate businesses where aspiring corporate businessmen may compete to occupy brokering positions, how snakeheads take up brokering positions is often a product of fortuitous circumstances and of their social resources. Also unlike legitimate businesses, where positions can be advertised and services procured through open channels, snakeheads within an organization cannot be replaced easily and the resources unique to specific smuggling tasks cannot be swapped or substituted.

However, small exchange relationships such as those of human smugglers depend on brokers' ability to link one another, and consequently the interests of all parties are realized. Although individual smuggling groups may lack the ability to respond to structural disruptions, their temporary alliances and dyadic interactions ensure that the enterprise as a whole can respond collectively and effectively to uncertain market conditions, reduce exposure to law enforcement activities, and offer favorable financial terms for individual snakeheads. The flexibility of the smuggling enterprise therefore does not necessarily reside within any given snakehead network, but rather in the entrepreneurial environment in general. The demand for these underground travel services continues to flourish in contemporary China. As a result, groups of entrepreneurs will rise to take advantage of it. Some of them will take up brokerage positions because of their positions in their social networks. Multiple cartwheel networks will then fill in the positions vacated by other collapsed networks. The business as a whole thus evolves and adapts.

From a law enforcement perspective, the implication of understanding the brokerage functions in human smuggling is clear. It is perhaps more effective to target these brokers than any prolonged investigations aimed at capturing a few major smuggling kingpins. Knowing the weaknesses of their structural arrangement, law enforcement efforts can therefore have an immediate and pronounced impact.

NOTE

1. The Senate bill (S.754—104th Congress) was introduced by Edward Kennedy, D-Mass., on May 3, 1995 and sought to amend the Immigration and Nationality Act to more effectively control US land borders, prevent the employment of illegal aliens, expedite the removal of illegal aliens, provide wiretap and asset forfeiture authority to combat alien smuggling and related crimes, and increase penalties for human smuggling activities.

REFERENCES

Burt, Ronald S. (1992). *Structural Holes: The Social Structure of Competition*. Cambridge, MA: Harvard University Press.

Burt, Ronald S. (2005). *Brokerage and Closure: An Introduction to Social Capital*. Oxford, UK: Oxford University Press.

Chao, Romero R. (2005). Transnational Chinese immigrant smuggling to the United States via Mexico and Cuba, 1882–1916. *Amerasia Journal* 30(3), 1–16.

Chin, Ko-lin (1999). *Smuggled Chinese: Clandestine Immigration to the United States*. Philadelphia: Temple University Press.

Chin, Ko-lin & Robert Kelly (1997). *Human Snakes: Illegal Chinese Immigrants in the United States*. Final Report, Grant SBR 93-11114, Law and Social Science Program, National Science Foundation.

Corcoran, Katherine (2011). Truckloads of migrants a billion-dollar business. *San Diego Union Tribune*, May 20, A8.

Landolt, Patricia & Wei Wei Da (2005). The spatially ruptured practices of migrant families: A comparison of immigrants from El Salvador and the People's Republic of China. *Current Sociology* 53, 625–653.

Lau, Angela & Sandra Dibble (1999). Illegal Chinese immigrants found in Baja—At least 82 have been detained. *San Diego Union Tribune*, August 25, A3.

Massey, Douglas S. & Rene Zenteno (1999). The dynamics of mass migration. *Proceedings of the National Academy of Sciences* 96(8), 5328–5335.

Massey, Douglas S., Jorge Durand, & Nolan J. Malone (2002). *Beyond Smoke and Mirrors: Mexican Immigration in an Era of Economic Integration*. New York: Russell Sage Foundation.

McCarthy, Terry (2000). Coming to America. *Time*, May 1, 42–45.

Morselli, Carlo & Julie Roy (2008). Brokerage qualifications in ringing operations. *Criminology* 46(1), 71–98.

Potter, Gary W. (1994). *Criminal Organizations: Vice, Racketeering, and Politics in an American City*. Prospect Heights, IL: Waveland.

Smith, Dwight C. (1980). Paragons, pariahs and pirates: A spectrum-based theory of enterprise. *Crime and Delinquency* 26(3), 358–386.

US Commission on Immigration Reform (1994). *U.S. Immigration Policy: A Report to Congress*. Washington, DC: US Government Printing Office.

Williamson, Oliver E. (1975). *Markets and Hierarchies: Analysis and Antitrust Implications*. New York: Free Press.

Woods, Audrey (2000). Deaths of 58 smuggling victims prompt major British inquiry. *San Diego Union Tribune*, June 20, A8.

Zhang, Sheldon X. (2007). *Smuggling and Trafficking in Human Beings: All Roads Lead to America*. Westport, CT: Praeger/Greenwood.

Zhang, Sheldon X. (2008). *Chinese Human Smuggling Organizations—Families, Social Networks, and Cultural Imperatives*. Palo Alto, CA: Stanford University Press.

Zhang, Sheldon & Ko-lin Chin (2002). Enter the dragon: Inside Chinese human smuggling organizations. *Criminology* 40, 737–768.

CHAPTER 7

Illegal Networks or Criminal Organizations

Structure, Power, and Facilitators in Cocaine Trafficking Structures

Andrea Giménez-Salinas Framis

The study of adult group offending has become a priority in criminological literature due to the reduced number of empirical studies carried out to understand this kind of deviance. Even if young co-offending has traditionally been one of the main topics in criminology, the core of adult criminal groups and their characteristics is an essential topic that has become more popular over the last few years. Even with the efforts of recent years, many questions remain partially unanswered. How do the offenders organize themselves? How are the roles distributed within the groups? What are the main structures in the most common illegal markets? How do organizations respond to disruption?

A considerable body of knowledge has examined drug dealing, especially from an ethnographic perspective (Adler, 1985, 1992; Reuter & Haaga, 1989; Dorn, Murji, & South, 1992; Natarajan & Belanger, 1998). These studies try to understand the subjects involved in different illegal markets, how they protect themselves, the roles they play, or their social organization. Regarding the organizations or networks involved in drug smuggling, we can distinguish among importers (high level) (Reuter, 1985; Reuter & Haaga, 1989), wholesale suppliers (mid-level), and retailers (lower level or street-level dealers) (Adler, 1985).

Few studies have been conducted on mid-level dealing to seek answers to the above questions. Nevertheless, existing evidence supports the notion that upper- and mid-level drug trafficking is not controlled by hierarchical transnational organized crime groups but by loose networks and small networks. Then again, the business is highly fragmented, consisting of a large number of entrepreneurial groups separately engaged in exploiting the lucrative opportunities presented by drug demand and whose relations patterns are based more on collaboration than competition (Pearson & Hobbs, 2001, 2003; Reuter, 2004; Natarajan, 2006).

This chapter presents the results of a study of four mid-level criminal organized groups operating in the Spanish cocaine market. The organized crime groups analyzed can be classified as mid-level (wholesale supplier) groups involved in large-scale cocaine distribution. Two are family-based groups with a more traditional structure and the other two have an ethnic element; illegal business being the common ground. The groups were investigated by the police (Guardia Civil[1]) between 2007 and 2009. The aim of the research was to compare the information provided by the police investigation with the information under social network analysis for the four groups, in order to reveal differences and similarities among the organized structures. To this end, three main areas have been analyzed: a) the structure of the mid-level groups; b) the key players and their roles; and c) the legal facilitators in the network.

CRIMINAL ORGANIZATIONS AND ILLEGAL NETWORKS

The core of criminal organizations is a new hot topic in criminological literature studying group offending. Decades ago, criminal organizations were mainly analyzed through the *corporate* model based on Weberian postulates (Cressey, 1972). This model tackles criminal organizations from several formal traits: centralized and organized hierarchy, clear division of work, assignment of functions on the basis of personal ability, and formal internal rules. In the following decade, some authors highlighted the inaccuracy of the model on the basis of the existing variety of organizations and the incorporation of changes and new trends in criminal organizations due to globalization and state scrutiny (Williams, 2001). In recent years, the study of organizations has taken a step forward with social network analysis (SNA). This method constitutes an alternative way of exploring criminal organizations by studying the social relationships within a network. SNA focuses on the nodes (subject, groups, etc.) or units in a network and the relationships between them, providing a more in-depth and contemporary understanding of patterns and characteristics of organized social groups (McIllwain, 1999; Morselli, 2009).

This chapter considers SNA as a complementary, not an exclusive, method of analyzing criminal organization. The *bureaucratic* model is a limited method to currently explain criminal networks operating in

European countries. Network representation is a more accurate method of explaining criminal enterprises operating in an interrelated world where relationships between them are more cooperative than competitive (Paoli, 2002). Both methods are still used and embrace different ways of applying the network concept. The first approach conceives the network as a form of organization in the midst of an organizational continuum from more hierarchical and complex organizations to a more horizontal and loosely connected group (networks) (Von Lampe, 2008). According to the second approach, the network transcends all forms of organization (Morselli, 2009).

This chapter will adopt the first approach, considering criminal organizations and illegal networks as different forms of organized crime groups. In this regard, if we examine the definitions of network organizations in contrast to those of criminal organizations under traditional approaches, we find the features outlined in Table 7.1.

In addition, many authors believe that organizations with an alternative rationale such as the network approach are resistant to identification and detection as a result of their structural advantages in relation to hierarchical and structured organizations (Zhang & Chin, 2003; Zaitch, 2002; Williams, 2001). Some of these advantages include: number of members, minor vertical bureaucratic structure, adaptability to circumstances and external threats (Benson & Decker, 2010), loose

Table 7.1 **Features of criminal organizations versus illegal networks**

Criminal organizations	Illegal networks
Hierarchical structure	Horizontal structure
Division of labor, specialization	Interchangeable operational roles
Promotional systems and recruitment procedures (merit or competency oriented)	Recruitment and placement based on the nature of the activity: prior working relationships, kinship/ethnicity, short-term assignments, contacts, etc. (Donald & Wilson, 2000; Schiray, 2001; Zaitch, 2002)
Formal and secret rules	Flexible and non-stable rules
Vulnerable structures	Resilient structures
Formal communication	Direct communication

connections between members, and reduced visibility (Reuter, 1985).

Internal Organization of Drug Smuggling

A considerable body of knowledge, especially ethnographic studies regarding drug dealing in lower levels, has revealed that groups involved in this activity are not criminal organizations as such. The kinds of subjects involved, their roles and methods to avoid prosecution and detection, the methods of corruption used and profits made are not features common to highly structured and organized criminal groups. Moreover, low-level drug smugglers are usually tightly bonded groups, with embedded ties based on kinship, territory, and other non-negotiable qualities where trust guarantees commitment beyond self-interest (Gambetta, 1988).

Several studies support these results in the earlier stages of the drug distribution process (mid- or upper-level dealing) (Adler, 1985, 1992; Reuter & Haaga, 1989; Dorn et al., 1992; Natarajan & Belanger, 1998; Desroches, 1999; Natarajan, 2000), although they provide little evidence of vertical hierarchies in drug smuggling. Other studies have identified not two (structured and poorly structured) but four main types of organization: corporations, communal businesses, family businesses, and freelance (Natarajan & Belanger, 1998).

Summarizing the results of the studies concerning the earlier stages (mid- and high-level dealing), they provide evidence of the following: a) illegal drug markets are not managed by large and very structured criminal syndicates but by small groups or loosely linked entrepreneurs (Natarajan & Belanger, 1998; Benson & Decker, 2010; Zaitch, 2002); b) members are involved in illegal markets because of opportunities and family or ethnic ties (Morselli, 2005; Kleemans & Van de Bunt, 1999); c) they have a flexible division of labor where operational roles in the organized crime groups are interchangeable and many of them can carry out multiple tasks; and d) mid-level brokers or wholesale suppliers play a significant role between importers and retailers. These brokers carry out their activities using their contacts.

With this evidence in mind, the following part of the chapter will describe the results of the analysis of four mid-level groups in the cocaine market in Spain. An insight into these groups will enable us to better understand whether they respond to the concept of criminal organization, well assimilated by police investigators, or whether they fit better into an illegal network profile. Through SNA, we will discern whether the network perspective supports the conclusions of the police investigations.

SOURCES AND RESEARCH DESIGN

This study analyzes data obtained from police files relating to four operations investigating criminal groups involved in cocaine trafficking, mainly in Madrid (Spain). The information gathered by the police for each group was collected from the records of the different police criminal investigations. The four operations are summarized below:

- Operation MAM (N = 58). The investigation started in 2006 when some Colombian citizens were detected introducing 50 kg of cocaine to be adulterated and distributed in Madrid (Spain). Ultimately, the group was involved in smuggling cocaine from Colombia through Brazil and Uruguay to be distributed in Madrid (Spain). This case involved a typical Spanish mid-level (wholesaler) cocaine group acting between a South American importer group and local retailers dealing in Madrid.
- Operation JUAN (N = 69). In 2009, the police detected a group smuggling cocaine from Mexico to Madrid. As the headquarters were in Mexico, the group was in charge of transporting the cocaine

to Spain for an estimated EUR 60 million according to the investigation. In this case, the group operated in close cooperation with another organization that would launder the proceeds of the drug distribution by this and other groups.

- Operation JADE (N = 62). In 2008, the group investigated was operating as a wholesale supplier and retail distributor of cocaine and heroin in a large distribution area in Madrid (Spain), where gypsy clans traditionally carry out similar activities. The group was in charge of acquiring, manipulating, and selling the drugs in the gypsy quarter.
- Operation ACER (N = 23). This investigation started in 2007 and involved a small family-based group. They distributed cocaine in Madrid (Spain) that was provided to them by other groups based in a northwest region of Spain, one of the most active areas in the country when it comes to the provision of cocaine from the countries of origin. This group even incorporated companies to invest and launder the proceeds of the unlawful activities: mainly real estate companies.

This research is based on both qualitative and quantitative information obtained using the following data-gathering instruments: a spreadsheet to gather information from investigation files (wiretappings, observations, searches, police reports, etc.) was designed with 74 variables regarding the following aspects—features of the organized group, illegal business undertaken, instrumental activities conducted, and profile of the members of the group. In addition, wiretappings were coded to identify the phone contacts and meetings detected and recorded during the investigation. Those sources of information were necessary to conduct SNA using UCINET software. The contacts and meetings between members have been analyzed using the one-mode network created in UCINET 6.

RESULTS

General Structure of the Criminal Groups

The analysis of the structure of an organized crime group is a complex task given the variety of qualitative and quantitative measures used by the researchers for this purpose (Natarajan, 2000). Nevertheless, SNA has additional values to assess the structure of the organizations in comparison to more hierarchical perspectives emphasizing an internal structure based on roles and positions. SNA gives weight to the existing relations among members, helping with the identification of some network structural characteristics and the most relevant members according to their contacts within the network.

As mentioned, one of the goals of the research was to understand the structure of the four organizations. In this regard, the structure has been analyzed to test the information provided by the police according to the investigation files. To this end, we compare the information of the structure provided by the investigation with that of SNA, using a matrix of contacts gathered from four networks. SNA has been used to identify the following aspects: centralization, density, and core/periphery.

- Network *centralization* provides information about the network structure, measuring the centrality of all nodes. A centralized network is dominated by one or several central nodes.
- *Density* is a measure of network cohesion and gives us the proportion of possible lines actually present in the graph.
- The *core periphery* model estimates the degree of coreness or closeness to the core of each player. It finds two classes of nodes—namely, a cohesive subgraph (the core) in which players are connected to each other in some maximal sense, and a class of player that is loosely connected to the cohesive subgraph by a lack of maximal cohesion with the core

(Borgatti & Everett, 1999: 377). Players in the core can coordinate their actions; those in the periphery cannot.

Finally, the key players and role distribution within the organized groups have been analyzed to compare police information results. We conducted SNA to identify the key members by means of centrality and betweenness measures. Degree centrality is based on the number of direct ties between one player and other players in the network and enables the identification of the central positions in the network (those members with most contacts). Conversely, betweenness highlights the importance of the intermediary position of players in a network (Sparrow, 1991).[2] This position is also a sign of power that is typical of a type of player acting as a key broker within the network. Moreover, analyzing the internal positions[3] enables us to compare the SNA measures with the police perception of key members and positions.

Operation MAM

Network Structure

According to the police files, the structure of the MAM group was threefold: the importer of cocaine from Colombia through Uruguay; the Spanish group (wholesale supplier) in charge of transporting, adulterating, and storing the drug; and the retailer group in charge of distributing the cocaine in Madrid (Spain). The police investigation concluded that the group had a hierarchical and complex structure and considered this to be an indicator of dangerousness.[4] Nevertheless, when using SNA with non-valued networks, we found that the measures provided did not lead to similar results. According to SNA measures, the entire network has a centralization of 22.5% and a density of 0.2%. Network density is very low in comparison with the densities provided by other similar networks (Ciel Network; Morselli,

2009). Finally, if we calculate the network's core, the result is 9 members (PCCP, JPPM, SNRM, HAMS, YPMG, CPGT, JDD, JJTE, and FR) out of 58, which means that 15% of the members have a strong relationship within the general structure. This description does not support the police structure; no such centralization is found, the network has a low density, and the network's core has a small pull of members sharing close relationship patterns, the rest of the members remaining in the periphery.

Figure 7.1 shows the network graph provided by SNA regarding a network including the three organizations.

Key Players and Role Distribution

This network illustrates the different members and their key roles according to their degree centrality and betweenness within the network (see Table 7.2 and Figure 7.1). First, we have the central player (JPPM), who has the highest degree centrality in the network (128.000). JPPM is a 60-year-old male from Ecuador with permanent residence in Madrid (Spain). He is the leader of the importer group and all members of this group depend on him to a great extent. Second, the broker role is carried out by SNRM (the head of the wholesale supplier group), who has the highest betweenness centrality (247.967). His broker role in Spain derives from his position in the market as a cocaine wholesale supplier to several retailers in the Spanish distribution market. Apart from these two important members, CPGT is also a relevant player as JPPM's coordinator. He also has a low-level betweenness but plays a key role between the two groups of the network.

Apart from the key players in the network, we have also analyzed the position of most of the other members to contrast police information regarding the network division of labor. The traditional chart in the criminal investigation showed a conventional

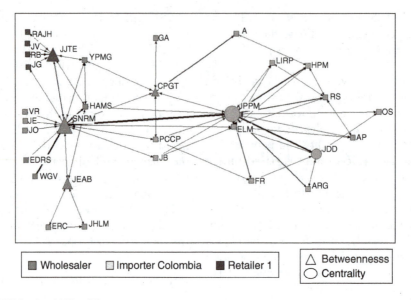

Figure 7.1 MAM network[a] (N = 58)

Note

a It can be that the graph shows fewer nodes than the number mentioned in the network description (N =). The reason is that not all nodes have contacts between them (same for all networks).

Table 7.2 Degree and betweenness centrality of the most important members

Member	Degree[a]	Betweenness
JPPM	128.000	145.000
JDD	35.000	3.000
SNRM	112.000	247.967
JJTE	34.000	85.000
JEAB	7.000	56.000
CPGT	15.000	52.550

Note

a Degree and betweenness measures have been calculated using valued networks. Network measures have been calculated using non-valued networks.

hierarchical distribution between positions where the most relevant members were the leaders of the three organized groups (importer—JPPM, wholesale supplier—SNRM, and retailer—JJTE), and the coordinators (FT, OS, FR, HPM, ELM, and PCPP). We also found operational tasks such as transport, adulteration, distribution or protection carried out by the following members: JDD, VAD, ELF, WGV, HAMS and YPMG.

From the analysis of tasks (see Figure 7.2), we found that the results essentially confirmed the police information and those members with a high degree centrality had higher positions in the network. In some cases, certain players (JDD and YPMG) had a higher degree centrality than the position described in the investigation, although the difference was insignificant. Nevertheless, one case is worth highlighting: CPGT is SNRM's wife, who the police files consider a member holding a secondary or auxiliary position. However, our analysis shows a key central role in the network according to her degree centrality. This is shown in Figure 7.2.

Operation JUAN

Network Structure

The JUAN network is composed of two autonomous branches according to the police files. The police operation started

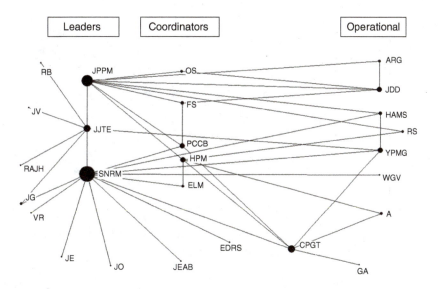

Figure 7.2 Distribution of roles by degree centrality in the MAM network

with a money-laundering investigation and ultimately led to the identification of a wholesale supplier group in charge of cocaine distribution in Madrid (Spain). It was also clear from the police files that the main organization was the group in charge of the illegal transportation of cocaine from Mexico (importer) to be distributed by a wholesale supplier in Spain. This group was classified by the police as high risk, due to the fact that it had access to weapons and its members were dangerous. In this case, the main importer was JLT and the head wholesale supplier was OJSR. Conversely, the laundering group that carried out this activity for more than one organization is exposed. Its leader (EHJ) was the owner of a jewelry store that was used as a screen company to conceal the laundering activities of some collaborators and many executors who changed the unlawfully obtained money to send it back to their countries of origin.

SNA of the whole network yielded the following results: low network centralization (21.34%) and very low density (0.4%). The core of the group is composed of 18 members out of a total of 69 (26%). In addition,

the network in Figure 7.3 does not confirm the police perception. It seems that the relationships between the two groups are more intense than those the police investigation uncovered and the links between the two organizations are not channeled through the main leaders, other members being connected directly and circumventing their own leaders.

Key Players and Role Distribution

By identifying the key players in the whole network, we have the following information: the most relevant members of the network are part of the money-laundering organization despite drug trafficking being the main activity perceived by the police.[5] As Table 7.3 shows, FDS has the highest degree centrality. He is a 31-year-old male, who is a coordinator and EJH's right-hand man, in charge of transportation and laundering the money in the jewelry store. In terms of betweenness, we have EHJ, who is a 40-year-old male, owner of the jewelry store in which the proceeds of cocaine trafficking is laundered. OJSR is also a key member and second in degree

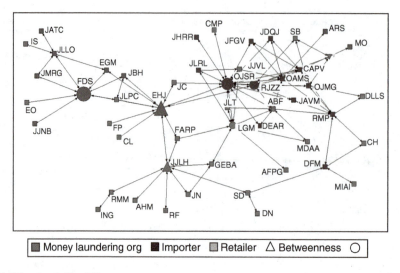

Figure 7.3 JUAN network (N = 69)

centrality and betweenness. He is the leader of the importer group. Table 7.3 provides the most significant scores.

Regarding the positions of the members of the JUAN network, the police files identify two hierarchical structures in which the two branches are clearly independent. The drug distribution branch is made up of three groups. The wholesale supplier had a coordination rank composed of FARP, JJVL, AEPG, and LGM. It was led by JLT and was in contact with the distributor group, led by OJSR, coordinated by JFVG, CAPV, RJZZ, and OJMG, and composed of a third group in charge of transport, protection, and logistics through SD, JHRR, DFM, RMP, and JAVM. Finally, the money-laundering group shows a more horizontal structure, with a leader

(EHJ), a coordinator (FDS), three members in charge of collecting money (JBH, JLLQ, and EGM) and 12 members in charge of laundering the money throughout the Spanish territory.

The distribution of positions in view of degree centrality in the JUAN network does not coincide with the police perception of two separate groups with different structures. The degree centrality of certain members does not correspond to their position in the organization. Some leaders, such as JLT, appear to have a minor degree centrality and many middle- and low-profile members have a lower or higher degree centrality according to their role in the organization (ABF, RMP, FARP, JJVL, and EGM). Figure 7.4 shows these differences.

Operation JADE

Network Structure

The aim of this operation was to remove three groups: a wholesale supplier of cocaine and heroin from a large distribution area in Madrid (Spain) called Cañada Real and two retailer groups. The main group was a

Table 7.3 Degree and betweenness centrality of the most important members

Members	Degree	Betweenness
FDS	114.000	209.000
OJSR	84.000	416.316
RJZZ	42.000	167.059
LGM	40.000	139.938
EHJ	46.000	604.667
JJLH	26.000	321.582

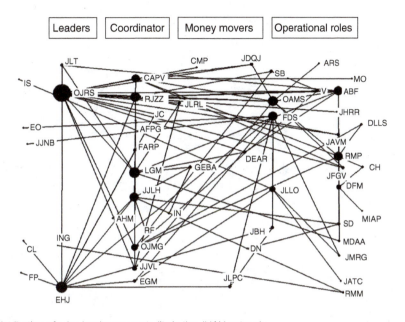

Figure 7.4 Distribution of roles by degree centrality in the JUAN network

family-based group with strong ethnic ties (Spanish gypsies), whose members been traditionally in charge of distributing heroin in marginal areas of large Spanish cities. JFM is the leader of the clan and is responsible for the distribution of cocaine imported from Peru by RBM. According to the police files, this is a typical Spanish wholesale supplier of cocaine and heroin network with a hierarchical structure and strong family ties. In this case, at the time of the investigation, the leader of the wholesale supplier group (JFM) was in jail for a previous offense, committed in 2008. Nevertheless, this situation did not prevent him from coordinating the business through two of his brothers, although mainly through JES. From the hierarchical chart prepared by the police, we could see an organization with a small hub characterized by strong family bonds (JFM, JES, AFM, and ABFM). The other collaborators had secondary roles.

By contrast, SNA of the network revealed a low level of centralization (17.3%) and density (2%). The core is also composed of 7 members out of a total of 62 (11%). The results show a more centralized network with a dense core of a few members that have intense contacts and a large amount of collaborators and members (Figure 7.5). This description is more similar to that provided in the police files, which characterized the network as hierarchical.

Key Players and Role Distribution

Within this family-based clan, FFM and RBM have the highest degree centrality, with similar results (49.000 and 46.000). FFM is a 49-year-old Spanish male (of gypsy descent), who is JES' main provider of heroin and the person in charge of distributing heroin in Cañada Real and other areas of Spain. RBM is the main importer of cocaine for the organization led by JES, while JFM is the former leader of the organization. RBM is a 38-year-old Dominican male with a Spanish nationality and a permanent resident in Madrid (Spain). Finally, it is worth noting that the former leader (JFM) comes fourth in terms of centrality, continuing in operation and in

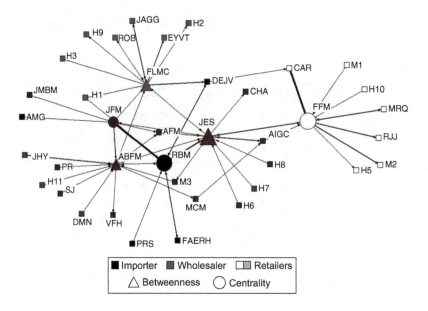

Figure 7.5 JADE network (N = 62)

communication despite being in jail, as shown in Table 7.4.

Regarding the broker role, JES has the highest betweenness score. JES is a 42-year-old Spanish male with a long police record for robbery, drug-trafficking (six arrests), and domestic violence. He coordinates drug distribution while his brother is in jail and keeps in contact with the main providers. Table 7.4 shows the key members in terms of degree and betweenness centrality.

If we consider the distribution of positions within the network, SNA offers no

important distinctions in relation to the information in the police files. Nevertheless, we can see JFM's important role at the time of the investigation, even from jail, from where he was able to keep his contacts and ensure immunity by bribing two police officers. This case is a clear example of how a network adjusts when its leader is removed. The interchangeable position of the three main family members enables the network to adapt to disruption (JFM, JES, and AFM).

Figure 7.6 shows the distribution of positions and roles[6] according to the degree centrality of the most relevant members. The general trend does not differ from the description provided by the police. The centrality of key members matches their position in the general network. Nevertheless, it is worth noting that many coordinators have similar results according to their significant position within the network. This can be explained by their family bonds and interchangeable roles and positions. The position in the chart of ABFM, JFM's son, is also noteworthy. He is a 14-year-old boy in charge of supervising the

Table 7.4 Degree and betweenness centrality of the most important members

Member	Degree	Betweenness
FFM	49.000	229.500
RBM	46.000	120.233
JES	39.000	406.067
JFM	32.000	106.067
FLMC	24.000	262.767
CAR	23.000	3.500
ABFM	23.000	241.367
DEJV	11.000	10.667

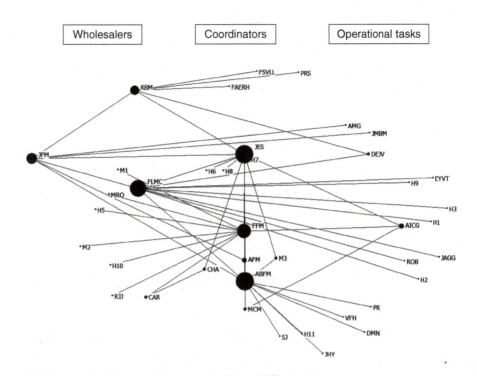

Figure 7.6 Distribution of positions by degree centrality in the JADE network

industrial premises where cocaine and heroin distribution take place.

Operation ACER

Network Structure

The network described in Figure 7.7 is also a Spanish family-based wholesale group involved in cocaine (from Colombia) distribution in three provinces in Spain. JFS is the main Colombian importer and SAR is a female who is head of the organization. JEPO is SAR's closest collaborator, and he transports drugs and collects money for SAR. According to the police investigation, this was a small group with a risky profile due to certain factors: use of weapons, complex structure, personal qualification, and dangerousness of its members. The police files show a centralized hierarchical structure with a central leader and JEPO

as the main coordinator. The other members depend greatly on her (SAR). Conversely, SNA shows a more centralized and hierarchical network as compared to the other three networks analyzed. This network has the highest centralization (41.7%) and density (14%). The core is composed of 8 members (MMM, SAR, and JEPO) out of a total of 23 (34%). The results show a more traditional profile and hierarchical structure where SAR is the central leader.

Key Players and Role Distribution

This is a small centralized family-based network in which SAR has a central and broker role and the highest degree centrality (71.000) and betweenness centrality (96.000) (see Table 7.5). She is a 44-year-old female in charge of the group and of keeping personal contacts with cocaine importers.

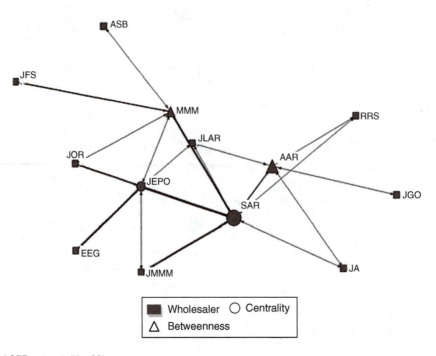

Figure 7.7 ACER network (N = 23)

Table 7.5 Degree and betweenness centrality of the most important members

Members	Out/In Degree	Betweenness
SAR	71.000	96.000
AAR	24.000	75.000
JEPO	46.000	60.250
MMM	31.000	42.250

She has an autonomous role in relation to the rest of the group, except for JEPO, her close collaborator. In terms of betweenness, ARR, who is SAR's sister and is in charge of the drug distribution together with her husband, ranks second (75.000). The third female involved in the network is SAR's mother (RRS), who is in charge of managing the money.

The conclusions of the study of positions within the network according to the degree centrality of its members are similar to those of the police. As we can see in Figure 7.8, the role distribution matches the police structure profile, except for AAR, who has a high degree centrality and is performing less important roles or positions within the organization. There could be two reasons for this. First, the family bonds in the network could explain the inclusion of a family member with a high degree centrality performing lesser positions within the network. Second, the role of females within criminal groups has always been less qualified than that of males, which could explain why women with a low qualification role can be so important in terms of degree centrality.

Legitimate Facilitators

The association of criminal groups with legitimate interests is a long-established fact. On the one hand, it is a source of resilience (Williams, 2001) and a strategy to avoid detection and disruption. On the other hand, organized crime enables legal professionals to complement legitimate funds with extra illegal income. This association

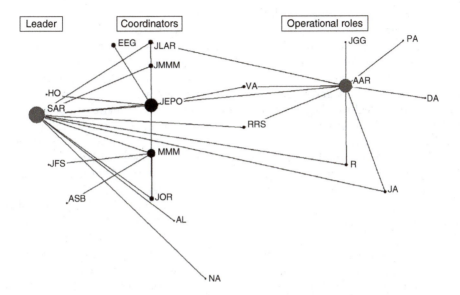

Figure 7.8 Distribution of roles by degree centrality in the ACER network

could encompass many groups but it focuses mainly: a) on public authorities through corruption at three levels: police departments, judicial institutions, and politicians; and b) on legitimate business in order to conceal the illegal nature of the activity or income by offering very beneficial opportunities to legitimate professionals. The latter case would include law-abiding businesses, accountants, legitimate businesspersons, or lawyers.

The police files of our four criminal groups reveal relationships with two types of legitimate players: public authorities and players involved in legitimate business activities. Regarding operation MAM, we found legal facilitators for cocaine transportation. In this case, the importer in Uruguay had at least one legal enterprise to conceal cocaine transportation to Spain. There is no evidence of a legal business in Spain to conceal illegal activities, although there is proof of corruption involving judicial authorities to obtain judicial immunity.

Operation JUAN is a classic case of money laundering being outsourced to another spe-

cialized organization. The organization in charge of money laundering is composed of some key players (lawyers and accountants) and many independent collaborators all over the Spanish territory in charge of laundering money for a commission before sending it back to the organized crime groups. A jewelry store owned by the head of the organization is the legal business concealing the movement of capital.

Finally, operation JADE is a local group in a gypsy ghetto where many similar clans live off illegal activities such as drug-trafficking. In this case, no legal outlet for the illegal business is necessary since the neighborhood is deeply involved in underworld activities. Community support for these types of activities provides a general consensus against illegal activities. What seems to be more effective in terms of protection is to avoid police detection and inspection. In operation JADE, this kind of protection came in the form of JFM's close contact with two police officers in charge of inspecting the market in the area. JFM, despite being in jail, maintained his personal contacts by bribing police officers in exchange for immunity.

Since ACER is a more traditional local group, it has its own legal facilitators to conceal the activity and launder illegal funds. The group has brothels and transportation companies to conceal the illegal activity and launder the proceeds of cocaine trafficking and other illegal activities.

Table 7.6 provides a summary of activities detected in the police investigation for each organization in terms of legal facilitators.

CONCLUSION

From the study of the structure of the four criminal groups and comparing the police investigation and the SNA results, we can conclude that the structure resulting from the police investigations overrates the hierarchical structure and positions within the criminal groups. As some other studies have suggested (Morselli, 2009; Natarajan, 2006; McIllwain, 1999), the results presented in this chapter also reveal more flexible and horizontal structures in groups classified by the police as hierarchical and complex structures. Therefore, the four structures could be described more as illegal networks than criminal organizations, except for ACER. Based on SNA of the four groups, three of the networks (MAM, JADE, and JUAN) have low levels of centralization and very low percentages of density (under 10%). This means that the network structure with a higher horizontal division of labor is the most common structure for the wholesale supply of cocaine in Spain. The only exception is ACER, which has the highest percentage of centralization and density. It is also the smallest network, characterized by a more traditional structure with a substantial centralization in the group's main leader (a woman in this case).

Regarding the key players in the networks, SNA offers the possibility of identifying the most relevant members of the network in terms of their degree centrality and betweenness. First, it is surprising that three networks have different members with betweenness and centrality scores. In general, members with the highest degree centrality are consistent with the hierarchical leaders of the network provided in the police files. In operations MAM and JADE, the cocaine importers are members with the highest centrality scores. In operation JUAN, the most central member is the second coordinator of the money-laundering group, while in operation ACER, the group is led by a woman. If we analyze the network's brokers, we can see that the most important members are leaders of middle groups (wholesaler suppliers) in charge of receiving the drugs and selling them to the retailers. This is consistent with other previous studies (Pearson & Hobbs, 2003; Desroches, 2005). In operation MAM, the broker is the leader of the distributor in Spain, while in operation JADE, the broker is also the leader of the distributing group, substituting the leader while he is in jail. In operation JUAN, the broker is the leader of the money-laundering group. Finally, in ACER, given the network's small size, the leader (SAR) shares the high degree centrality and betweenness.

From the analysis of the members' degree centrality and the roles performed in the network, SNA confirmed police intuition or perception regarding the positions and roles

Table 7.6 Administrative and economic facilitators in drug trafficking

Operation	Administrative penetration	Economic penetration
MAM	Judicial corruption	Legal business in Uruguay
JUAN	No indication	Money laundering outsourced
JADE	Police corruption	Illegal background
ACER	No indication	Legal business in Spain

performed by the most important members in the network. Nevertheless, from the graphs representing the ACER and JUAN operations, it is interesting to look at the lower-level positions in the organization. Some of the lower members in the police files were overrated according to their relevance in terms of degree centrality. This kind of analysis could give added value to police investigations to identify relevant members in less qualified positions or in the network periphery. All these conclusions must be interpreted bearing in mind the characteristic limitations of SNA in relation to the information available in police files about clandestine networks. This information tends to be limited and influenced by the police investigation.

By integrating all the results provided in this chapter regarding the groups, we arrive at a profile for each network according to the classification. The first group (MAM) is a typical organized criminal group of wholesale suppliers in which the cocaine importer and wholesale supplier are key members. This could be classified as a *communal business*. The structure analysis shows a horizontal network where members share their own resources to develop the illegal activity (Haller, 1990). We also have operation JADE, in which the common structure is not only business-orientated but also family-based, where tradition has an influence on the network structure (*family business*). Regarding JUAN, it is an organized group that could be considered a *corporation-type business*. As mentioned previously, the economic business seems to be the main activity, finding provision from other groups involved in other illegal activities. Finally, the ACER network seems to be a family business with a more hierarchical structure. Even if it is also family-based, it has the most traditional structure with a high degree centrality concentrated in one leader, while the rest of the group is subject to the leader's guidance. In this case, family bonds and trust are essential.

The last part of the chapter analyzes the legal facilitators providing additional protection or assisting the illegal business—in other words, the existing association with legitimate businesses or politics. The results show that all the networks had legal facilitators that supported the illegal business and prevented external detection. MAM shows the most sophisticated strategies with political and economic connections: judicial corruption was detected in Spain and legal enterprises were used in Uruguay to conceal the illegal transportation of cocaine. Operation ACER has a legitimate business through which the proceeds of the illegal activities are laundered. Operation JUAN only appears to have legitimate connections to conceal legal earnings in its money-laundering branch. Finally, operation JADE is a group rooted in a local community which lives off an informal economy. This is an example of how counterproductive an association with a legitimate business can be in certain criminal backgrounds. In this case, the criminal facilitators include community support, acceptance by the local authorities, and personal contacts.

Finally, this analysis supports the use of SNA for the study of the structure of organized crime groups, the powerful and broker members, and the significance of external cooperators. The additional information provided by this methodology is very useful to have a better understanding of the organized crime groups active in the main illegal markets and to help criminal investigations.

NOTES

1. The Guardia Civil is one of two national police forces in Spain. It is mainly in charge of investigating crimes in rural areas and investigates 60% of crimes committed in Spain.
2. Betweenness centrality is the fraction of all shortest paths that pass through a vertex along the shortest path of the network.
3. We understand position to mean the status or hierarchical role of a member of the organization. Through this information, our aim was to compare the hierarchical position assigned by the police with the result of SNA.

4. The questionnaire created to gather police information contains a section where the investigator is asked to assess the dangerousness of the organization from 0 to 5. The investigator is requested to refer to the indicators from the investigation that he/she has taken into account to reach his/her decision.

5. This could be biased because the contacts of the money-laundering group were overrepresented in the matrix.

6. In this case, we have divided the chart into three categories of position and have included wholesalers in the first hierarchical position of the entire network.

REFERENCES

Adler, P.A. (1985). *Wheeling and Dealing: An Ethnography of an Upper-level Dealing and Smuggling Community*. New York: Columbia University Press.

Adler, P.A. (1992). The "post" phase of deviant careers: Reintegrating drug traffickers. *Deviant Behavior* 13, 103–126.

Benson, J.S. & S.H. Decker (2010). The organizational structure of international drug smuggling. *Journal of Criminal Justice* 38, 130–138.

Borgatti, S.P. & M.G. Everett (1999). Models of core/periphery structures. *Social Networks* 21, 375–395.

Cressey, D. (1972). *Criminal Organizations: Its Elementary Forms*. New York: Harper and Row.

Desroches, F. (1999) Wholesale drug dealers. Paper presented to panel on "The structure and operation of illegal commodity markets." *Annual Meeting of the American Society of Criminology*, Toronto.

Desroches, F. (2005). *The Crime that Pays: Drug Trafficking and Organized Crime in Canada*. Toronto: Canadian Scholar's Press.

Donald, I. & A. Wilson (2000). Ram raiding: Criminals working in groups. In D. Canter & L. Allison (eds.), *The Social Psychology of Crime* (vol. III, pp. 127–152). Burlington, VT: Ashgate.

Dorn, N., K. Murji, & N. South (1992). *Traffickers: Drug Markets and Law Enforcement*. London: Routledge.

Gambetta, D. (1988). Mafia: The price of distrust. In D. Gambetta, *Trust: Making and Breaking Cooperative Relations* (pp. 158–175). Oxford: Blackwell.

Haller, M.H. (1990). Illegal enterprise: A theoretical and historical interpretation. *Criminology* 28, 207–235.

Kleemans, E.R. & E.G. Van De Bunt (1999). Social embeddedness of organized crime. *Transnational Organized Crime* 5, 1, 19–36.

McIllwain, J.S. (1999). Organized crime: A social network approach. *Crime, Law and Social Change* 32, 301–324.

Morselli, C. (2005). *Contacts, Opportunities and Criminal Enterprise*. Toronto, Ontario: University of Toronto Press.

Morselli, C. (2009). *Inside Criminal Networks*. New York: Springer.

Natarajan, M. (2000). Understanding the structure of a drug trafficking organization: A conversational analysis. *Crime Prevention Studies* 11, 273–298.

Natarajan, M. (2006). Understanding the structure of a large heroin distribution network: A quantitative analysis of qualitative data. *Journal of Quantitative Criminology* 22, 171–192.

Natarajan, M. & M. Belanger (1998). Varieties of upper-level drug dealing organizations: A typology of cases prosecuted in New York City. *Journal of Drug Issues* 28(4), 1005–1026.

Paoli, L. (2002). The paradoxes of organized crime. *Crime, Law & Social Change* 37, 51–97.

Pearson, G. & D. Hobbs (2001). Middle market drug distribution. *Home Office* 9. Research Study No. 227. London: Home Office.

Pearson, G. & D. Hobbs (2003). Kin pin? A case study of a middle market drug broker. *Howard Journal of Criminal Justice* 42(4), 335–347.

Reuter, P.H. (1985). *Organization of Illegal Markets: An Economic Analysis*. Washington, DC: National Institute of Justice.

Reuter, P. (2004). The political economy of drug smuggling. In M. Vellinga (ed.), *The Political Economy of the Drug Industry* (pp. 129–147). Gainesville, FL: University Press of Florida.

Reuter, P.H. & J. Haaga (1989). *The Organization of High Level Drug Markets: An Exploratory Study*. Santa Monica, CA: Rand.

Schiray, M. (2001). Introduction: Drug trafficking, organized crime, and public policy for drug control. *International Social Science Journal* 53, 351–358.

Sparrow, M.K. (1991). The application of network analysis to criminal intelligence. An assessment of the prospects. *Social Networks* 13, 251–274.

Von Lampe, K. (2008). Organized crime in Europe: Conceptions and realities. *Policing: A Journal of Policy and Practice* 2(1), 7–17.

Williams, P. (2001). Transnational criminal networks. In J. Arquilla & D. Ronfeldt (eds.), *Networks and Netwars: The Future of Terror, Crime and Militancy* (pp. 61–97). Santa Monica, CA: RAND.

Zaitch, D. (2002). *Trafficking Cocaine: Colombian Drug Entrepreneurs in the Netherlands*. The Hague, Netherlands: Kluwer.

Zhang, S. & K. Chin (2003). The declining significance of triad societies in transnational illegal activities: A structural deficiency perspective. *British Journal of Criminology* 43(3), 469–488.

CHAPTER 8

Dismantling Criminal Networks

Can Node Attributes Play a Role?

David A. Bright, Catherine Greenhill, and Natalya Levenkova

Criminal groups involved in the trade of illicit commodities (e.g., drugs, arms, people) and in terrorist activities contribute to health and social harms in the Australian and international communities. Internationally, there is growing recognition of the need to more clearly describe the operation of criminal networks, and to empirically investigate the effectiveness of law enforcement strategies aimed at dismantling criminal networks.

Particularly since the 2001 terrorist attacks, there has been a growing focus in law enforcement and research communities on conceptualizing criminal groups as networks. The shift to thinking about criminal groups as networks promises to improve our understanding of such groups and enhance law enforcement interventions. Law enforcement intervention predicated on outdated notions of illicit groups as hierarchies rather than networks may focus on ineffective strategies, such as removing individuals thought to be in positions of authority. In particular, the effectiveness of law enforcement interventions against criminal networks may be instructed by research which describes the structure of such networks, and identifies factors which influence the resilience and vulnerability of criminal networks to law enforcement interventions.

In this chapter, we examine a case study of a criminal network by describing the global structure of the network. We will use simulations to investigate different strategies for dis-

mantling the networks and apply two "measures of disruption" to evaluate the effectiveness of these strategies. Specifically, we compare law enforcement strategies which focus on centrality scores with those which focus on attributes of individuals in the network. The motivation for this work is to explore which factor or combination of factors law enforcement should focus on when targeting nodes with the aim of dismantling the network. We acknowledge that this approach presupposes that law enforcement has collected information on the network and is aware of all players within the network. A large proportion of law enforcement resources are directed into identifying individuals involved and the connections between them. The current project focuses on the strategic approaches law enforcement selects once they have collected sufficient knowledge and intelligence about a discrete criminal network. The current study adds to the series of strategic cases, against which other cases can be compared. It follows work by Morselli and Petit (2007) on heroin importation in Canada, and Natarajan (2006) on heroin trafficking and dealing in New York.

First, we turn to the relationship between network structure and the resilience and vulnerability of such networks.

NETWORK STRUCTURE

Existing theoretical accounts and empirical results suggest that networks can be divided into two types based on structure: exponential and scale-free (Albert, Jeong, & Barabasi, 2000). Exponential networks (also called Poisson networks) are structurally homogenous, with the majority of nodes having approximately the same number of links. In other words, nodes show some variation in the number of links they possess as compared to the average node (i.e., the peak of the bell curve), but it is very unlikely to find nodes with a very much larger or smaller number of links compared with the average node. Scale-free networks, on the other hand, are inhomogeneous—the majority of nodes have proportionately few links and a small minority of nodes has a very large number of links (known as hubs). A plot of the number of links (k) to number of nodes with k links would follow a "heavy-tailed" distribution (see Figure 8.1): many nodes have a small number of links (the left of the graph) and few have a very large number of links (the right of the graph).

Examples of scale-free networks include the World Wide Web (Albert, Jeong, & Barabasi, 1999), the physical structure of the internet (Faloutsos, Faloutsos, & Faloutsos, 1999), protein–protein interaction networks (Dorogovtsev & Mendes, 2001), and (at least some) social networks. Examples of scale-free social networks include: sexual relationships in Sweden (Liljeros, Edling, Amaral, Stanley, & Aberg, 2001), networks of people connected by email (Ebel, Mielsch, & Bornholdt, 2002), and networks of scientific papers connected by citations (Redner, 2005).

The structure of networks has important implications for the resilience and vulnerability of networks and, in particular, for whether such networks can be dismantled by removal of well-connected nodes (called hubs).

Implications of Scale-free Structure for Network Vulnerability

In scale-free networks, network connectivity is maintained by a few highly connected hubs whose removal can drastically alter network topography. These hubs are typically located on many of the paths between other pairs of nodes in the network. Although few in number, these hubs can be conceptualized as the "glue" which binds networks together. The structure of scale-free networks makes them resistant to accidental or random failure (Albert et al., 2000; Bollobás & Riordan, 2004; Crucitti, Latora, Marchiori, & Rapisarda, 2003). This is because the random removal of nodes will take out mainly less-connected ones because they are far more numerous. The elimination of nodes with few connections does not usually exert a large impact on network topography. However, the simultaneous removal of only a few hubs (representing a small proportion of the entire network) can collapse an entire networked system (Bollobás & Riordan, 2004; Newman, 2010; Morselli & Roy, 2008; Morselli, 2009).

While in many areas (e.g., internet topography, electricity grids) the focus is on ensuring network resilience, in the study of criminal networks, real-world policy implications flow from identifying areas of weakness in networks which can be exploited by law enforcement agencies. Despite the implications for the development of law enforcement

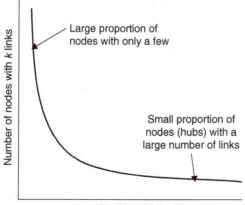

Figure 8.1 The distribution of nodes and links in scale-free networks

interventions, there has been very little previous research on dismantling criminal networks.

Morselli and Petit (2007) evaluated the impact of a surveillance and seizure operation on a drug trafficking network. The project evaluated the impact of this intervention on network structure. By virtue of the type of law enforcement intervention involved, it did not examine the impact of removal of nodes as there were no arrests until the intervention was concluded. Nonetheless, Morselli and Petit (2007) found that over time and law enforcement pressure, the centralization of the network decreased and that one node that was initially highly central became less so over time. Although this study examined the impact of law enforcement on a criminal network, it did not investigate the impact of node removal on overall network structure. We are aware of only three previous studies which have done so (Keegan, Ahmed, Williams, Srivastava, & Contractor, 2010; Xu & Chen, 2009; Morselli & Roy, 2008).

Using simulation methodology, Xu and Chen (2009) examined terrorist, meth trafficking, and gang networks. They found that these networks had scale-free properties and also exhibited characteristics of "small-world" networks (i.e., high clustering compared to random graphs with the same average degree centrality). They simulated attacks on hubs (nodes with high degree centrality) and attacks on bridges (nodes with high betweenness centrality). Network fragmentation following sequential node-removal was indicated by measuring: the fraction of nodes in the largest connected component, average size of remaining components, and average shortest path lengths between pairs of nodes. They found that both hub and bridge attacks were effective in dismantling the networks; though all three networks were more sensitive to attacks targeting bridges than hubs.

Keegan et al. (2010) examined the resilience of online gaming (1,600 nodes) and drug trafficking (110 nodes) networks, and compared random failure with attacks targeted at hubs (i.e., sequential removal of nodes by degree centrality scores). They found that the online gaming network had a scale-free structure. As measures of network fragmentation, they used the fraction of nodes in the largest connected component and the fraction of nodes which were isolates. They found similar resilience to degree and random attack when fewer than 1% of nodes were removed. However, removing 5% of nodes by attacking hubs fragmented the network; in contrast, the removal of 5% of nodes by random failure did not lead to fragmentation.

Taken together, these two studies suggest that criminal networks, like other networks, may be scale-free in structure and therefore vulnerable to law enforcement interventions which target hubs. However, in social networks, the nodes are people (as opposed to networks made up of telegraph poles or web pages) and may range in their skills, knowledge, and other critical characteristics (e.g., capacity to avoid detection by law enforcement). Therefore, for social networks, the impact of node-level attributes is an important, yet under-researched factor in terms of network vulnerability and resilience. Indeed, one criticism of the previous work on criminal network structure and vulnerability (e.g., Keegan et al., 2010; Xu & Chen, 2009) is that it does not take into account the attributes of individuals in the networks (e.g., Robins, 2009; Robins & Kashima, 2008). Instead, each node is treated as being identical, separate and apart from centrality scores. However, nodes (that is, individuals) can be critical for reasons unrelated to centrality. For example, they may have exclusive access to resources/knowledge (e.g., chemicals), play crucial roles (e.g., managing clan lab site), or be a critical link between the licit and illicit worlds (e.g., baggage handlers, corrupt police). Robins (2009) argues that network analysis should include not just an analysis of traditional features such as centrality scores, but should also explore features of individuals within the network. He describes five levels of factors relevant to networks: individual-level factors, dyadic-level factors, node-positioning network effects, localized network structural features, and global network features. Individual-level factors include capacities such as skills, expertise, information, and knowledge. In a similar vein, Schwartz and Rouselle (2009) suggest the use of attribute weights for nodes with greater weights reflecting possession of more resources (e.g., information, skills, money). According to their model, actors with higher attribute weights and more connections add relatively more to network capital than those with lower attribute weights and fewer connections. Schwartz and Rouselle (2009) recommend the use of attribute and link weights to develop law enforcement intervention and intelligence priorities.

Some previous research has described the roles of individuals within criminal networks, but has not explored the implications of such roles for the network's vulnerability to law enforcement. For example, Natarajan (2006) conducted a "role analysis" of a heroin importation network in addition to more traditional network analyses, finding several roles in the network, including retailers, sellers, brokers, and secretaries. In another study, Morselli and Roy (2008) employed crime scripts in which five key roles were needed in order to complete the task (stolen vehicle exportation). Similarly, Bright, Hughes, and Chalmers (2012) used a role analysis of a methamphetamine network, finding several roles, including workers, specialists, wholesale-level dealers, and managers. However, previous research has not examined the impact on network typology of law enforcement interventions which target nodes based on centrality scores (*node-positioning effects* under Robins' framework) and/or functional roles performed by individuals in the network (*individual-level effects*, according to the framework outlined by Robins), using

methods such as those described by Schwartz and Rouselle (2009). Therefore, to fill this gap in the literature, the current study will investigate whether, when the aim of law enforcement is to dismantle the network, law enforcement should target individuals based on centrality scores or based on their role in the network (including the skills and knowledge they possess), or perhaps some combination of the two.

The aims of the current study are to use a case study of a criminal network: 1) to determine whether the network is scale-free; and 2) to investigate whether law enforcement should target nodes in criminal networks based on centrality scores (i.e., hubs), on node attribute information, or some combination of the two.

METHOD

For criminal networks, the collection of complete datasets in realistic contexts is difficult. For example, trial transcripts cost money, and gaining access to law enforcement data is likely to involve a lengthy approval process. In the current study, we used judges' comments as the primary source of data. Judges' sentencing comments offer a viable alternative and we have used this source in previous research on criminal networks (e.g., Bright, Greenhill, & Levenkova, 2010; Bright et al., 2012). In criminal cases, judges' sentencing comments convey the judges' justifications for a sentencing decision. They typically include the name of the person sentenced and a summary of the established facts in the case (behaviors, locations, names, dates), including the names of criminal associates.

For the current study, we used an existing dataset described in a previous paper (Bright et al., 2012). The method used to extract and analyze the data was as follows: a search was conducted on the NSW Lawlink website for criminal cases between January 1999 and May 1999 using two search terms ("methamphetamine" and "methylamphetamine"; the aim was to find a criminal network involved in the manufacture and trafficking of methamphetamine for a related project). Cases were included if they involved the manufacture and distribution (including importation) of the drug. A total of 61 cases were found which met the inclusion criteria. Each case was read by one of the researchers. The review resulted in the identification of three groups involved in manufacture/trafficking/importation of methamphetamine. We selected the largest group for further analysis. Eleven cases were identified which made reference to individuals connected with this group. SNA and network mapping was conducted using the software programs Visone and UCINET.

Previous research using the same dataset identified seven roles for 35 of the 36 network members. There was insufficient information on one individual, so this node was not given a role (see Bright et al., 2012). Roles were determined based on the main set of activities or responsibilities for the different network participants, as described in judges' sentencing comments. Table 8.1 shows the seven roles and a description for each. A network map is displayed in Figure 8.2, with roles indicated by shape and shading.

Our first aim was to examine whether the structure of the network could be classified as scale-free or exponential. We used two methods to test whether the two networks exhibited a scale-free structure: 1) we compared mathematical properties of the network to random graph equivalents, and 2) we applied a goodness-of-fit test to check whether the degree distribution of the network is

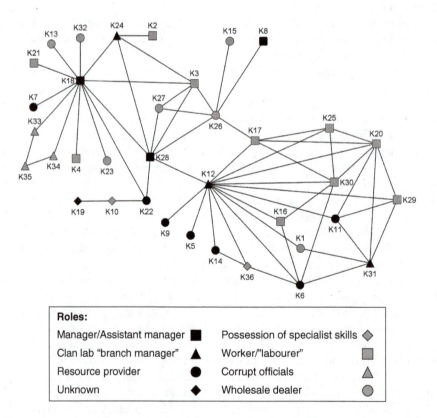

Figure 8.2 Network map of the methamphetamine trafficking network, showing roles

Table 8.1 Descriptions of the roles played by individuals in the network

Role	Descriptor
Managers	Designated tasks to others, provided the funds for parts of the drug trafficking operation, or to whom other individuals reported
Clan lab managers	Managed the operation of clandestine laboratory sites
Wholesale dealers	Responsible for selling methamphetamine in single to multiple kilogram lots
Resource providers	Sourced chemicals and equipment required for the manufacture of the drug
Specialists	Possessed specialist knowledge and skill in the manufacture of methamphetamine
Workers/laborers	Paid a wage to complete tasks or follow orders
Corrupt officials	Occupied government positions and received bribes to behave in corrupt ways

consistent with a power-law distribution (with cut-off).

Next, to examine the impact of law enforcement interventions, we conducted four sets of simulations. A computer simulation needs numerical data in order to perform calculations. Therefore, in order to take the role of each node into account, the roles must somehow be quantified. Our approach to this was to assign a weight to each node, where the weight is inversely proportional to the number of individuals in the syndicate with the same role. Hence the weight is a proxy for how difficult it might be to replace that individual, were they to be removed from the network (i.e., arrested). For example, there are two managers in the network, so they are both assigned a weight of 0.5. There are 10 workers in the network, so they all receive a weight of 0.1. While we acknowledge that this is simplistic, and that there are many other ways to quantify how important nodes are

in the network, we believe that these weights provide an educated guess at the importance of each node, in the absence of further information. The node with unknown role was assigned a weight of 0. The weights of each node are shown in Table 8.2.

We used four different law enforcement simulations to examine the differential impact of targeting criminal networks based on centrality scores, roles, a mix of centrality/role information, and a random strategy. The four different rules we used in the simulations were as follows:

- Random attack: Nodes are targeted in a random order. Although it could be argued that random removal of nodes might simulate "random" law enforcement interventions (e.g., stop and search; border detection), it is better conceived as a baseline comparison for targeted intervention. Random removal is relatively

Table 8.2 Roles and associated weights assigned to nodes in the network

Role	Nodes with that role	Weight of each of these nodes
Manager/Assistant manager	K18, K28	1/2
Possession of specialist skills	K10, K36	1/2
Clan lab "branch manager"	K12, K24, K31	1/3
Corrupt official	K33, K34, K35	1/3
Wholesale dealer	K1, K13, K15, K23, K26, K27, K32	1/7
Resource provider	K5, K6, K7, K8, K9, K11, K14, K22	1/8
Worker/"laburer"	K2, K3, K4, K16, K17, K20, K21, K25, K29, K30	1/10
Unknown role	K19	0

easy as no knowledge of the network structure is required. If some individuals are hard to locate, with a random strategy, any person will suffice as a target (Carley, 2006);

- Degree attack: The node of highest remaining degree centrality score was selected for removal;
- Weight attack: The node with the highest remaining weight was removed from the network; and
- Mixed strategy: The degree attack and weight attack can be combined to produce a family of mixed strategies. For a given constant c between 0 and 1, we define the score of a node v in the current network to be:

$$S(v) = (1 - c)\, d(v) + c\, B\, w(v)$$

where $d(v)$ denotes the degree centrality of node v in the current network, $w(v)$ denotes the weight of node v, and B is a constant chosen so that, over the initial network, the average contribution of two terms is equal. (For the methamphetamine network, we used $B = 124/7$.) When $c = 0$, we obtain degree attack, and when $c = 1$, we obtain weight attack. For intermediate values of c, we have a combination of the two. For example, when $c = 0.5$, role and centrality scores contribute equally to the selection of nodes to be removed. We investigated many possible combinations of weight and degree attack (c) to find the most effective combination. For the given network, setting $c = 0.1$ gave the best results. (This is explained and quantified in the next section.) So we only report on the mixed strategy with $c = 0.1$. For this value of c, 10% of node selection is based on role and 90% is based on centrality score.

In each simulation, at each time step, a node of the current network is chosen according to some rule and deleted from the network. In the case of a tie (e.g., for maximum degree, or for maximum weight), a node with the maximal value was chosen randomly. We performed 100 runs of each simulation, always starting the methamphetamine network as the initial network.

The vulnerability of dark networks to being dismantled by law enforcement can be measured in various ways. In earlier work (Bright et al., 2010), we investigated the following measures of fragmentation for the degree targeting and random targeting simulations: the number of nodes in the largest connected component, the number of isolated nodes, maximum degree centrality, and the number of connected components. For each of these measures, degree targeting significantly outperformed random targeting.

In the current study, we use two outcome measures for the connectivity of the network: one which ignores role information, and one which tries to take role information into account. A connected component in a network is a maximal set of nodes such that all pairs of nodes in the set are joined by a path in the network. Let $n(G)$ denote the number of nodes in the largest connected component of the current network G. This measure (and the other fragmentation measures mentioned above) only considers the topological structure of the network and ignores individual attributes of the nodes, such as role. But we wish to investigate how individual attributes, such as roles, can affect the choice and performance of intervention strategies. Therefore, it is desirable, and arguably appropriate, to include role information in our method for measuring the success of the intervention strategies. This led us to investigate another measure, which we call the disruption function. For the current network G, the disruption function is given by:

$$n(G) + K\, w(G),$$

where $w(G)$ is the maximum, over all connected components, of the sum of the weights of the nodes in that component. The disruption function is given by the number of nodes in the largest connected component, plus a constant multiplied by the largest total weight among all connected components. Note that the heaviest component need not be the largest connected component. In this way, the disruption function is a composite measure of fragmentation and the "irreplaceability" of the remaining connected nodes and, hence, takes both topological and individual-level data into account. The constant K is chosen so that when G is the initial network, the contribution from both terms is equal. For the methamphetamine network, this is achieved by setting $K = 36/7$.

For each of our four simulations, both of these measures were calculated after every node deletion in each run, and then averaged over the 100 runs. The values for the four simulations were then plotted together in a graph, for each of the two measures.

RESULTS

Network Structure

One way to examine the mathematical properties of real-world networks is to compare them with their random graph equivalents. Random graphs are constructed by making connections between nodes using a pre-set probability p. For example, if $p = 0.5$ then, for each pair of nodes in the network, there is a 50% probability that they will be connected. To produce equivalent random graphs against which to compare our real-world networks, the probability is calibrated to give the same average degree in the random graph as for the real-world network. In the methamphetamine trafficking network, there were 36 nodes, 62 edges, and an average degree centrality score of 3.444. We used probability $p = 0.09841$ to give the same average degree in the corresponding random graph. The resulting graph is an "exponential network" in the sense of Albert et al. (1999). In this random

graph, the probability that there is a node with degree centrality of 14 is less than 7.6×10^{-5} (less than an eight in 100, 000 chance) and the probability that there exists a node with degree 14 and a node with degree 12 (as in the methamphetamine network) is less than 3.09×10^{-7} (an approximately three in 10 million chance). So the methamphetamine trafficking network is very far from being like an exponential network.

To further test whether the network could be said to be scale-free, a goodness-of-fit test was applied to the data, following the method described in Clauset, Shalizi, and Newman (2009). The outcome of this test suggests that the degree distribution of the methamphetamine network (for degrees 2 and above) is consistent with a power-law distribution with cut-off. Confidence in this conclusion is measured by the p-value, which for our network was around 0.2. (The hypothesis of a power-law distribution should be rejected if the p-value is less than 0.1.)

Law Enforcement Simulations

First, we investigated the dependence of the disruption function on the parameter c, in order to find a near-optimal value of c (at least for the given network). Note that the disruption function takes high values when the network is still well connected and contains hard-to-replace nodes. On the other hand, a low value of the disruption function indicates that the network does not contain large connected components or smaller components containing high-weight nodes. Therefore, a low area under the disruption curve corresponds to efficient dismantling of the network, as measured by the disruption function. The area under the curve of the disruption function was calculated for many different values of c and averaged over 100 runs for each value of c (see Figure 8.3). We see that the area under the disruption function was lowest for values of c around 0.1. Therefore, we chose to work with $c = 0.1$ as a convenient value.

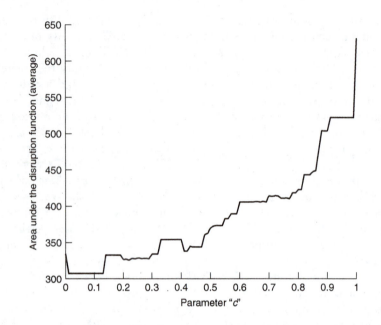

Figure 8.3 Average area under the disruption function, for various values of c

Next we performed 100 runs of each of our simulations and measured fragmentation of the network at each step by calculating the size of the largest connected component (see Figure 8.4). The x axis shows the number of time steps which have occurred, which equals the number of nodes which have been deleted from the network. The y axis shows the average size of the largest connected component after each deletion, averaged over 100 runs of the simulation. There are four plots shown, corresponding to the four strategies.

Just by viewing this plot, we see that random targeting is ineffective compared with

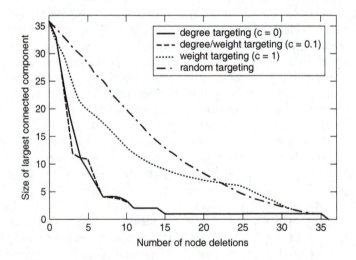

Figure 8.4 The four simulations, measured by the size of the largest connected component

the three other strategies. The best strategies (as measured by the size of the largest connected component) appear to be degree targeting and the mixed strategy. This can be quantified by comparing the area under each curve. These areas are 470.31 for random targeting, 373.43 for weight targeting, 160.60 for degree targeting, and 158.99 for the mixed strategy. This confirms the visual impression that the degree targeting and mixed strategy have a similar performance, and that both outperform the other two strategies (targeting based on role only, and random targeting).

Finally, we performed 100 runs of each of our simulations, calculating the disruption function of the network at each step. Figure 8.5 shows a plot of the average value of this function over the four simulations. Again, the x axis shows the number of time steps which have passed, which equals the number of nodes which have been deleted. The y axis shows the average value of the disruption function after each deletion, where the average is taken over 100 runs in each simulation. Four plots are again shown, corresponding to our four strategies.

Viewing the plot, we see that the best performance (as measured by the disruption function) is obtained using the degree targeting and mixed strategies, with these being very similar. In fact, the curve for the mixed strategy lies below the curve for the degree strategy most of the time, which suggests that the mixed strategy performed the best overall. The random strategy is far worse than all the others. The effectiveness of targeting based on role only falls between random targeting and the degree/mixed interventions. We quantify this by calculating the area under each curve, giving the following areas: 939.20 for random targeting, 635.19 for weight targeting, 335.25 for degree targeting, and 307.58 for the mixed strategy. This confirms that the mixed strategy was the best in this case.

CONCLUSION

The current study aims to examine whether criminal networks show evidence of being scale-free in structure, and to estimate the differential effectiveness of different law enforcement strategies aimed at dismantling criminal networks. We used a case study of

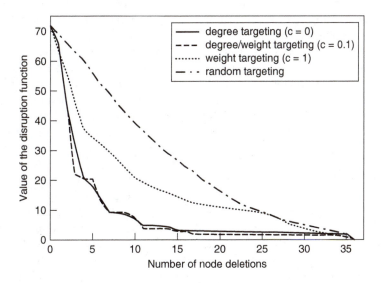

Figure 8.5 The four simulations, measured using the disruption function

an Australian methamphetamine trafficking network.

We performed some calculations to compare the degree distribution of the methamphetamine network with the expected degree distribution of a random graph with the same density of links. Our calculations show that the methamphetamine network is not an "exponential network, " as the nodes of high degree are extremely unlikely to exist in a random graph with the same average degree. Most real-world networks seem to be either exponential or scale-free (Albert et al., 2000). By applying a goodness-of-fit test, we confirmed that a power-law distribution is a plausible hypothesis for the degree distribution of the methamphetamine network. Hence the network can be said to be scale-free (though this term is usually applied to much larger networks).

Scale-free networks are vulnerable to being dismantled by deleting nodes with many connections (i.e., hubs). Our simulations examine whether law enforcement should target hubs, or whether including information about node attributes is a more effective strategy. In our simulations, the degree targeting strategy proved very effective at fragmenting the network, with respect to both measures (size of largest component, and the disruption function). This is consistent with the finding that the network may be scale-free in structure and with previous research (e.g., Keegan et al., 2010). It is somewhat surprising that the mixed strategy achieved an improvement over degree targeting when measured using the maximum component size, since this is a purely topological measure. We believe that this improvement is an artifact of the properties of the methamphetamine network. Careful study of Figure 8.4 reveals that the curve for the mixed strategy dips below the curve for the degree targeting at the third step (after the third deletion). By the fourth deletion, the two curves meet and thereafter the curve for degree targeting is always below or meeting the mixed strategy curve. So the

improvement obtained by the mixed strategy is entirely due to the choices made in the third step of the simulation. We investigate this further below.

Under both strategies, the first two nodes which are deleted are always K12 and K18 (in that order). After these deletions, there are 22 nodes in the maximum connected component of the remaining network. Then the degree targeting strategy will randomly choose a node of highest remaining degree, namely K20 or K28 (both of degree 7). Each of these nodes is chosen with probability 0.5 and is deleted, leading to a network with a maximum connected component of size 21 or 18. The average over 100 runs of the maximum component size at this step will be close to 19.5 (which equals the average of 21 and 18). However, at the third step, the node with the highest score in the mixed strategy is K26. Hence this node will be deleted at the third step, leading to a network with a maximum connected component size of 11. This fairly dramatic improvement (reducing the size of the largest component from 22 to 11 in one step) is due to an important structural property of this particular criminal network. As can be seen from Figure 8.2, deleting the links from K17 to K26 and from K12 to K28 will disconnect the network into two pieces of roughly equal size. This can also be achieved by deleting one node from each of these two links, such as K12 and K26. In graph theory terminology, the set containing K12 and K26 is a *cut set*, meaning that deleting these nodes creates a disconnected graph. It is a very useful cut set for fragmenting the network because each remaining component is much smaller than the original network (around half the size). By chance, the mixed strategy manages to delete such a cut set in the first three steps, thereby producing a steep drop in the size of the largest connected component.

It is clear from Figures 8.4 and 8.5 that random targeting is much less effective than degree targeting, irrespective of whether effectiveness is measured using the size of the largest connected component or the disruption function. To quantify this, we calculated the ratios of the areas under the curve for random targeting versus degree targeting. This ratio equals 3.22 with respect to the maximum component size measure (Figure 8.4) and equals 3.25 with respect to the disruption function (Figure 8.5). For this network, and using these two measures, degree targeting was three times more effective than random targeting.

As mentioned previously, the mixed strategy performed (slightly) better relative to the degree strategy. The ratio of the areas under the curve for the degree targeting versus mixed strategy was 1.006 with respect to the maximum component size measure (Figure 8.4) and was 1.092 with respect to the disruption function (Figure 8.5). It is not surprising that this small improvement is larger when measured by the disruption function, given that the disruption function takes role information into account when measuring fragmentation.

It should be noted that we used the value c = 0.1 since this gave optimal performance for the given network, as shown in Figure 8.3. It is noteworthy that this value c is quite small, meaning that the mixed strategy only takes role information into account to a limited extent. This could be an artifact of the particular network studied.

Overall, law enforcement strategies which targeted nodes based on centrality scores and on a combination of centrality scores and roles of individuals were most effective. Law enforcement interventions which use role information only and which do not consider centrality scores were relatively ineffective at dismantling the network. Interestingly, adding role information to centrality scores increased the effectiveness of law enforcement interventions in dismantling the network when the outcome measure incorporated the roles or ease with which individuals could be replaced (the disruption function).

The results of the study suggest that, to effectively target and dismantle criminal networks, law enforcement should consider node-level features (such as the roles played by individuals in the network) in addition to node topography features, such as centrality scores. Indeed, the results suggest that only using role information to determine nodes to target is less effective than using either centrality scores or centrality scores in concert with individual attributes (such as roles). The results underscore the utility of measures of centrality in choosing individuals to target when the aim is to dismantle criminal networks. Scale-free network structure suggests that targeting informed by centrality scores is important. Law enforcement targeting which does not use centrality scores to guide arrests is likely to be ineffective (when the aim is to dismantle criminal networks). However, the study provides some early evidence that including information on node attributes may enhance law enforcement effectiveness.

To make cost-effective arrests, law enforcement agencies require resources which facilitate the gathering of quality intelligence, sophisticated SNA, and interventions targeted at vulnerable areas (i.e., hubs). These processes are resource heavy. In recent media interviews (Australian Broadcasting Corporation, 2010). Australian Crime Commission Chief Executive Officer and ex-officers suggested that law enforcement is currently under-resourced to engage effectively in these endeavors. Also, there may be political pressure on law enforcement agencies to seize drugs and money, make arrests etc. as indicators of success, rather than to engage in prolonged intelligence gathering, costly investigations, and interventions designed to dismantle a criminal network. If future research supports the results of this preliminary research, it would suggest that resources directed into longer-term intelligence gathering, SNA of criminal networks (i.e., including calculation of centrality measures and node-level attribute information), and targeting vulnerabilities within criminal networks may produce cost-effective results. This requires further research using economic analyses which can incorporate the costs inherent in high-volume surveillance and intelligence-gathering operations.

Furthermore, there are no clear and accepted methodologies which measure the effectiveness of law enforcement interventions aimed at dismantling criminal networks. On the other hand, trends in seizures and arrests are routinely reported and are often used (somewhat erroneously) as measures of law enforcement effectiveness. This surfaces the need for the development of alternate performance indicators which can accurately reflect other law enforcement goals, such as the dismantling of criminal networks. The measures we used in this study show promise as measures of law enforcement effectiveness where the aim is to dismantle criminal networks.

There are a number of important limitations of this study and for the generalizability of the results to real-world criminal networks: 1) Networks are multimodal (include people, events, locations, resources). However, for the current study, we used only static connections between people, and did not collect information on the type or strength of links; 2) Criminal justice/law enforcement data can include intentional misinformation (e.g., aliases) and inaccuracies (e.g., typographic errors); 3) Law enforcement and criminal justice data, such as those used in this study, are often incomplete. The network used in this study may be only a part of a larger network which remains hidden; 4) Degree centrality scores for particular nodes may be artificially inflated by the amount of information gathered on particular nodes during the investigation, and may not reflect the extent of "real" connectedness; 5) The network that we studied is very small, with only 36 nodes. The mathematical techniques used in our analyses are limited by the small size of the network; 6) There are many ways to quantify role information and to measure fragmenta-

tion of a network: we feel that the choices that we made were logical; however, other choices may also be valid and may lead to different results; 7) The simulations assumed that no new connections are made in response to node removal. Illicit networks are known to be resilient (Ayling, 2009; Bakker, Raab, & Milward, 2010; Carley, 2006) and can respond or adapt to law enforcement interventions in a number of ways: by replacing nodes or links, by laying low, by recruiting new members, by joining other groups, or through the emergence of new leaders (Carley, Lee, & Krackhardt, 2002). In fact, even if all well-connected nodes are removed, just a few remaining nodes might re-establish communication (Williams, 2001). The simulation did not take account of this possibility; 8) The conclusions are limited to the network we examined: the methamphetamine trafficking network. Further research is required to determine the generalizability of our results; 9) The aims of law enforcement are diverse. In this project, we evaluated the extent to which law enforcement interventions (arrests) can dismantle a criminal network. However, law enforcement may seek to accomplish goals other than dismantling a network. For example, the aim may be to incapacitate the network so that the groups can no longer act illicitly, or to breach trust within the network such that the network disintegrates via internal distrust and conflict.

Despite the limitations, the simulation methodology we employed here can provide insights into the structural and functional damage that can be done to dark networks by targeted removal of nodes. It has the potential to demonstrate the utility of targeted node removal as a law enforcement intervention, especially compared with the removal of nodes such as drug couriers, wholesale dealers, or other individuals who are easily replaceable and are not well connected with other nodes in the network, but may simply be more "visible." In addition, it provides a potential method for measuring the effectiveness of law enforcement interventions which aim to dismantle criminal networks.

Research looking at the vulnerability and resilience of criminal networks is in its infancy. This chapter represents an important progression in the literature, but more research is needed. Improved strategies may be obtained by taking more information from the network into account, such as looking for small cut sets which achieve a steep drop in the size of the largest connected component. Furthermore, alternate methods to measure connectedness—for example, frequency of contact (e.g., number of phone calls)—could be used to quantify strength of relationships. There is also a need to replicate this work with larger, more complex networks, and with a variety of criminal networks (terrorist networks, arms traffickers, people smugglers/traffickers, etc.). Insights may be gained from performing simulations on random scale-free (or other) networks, using some random distribution of role data. Future research should utilize dynamic modeling which incorporates network responses/adaptation (e.g., previously unconnected nodes connect; recruitment), and individual/node-level characteristics (e.g., resilience, adaptability). Finally, the current chapter utilized a relatively unsophisticated method of quantifying role information. Future research should utilize more detailed data sources and attempt to use more sophisticated node attribute data (Robins, 2009; Robins & Kashima, 2008).

REFERENCES

Albert, R., H. Jeong, & A.L. Barabasi (1999). Diameter of the World-Wide Web. *Nature* 401, 130–131.

Albert, R., H. Jeong, & A.L. Barabasi (2000). Letters to Nature: Error and attack tolerance of complex networks. *Nature* 406, 378–382.

Australian Broadcasting Corporation (2010). *Crime Incorporated*. Four Corners, August 30.

Ayling, J. (2009). Criminal organizations and resilience. *International Journal of Law, Crime and Justice* 37(4), 182–196.

Bakker, R.M., J. Raab, & H.B. Milward (2010). A preliminary theory of dark network reslience. *Journal of Policy Analysis and Management* 31, 33–62.

Bollobás, B. & O. Riordan (2004). Robustness and vulnerability of scale-free random graphs. *Internet Mathematics*, 1(1), 1–35. doi: 10.1080/15427951.2004.10129080

Bright, D.A., C. Greenhill, & N. Levenkova (2010). *Attack of the Nodes: Scale-Free Criminal Networks and Vulnerability to Targeted Law Enforcement Interventions*. Paper presented at the 2nd Illicit Networks Workshop, Wollongong, Australia.

Bright, D.A., C.E. Hughes, & J. Chalmers (2012). Illuminating dark networks: A social network analysis of an Australian drug trafficking syndicate. *Crime, Law, and Social Change* 57(2), 151–176.

Carley, K.M. (2006). Destabalization of covert networks. *Computational and Mathematical Organization Theory* 12, 51–66.

Carley, K.M., J. Lee, & D. Krackhardt (2002). Destabilizing networks. *Connections* 24, 79–92.

Clauset, A., C.R. Shalizi, & M.E.J. Newman (2009). Power-law distributions in empirical data. *SIAM Review* 51, 661–703.

Crucitti, P., V. Latora, M. Marchiori, & A. Rapisarda (2003). Efficiency of scale-free networks: Error and attack tolerance. *Physica A: Statistical Mechanics and its Applications* 320, 622–642.

Dorogovtsev, J.F.F. & A.N. Mendes (2001). Scaling properties of scale-free evolving networks: Continuous approach. *Physical Review E* 63(5), 056125.

Ebel, H., L.-I. Mielsch, & S. Bornholdt (2002). Scale-free topology of e-mail networks. *Physical Review E* 66(3), 035103.

Faloutsos, M., P. Faloutsos, & C. Faloutsos (1999). On power-law relationships of the internet topology, ACM SIGCOMM '99. *Computer Communications Review* 29, 251–263.

Keegan, B., M.A. Ahmed, D. Williams, J. Srivastava, & N. Contractor (2010). *Dark Gold: Statistical Properties of Clandestine Networks in Massively Muliplayer Online Games*. Paper presented at the 2010 IEEE Second International Conference on Social Computing, IEEE Computer Society, Los Alamitos, CA, USA.

Liljeros, F., C.R. Edling, L.A.N. Amaral, H.E.

Stanley, & Y. Aberg (2001). The web of human sexual contacts. *Nature* 411(6840), 907–908.

Morselli, C. (2009). *Inside Criminal Networks*. New York: Springer.

Morselli, C. & K. Petit (2007). Law-enforcement disruption of a drug importation network. *Global Crime* 8(2), 109–130.

Morselli, C. & J. Roy (2008). Brokerage qualifications in ringing operations. *Criminology* 46, 71–98.

Natarajan, M. (2006). Understanding the structure of a large heroin distribution network: A quantitative analysis of qualitative data. *Journal of Quantitative Criminology* 22(2), 171–192.

Newman, M.E.J. (2010). Random graphs as models of networks. In S. Bornholdt & H.G. Schuster (eds.), *Handbook of Graphs and Networks: From the Genome to the Internet* (pp. 35–68). Weinheim: Wiley-VCH Verlag.

Redner, S. (2005). Citation statistics from 110 years of Physical Review. *Physics Today* 58, 49–54.

Robins, G. (2009). Understanding individual behaviors within covert networks: The interplay of individual qualities, psychological predispositions, and network effects. *Trends in Organized Crime* 12(2), 166–187.

Robins, G. & Y. Kashima (2008). Social psychology and social networks: Individuals and social systems. *Asian Journal of Social Psychology* 11(1), 1–12.

Schwartz, D.M. & D.A. Rouselle (2009). Using social network analysis to target criminal networks. *Trends in Organized Crime* 12, 188–207.

Williams, P. (2001). Transnational criminal networks. In D.F.R. John Arquilla (ed.), *Networks and Netwars: The Future of Terror, Crime, and Militancy* (pp. 61–97). Santa Monica: RAND.

Xu, J. & H. Chen (2009). Untangling criminal networks: A case study. In H. Chen, R. Miranda, D. Zeng, C. Demchak, J. Schroeder, & T. Madhusudan (eds.), *Intelligence and Security Informatics* (p. 958). Berlin, Heidelberg: Springer.

CHAPTER 9

Strategic Positioning in Mafia Networks

Francesco Calderoni

Individuals in criminal groups are constantly faced with a trade-off between security (minimizing risks) and efficiency (maximizing opportunities/profits). Individuals achieving a good balance in this trade-off—i.e., those managing to maintain control over criminal opportunities and activities while reducing the risk of detection—are strategically positioned and more likely to succeed in their criminal careers (Bouchard & Nguyen, 2010: 132; Morselli, Giguère, & Petit, 2007).

The security/efficiency trade-off is a consequence of the structure of criminal markets, such as those for drugs. The literature on drug markets highlights that criminal groups adapt to market conditions and particularly to the need to minimize the risks of apprehension while maximizing the profits generated by the traffic. Studies have shown that drug markets are particularly flexible and dynamic environments (Benson & Decker, 2010; Bouchard & Ouellet, 2011: 70–71; Desroches, 2003; Dorn, Levi, & King, 2005: 14–15; Dorn, Murji, & South, 1992: ix; Paoli, 2004: 201; Pearson & Hobbs, 2001: 11–12; Reuter, 2009; Reuter & Haaga, 1989: 54–55). The characteristics of such markets inevitably influence the type of criminal groups operating within them (Reuter, 1983; Paoli, 2004: 203). Several constraints related to the illegality of the product make it difficult for large criminal enterprises to form and continue for longer periods. By contrast, small, inconstant groups are formed, with partner-

ships changing frequently (Reuter, 1983; Eck & Gersh, 2000). Larger structured groups, such as mafia-type groups, are exceptional (Reuter, 2009: 16). Whenever they participate in drug markets, mafia-type organizations do not seem to achieve monopoly positions (Becchi, 1996: 125–127; Paoli, 2002a: 145–147; Varese, 2006a: 433–438). Instead, they adapt to the dynamic environment with a very limited importance of their internal formal hierarchies (Paoli, 2004: 198–199).

Identification of the most important individuals in criminal networks has received particular attention since the 1980s (Lupsha, 1980; Davis, 1981: 18; Lupsha, 1983; Ianni & Reuss-Ianni, 1990: 76–77). This is hardly surprising, given the implications of such endeavors from both a research and a policy perspective. The most recent contributions on the structure of criminal organizations and particularly on strategic positioning have increasingly included the application of social network analysis (hereinafter SNA) approaches and methods (Natarajan, 2000; Xu & Chen, 2003; Natarajan, 2006; Varese, 2006b; Morselli & Giguère, 2006; Morselli & Petit, 2007; Morselli et al., 2007; Morselli & Roy, 2008; Malm, Kinney, & Pollard, 2008; Heber, 2009; Morselli, 2009a, 2009b; Bouchard & Nguyen, 2010; Morselli, 2010; Bouchard & Ouellet, 2011; Bright, Hughes, & Chalmers, 2012). The application of SNA to drug trafficking groups has led to important advances in the field by making it possible to determine the strategic positioning of specific criminals who have proved successful in balancing security and efficiency.

Most SNA techniques use the key concept of centrality to identify the most important subjects in a network. Several measures of centrality have been developed for different purposes, the choice depending on the type of data and the research objectives (Hanneman & Riddle, 2005: 147; McGloin & Kirk, 2010: 219–220; Morselli, 2009b: 38; Scott, 2000: 82; Wasserman & Faust, 1994: 169).

The literature on illicit networks has argued that degree and betweenness centrality scores may have different meanings among criminal networks. Interestingly, the most common and straightforward measure of centrality—degree centrality (i.e., the number of a node's direct contacts)—may be particularly misleading in identifying the most important nodes in criminal networks. In particular, degree centrality reflects active involvement in a network's activities, but in the case of criminal networks it has been argued that "degree centrality makes a person vulnerable" (Baker & Faulkner, 1993: 854). Indeed, having a high number of direct contacts makes a node particularly visible and consequently an easy target for law enforcement. Alternatively, betweenness centrality has been considered a more suitable measure (Sparrow, 1991: 264–265). Betweenness centrality calculates the number of times a node lies in the shortest path between two other nodes in the same network. In the context of criminal networks, it may prove more effective in revealing strategic positioning, since it signals less visibility and more indirect control over the flow of information (Morselli, 2009b: 39–40, 2010). Accordingly, strategically positioned individuals in criminal networks are likely to have lower degree and higher betweenness centrality scores (Morselli, 2010). This strategic positioning pattern has two advantages. First, it allows for better control over the criminal activities, so that it should differentiate the criminal leaders from the other individuals. Second, it affords better protection from detection and conviction, along with lower sentencing.

This interpretation has been supported by empirical evidence. Baker and Faulkner (1993) showed that degree centrality increased the chances of conviction and the penalties in price-fixing conspiracies. In his studies on the Hells Angels in Quebec, Morselli found that subjects with higher status within the motorcycle group had higher betweenness centrality and lower degree centrality compared with middle- and low-status members (Morselli, 2009a, 2009b). More recently, he also found that "the highest proportion of arrests was found in the high degree centrality/low-betweenness-centrality group" (Morselli, 2010: 389). In another study, Morselli found that members of the Bo-Gars gang had lower direct, but higher indirect connectivity than did other gangs and non-gang members. This was reflected in lower arrest rates (Morselli, 2009b: 156–157). Bouchard and Nguyen (2010) studied cannabis cultivation in Quebec and argued that personal network characteristics (e.g., youth vs. adult network, network size) influence detection and arrest.

Unfortunately, the above-mentioned studies depended on a particular distribution of the centrality measures, and specifically on a limited overlap between them. For example, in the case of Morselli's study on the Hells Angels, the two centrality measures were significantly and positively correlated, but with a limited amount of covariance (Pearson's r = 0.4) (Morselli, 2010: 388). This revealed that direct and indirect connectivity in the network followed different routes and made it possible to identify strategic positioning patterns.

In most criminal groups, centrality measures may not enable the identification of strategic positioning of individuals. Indeed, in many cases "criminal network participants are balancing both forms of centrality" (Morselli, 2010: 386). Centrality measures may have very similar structures with high positive correlation, to the point that the overlap between degree and betweenness centrality leaves little room for identifying strategic positioning. This implies that SNA methods alone may not permit identification of strategically positioned individuals, although such patterns may actually exist.

Other complementary research strategies can contribute to uncovering strategic positioning patterns whenever the distributions of degree and betweenness centrality overlap. Several studies have identified the main tasks, the status, and other characteristics of individuals in criminal networks by analyzing the content of intercepted conversations or other judicial sources (Natarajan, 2000, 2006; Varese, 2006b; Campana, 2011; Varese, 2012; Bright et al., 2012). Indeed, content analysis integrates well with SNA methods, and criminal network scholars have acknowledged it to be "the next step toward enriching the various analyses conducted throughout this book" (Morselli, 2009b: 164). A few studies have coupled network analysis with the content analysis of judicial documents in order to explore the functioning of criminal networks. For example, Natarajan identified the different tasks or roles in two New York criminal organizations trafficking cocaine (2000) and heroin (2006) by analyzing a sample of intercepted conversations. She further measured the status of each individual in the network by means of a six-item coding guide.[1] Varese (2006b) analyzed a Russian criminal organization attempting to establish a branch in Rome with the main purpose of laundering money and investing in the legal economy. The study estimated the informal hierarchy of the group by analyzing the number of times an individual gave orders, expressed dissatisfaction, and threatened his/her interlocutor (Varese 2006b: 27). More recently, Bright and colleagues (2012) have studied the organization of a group involved in the production and distribution of methamphetamine in New South Wales, Australia. The authors identified dif-

ferent tasks within the organization through analysis of the court's sentencing comments. Although these studies were not directly concerned with analysis of the strategic positioning of individuals, they demonstrate the usefulness of different approaches in identifying tasks and roles and providing further insight into the social organization of criminal networks. At the same time, the diversity of the methods adopted suggests that there are no general rules and that methods should be carefully designed to take account of the specific criminal activities, and even the types of drug trafficked by the groups analyzed.

The aim of the research reported in what follows was to identify strategic positioning patterns in two drug trafficking networks where degree and betweenness centrality scores were closely correlated. Multiple research strategies intended to identify hierarchy, task, and status were applied to two groups belonging to the 'Ndrangheta, a mafia-type organization from Calabria, a Southern Italian region. The first objective was to identify strategic positioning in the criminal networks, overcoming the difficulties generated by the nearly complete overlap between degree and betweenness centrality. The second objective was to verify whether the structure identified also reflected the arrest, conviction, and sentencing of individuals.

THE 'NDRANGHETA AND NETWORK POSITIONING

The historical origins of the 'Ndrangheta reach back to the nineteenth century, although some evidence suggests that it may have had precursors even before that period (Ciconte, 1992; Gratteri & Nicaso, 2009: 25). The basic unit of the 'Ndrangheta is called 'ndrina. Unlike the Sicilian Cosa Nostra, the 'ndrine mostly consist of members of the same blood family, a characteristic which strengthens the cohesion of the criminal group (Paoli, 2003; Varese, 2006a). The 'ndrine from the same area form a *locale,* which controls a specific territory. The 'Ndrangheta further enhances the strength of the *'ndrine* and *locali* by fostering a shared culture based on rituals, affiliation ceremonies, formal ranks, and mythology.[2] Familial, cultural, and hierarchical ties reinforce trust among the members and give the 'Ndrangheta exceptional solidity (Paoli, 2003). As proof of this, very few *pentiti* (collaborators with justice) come from the 'Ndrangheta, as opposed to the Sicilian Mafia or the Neapolitan Camorra (Paoli, 1994: 216).

One of the main criminal activities of the 'Ndrangheta is the trafficking of cocaine. The 'Ndrangheta has exploited its organizational structure to establish solid partnerships with Colombian cocaine suppliers (Paoli, 1994: 222–223). Several official reports maintain that the 'Ndrangheta has achieved a primary role in the Italian cocaine market, outmatching other mafia-type organizations, such as the Sicilian Mafia and the Neapolitan Camorra (CPA, 2008; Paoli, 2004: 201).

Analysis of the structure of two 'Ndrangheta drug trafficking organizations provides an interesting opportunity to identify strategic positioning patterns within two highly structured criminal groups. Indeed, the 'Ndrangheta normally operates with a clear division of tasks among the members of the organization. Furthermore, its structured nature, typical of mafia-type organizations, implies that different levels of leadership or social status may be identified by examining either the formal ranks assigned to the members or the informal hierarchy that may be observed from the content analysis of the conversations.

METHODOLOGY

Case Studies and Data Sources

This research consisted of two case studies relating to two investigations coordinated by the Antimafia Prosecutor's Office of

Reggio Calabria (Operation Chalonero and Operation Stupor Mundi).[3] Information on the two cases came from multiple sources, including judicial files (e.g., arrest warrants, final judgments) and other sources (the literature, official reports by law enforcement agencies or prosecution offices, and news reports).

Operation Chalonero was conducted by the *Carabinieri* of the Provincial Command of Reggio Calabria. The investigation lasted several years and ended in January 2007 with the arrest of 16 people ordered by the Court of Reggio Calabria. The phone interceptions covered the period from August 2003 to June 2004. Operation Chalonero focused on criminal groups belonging to the 'Ndrangheta and trafficking cocaine from South America to Italy, through Spain. The drug was sold in Italy, particularly in the areas of Milan, Florence, Bologna, Rome, and in Calabria (DIA, 2007: 106).

Operation Stupor Mundi was conducted by the Antidrug Operational Group of the *Guardia di Finanza* of Reggio Calabria. The investigation lasted for a number of years and ended in May 2007 with the arrest of 38 people on order by the Court of Reggio Calabria. The phone interceptions covered the period from June 2002 to April 2004. The operation focused on criminal groups belonging to the 'Ndrangheta and trafficking cocaine from South America to Italy, through Spain and the Netherlands. The drug was sold in Italy, particularly in the areas of Milan, Turin, Rome, and in Calabria (CPA, 2008: 195 and 235).

The main analyses were conducted on the information contained in two court orders issued by the preliminary investigation judge (*Giudice per le indagini preliminari*) upon request by the prosecution. From a comparative perspective, court orders of this kind are broadly similar to arrest warrants in other jurisdictions. The two documents provided data on the accused individuals (e.g., name, birth date, residence, citizenship) and their activities.[4] In particular, they reported data on the communication flows among the members of the two networks and a number of conversations that were partly or entirely transcribed. Furthermore, the documents provided information on whether each individual was targeted by the investigation and arrested at the end of the operations (see Table 9.1).[5]

Additional sources provided information about the outcomes of the criminal proceedings. Several judgments were collected in cooperation with the Antimafia Prosecutor's Office of Reggio Calabria. Unfortunately, information about conviction and sentencing was available only for a limited number of individuals. This was because, in the Italian criminal justice system, once an investigation has been closed, the development of the proceedings may take different paths for the accused persons and may last several years. Indeed, for Chalonero, two first-grade judgments and one appeal judgment were available. For Stupor Mundi, three first-grade judgments were collected.[6] Overall, the decisions collected provided information about the acquittal or conviction of around 17 individuals out of 46 accused for Chalonero, and 40 out of 45 accused for Stupor Mundi, respectively (Table 9.1).

The Analyses of the Two Groups

The research used various methods, some of them based on previous studies on drug trafficking and other criminal groups (Natarajan, 2000; Varese, 2006b; Natarajan, 2006; Morselli, 2009b, 2010). For each investigation, the analyses focused on a subset of individuals. Indeed, relational information

(participation in phone calls and/or in meetings) was available for 92 and 128 individuals for Chalonero and Stupor Mundi, respectively.[7] However, a preliminary analysis showed that most individuals participated only marginally in the networks. A number of individuals were in contact with only one other subject and participated in a low number of communications. By contrast, a limited number of individuals had a very high number of contacts and participated in a high number of communications. The results were consistent with the findings of previous research. Several studies have found that a small proportion of the individuals in a criminal group account for the majority of the communications (Natarajan, 2000: 277, 2006: 179; Morselli, 2009b: 51). Given the concentration of the contacts, and in line with the literature, it was decided to remove from the analysis the individuals with only one contact, and to exclude those with very limited participation in the group's activities. Consequently, the study concentrated on two subsets of 61 and 73 individuals for Chalonero and Stupor Mundi, respectively.[8]

The first analysis aimed at identifying the main task of each individual within the two groups (Natarajan, 2000, 2006; Morselli & Giguère, 2006; Bright et al., 2012). As argued by previous studies, individuals in charge of organizing smuggling operations and connecting producers/suppliers with buyers have key brokering roles in criminal networks. For this reason, the analysis identified a key group of traffickers in both groups. Other tasks (as suppliers, buyers, couriers, support personnel, and retailers) were identified and

Table 9.1 Information on the different stages of the criminal proceedings

	Accused	N/acc.	Total	Arrested	N/arr.	Total	Convicted	Acquitted	N/a	Total
Stupor Mundi	45	28	73	38	7	45	26	14	5	45
Chalonero	46	15	61	11	35	46	12	5	29	46

they revealed important similarities between the two organizations (Table 9.2).

The purpose of the second analysis was to identify the importance of each individual within the two criminal groups using methodologies different from SNA. To this end, two different strategies were followed. The *first strategy* relied on information from the prosecution and the court. Indeed, the court orders for both operations provided information about the organizational structure of the 'Ndrangheta groups, and specifically about their members and bosses (Table 9.2).[9] The above-mentioned classification had the advantage of selecting a restricted number of individuals as the criminal leaders. Conversely, it had the disadvantage of relying heavily on information from the prosecution and the court, with very limited possibilities to verify its reliability and accuracy. To overcome this problem, the *second strategy* centered on the assessment of the relative status of the individuals, drawing on previous literature (Natarajan, 2000, 2006). The analysis applied a six-code scheme to the communications among the individuals in the groups.[10] The coding scheme was applied to one conversation for every couple of individuals for which conversations were available in the court orders.[11] Each individual was attributed a status score resulting from application of the coding scheme (one point for the presence of each of the above-listed codes).[12] In the case of individuals with status scores from multiple conversations, the status score was the mean of the scores of the single conversations. Furthermore, the individuals in each group were divided into three status classes according to their status scores (Table 9.2).[13]

Finally, SNA methods were applied to the two criminal groups (Table 9.3).[14] They extracted information about phone calls and meetings from the two court orders and created two valued, square matrices, indicating whether any two individuals were in contact

Table 9.2 Number of individuals per task, hierarchy, and status

		Chalonero	*Stupor Mundi*
	Total individuals	61	73
General information	Foreigner	12	2
	Female	4	4
Task	Supplier	—	14
	Trafficker	16	9
	Buyer	19	15
	Courier	12	N/a
	Support	26	16
	Retailer	—	14
Hierarchy	Non-member	44	37
	'Ndrangheta member	12	30
	Boss	5	6
Status class	High status	10	23
	Medium status	29	18
	Low status	22	32
Status score	Min score	2	1.7
	Max score	4	4.5
	Mean score	2.8	2.6
	St. dev.	0.6	0.6

and how many communications occurred between them. Also, valued matrices were transformed into binary matrices to perform some routines.[15]

Consistently with the purpose of identifying strategic positioning patterns within the two groups, degree and betweenness centrality were calculated. Degree centrality was measured on both binary and valued networks, the latter indicating the number of contacts instead of the mere presence of a contact. In addition, the analysis calculated the clustering coefficient for each node. This measures the density of the neighborhood of each node (i.e., all the nodes directly connected to a given node) (Hanneman & Riddle, 2005: 124). The clustering coefficient measures the likelihood that two individuals connected to the same third individual are themselves connected (Morselli, 2009b: 40–41). Although Morselli suggested that it should be considered a measure of direct connectivity, (such as degree or eigenvector centrality), this research used it in a different way (Morselli, 2009b: 136–137). Indeed, having a high coefficient means that a node's contacts are also in contact with each other. Conversely, a low score implies that the density of the neighborhood of a node is low. In the context of a criminal organization, having scarcely connected contacts may be an advantage, meaning that a node bridges various individuals which are not in contact. Furthermore, higher clustering may imply low secrecy, since information may be shared among the other nodes.[16]

As already anticipated, in both networks, the three centrality measures (degree, valued degree, and betweenness) were closely correlated.[17] This made it impossible to take the traditional approach to the identification of strategic positions within criminal networks and required the development of new research strategies.

RESULTS

Strategic Positioning in the 'Ndrangheta

In both networks, traffickers and bosses had higher status scores than other individuals (Table 9.4). As for the traffickers, this finding reveals that this specific task is of vital importance in drug-trafficking organizations, including mafia-type ones. This is because they may be more experienced and skilled than other criminals and this would be revealed also by their higher status. This comes as no surprise. Traffickers are similar to brokers in criminal networks, a function whose importance has been abundantly highlighted in the literature (Morselli, 2009b: 15; Coles, 2001).[18] Similarly, bosses had higher status than simple 'Ndrangheta members and non-members (although the difference was not statistically significant in Chalonero, probably because of the limited number of 'Ndrangheta members and bosses). Interestingly, in both groups all bosses were traffickers.

The introduction of network measures into the analysis yielded a more complex

Table 9.3 Network measures, descriptive statistics

	Chalonero					Stupor Mundi				
	Degree	Val. deg.	Betw.	Clus. coeff.	No. pairs	Degree	Val. deg.	Betw.	Clus. coeff.	No. pairs
Min	0.03	2.00	0.00	0.08	1.00	0.01	1.00	0.00	0.09	0.00
Max	0.62	294.00	0.75	1.00	666.0	0.71	947.00	0.51	1.00	1275.0
Avg.	0.07	16.95	0.03	0.77	19.9	0.08	52.55	0.02	0.74	42.6
St.dv	0.08	39.42	0.10	0.29	85.5	0.10	138.45	0.07	0.28	159.3

Note
Degree and betweenness are normalized values.

Table 9.4 Mean status score by task and by hierarchy in both groups

		Chalonero		Stupor Mundi	
		N	Mean status sc.	N	Mean status sc.
Task	N/trafficker	52	2.70*	57	2.43**
	Trafficker	9	**3.16***	16	**2.98***
Hierarchy	N/member	49	2.71	43	2.50**
	Member	7	2.91	24	2.43**
	Boss	5	**3.2**	6	**3.38***

Note
** p < 0.01, * p < 0.05

picture (Table 9.5). In both groups, traffickers, bosses, and members of the 'Ndrangheta showed higher centrality. They had more contacts and also more frequent communications (valued degree). Furthermore, betweenness centrality scores were very high for traffickers, and even higher for bosses. Overall, a small set of traffickers/bosses is central to the flow of information in both criminal networks. This indicates that these individuals play a crucial role in connecting different nodes through the drug-trafficking operations. In part, the findings support the view that the specific activities within the drug-trafficking chain account for the positioning of the individuals within the network and provide evidence of the adaptation of mafia-type organizations to the criminal markets in which they operate (Paoli, 2002b, 2004).

Although straightforward, this picture seem to contrast with the model of a hierarchical organization as hypothesized in the literature and as could be expected given the characteristics of the 'Ndrangheta. In hierarchical networks, it is likely that leaders are only in contact with a limited number of lieutenants or collaborators, so that they can maintain indirect control over the criminal activities while minimizing their visibility (Jackson, Herbrink, & Jansen, 1996). By contrast, in the two 'Ndrangheta groups, the bosses were directly involved in the criminal activities. Indeed, the results show no traces

of differences among the different centrality measures. Traffickers, bosses, and members of the 'Ndrangheta were remarkably higher in both betweenness and degree centrality than other individuals.

Two interpretations, not necessarily mutually exclusive, may explain this finding. First, the theoretical hypothesis formulated by Jackson and colleagues (1996), based on delegation, division of tasks, and minimal involvement of criminal leaders, may have overlooked the specific features of drug-trafficking. In drug markets, the illicit nature of the activities entails that security (direct control of the activities by bosses) prevails over efficiency (indirect control and delegation). Although delegation allows more efficient management of the activities, it should not be regarded as a more secure approach because it increases the risks of information diffusion and detection. Delegation and indirect control are a luxury that criminal organizations can rarely afford. The findings from Chalonero and Stupor Mundi suggest that mafia-type organizations are no exception to this rule. Traffickers and bosses maintained close control of the activities, giving priority to security over more efficient organizational structures. This interpretation confirms that "covert networks are not generally capable of trading efficiency for security" (Morselli et al., 2007: 151) and that they tend to prioritize security in the form of direct control by bosses/traffickers.

Table 9.5 Mean individual network measures by task, status class, hierarchy, and traffickers-by-status class

| | | Chalonero | | | | | | Stupor Mundi | | | | | |
		N	Degree	Valued degree	Betweenness	Clus. coeff.	N.pairs	N	Degree	Valued degree	Betweenness	Clus. coeff.	N.pairs
Task	N/trafficker	52	0.050**	8.4**	0.014**	0.838**	3.8**	57	0.053**	17.6**	0.004**	0.814**	8.0**
	Trafficker	9	**0.198****	**66.6****	**0.138****	0.404**	112.6**	16	**0.191****	**177.0****	**0.071****	0.468**	**165.6****
Hier.	N/member	49	0.047**	6.6**	0.003**	0.871**	3.3**	43	0.047**	10.3**	0.005**	0.838**	5.8**
	Member	7	0.102**	28.0**	0.040**	0.493**	19.7**	24	0.101**	64.0**	0.018**	0.649**	41.0**
	Boss	5	**0.274****	**103.2****	**0.222****	0.217**	**183.0****	6	**0.278****	**309.2****	**0.118****	0.358**	**312.7****
Status class	High st.	10	0.075	15.6	0.027	**0.717**	14.0	23	0.093	62.5	0.023	**0.643**	42.2
	Medium st.	29	**0.089**	**24.6**	**0.042**	0.720	34.4	18	**0.095**	**74.0**	**0.032**	0.780	80.7
	Low st.	22	0.048	7.4	0.003	0.870	3.4	32	0.070	33.3	0.008	0.782	21.5
Traff.*Status	Traf*hi. st.	3	0.122	25.7	0.036	0.516	33.3	10	0.144	119.8	0.046	**0.466**	**87.1**
	Traf*med st.	6	**0.236**	**87.0**	**0.189**	0.349	152.2	1	**0.708**	**947.0**	**0.505**	0.094	1275.0
	Traf*low st.	0	N/a					5	**0.181**	**137.6**	0.034	0.549	100.6

Notes
** p < 0.01, * p < 0.05
The differences for traffickers*status were not statistically significant due to the extremely low number of cases.

Second, the networks observed may have been influenced by law enforcement perception. In part, this is not surprising, since the data were drawn from law enforcement sources and collected for purposes different from the analysis of the structure of the groups from a network perspective. Police surveillance may have focused on the most visible actors, and this may further explain why all bosses were also traffickers. Prosecution as bosses of the two groups may have been influenced by the visibility of individuals rather than their actual importance within the criminal organizations. Indeed, the content analysis of the conversations revealed that individuals identified as bosses frequently did not receive particular respect from other individuals. For example, they frequently received orders and treated other individuals with deference.

The inclusion of the results of the status analysis provided important insights allowing identification of the strategic positions of some individuals (Table 9.5). In particular, in both groups, individuals in the high-status class were not the most central nodes. Conversely, individuals with medium status had higher centrality scores (although the differences of the means were not statistically different, possibly due to the low number of cases).

In both groups, high-status individuals were strategically positioned. They were generally more detached from the core of the criminal activities, letting medium-status individuals occupy central positions. Furthermore, in Chalonero and Stupor Mundi, high-status individuals had lower clustering coefficients, although they generally had smaller neighborhoods. This is counterintuitive, since the clustering coefficient is generally indirectly correlated to the size of a node's neighborhood. Conversely, medium-status individuals had larger neighborhoods, but also higher clustering coefficients. This may indicate that such nodes are redundant and that their actual brokering power is more limited than that of high-status nodes. The latter were connecting subjects who were less connected among themselves. This pattern further points up their strategic position within the two criminal networks.

Closer analysis of traffickers within different status classes provides additional support for this finding (Table 9.5). In Chalonero, medium-status traffickers had higher centrality scores than did the high-status individuals (there were no low-status traffickers). In Stupor Mundi, high-status traffickers had centrality scores lower than the only medium-status trafficker and even lower than low-status traffickers. Furthermore, their clustering coefficient was lower, although with neighborhoods smaller than those of the other traffickers.

The strategic positioning pattern is recognizable in Figure 9.1 and Figure 9.2. The nodes were plotted against their status score and task. In both networks, traffickers were strongly connected with each other and communicated very frequently (solid black and solid grey lines). High-status individuals maintained fewer frequent contacts, remaining in a more detached position.

The network structure emerging from the analyses suggests that a specific pattern of network positioning was in place in the 'Ndrangheta groups. However, this could not be identified solely through analysis of degree and betweenness centrality, as suggested by the previous literature (Baker & Faulkner, 1993; Morselli, 2010, 2009a, 2009b: chap. 9). In the two 'Ndrangheta networks, individuals with medium status had higher direct and indirect connectivity than high-status individuals. These, in turn, were less central, but frequently had more strategic (less redundant) connections, as highlighted by lower clustering coefficients. This pattern appears consistent with the hypothesis that more important individuals may prefer to remain more detached from the operational core of the criminal activities in order to reduce the risk of detection (Morselli, 2010).

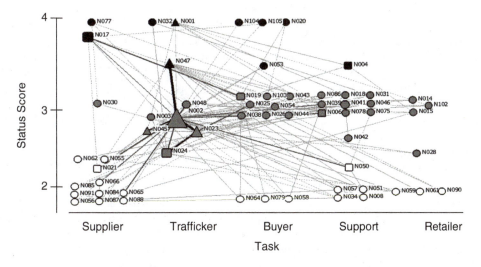

Figure 9.1 Chalonero. Status score by task[a]

Notes

a Node colors: black = high-status class; grey = medium-status class; white = low-status class
  Node shapes: triangle = boss; rounded square = member of the 'Ndrangheta; circle = non-member
  Node size: betweenness centrality
  Lines: solid black lines = ties with value > average valued degree (17); solid grey lines = ties with value > ½ valued degree (8); dotted grey lines = other ties

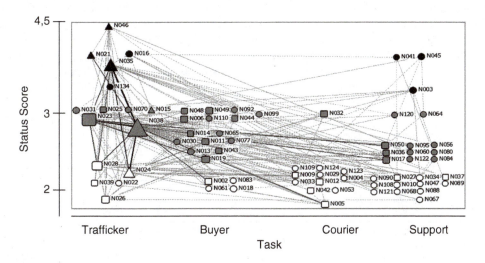

Figure 9.2 Stupor Mundi. Status score by task[a]

Notes

a Node colors: black = high-status class; grey = medium-status class; white = low-status class
  Node shapes: triangle = boss; rounded square = member of the 'Ndrangheta; circle = non-member
  Node size: betweenness centrality
  Lines: solid black lines = ties with value > average valued degree (53); solid grey lines = ties with value > ½ valued degree (27); dotted grey lines = other ties

The structure observed in the two groups gave the 'Ndrangheta organizations particular strength and resilience. Medium-status individuals were more central, but also more easily expendable and replaceable with other, readily available, affiliates to restore the criminal trade (Carley, Krackhardt, & Lee, 2002). For example, in Stupor Mundi, N24 was arrested by the police during a smuggling operation. Other traffickers, such as N25 (N24's brother) and N28, quickly mobilized and replaced the arrested node in the trafficking of cocaine.

The pattern observed allowed high-status individuals to reduce their visibility in the criminal activities. However, their low betweenness centrality suggests that they probably had different ways to control the activities of the organization. Their higher social status in the criminal groups probably enabled them to exert control with a limited amount of communications. This is consistent with Paoli (2002b), who argued that mafia-type organizations are rooted in particularly strong relations based on shared culture and kinship. Criminals are always embedded in wider social networks extending well beyond the boundaries of the networks that can be identified by analyzing one or more single investigations. SNA measures alone can

hardly capture the social capital and status of criminals, especially when they are embedded in very complex criminal organizations, such as mafia-type groups. The status analysis performed in this study has uncovered a part of these social relations, something which would not have emerged from the mere analysis of the social network.

Strategic Positioning and Outcomes of the Investigations and Trials

The strategic positioning patterns identified in the previous sections were verified against the outcomes of the investigations (accusation and arrest) and the trials (acquittal, conviction, and sentence).

In regard to the outcome investigations, individuals in both groups were classified as non-accused, accused-not-arrested, and arrested. Table 9.6 shows that that traffickers, members of the 'Ndrangheta, and bosses were always accused (except for 2 out of 16 traffickers in Stupor Mundi). Almost all bosses and members of the 'Ndrangheta were arrested (except for one member in Chalonero). Traffickers were arrested much more frequently than non-traffickers. The data on status appear less straightforward. Overall, the bivariate analysis of the status classes and

Table 9.6 Task, hierarchy, and status class per accused, accused (not arrested), and arrested individuals

		Chalonero				Stupor Mundi			
		N/accused	Accused	Arrested	$\chi^2(p)$	N/accused	Accused	Arrested	$\chi^2(p)$
Task	Non-trafficker	15	32	5	17.5**	26	6	25	7.2*
	Trafficker	0	3	6		2	1	13	
Hierarchy	Non-member	15	34	0	55.8**	28	7	8	46.9**
	Member	0	1	6		0	0	24	
	Boss	0	0	5		0	0	6	
Status	High st.	3	3	4	7.8**	7	2	14	1.7
	Medium st.	5	18	6		8	1	9	
	Low st.	7	14	1		13	4	15	
Total		15	35	11		28	7	38	

Note
** p < 0.01, * p < 0.05

the outcomes of the investigation provided a statistically significant, but weaker, chi-square than task and hierarchy for Chalon-ero and non-significant results for Stupor Mundi. This may suggest that the status was less decisive in determining the outcomes of the investigations. While law enforcement focused on traffickers and members/bosses of the 'Ndrangheta, the status of individuals was less associated with accusation and arrest.

Examination of the outcomes of the trials provides further insights. As already mentioned, information about the acquittal/conviction was available only for a limited number of individuals in the two groups. For this reason, the analysis of the judicial outcome concentrated only on Stupor Mundi, where information on conviction was available for 40 out of 45 accused individuals.

The data show that traffickers, members of the 'Ndrangheta, and bosses were frequently convicted (but the difference was statistically significant only for trafficker/non-trafficker at $p > 0.1$) (Table 9.7). In addition, non-traffickers and non-members of the 'Ndrangheta had high conviction rates (both above 50%). For traffickers, members, and bosses of the 'Ndrangheta, the mean sentence in months was higher than for other individuals (Table 9.8). Interestingly, a different pat-tern emerges when one considers the status classes. Here, low-status individuals were more frequently convicted. Low-status individuals appear extremely vulnerable as to their conviction rate (14 out of 19). Indeed, this may be due to their limited skills in reducing the risks associated with drug-traf-ficking. Conversely, they received lower sentences (on average approximately seven years and nine months of imprisonment). Regarding sentencing, medium-status individuals received the severest penalties (on average approximately 12 years and three months), but with a conviction rate lower than that of the low-status class (5 out of 10). This is consistent with the more central position in the criminal network, which in the case of conviction may result in very severe punishment. High-status individuals were convicted slightly more frequently than medium status ones (7 out of 11). However, their mean sentence was significantly lower (approximately nine years and three months), with a difference of nearly 36 months.

Overall, the results concerning the outcomes of the investigations and of the trials show that the strategic positioning patterns identified in the previous section also affected the judicial outcomes of the two operations. In particular, high-status individuals, maintaining a more detached position within the

Table 9.7 Conviction per task, hierarchy, and status class in Stupor Mundi network

		Acquitted	Convicted	$\chi^2(p)$
N		14	26	
Task	Non-trafficker	13	17	3.6!
	Trafficker	1	9	
Hierarchy	Non-member	6	7	1.1
	Member	7	16	
	Boss	1	3	
Status class	High status	4	7	1.6
	Medium status	5	5	
	Low status	5	14	

Note
** $p < 0.01$, * $p < 0.05$, ! $p < 0.10$

Table 9.8 Mean sentence (in months) per task, hierarchy, and status class in Stupor Mundi network

		Mean sentence (months)
Task	Non-trafficker	92.9**
	Trafficker	**138.1****
Hierarchy	Non-member	86.1**
	Member	96.5**
	Boss	225.3**
Status class	High status	111.7
	Medium status	**147.2**
	Low status	93.2

Note
** $p < 0.01$, * $p < 0.05$

network of Stupor Mundi, received sentences shorter than those of medium-status individuals (the most active players in the network), and had conviction rates lower than those of low-status individuals (the subjects usually tasked with the most risky activities, such as courier work). These findings further contribute to the existing literature on strategic positioning in criminal networks and its impact on judicial outcomes of criminal cases (Baker & Faulkner, 1993; Morselli, 2009b, 2009a, 2010; Bouchard & Nguyen, 2010). They confirm that strategic positioning patterns can be uncovered in complex criminal organizations and that these patterns are reflected in the judicial outcomes of cases. Specific positioning by some individuals may provide better protection against arrest and longer sentences. The identification and analysis of such patterns is a new direction for a more detailed understanding of the functioning of criminal organizations. The implications go beyond mere academic debate. Indeed, identification of strategically positioned individuals, especially when they are not the alleged bosses or traffickers, may enable law enforcement and prosecution agencies to disrupt criminal organizations more efficiently and permanently.

Furthermore, this study has identified

strategic positioning patterns by means of a new method which integrates analysis of the contents of intercepted conversations with network analysis measures. Whilst most previous studies have relied on the (probably exceptional) different distributions of degree and betweenness centrality (Morselli, 2009a, 2009b, 2010), this study has overcome this condition by suggesting that centrality can be complemented with other measures of individuals' importance which do not rely on network analysis methods.

Limitations

The analyses presented in this study had some limitations which mostly concerned the reliability of criminal justice sources for the analyses performed. This issue is common to most studies on criminal networks (and indeed to any study relying on such sources), and the literature frequently discusses it at length (Malm & Bichler, 2011: 20–22; Morselli, 2009b: 41–50; Xu & Chen, 2008: 63; von Lampe, 2009). The growing body of studies that use similar judicial sources for similar analyses suggests that the methodology of the present study is reasonably fit for this purpose (Natarajan & Belanger, 1998; Natarajan, 2000; Morselli & Giguère, 2006; Natarajan, 2006; Varese, 2006b; Morselli et al., 2007; Morselli & Petit, 2007; Malm et al., 2008; Morselli, 2009a; Heber, 2009; Malm, Bichler, & Van De Walle, 2009; Morselli, 2010; Natarajan, Zanella, & Yu, 2010; Campana, 2011). In particular, some contributions suggest that network properties and measures are strong even if randomly tested for missing data (Xu & Chen, 2008: 63–64; Morselli, 2009b: 48).

Nevertheless, some caveats are necessary. As with most judicial documents, the data collection served mainly criminal procedural and evidentiary purposes. The sources were inevitably affected by the point of view of the police and the prosecution. This influence was taken into account above when presenting the analysis of the hierarchy of the two groups. However, law enforcement strategies may have further influenced the boundaries and characteristics of the groups investigated (von Lampe, 2009: 95). Furthermore, some parts of the criminal groups may have been omitted and/or overlooked, either because of the criminals' strategies to deflect attention or because of the limited resources available to law enforcement.

This study has inevitably been susceptible to the above problems, but some elements suggest that they were acceptably limited for the two groups studied. First, Chalonero and Stupor Mundi were long-lasting investigations, so that the possibility that important individuals in the networks were missed should be relatively low (Morselli, 2009b: 49). Second, the direct analysis of conversations adopted for the identification of task and status scores made it possible to focus directly on intercepted conversations. Although the selection of the conversations included in the court orders depended on the choices made by the prosecution and the court, it seems unlikely that conversations containing particularly important information about the criminal activities were omitted. In any case, directed analysis of the conversations made it possible to restrict the influence of the criminal justice system on the results. Finally, the analysis of two broadly similar groups was intended to limit the risk of a selection bias.

CONCLUSIONS

This study has analyzed two 'Ndrangheta drug-trafficking networks and their internal structures. Differently from previous research, centrality measures showed very high correlations in the networks observed. It was therefore not possible to identify strategic positioning patterns solely by means of centrality measures. For this reason, the study adopted multiple methodologies to identify the tasks and importance of the individuals in the criminal groups. The analyses showed

that traffickers, members of the 'Ndrangheta, and bosses were more involved in the criminal activities and had higher centrality scores than did other members. Although of interest, these findings did not show any trace of strategic positioning. Conversely, the inclusion of the status of the individuals, based on the content analysis of the conversations, made it possible to identify different patterns of network positioning. In both networks, individuals with high status remained more detached from the core of the criminal activities, leaving medium-status individuals in central, and more vulnerable, positions. The identified strategic positioning patterns provided the 'Ndrangheta networks with particular strength. Indeed, medium-status individuals could be (and on one occasion actually were) expendable and replaceable with other affiliates, so that the criminal activities could be rapidly resumed at the previous levels. High-status individuals proved to have particularly strategic connections (lower clustering coefficients despite the smaller size of their neighborhoods). Further research could explore whether these connections function as weak ties providing more opportunities and resources than the stronger ties of medium-status individuals (Granovetter, 1973, 1983).

The study has also verified the impact of the strategic positions against the outcomes of the investigations (accusation and arrest) and of the trials (acquittal or conviction). Whilst in both groups task and hierarchy were strongly associated with higher accusation and arrest rates, this was not the same for the status of individuals. This suggests that individuals with higher status were not more frequently accused and arrested than traffickers and bosses. Moreover, in Stupor Mundi, high-status individuals were not more frequently convicted than others, and they received shorter mean sentences than did medium-status individuals.

These results have several implications. The adoption of multiple analytical strategies resulted in a triangulation of methods which yielded additional insight and control over the reliability of the results. Reliance on one single method may furnish only limited understanding of the structure of a criminal organization. If possible, complementary strategies should always be used.

The increasing interest in SNA methods should not lead to an overemphasis on merely quantitative approaches in the analysis of a single criminal network. Although SNA has interesting analytical potential, it should be always carefully used in combination with a qualitative understanding of the structure of a criminal network. In the two cases studies, mere reliance on SNA would not have identified any strategic positioning in the two groups. Even worse, it would have identified as more important (i.e., more central) a number of individuals who, although in control of the drug-trafficking activities, proved not to be the most important actors according to their social status. Among possible qualitative complementary methods, direct analysis of transcripts and communications yielded interesting results. It furnished better understanding of the social structure of the two groups than would have been forthcoming from mere reliance on the criminal justice system's identification of bosses.

There is a need for further studies on the structure of criminal organizations and the strategic positioning of individuals. At present, there are very few scholarly works on the structure of organized crime networks. More studies, on a variety of criminal organizations, are required to achieve a critical mass of knowledge in this field. Indeed, similarities among criminal networks are probably as frequent as the differences, and they are equally important for a better understanding of criminal networks. Unfortunately, academic practices sometimes seem to discourage this process. Academics should be careful not to mistake the advancement of knowledge for the necessary production of new, unprecedented results. More frequently than expected, replication of similar analyses on different criminal networks may provide interesting results.

NOTES

1. The six items were: a) express satisfaction; b) request information; c) not provide information; d) give orders; e) not seek clarification of orders; and f) not use the word "sir" when talking to others (Natarajan, 2006: 181, see also 2000: 279).

2. Seizures have been made of written "regulations" which describe the rules of the organization and its secret oaths (Gratteri & Nicaso, 2009; Malafarina, 1978; Paoli, 2003). The 'Ndrangheta has specific ranks for its members, with an elaborate formal hierarchy consisting of two main layers: the higher society (*società maggiore*) and lower society (*società minore*). There are multiple ranks within each layer (Paoli, 2003).

3. The two investigations were identified in cooperation with the Antimafia Investigative Directorate (Direzione Investigativa Antimafia in Italian, hereinafter DIA), a law enforcement agency specialized in the investigation of mafia-type cases. The DIA provided access to a number of judicial documents relating to approximately a dozen major investigations characterized by the involvement of the 'Ndrangheta in drug trafficking. The two operations were selected in order to be broadly comparable (in terms of the size and type of criminal activities).

4. Accused persons are individuals charged with a specific crime by the prosecution. In a comparative perspective, they may be regarded as suspects. Accused persons can be arrested (i.e., remanded in custody or pretrial detention) whenever the crime is an arrestable offense, the prosecution demonstrates that there is a reasonable belief that they have committed the crime, and there is the risk that the accused may commit further crimes, flee, or suppress evidence. The arrest is ordered by a judicial authority (the preliminary investigation judge) upon request by the prosecution.

5. In the Italian criminal justice system, criminal investigations actually finish some time after the arrest of the most dangerous suspects, once the prosecution has wrapped up the evidence and formulated the indictment (*richiesta di rinvio a giudizio*).

6. The Italian criminal proceedings enables up to three grades of judgment by different courts. For the two case studies, first-grade judgments are issued by tribunals (either by a panel of three judges or, if the defendant opts for a special, usually quicker, trial, by the preliminary hearing judge). These decisions may be appealed before a Court of Appeal, which issues an appeal judgment either confirming or modifying the previous one. Appeal judgments may be further challenged before the *Corte di Cassazione*, the highest Italian criminal court.

7. For each operation, the analysis coded each indi-

vidual as N1, N2, . . . in order to prevent direct identification.

8. Similar "trimming" operations are routinely conducted in criminal network studies (Natarajan, 2000, 2006; Morselli, 2009a: 152)

9. This is because, in both cases, the most important charge was that of belonging to a drug-trafficking organization. The court orders included the court's assessment of the evidence relating to this charge and therefore allowed classification of each individual in the two groups as either a member of the 'Ndrangheta or a non-member. Furthermore, the prosecution and the court also identified the leaders of each criminal organization. This is because Italian criminal law attaches particular importance to leadership roles within organized drug-trafficking groups, and applies higher penalties to them. This enabled the classification of five individuals as "bosses" in Chalonero and six in Stupor Mundi.

10. The coding scheme was as follows: a) express (dis)satisfaction; b) request information; c) not provide information; d) give orders; e) not seek clarification of orders; and f) not use the third person singular or second person plural when talking to others.

11. The second conversation for every dyad was randomly selected. When a dyad was involved in a single conversation only, the analysis focused on that conversation. For some individuals, there were no conversations available. This was because these individuals had participated in meetings but not in conversations. For these individuals (N = 17 and N = 27 for Chalonero and Stupor Mundi, respectively), the status score was attributed on the basis of detailed analysis of the overall context described in the court order. In particular, the study attributed the status score on the basis of the considerations of the court and of the prosecution and of the status of individuals performing the same task or with the same role within each criminal network. For example, in Chalonero, N1 was a fugitive, and he did not participate in telephone calls in order to avoid being tracked and arrested. At the same time, he was the boss of the organization, as evident from both the considerations of the court and the fact that his agreement was required for major decisions. For this reason, he received a status score of 4, equal to that of the highest-status individuals identified in the same operation.

12. Two coders independently coded a sample of conversations to assess the reliability of the coding scheme. The mean correlation between the two coders was 0.85, in line with Natarajan's studies (2006: 182; 2000: 280).

13. The medium-status class included subjects with status scores within the mean +/– a half standard deviation; the low-status class comprised status scores lower than the mean minus half standard deviation, and the high-status class included individuals with a status score higher than the mean plus half standard deviation. The classes' ranges were very similar between the two networks. The thresholds were 2.5 and 3.1 for Chalonero and 2.2 and 2.9 for Stupor Mundi.

14. The network analysis was performed using the Ucinet 6 (Borgatti, Everett, & Freeman, 2002).

15. The network analysis was performed on undirected matrixes. The use of directed matrices would have excluded an important set of information—i.e., the data on meetings—which could not be gathered in directed form.

16. The clustering coefficient is strongly influenced by the size of a node's neighborhood. With a high number of direct contacts, it is less likely that they will be densely connected. For this reason, the clustering coefficient is always presented along with the number of pairs (i.e., the number of possible combinations among a node's direct contacts).

17. Pearson's r ranged from 0.946 to 0.978 in Chalonero and from 0.909 to 0.966 in Stupor Mundi. All correlations were statistically significant at the 0.01 level.

18. "Brokers are neither patrons nor clients. They play in between and what past research has demonstrated is that individuals who are capable of maintaining such a stance are generally well-respected, higher achievers, and strategic participants in the networks that surround them" (Morselli, 2009b: 17).

REFERENCES

Baker, Wayne E. & Robert R. Faulkner (1993). The social organization of conspiracy: Illegal networks in the heavy electrical equipment industry. *American Sociological Review* 58(6), 837–860.

Becchi, Ada (1996). Italy: "Mafia-dominated Drug Market"? In Nicholas Dorn, Jorgen Jepsen, & Ernesto U. Savona (eds.), *European Drug Policies and Enforcement* (pp. 119–130). Basingstoke and London: Macmillan.

Benson, Jana S. & Scott H. Decker (2010). The organizational structure of international drug smuggling. *Journal of Criminal Justice* 38(2), 130–138.

Borgatti, Steve P., Martin G. Everett, & Linton C. Freeman (2002). *Ucinet 6 for Windows: Software for Social Network Analysis*. Harvard: Analytic Technologies

Bouchard, Martin & Holly Nguyen (2010). Is it who you know, or how many that counts? Criminal networks and cost avoidance in a sample of young offenders. *Justice Quarterly* 27(1), 130–158.

Bouchard, Martin & Frederic Ouellet (2011). Is small beautiful? The link between risks and size in illegal drug markets. *Global Crime* 12(1), 70–86.

Bright, David A., Caitlin E. Hughes, & Jenny

Chalmers. (2012). Illuminating dark networks: A social network analysis of an Australian drug trafficking syndicate. *Crime, Law and Social Change* 57(2), 151–176.

Campana, Paolo. (2011). Eavesdropping on the Mob: The functional diversification of Mafia activities across territories. *European Journal of Criminology* 8(3), 213–228.

Carley, Kathleen M., David Krackhardt, & Ju-Sung Lee (2002). Destabilizing networks. *Connections* 24(3), 79–92.

Ciconte, Enzo (1992). *"Ndrangheta dall" Unità a oggi*. Rome & Bari: Laterza.

Coles, Nigel (2001). It's not what you know—it's who you know that counts. Analysing serious crime groups as social networks. *British Journal of Criminology* 41(4), 580–594.

CPA (2008). *Relazione annuale sulla 'ndrangheta—Relatore On. Francesco Forgione*. Roma: Commissione Parlamentare di inchiesta sul fenomeno della criminalità organizzata mafiosa o similare.

Davis, Roger H. (1981). Social network analysis: An aid in conspiracy investigations. *FBI Law Enforcement Bulletin* 50(12), 11–19.

Desroches, Frederick J. (2003). Drug trafficking and organized crime in Canada: A study of high-level drug networks. In Margaret E. Beare (ed.), *Critical Reflections on Transnational Organized Crime, Money Laundering and Corruption* (pp. 237–255). Toronto: University of Toronto Press.

DIA (2007). *Relazione del Ministro dell'Interno al Parlamento sull'attività svolta e sui risultati conseguiti dalla Direzione Investigativa Antimafia—I semestre 2007*. Rome: Ministry of Interior.

Dorn, Nicholas, Michael Levi, & Leslie King (2005). *Literature Review on Upper Level Drug Trafficking*. London: Home Office Research, Development and Statistics Directorate.

Dorn, Nicholas, Karim Murji, & Nigel South (eds.) (1992). *Traffickers: Drug Markets and Law Enforcement*. London: Routledge.

Eck, John E. & Jeffrey S. Gersh (2000). Drug trafficking as a cottage industry. In Mangai Natarajan & Mike Hough (eds.), *Illegal Drug Markets: From Research to Prevention Policy, Crime Prevention Studies* (pp. 241–271). Boulder, CO: Lynne Rienner Publishers.

Granovetter, Mark S. (1973). The strength of weak ties. *American Journal of Sociology* 78(6), 1360–1380.

Granovetter, Mark S. (1983). The strength of weak ties: A network theory revisited. *Sociological Theory* 1(1), 201.

Gratteri, Nicola & Antonio Nicaso (2009). *Fratelli di sangue* (2nd ed.). Milan: Mondadori.

Hanneman, Robert A. & Mark Riddle (2005). *Introduction to Social Networks Methods*. Riverside, CA: University of California, Riverside Retrieved from www.faculty.ucr.edu/~hanneman/nettext/.

Heber, Anita (2009). The networks of drug offenders. *Trends in Organized Crime* 12(1), 1–20.

Ianni, Francis A.J. & Elizabeth Reuss-Ianni (1990). Network analysis. In Paul P. Andrews & Marilyn B. Peterson (eds.), *Criminal Intelligence Analysis* (pp. 67–84). Loomis, CA: Palmer Enterprises.

Jackson, Janet L., Janet C.M. Herbrink, & Robert W.J. Jansen (1996). Examining criminal organizations: Possible methodologies. *Transnational Organized Crime* 2(4), 83–105.

Lupsha, Peter (1980). Steps toward a strategic analysis of organized crime. *The Police Chief*, May.

Lupsha, Peter (1983). Networks vs. networking: Analysis of an organized crime group. In Gordon P. Waldo (ed.), *Career Criminals* (pp. 59–87). Beverly Hills, CA: Sage.

Malafarina, Luigi (1978). *Il codice della 'ndrangheta*. Reggio Calabria: Parallelo 38.

Malm, Aili E. & Gisela Bichler (2011). Networks of collaborating criminals: Assessing the structural vulnerability of drug markets. *Journal of Research in Crime and Delinquency* 48(2), 271–297.

Malm, Aili E., Gisela Bichler, & Stephanie Van De Walle (2009). Comparing the ties that bind criminal networks: Is blood thicker than water? *Security Journal* 23(1), 52–74.

Malm, Aili E., J. Bryan Kinney, & Nahanni R. Pollard (2008). Social network and distance correlates of criminal associates involved in illicit drug production. *Security Journal* 21(1–2), 77–94.

McGloin, Jean Marie & David S. Kirk (2010). Social network analysis. In A.R. Piquero & D. Weisburd (eds.), *Handbook of Quantitative Criminology* (pp. 209–224). New York: Springer.

Morselli, Carlo (2009a). Hells Angels in Springtime. *Trends in Organized Crime* 12(2), 145–158.

Morselli, Carlo (2009b). *Inside Criminal Networks*. New York: Springer.

Morselli, Carlo (2010). Assessing vulnerable and strategic positions in a criminal network. *Journal of Contemporary Criminal Justice* 26(4), 382–392.

Morselli, Carlo & Cynthia Giguère (2006). Legitimate strengths in criminal networks. *Crime, Law and Social Change* 43(3), 185–200.

Morselli, Carlo & Katia Petit (2007). Law-enforcement disruption of a drug importation network. *Global Crime* 8(2), 109–130.

Morselli, Carlo & Julie Roy (2008). Brokerage qualifications in ringing operations. *Criminology* 46(1), 71–98.

Morselli, Carlo, Cynthia Giguère, & Katia Petit (2007). The efficiency/security trade-off in criminal networks. *Social Networks* 29(1), 143–153.

Natarajan, Mangai (2000). Understanding the structure of a drug trafficking organization: A conversational analysis. In Mangai Natarajan & Mike Hough (eds.), *Illegal Drug Markets: From Research to Prevention Policy*, vol. 11, *Crime Prevention Studies* (pp. 273–298). Monsey, NY: Criminal Justice Press/Willow Tree Press.

Natarajan, Mangai (2006). Understanding the structure of a large heroin distribution network: A quantitative analysis of qualitative data. *Journal of Quantitative Criminology* 22(2), 171–192.

Natarajan, Mangai & Mathieu Belanger (1998). Varieties of drug trafficking organizations: A typology of cases prosecuted in New York City. *Journal of Drug Issues* 28(4), 1005–1026.

Natarajan, Mangai, Marco Zanella, & Christopher Yu (2010). How organized is drug trafficking? Presentation at the 19th Environmental Criminology and Crime Analysis Conference, 5–8 July, Brisbane, Australia.

Paoli, Letizia (1994). An underestimated criminal phenomenon: The Calabrian 'Ndrangheta. *European Journal of Crime, Criminal Law and Criminal Justice* 2(3), 212–238.

Paoli, Letizia (2002a). "Flexible hierarchies and dynamic disorder": The drug distribution system in Frankfurt and Milan. *Drugs: Education, Prevention, and Policy* 9(2), 143–151.

Paoli, Letizia (2002b). The paradoxes of organized crime. *Crime, Law and Social Change* 37, 51–97.

Paoli, Letizia (2003). *Mafia Brotherhoods: Organized Crime, Italian Style*. Oxford: Oxford University Press.

Paoli, Letizia (2004). The illegal drugs market. *Journal of Modern Italian Studies* 9(2), 186.

Pearson, Geoffrey & Dick Hobbs (2001). *Middle Market Drug Distribution*. London: Home Office Research, Development and Statistics Directorate.

Reuter, Peter (1983). *Disorganized Crime: The Economics of the Visible Hand*. Cambridge, MA: MIT Press.

Reuter, Peter (2009). *Assessing the Operation of the Global Drug Market Report 1*. Cambridge, UK: RAND Europe.

Reuter, Peter & Kohn Haaga (1989). *The Organization of High-Level Drug Markets: An Exploratory Study*. Santa Monica, CA: RAND.

Scott, John P. (2000). *Social Network Analysis: A Handbook* (2nd ed.). London: Sage.

Sparrow, Malcolm K. (1991). The application of network analysis to criminal intelligence: An assessment of the prospects. *Social Networks* 13(3), 251–274.

Varese, Federico (2006a). How mafias migrate: The case of the 'Ndrangheta in Northern Italy. *Law & Society Review* 40(2), 411–444.

Varese, Federico (2006b). The structure of a criminal network examined: The Russian Mafia in Rome. *Oxford Legal Studies Research Paper* No. 21.

Varese, Federico (2012). How mafias take advantage of globalization: The Russian Mafia in Italy. *British Journal of Criminology* 52(2), 235–253.

von Lampe, Klaus (2009). Human capital and social capital in criminal networks: Introduction to the special issue on the 7th Blankensee Colloquium. *Trends in Organized Crime* 12(2), 93–100.

Wasserman, Stanley & Katherine Faust (1994). *Social Network Analysis: Methods and Applications*. Cambridge, UK: Cambridge University Press.

Xu, Jennifer & Hsinchun Chen (2003). Untangling criminal networks: A case study. In H. Chen, R. Miranda, D. Zeng, C. Demchak, J. Schroeder, & T. Madhusudan (eds.) *Intelligence and Security Informatics*, vol. 2665 (pp. 232–248). Berlin, Heidelberg: Springer Berlin Heidelberg.

Xu, Jennifer & Hsinchun Chen (2008). The topology of dark networks. *Communications of the ACM*, October, 58–65.

CHAPTER 10

Drug Trafficking Networks in the World Economy

Rémi Boivin

Macro-level features are largely neglected in most analyses of crime networks. The focus is generally put on relations between individuals (or small groups of individuals) rather than the context in which they operate. Yet, contextual factors may be crucial for a complete understanding of criminal activity. Al Capone is one of many examples (see Papachristos in this book): his career as a member of a large criminal syndicate would not have been the same if the Eighteenth Amendment had not mandated a national ban on alcohol.

Furthermore, some criminal activities must be understood in a relational perspective. Recently, Naylor (2003) proposed a definition of market-based offenses that borrows the language of networks. He stated that trafficking consists of multilateral exchanges of inherently illegal goods between producers, distributors and consumers in a market-like context. Two elements of Naylor's definition are particularly relevant to the study of transnational drug trafficking. First, drug trafficking involves the movement of an illegal commodity from source to user. The chain between the two comprises a given number of intermediaries. This could be referred to as the "economic" element because it is centered on the commodity trade. Second, those exchanges occur in specific social and political contexts; the commodity itself is secondary. The contextual element of drug trafficking has been the subject of many analyses in geopolitics. The study of transnational drug trafficking thus remains multidisciplinary and quite separated: it combines notions borrowed from sociology, anthropology, economics, and politics.

This chapter provides a rare attempt to analyze global transnational drug trafficking networks.[1] Network analysis techniques should be used when dealing with relational data—in this case, illegal drug flows between countries. The chapter also aims to illustrate that individual or group networks are embedded in larger social, political, and economic contexts.

TRANSNATIONAL DRUG TRAFFICKING AS TRADE NETWORKS

In the last 25 years, researchers have demonstrated that drug trade networks have a lot in common with legal markets. Economic analyses of transnational trafficking demonstrated the fundamental inequality among participants of the trade. Peter Reuter and colleagues demonstrated that production costs were negligible compared to retail prices of cocaine in the US, a situation very similar to legal commodities (Caulkins & Reuter, 1998, 2010; Reuter & Kleiman, 1986). Most capital gain comes from risk compensation at importation (Reuter & Greenfield, 2001) and at retail sale (Caulkins & Reuter, 1998; Levitt & Venkatesh, 2000). Profit per person is high for upper- and middle-level traffickers but most of the accounting profits are divided among a large number of low-level dealers. At the country level, those analyses imply: 1) that crop destruction strategies aiming to raise prices in destination countries are doomed from the start and 2) that transnational drug trafficking involves the transfer of money to source and transit countries—or at least to individuals operating in foreign countries.

Which countries benefit from the drug trade? And why? Geopolitics are useful to explain the historical role played by Afghanistan in the production of opium poppy (Chouvy, 2010), the frequent use of Spain as a transit country toward Europe (Sands, 2007), or the development of a cocaine industry in Colombia (Kenney, 2007; Thoumi, 1995). In all cases, drug trafficking emerged and remained in place because of a combination of economic, geographic, cultural, and political factors. An interesting feature is that countries that apparently benefit from the drug trade rarely occupy key positions in the global economy.

Such studies illustrate the strengths and limitations of current research on transnational drug trafficking. Economic analyses showed that a considerable number of individuals and countries benefit from the trade of illegal drugs. Geopolitics reminded us that the trade was made possible because specific conditions prevailed. Both perspectives need to be combined to fully understand the structure of drug trafficking networks. In a previous paper (Boivin, 2010), I argued that the world-system perspective (Wallerstein, 1974) offers a theoretical framework that allows a global-level analysis of drug trafficking. It was based on two insights common to both geopolitical and economic analyses of drug trafficking. First, drug trafficking is a set of commodity chains, i.e., "network[s] of labor and production processes whose end result is a finished commodity" (Hopkins & Wallerstein, 1982: 59). As a consequence, most empirical work on world systems uses relational data and network analysis techniques

(Chase-Dunn & Grimes, 1995; Kick & Davis, 2001; Kim & Shin, 2002; Mahutga, 2006; Nemeth & Smith, 1985; Smith & White, 1992; Snyder & Kick, 1979). Drug trafficking requires a structure of criminal opportunities, no matter how formal or informal it is. Network analysis seeks structure without assuming that participants are fully aware of their position (Morselli, 2009).

Second, countries involved in the drug trade become interdependent. Countries occupy a relatively steady position in the trade because of a variety of economic, political, cultural, and geographical factors (Farrell, Mansur, & Tullis, 1996; Paoli, Greenfield, & Reuter, 2009; Reuter & Kleiman, 1986). For example, the Netherlands has been a transit point for both legal and illegal commodities because of its strategic position in Europe and its important ports. Also, local events may have significant impacts on distant countries: the Taliban crackdown against opium poppy cultivation in Afghanistan (Farrell & Thorne, 2005) caused slight diminutions of purity in Europe and Turkey (Paoli et al., 2009) and contributed to heroin shortages in Australia and Canada (Jiggens, 2008; Prunckun, 2006; Smithson, 2006; Wood, Stoltz, Li, Montaner, & Kerr, 2006a, 2006b). Countries are not isolated from one another; the drug trade must be analyzed in a relational perspective.

So drug markets are similar to other commercial trades in many ways. Should it be assumed that illegal drugs are just another type of commodity and that key players of the global legal trade are also strategically positioned in black markets? This chapter explores such questions using network methods to analyze flows of illegal drugs between countries. It aims to compare general features of legal trade networks and drug trafficking networks. It is argued that a popular theoretical framework used to analyze the evolution of global markets (the world-systems perspective) can be applied to illegal markets with unexpected implications.

Building the Networks

Two types of relational data were used to build separate networks of exchanges of cocaine, heroin, and marijuana between countries. The first is a collection of seizures of "significant" quantities of drugs between 1998 and 2007.[2] The dataset provides detailed information on a large number of cases, including origin and/or destination countries (N = 20, 527 dyads). Seizures were reported to the United Nations Office on Drugs and Crime (UNODC) on a voluntary basis; as a consequence, key players of the drug trade are not included in the UNODC dataset. The networks were completed with observational data reported by various international organizations involved in drug trafficking surveillance or control.[3] Overall, the networks cover most countries of the world (N = 194). More details on the construction of the drug trafficking networks are available elsewhere (Boivin, 2011).

Below, global drug trades are compared to legitimate markets. The UN collects detailed country-level commodity trade statistics. The COMTRADE database includes the annual value of imports and exports between countries and areas for different types of commodities. Import data for 2000 are used because they have traditionally been considered more reliable than export data (Linneman, 1966). Total values were dichotomized (1 = presence of trade).

This study is based on the world-system perspective. An important step was to determine the position of every country in the legitimate world economy. Following Mahutga (2006), it was indicated by the total value of trade for a given country (more trade = closer to the core). Country position is best conceptualized as a continuum between core and peripheral countries (Chase-Dunn, 1989). The core, or center, of the world economy comprises developed countries with important production resources; they have the potential to produce almost any kind of commodities. At the opposite end, most peripheral countries have limited production capacities. They export large amounts of raw materials at low costs (and low benefits for exporting countries), and rely on imports for specialized commodities. Semi-peripheral countries are somewhere in the middle: they typically have a more diversified production than peripheral countries, but are dependent at some point on other countries for their supply of many commodities. Four groups of countries were formed: core, strong semi-periphery, weak semi-periphery, and periphery.

THE STRUCTURE OF DRUG TRAFFICKING

This section is organized around the three main propositions of the world-system perspective (Chase-Dunn, 1989, 2002; Wallerstein, 1974, 1979). These propositions provide a simplification of the framework but capture its core features (Boivin, 2010). Legal markets are compared to cocaine, heroin, and marijuana trade networks.

The world-system perspective relies on the assumption that there is a large social system that comprises borders, structures, member groups, rules of legitimation, and coherence. This system stretches over national borders (Wallerstein, 1974). Constituting members (usually countries or states) form a global trade network "built" on political and economical agreements (Chase-Dunn, 1989, 2002; Wallerstein, 1979).

Two types of world-systems have existed: world empires and world economies (Wallerstein, 1974). World empires consist of a single political system while world economies have multiple central authorities. In theory, many world systems can co-exist; however, today's world economy covers most countries. The boundaries of world systems are directly related to transport and communication possibilities. The world-system perspective does not deny the increasing unification of the world's individuals and societies—the globalization of the world: it simply suggests that the process started well before World War II. In other words, world systems are dynamic in nature and structural changes have been observed and remain possible (Chase-Dunn, 1989).

Drug markets have distinctive features. The cocaine market is very similar to a world empire because it is centered on a single area of production (South America). At the opposite, the marijuana market is an extreme example of a world economy because it is grown in virtually all countries of the world. As such, the marijuana market has more things in common with present legal trades than cocaine and heroin. However, marijuana trafficking is mostly regional, as Table 10.1 demonstrates.

It appears necessary to look beyond countries to understand drug trafficking. A single route comprises several countries and a single country can play different roles in several routes. Furthermore, countries are not connected randomly: the geographical distance between connected countries displays important variations from one market to the other. In a world-system perspective, commodity availability and transport opportunities can explain the extent of a market (Wallerstein, 1974). Since marijuana and, to a lesser extent, heroin are available from more than one source, it is not necessary to develop means of transport that are as elaborate and varied than those for cocaine.

In legal markets, using the same route for different commodities is commonplace. The world-system perspective considers specific phenomena as structural consequences of the system rather than a carefully planned strategy. For example, using the same routes for different commodities could be explained by the geographical distance between source and destination countries. The number of options decreases when approaching destination. In that view, it is surprising that few trafficking routes appear to be used for different drugs. Two or three types of drugs appear to be transported between only 132 pairs of countries. The vast majority of pairs (N = 694; 84.0%) are solely used for the transport of one type of drug, which differentiates drug markets from legal trades.

Core–Periphery Divisions

Wallerstein and colleagues suggest that the present world economy is fundamentally capitalist because it fuels on a perpetual search for profit (Wallerstein, 1974). Eventually, the system expands to the point where actors are forced to organize production instead of simply buying and selling at the best price (Chase-Dunn, 1989). As stated above, constituting members form a more or less formal trade network that results in the establishment of unequal economic relations, where some countries have more benefits than others. The world system favors core over peripheral countries and, to a lesser extent, semi-peripheral countries (Chase-Dunn, 1989; Wallerstein, 1974, 1979).

Core countries collect more wealth at the expense of other countries. Peripheral and semi-peripheral countries are not able to produce necessary specialized commodities and rely on core countries, which sell at a high price. In return, core countries import raw materials from peripheral countries at low costs. The position in the system is thus a direct function of production means. This structure ensures the stability of the system, even if countries tend to limit their importations and to develop foreign markets in order to improve their position in the system (van Rossem, 1996). The primary consequence of the system is that core countries are the

Table 10.1 Proportion of exchanges between countries of the same region or continent

	Cocaine	Heroin	Marijuana
Pairs of countries	418	370	193
Same continent	47.6%	62.4%	72.5%
Same region	32.3%	38.9%	57.5%

source of most exchanges of legal commodities (Table 10.2). Peripheral countries are importers in 4.5% of the total commodity trade, and exporters in only 0.3% of exchanges. Peripheral countries are dependent on core countries for their supply in numerous commodities.

Drug markets display similarities but also significant differences. For example, drug markets are obviously capitalist. When questioned, high-level traffickers invariably mention monetary gain as an important motivation (Decker & Chapman, 2008; Desroches, 2005, 2007). The analysis of drug prices also proved that: 1) prices are higher than they would be in a legal market (Miron, 2003) and 2) the gap between legal and illegal prices is largely attributable to risk compensation rather than production/transportation costs (Caulkins & Reuter, 1998).

However, drug markets differ from legal trade in three important ways. First, peripheral countries are more involved in the drug trade (see Table 10.3 for cocaine). In sharp contrast to legal trade, peripheral countries are the source of more than 40% of exchanges of cocaine, heroin, and marijuana, while core countries are exporters in less than 25% of cases. Second, most exchanges of drugs are between equivalent countries or directed toward core countries (Table 10.4). Third, core countries depend on peripheral and semi-peripheral countries for their supply in plant-based drugs. The whole production of cocaine and heroin and 82.6% of marijuana exporters are located in peripheral or weak semi-peripheral countries. For various reasons—starting with active drug law enforcement—core countries are not able to meet the national demand for drugs. Consequently,

Table 10.2 Exchanges of legal commodities between categories of countries, year 2000 (% of total US$ value)

		Importers (receivers)				Total
		Core	Strong semi-periphery	Weak semi-periphery	Periphery	
Exporters (senders)	Core	45.3%	23.0%	5.6%	4.1%	78.0%
	Strong semi-periphery	16.5%	2.7%	0.6%	0.4%	20.2%
	Weak semi-periphery	1.5%	0.1%	0.0%	0.0%	1.6%
	Periphery	0.2%	0.1%	0.0%	0.0%	0.3%
	Total	63.5%	25.9%	6.2%	4.5%	100%

Source: Mahutga (2006)

Table 10.3 Exchanges of cocaine between categories of countries, year 1998–2007 (% of pairs of countries)

		Importers (receivers)				Total
		Core	Strong semi-periphery	Weak semi-periphery	Periphery	
Exporters (senders)	Core	13.1%	5.0%	6.2%	1.5%	25.8%
	Strong semi-periphery	3.1%	1.5%	1.5%	1.5%	7.6%
	Weak semi-periphery	12.7%	3.1%	2.7%	7.3%	25.8%
	Periphery	27.0%	5.0%	3.5%	5.0%	40.5%
	Total	55.9%	14.6%	13.9%	15.3%	100%

Table 10.4 Direction of commodity trade between categories of countries (% of pairs of countries)

	Legal commodities	Cocaine	Heroin	Marijuana
Toward core	18.3%	51.4%	47.3%	39.4%
Same position	48.0%	27.0%	36.8%	45.6%
Toward periphery	33.7%	21.6%	15.9%	15.0%
Total	100%	100%	100%	100%

countries that are generally disadvantaged in commodity trades occupy key positions in drug markets. Capitalist motivations and trade inequality are features of both legal and illegal markets, but the structure appears to be almost opposite.

States Play a Crucial Role in the Formation of World Systems

The third proposition of the world-system perspective is widely accepted: states define rules of circulation at their borders (Wallerstein, 2004). Those rules are applied to commodities, assets, and individuals. Consequently, political decisions allow the establishment of transnational trade networks. Laws and economic agreements are adopted to facilitate transnational commodity trade. In the world economy, the most powerful countries are those that have a large number of diversified relations with other countries (Mahutga, 2006). For example, core countries maintain commercial relations with most countries of the world and thus are not dependent on a small number of trade partners. Thereby, the density of the world

(legal) trade network is high[4] (De Benedictis & Tajoli, 2009).

Table 10.5 shows the density of six world trade networks for the year 2000. The density of the world economy was calculated by De Benedictis and Tajoli (2009) and includes all types of legal commodities. However, the analysis of all international trade is not necessarily relevant to the argument because it includes very different types of commodities. Two types of commodities were selected for further analyses. Like illegal drugs, coffee and chocolate are addictive plant-based products that require few transformations. What makes comparisons even more interesting is that both legal products are mainly grown in peripheral countries (Reuter & Greenfield, 2001). Coffee and chocolate data were taken from the UN COMTRADE and include both raw and transformed products.

Results suggest again that the structure of the trade is quite different. In the case of illegal drugs, states decided to ban possession, production, and trafficking, but cannot fully enforce drug laws. This situation makes the drug trade different from most trades. Laws are meant to disrupt commercial activities

Table 10.5 The density of total, chocolate, coffee, cocaine, heroin, and marijuana trade networks, year 2000

	Number of countries (n)	Potential links (n*(n−1))	Observed links	Density (%)
Coffee	161	25,760	5620	21.8
Chocolate	162	26,082	3834	14.7
Total (legal)	176	30,800	11,938	38.8
Cocaine	118	13,806	445	3.2
Heroin	134	17,822	370	2.1
Marijuana	194	37,442	193	0.5

instead of protecting traders. Drug trafficking is a risky business: traffickers can be arrested/convicted, loads can be seized, and violence can arise as a way to settle disagreements. As a result, cocaine, heroin, and marijuana trade networks are much less dense than coffee and chocolate. Drug routes should probably be analyzed in terms of effectiveness rather than variety. Efficient routes secure drug supply: a drug needs to be available to be purchased. Conversely, the threat of law enforcement makes it almost necessary to establish more than one route. In short, only one route is needed to secure drug supply, but a variety of routes should make drug markets more resilient (Bouchard, 2007). The density of cocaine and heroin networks is higher close to source countries, due to the limited number of possibilities—a typical feature of monopolies. The heroin network is spread out but less dense than the smaller cocaine network. The marijuana network is not very dense because there is significant domestic production in many countries.

CONCLUSION

In theory, the world-system perspective predicts that raw materials would be exchanged at low prices from peripheral countries to core countries. Most legal commodities could be grown or produced in core countries but it is more profitable to import cheap materials. Similarly, cocaine, heroin, and marijuana are easy-to-grow, plant-based drugs that require relatively basic transformations. At the same time, law enforcement efforts are more intense in core countries. As a result, core countries are not able to produce enough drugs to meet domestic demand and must rely on imports from less developed countries. In a separate paper, I analyzed drug prices and mark-ups and found that the value of cocaine and heroin increases more sharply when exchanges are directed toward core countries (Boivin, 2011). In other words, core countries depend upon peripheral and semi-peripheral coun-

tries to access two popular commodities—cocaine and heroin. The trade network is turned upside down.

Caulkins and Reuter (1998) showed that production and transformation costs represent a small proportion of the retail price of drugs and that the value of drugs increases more quickly after importation in destination countries. Consequently, drug trafficking is more profitable for local criminals. Still, transactions after importation involve a redistribution of wealth inside destination countries, while transnational trafficking generates money transfers toward foreign criminals—an economic gain for producers and brokers operating in peripheral and semi-peripheral countries (Naylor, 2003).

Furthermore, marijuana networks differ in many aspects. The production of cannabis is widespread—from core to periphery. Most observers explain the expansion of marijuana production in core countries as a convergence of technological innovations (e.g., hydroponics), a growing tolerance toward consumption and less active and/or efficient law enforcement efforts (Bouchard, 2007; Bouchard & Dion, 2009; Clements, 2006; Weisheit, 1992). A world-system interpretation of the expansion would be that core countries are trying to limit their dependence on otherwise "dominated" countries. With important domestic production of a very popular drug, core countries maintain their position in the world economy, even if the product itself is illegal.

However, protectionism is not sufficient to explain domestic production of illegal drugs. The absence of cocaine and heroin production in core countries provides a strong example: producing small quantities of drugs requires very large quantities of coca or opium poppy, which means large-scale outdoor cultivation. While corruption and less intense drug law enforcement allow this kind of cultivation in some peripheral countries, the same situation is inconceivable in core countries.

The world-system approach applied to illegal drug trafficking highlights the fact that drug trafficking involves a series of exchanges between individuals operating in different countries. Macro-level analyses of trafficking should thus be based on relational rather than traditional non-relational data (for a similar argument, see Paoli et al., 2009, and Zaitch, 2002). It also supports the idea that drug trafficking is primarily a commercial activity between willing buyers and sellers (Naylor, 2003). Recreational drugs are an attractive market for peripheral countries: core countries are not able to supply the numerous local consumers—a situation usually characteristic of rare or luxury goods (e.g., diamonds). The main difference is that a complex human decision (the prohibition of cocaine and heroin) rather than nature is creating opportunities for countries that are generally disadvantaged. During the 1980s, cocaine trafficking significantly contributed to maintain the economic situation of Bolivia, Peru, and Colombia (Craig, 1987; Thoumi, 1995). Illegal drugs are certainly not necessary to ensure the development of societies but they can become a significant economic, political, and military issue (Cornell, 2005). Controlling the production and availability of this commodity provides a strategic advantage over other countries. And numerous criminal entrepreneurs are trying to make the most of it.

NOTES

1. The network terminology was used by Paoli, Greenfield, and Reuter (2009) to analyze the world heroin market but the authors did not provide a formal network analysis of the trade.
2. The defined thresholds of significant quantities used by UNODC are as follows: 1 kilogram or more for marijuana and 100 grams or more for cocaine and heroin.
3. I conducted a systematic review of information contained in 48 annual reports and country overviews published by the UNODC, the Bureau of International Narcotics and Law Enforcement Affairs (BINLEA), the International Narcotics Control Board (INCB), and the European Monitoring Center for Drugs and Drug Addiction (EMCDDA).
4. The density of a network is the number of links in a network, expressed as a proportion of the maximal number of links (De Benedictis & Tajoli, 2009). A network in which all possible links are active has a density of 1.

REFERENCES

Boivin, R. (2010). Le monde à l'envers? Vers une approche structurelle du trafic transnational de drogues illicites. *Déviance et Société* 34(1), 93–114.

Boivin, R. (2011). *Le Monde à L'envers: Analyse de la Structure du Trafic Transnational de Drogues Illicites*. Doctoral dissertation, School of Criminology, Université de Montréal.

Bouchard, M. (2007). On the resilience of illegal drug markets. *Global Crime* 8(4), 325–344.

Bouchard, M. & C.B. Dion (2009). Growers and facilitators: Probing the role of entrepreneurs in the development of the cannabis cultivation industry. *Journal of Small Business and Entrepreneurship* 22(1), 25–38.

Caulkins, J. & P. Reuter (1998). What price data tells us about drug markets. *Journal of Drug Issues* 28(3), 593–612.

Caulkins, J.P. & P. Reuter (2010). How drug enforcement affects drug prices. In M. Tonry (ed.), *Crime and Justice: An Annual Review of Research*, vol. 39 (pp. 213–271), Chicago: University of Chicago Press.

Chase-Dunn, C. (1989). *Global Formation*. Cambridge, MA: Basil Blackwell.

Chase-Dunn, C. (2002). World-systems theorizing. In J.H. Turner (ed.), *Handbook of Sociological Theory* (pp. 589–612). New York: Kluwer Academic/Plenum Publishers.

Chase-Dunn, C. & P. Grimes (1995). World-systems analysis. *Annual Review of Sociology* 21, 387–417.

Chouvy, P.-A. (2010). *Opium: Uncovering the Politics of the Poppy*. Cambridge, MA: Harvard University Press.

Clements, K.W. (2006). Pricing and packaging: The case of marijuana. *Journal of Business* 79(4), 2019–2044.

Cornell, S.E. (2005). The interaction of narcotics and conflict. *Journal of Peace Research* 42(6), 751–760.

Craig, R. B. (1987). Illicit drug trafficking: Implications for South American source countries.

Journal of Interamerican Studies and World Affairs 29(2), 1–34.

de Benedictis, L. & L. Tajoli (2009). *The World Trade Network*. Working Paper 51–2009, Macerata University, Department of Finance and Economic Sciences.

Decker, S.H. & M.T. Chapman (2008). *Drug Smugglers on Drug Smuggling*. Philadelphia: Temple University Press.

Desroches, F.J. (2005). *The Crime That Pays: Drug Trafficking and Organized Crime in Canada*. Toronto: Canadian Scholars' Press Inc.

Desroches, F. (2007). Research on upper-level drug trafficking: A review. *Journal of Drug Issues* 37(4), 827–844.

Farrell, G. & J. Thorne (2005). Where have all the flowers gone?: Evaluation of the Taliban crackdown against opium poppy cultivation in Afghanistan. *International Journal of Drug Policy* 16, 81–91.

Farrell, G., K. Mansur, & M. Tullis (1996). Cocaine and heroin in Europe 1983–1993: A cross-national comparison of trafficking and prices. *The British Journal of Criminology* 36(2), 255–281.

Hopkins, T.K. & I. Wallerstein (1982). Patterns of development of the modern world-system. In T.K. Hopkins & I. Wallerstein (eds.), *World-Systems Analysis: Theory and Methodology* (pp. 41–82). Beverly Hills: Sage Publications.

Jiggens, J. (2008). Australian heroin seizures and the causes of the 2001 heroin shortage. *International Journal of Drug Policy* 19(4), 273–278.

Kenney, M. (2007). The architecture of drug trafficking: Network forms of organisation in the Colombian cocaine trade. *Global Crime* 8(3), 233–259.

Kick, E.L. & B.L. Davis (2001). World-system structure and change. *American Behavioral Scientist* 44(10), 1561–1578.

Kim S. & E.H. Shin (2002). A longitudinal analysis of globalization and regionalization in international trade: A social network approach. *Social Forces* 81(2), 445–471.

Levitt, S. & S.A. Venkatesh (2000). An economic analysis of a drug-selling gang's finances. *The Quarterly Journal of Economics* 115(3), 755–789.

Linneman, H. (1966). *An Econometric Study of International Trade Flows*. Amsterdam: North-Holland.

Mahutga, M.C. (2006). The persistence of structural inequality? A network analysis of international trade, 1965–2000. *Social Forces* 84(4), 1863–1889.

Miron, J.A. (2003). The effect of drug prohibition on drug prices: Evidence from the markets for cocaine and heroin. *The Review of Economics and Statistics* 85(3), 522–530.

Morselli, C. (2009). *Inside Criminal Networks*. New York: Springer.

Naylor, R.T. (2003). Towards a general theory of profit-driven crimes. *British Journal of Criminology* 43, 81–101.

Nemeth, R.J. & D.A. Smith (1985). International trade and world-system structure: A multiple network analysis. *Review* 8(4), 517–560.

Paoli, L., V.A. Greenfield, & P. Reuter (2009). *The World Heroin Market: Can Supply Be Cut?* New York: Oxford University Press.

Prunckun, H. (2006). A rush to judgement?: The origin of the 2001 Australian "heroin drought" and its implications for the future of drug law enforcement. *Global Crime* 7(2), 247–255.

Reuter, P. & V. Greenfield (2001). Measuring global drug markets: How good are the numbers and why should we care about them? *World Economics* 2(4), 159–173.

Reuter, P. & M.A.R. Kleiman (1986). Risks and prices: An economic analysis of drug enforcement. In N. Morris & M. Tonry (eds.), *Crime and Justice: An Annual Review of Research*, vol. 7 (pp. 289–340). Chicago: University of Chicago Press.

Sands, J. (2007). Organized crime and illicit activities in Spain: Causes and facilitating factors. *Mediterranean Politics* 12(2), 211–232.

Smith, D.A. & D.S. White (1992). Structure and dynamics of the global economy: Network analysis of international trade 1965–1980. *Social Forces* 70(4), 857–893.

Smithson, M. (2006). A little (more) knowledge: Comments on Wood et al. (2006). *Addiction* 101(5), 622–623.

Snyder, D. & E.L. Kick (1979). Structural position in the world system and economic growth, 1955–1970: A multiple-network analysis of transnational interactions. *American Journal of Sociology* 84(5), 1096–1126.

Thoumi, F.E. (1995). *Political Economy and Illegal Drugs in Colombia*. Boulder, CO: Lynne Rienner.

Van Rossem, R. (1996). The world-system paradigm as general theory of development: A cross-national test. *American Sociological Review* 61(3), 508–527.

Wallerstein, I. (1974). *The Modern World-System I: Capitalist Agriculture and the Origins of the European World-Economy in the Sixteenth Century.* New York: Academic Press.

Wallerstein, I. (1979). *The Capitalist World-Economy.* Cambridge: Cambridge University Press.

Wallerstein, I. (2004). *World-Systems Analysis: An introduction.* Durham, NC, and London: Duke University Press.

Weisheit, R.A. (1992). *Domestic Marijuana: A Neglected Industry.* Westport, CT: Greenwood Press.

Wood, E., J.-A. Stoltz, K. Li, J. Montaner, & T. Kerr (2006a). The cause of the Australian heroin shortage: Time to reconsider? *Addiction* 101(5), 623–625.

Wood, E., J.-A. Stoltz, K. Li, J. Montaner, & T. Kerr (2006b). Changes in Canadian heroin supply coinciding with the Australian heroin shortage. *Addiction* 101(5), 689–695.

Zaitch, D. (2002). From Cali to Rotterdam: Perceptions of Colombian cocaine traffickers on the Dutch port. *Crime, Law and Social Change* 38(3), 239–266.

PART III

Cybercrime Networks

CHAPTER 11

Skills and Trust

A Tour Inside the Hard Drives of Computer Hackers

Benoit Dupont[1]

Stories of the exploits of computer hackers who have broken into supposedly secure government and corporate information systems appear almost daily on the front pages of newspapers and technology websites, yet we know very little about the individuals behind these headlines. They are often caricatured as socially inept (Denning, cited in Leeson & Coyne, 2005: 518) but intellectually gifted teenagers who unleash a technical apocalypse on their helpless victims from the solitary confines of their parents' basements, a representation fueled to a large extent by Hollywood movies.[2] This stereotype is helped by the very limited number of arrests made by the police, and the even smaller number of cases that go to trial, as most of the accused plead guilty in order to negotiate a favorable arrangement with prosecutors. The resulting lack of real-life accounts describing malicious computer hackers and how they operate means that policy makers and criminal justice practitioners as well as members of the public rely on fictional depictions or self-aggrandizing autobiographies (Mitnick & Simon, 2011; Calce & Silverman, 2008) to make sense of this new class of offenders.

Academic publications are unlikely to alter this stereotype any time soon. Not only are they disproportionally few compared to those in the general media but most of the academic literature on the subject originates from computer science researchers who focus on the technical or economic aspects of hack-

ing and demonstrate little interest in its social dimension. A few psychologists (Schell, Dodge, & Moutsatsos, 2002; Rogers, 2006; Young, Zhang, & Prybutok, 2007), sociologists (Jordan & Taylor, 2008; Turgeman-Goldschmidt, 2009), anthropologists (Coleman & Golub, 2008), and criminologists (Hollinger, 1991; Yar, 2005; Holt, 2009) have sought to fill this knowledge gap and debunk the myths and stereotypes attached to the hacker subculture, producing taxonomies, looking for motivations, and assessing the significance of hacking in our technology-dependent societies. But only two of these studies (Meyer, 1989; Holt, 2009) have examined the social organization of computer hackers, emphasizing the existence of cooperative working relationships and their limitations. Nor is it always clear in the above-mentioned studies to what extent respondents are in fact involved in criminal activities.

Surveys and semi-structured interviews (conducted either face-to-face or online) have been the prevailing modes of data collection in this field of research and hacker conventions have been particularly fertile grounds for meeting prospective respondents. The downside of this sampling strategy is that the self-selection process resulting from the decision to attend such highly publicized conferences (Defcon, for example, had 10,000 attendees in 2011) might create a bias toward "white-hat" hackers who feel comfortable mingling with intelligence and law enforcement agents. Identifying, recruiting, and interviewing informants who are part of the criminal offender population has always presented a number of practical and ethical dilemmas for ethnographic researchers (Hobbs, 1995: 2; Shover, 1996: 193; Wright & Decker, 1997: 3). Academics studying malicious hackers fortunately avoid the risks encountered by those who study armed robbers but the possibility of exaggerated and deceptive responses is substantial.

This chapter seeks to expand our knowledge of the social norms and practices that govern interactions between malicious hackers through a case study based on the seized communication logs of 10 confirmed co-offenders. After presenting the data, discussing the types of analysis that were performed, and describing how the material became available to the author, the remaining sections focus on the two variables that define this criminal network's performance: skills and trust. The skills under consideration are the three different sets of cognitive and practical abilities that malicious hackers need in order to succeed financially. Monetization and social skills, in addition to technical skills, play key roles in profit-oriented malicious hacking and explain why earning a decent living in the computer underground remains a laborious endeavor, even for advanced hackers. Trust, which facilitates the diffusion of technical, monetization, and social skills and fosters collaboration, was found to be much lower in this network than is generally assumed in the literature on hacking. In fact, over the two years for which data is available, this network showed significant lack of trust that erupted into direct aggressions between members without any discernible external pressures to explain this rapid erosion. The need for monetization and social skills as well as the lack of trust between members may partly explain why hacker networks are so ephemeral and vulnerable to law enforcement disruption.

OFFENDERS' PROFILES, DATA ACQUISITION, AND METHODOLOGY

Before proceeding to a more substantial analysis, it is important to discuss three characteristics of the data. First, the sample of hackers being studied was not self-selected or made up of volunteers met online or at various conferences, whose criminal background is hard to authenticate. The hackers involved had been identified by police investigators as suspects in various computer crimes under the Canadian criminal code and, given this, it was not considered necessary to independently determine the extent of their involvement in malicious and illicit activities. Second, the hackers concerned had been the main focus of an extended police investigation (more than two years), which ended with arrests and equipment seizures that provided a retrospective and unbiased glimpse into their daily routines. Their hard drives were analyzed by investigators in search of evidence and large amounts of data from their communication logs were extracted with the use of advanced forensic tools. Access to these logs means that the data presented here do not depend on respondents' imprecise recollections or hyperbole (Grabosky, 2007), but truly reflects their interactions with co-offenders and the evolution of these exchanges. The bias inherent in qualitative interviews about past events is neutralized by access to what amounts to a virtual time-travel machine, allowing private conversations between co-offenders, conducted in an atmosphere free of external interferences, to be reliably captured for systematic analysis. Third, the hackers who make up this sample belonged to the same network, meaning that they had maintained collaborative ties for at least two years. Even if the strength of these ties fluctuated greatly over the reference period, this is, to my knowledge, the first time the inner workings of a hacker network have been studied through a mixed-method approach over such an extended period of time.

In a democracy, such intrusive data can only be collected by a law enforcement organization operating under proper judicial authority. Hence, this research would have been impossible without the support of the Sûreté du Québec (SQ), the police force for the Canadian province of Quebec. In February 2008, the SQ's cybercrime unit arrested 17 suspects in 12 locations in what became known as Operation Basique. This investigation began in 2005 as an intelligence project looking at the hacking underground, but it soon focused on this particular hacker network when it became apparent that its members operated large botnets of compromised computers. A botnet is usually defined as a group of infected machines under the influence of malware code controlled by an individual known as a "botmaster" (Abu Rajab, Zarfoss, Monrose, & Terzis, 2006: 42; Gu, Perdisci, Zhang, & Lee, 2008: 139). Botnets have been characterized as "compulsory military service for Windows boxes [computers]" (Stromberg, cited in Zarfoss, 2007: 11), although Apple computers are far from immune (Perlroth, 2012). These armies of "zombie" machines are versatile and powerful tools that can be used to launch distributed denial of service attacks, spam, and phishing campaigns, and to steal confidential information or carry out click frauds. The largest known botnets, such as Mariposa, Conficker, Rustock, Grum, DNS Changer, or Coreflood, were able to corral millions of machines to their service.

Members of the Basique network did not operate at this level but were nevertheless serious players on the hacking scene. The investigators who analyzed their hard drives were able to identify more than a hundred botnets controlled by this group, comprising 630,000 IP addresses in 120 different countries. Of the 17 suspects initially arrested, 10 were later charged and all of them eventually pleaded guilty to charges such as unauthorized use of computers, possession and use of passwords, mischief in relation to data, fraud, and possession of credit card data. Nine of them were sentenced to periods of home detention ranging from 15 to 18 months, complemented with some community work. One notable exception was the person perceived to be the leader of the group, who received a two-year jail term and three-year probation, possibly the harshest sentence handed down for computer-related offenses in Canadian judicial history. These 10 convicted hackers make up the criminal network analyzed in this chapter.

The demographic profile of these 10 hackers largely agrees with that provided in the literature as all of them were male and their average age at the time of arrest was 20.4 years (range: 17–25). Although only two were minors when arrested, most of the others stated in their initial police interview that they had become interested in hacking as early as eight years old and had become acquainted with botnets by their early teens. Although the sample cannot be considered representative, this particular group seems to corroborate the stereotype of a hacking subculture essentially populated by young males. Young women appeared regularly in communication logs but as former, current, or potential girlfriends who required technical help or prompted network members to attack people against whom they bore a grudge, never as botnet creators or operators.

This sample differs from typical representations of the hacking community (Turgeman-Goldschmidt, 2009: 324) in its involvement in other types of criminal offenses and the occupational orientation of its members. Half of the arrested hackers (five) had previous police records for drug-related offenses (three), theft (two), or assault (two) and were therefore already involved in low-level non-technological crimes. Half of them also repeatedly discussed their drug-consumption habits (mainly cannabis) in the seized logs. Among the five hackers who had steady jobs, only one was employed in the computer industry. The other four worked in trade or manual labor on a family farm, in the logging industry, in a plastics factory, and in a door and window installation company. A sixth hacker was receiving social welfare benefits, although he worked in a variety of undeclared menial jobs. Of the four remaining hackers, two were studying computer science and two had an unknown status. The two features of early involvement in various forms of petty crime and a blue-collar occupational profile contradict the stereotype of the hacker as a computer geek, destined to join the ranks of internet or security start-ups after a decisive encounter with the criminal justice system. In this network, hacking was a pastime that provided a sense of freedom and excitement to individuals whose professional and personal prospects were dim. Indeed, three came from dysfunctional families where one or both parents had a criminal record, in some cases for very serious violent offenses, such as attempted murder. For these individuals, hacking is best described as the extension or diversification of a burgeoning criminal trajectory rather than a misstep in an otherwise uneventful biography.

The original data provided by the SQ consisted of 4,714 one-to-one conversations extracted from the hackers' hard drives, conducted via a synchronous online messaging technology known as IRC (Internet Relay Chat). IRC is a very popular communication tool for hackers, who use dedicated channels to learn new skills, brag about their exploits, and trade illicit goods and services (Franklin, Paxson, Perrig, & Savage, 2007). The majority of IRC channels are used by legitimate individuals who appreciate its interactive features (Werry, 1996). Hackers themselves frequently use IRC for purely social purposes. For example, while the 4,714 conversations mentioned above involved 761 individuals (in addition to the 10 hackers), 95.1% of these users were apparently not involved in illicit activities (Décary-Hétu & Dupont, 2012) but were friends and family members or complete strangers with a common

hobby. The seized logs also included public discussions that took place on freely accessible hacking channels and implicated numerous individuals in illegal hacking activities, but offenders are aware that these channels are monitored by law enforcement agencies and usually avoid implicating themselves. Such forums act more as meeting points that provide initial contacts which can then be followed up by private conversations. In order to focus on the most serious content and avoid being drowned in large volumes of useless data, it was decided to restrict the analysis to private IRC discussions between the 10 arrested hackers (which yielded 113 chat logs) and between these hackers and other individuals if conversations contained certain keywords or technical references suggesting malicious activities (89 additional chat logs).[3] Overall, 202 text files containing almost a quarter of a million words (243,978 to be precise) were coded and analyzed in order to understand how this network operated. A qualitative data analysis software called QDA Miner facilitated the coding, annotating, and retrieval of this large dataset. The social network analysis component of that project relied on the UCINET software package (Borgatti, Everett, & Freeman, 2002). In order to maintain the privacy of the arrested hackers and their interlocutors, an identifying number was randomly allocated to each discrete nickname extracted from the IRC logs.

Although these logs represent only a fraction of the data seized by investigators (0.01% of the 348MB of text files retrieved from the hackers' hard drives), their content can confidently be characterized as the most informative. IRC channels are routinely used by botmasters to receive information from and send commands to machines they have infected all over the world (Stone-Gross et al., 2009) and a large number of the remaining logs contained automatically generated lines of computer code that are of little value for the purpose of this research.

The data under consideration must obviously be interpreted with care, as they may suffer from a number of biases. The chats logs could have been erased at regular intervals by security-minded hackers in order to suppress evidence in case of an arrest, reducing our ability to grasp the true extent of these prudent offenders' skills. But in order to be completely effective, this precaution would need to be taken by each of the individuals concerned, which is rarely the case. Logs might also have been erased involuntarily as the result of a hardware failure and a lack of backup, unfortunate incidents that can strike even the most proficient hackers. Alternatively, the recent purchase of new equipment might mean that all archived data in old machines had been disposed of and thus was unavailable for further analysis. As well, identification of individuals was not always straightforward. While it was sometimes possible in the qualitative analysis to uncover instances where an arrested hacker had used multiple nicknames and his various numerical identifiers could thus be recoded, this process could not be implemented for all protagonists and the same person could very well be represented as multiple nodes (one node per nickname). Finally, the timestamps used to record the day and time at which online conversations occurred were automatically assigned by the hackers' machines, but a de-synchronized or incorrectly set internal clock could distort the chronology of events. With these caveats in mind, we can proceed to the first stage of the data analysis and consider the level of expertise demonstrated by these hackers as well as the different types of skills exhibited by network members.

THE UNEQUAL DISTRIBUTION OF TECHNICAL, MONETIZATION, AND SOCIAL SKILLS

As explained previously, botnets are versatile and powerful illicit tools that can provide significant profits to their operators. A number of empirical studies relying on leaked or manipulated data from command and control (C&C) servers used to coordinate large armies of compromised computers have estimated that the most successful botmasters generate revenues of up to US$3.5 million per year, mostly from spam sent on behalf of online pharmacies (Anderson et al., 2012; McCoy et al., 2012). However, researchers have found that profits are much more modest for the majority of bot herders, whose median incomes range from a few hundred to a few thousand dollars a year, depending on their strategies (Herley & Florêncio, 2009; McCoy et al., 2012). So, despite media and industry reports that stress the ease with which botnets can be purchased or rented online (Ollmann, 2008; Danchev, 2010; Krebs, 2011; Leyden, 2011), most hackers still find it difficult to benefit financially from this widely available technology. The economics of botnets and underground markets certainly explain in part why it is so hard for botmasters to turn a profit (Herley & Florêncio, 2008; Anderson et al., 2012), but I suggest that considering the mix of skills that botmasters possess or lack is also important in understanding their success or failure. Using the typology developed by Copes and Vieraitis (2008) for identity thieves, malicious hackers who want to succeed financially need three types of skills: 1) technical, 2) monetization ("system knowledge" in Copes and Vieraitis's terminology), and 3) social. Consideration of how the arrested hackers performed, individually and collectively, in each category shows that technical skills are crucial but not sufficient, and that monetization and social skills are in much more limited supply than technical skills.

Technical Skills

In the context of this particular hacker network, technical skills are the technical expertise or knowledge that can be mobilized for the development, deployment, and maintenance of a large pool of stable and stealthy robots. While the most talented hackers are able to create original botnets, most botmasters prefer to download existing malicious code from various internet forums and modify these generic applications in order to suit their needs. Many "families" of botnets have evolved over the years and share a common codebase, with new extensions and functionalities constantly added, the most popular being Agobot, SDBot, SpyBot, or GT Bot (Barford & Yegneswaran, 2007). The arrested hackers favored SDBot and variants such as JrBot and RxBot, as well as a rarer type of bot known as Kaiten. According to the Honeynet Project, a non-profit security organization that investigates computer attacks, none of these two botnet families are considered particularly sophisticated (Bächer, Holz, Kötter, & Wicherski, 2008). Both have been widely available since early 2000, which suggests that the arrested hackers preferred to deal with more established "products" for which there are numerous online tutorials. The arrested hackers' machines revealed no trace of the more elaborate ZeuS botnet, which is specifically designed to harvest online banking credentials and appeared in the wild as early as 2007 under the name NTOS (Lemos, 2010), a clear indication that our hackers do not fit the "early adopter" or "innovator" profiles.

Of the 10 hackers, one stood out as the technical leader of this network. N378 was able to significantly modify the malware codebase he downloaded from the internet. He was also very effective at propagating his malicious code and at the time of his arrest he controlled almost half the compromised machines infected by this network (291,000 bots). His technical expertise was undisputed among other network members, and he acted as a mentor and teacher for less technically advanced hackers. He also shared some of his custom-built code and, in a few instances, provided access to the C&C servers that controlled his bot army to let co-offenders use his attack capabilities. Police investigators claim

that he had used this technical expertise to launch 153 DDoS (denial of service) attacks over the two years preceding his arrest and more than 2,000 passwords and 500 credit card numbers were in his possession when he was arrested.

The remaining members of this hacker network were much more modest in their technical prowess, with a median number of 60,197 controlled bots, and a low of 314 infected machines for N142. If these hackers were avid attackers, their technical skills limited their ability to steal credit card numbers and banking credentials from their victims. A good example is N286, who controlled 104,000 bots but had only managed to obtain nine credit card numbers. These hackers also found it difficult to maintain their infrastructure, as their bots and C&C servers, which were all hosted on compromised machines, were frequently detected and removed by their victims. On a number of occasions, N1 and N142 lost all of their bots in this fashion and turned to N378 to ask him to spare a few of his bots so that they could immediately resume their activities (a request that was denied in both instances).

The uneven distribution of expertise among network members did not seem to be compensated for through the purchase or rental of easy-to-use malware packages—what security industry analysts call the "malware as a service" model, where, for a fee, malware developers offer aspiring slow or lazy hackers advice, technical support, and money-back guarantees as well as upgrades (Gilman, 2009). None of the network members operated the types of botnets found for sale on underground markets (such as ZeuS) and their socio-demographic profiles suggest it is unlikely that they would have had the necessary funds for such an investment as some of the most sophisticated malware kits can cost up to a few thousand dollars (Stevens & Jackson, 2010).

The technical skills required to set up and operate a large botnet are far from insignificant and only those ready to invest significant amounts of time or money can move beyond an initial experimentation phase. Talent also plays an important role and, above a certain level of complexity, motivation alone is not sufficient to acquire the necessary skills. This is not to say that hackers who display rudimentary technical expertise cannot cause substantial damage to computer systems, as the activities of this network make abundantly clear, but these apprentices are largely empowered by mentors who tend to shape their network's technical capability. Finding and removing these few technical leaders is likely to be one of the most reliable ways to disrupt hacker networks, as they are difficult to replace.

Monetization Skills

Knowing how to conscript thousands of vulnerable machines will allow a hacker to carry out attacks against an adversary's computer system or to steal banking credentials, but in order to convert these abilities into income, a second category of skills is required. Copes and Vieraitis (2008: 102) define system knowledge as the "understanding [of] how banks and credit agencies operate and . . . which stores require identification." The characterization of monetization skills used here involves a broader range of knowledge that includes—but is not limited to—the approximate value that various bits of stolen information can fetch on underground markets, the online forums where stolen data can be traded, botnets can be rented, or co-offenders can be recruited in order to siphon credit card and bank accounts, the alternative financial tools that govern money transfers between illicit actors (who do not accept credit card payments), and the informal rules that govern these exchanges and protect dealers against the numerous "rippers" who haunt these markets (Herley & Florêncio, 2009; Motoyama, McCoy, Levchenko, Savage, & Voelker, 2011), as well as the security procedures that are implemented by online and brick-and-mortar retailers or banking institutions in order to prevent fraud and account takeovers (Newman & Clarke, 2003).

Although the most capable members of this network displayed technical skills above the script-kiddie level, they were very limited in their monetization skills. Even N378, the network's technical leader, who sorely needed money, experienced difficulties in converting apparently straightforward opportunities into cash, as the following discussion with N1077 (who was not a network member) illustrates:

[23:38] <1077> I have 18 cards waiting
[23:38] <1077> I send you 500$ by WU [Western Union, one of the preferred money transfer solutions among internet fraudsters] for each card that works as expected
[23:38] <1077> 2k cash and 2k shopping
[23:38] <378> lol [laugh out loud]
[23:38] <1077> I cashout 1k for the card's owner
[23:38] <378> this is another business
[23:39] <1077> I end up with 500 and you too
[23:39] <378> today
[23:39] <378> the police
[23:39] <378> seized
[23:39] <378> my car
[23:39] <378> for the second
[23:39] <378> time
[23:39] <378> this month
[23:39] <1077> lol why
[23:44] <378> you need the login
[23:44] <378> the password
[23:44] <378> social insurance
[23:44] <1077> wooo
[23:44] <1077> no
[23:44] <1077> I don't have this
[23:44] <378> just the last 3 numbers
[23:44] <378> and his birthdate
[23:44] <378> and the account needs to be activated

[23:44] <378> I hope you knew that..?

[23:44] <1077> I tell you I have the card with the embossed numbers and the dob [date of birth] that's it I know a guy who is able to do all this with the info I have

[23:45] <378> otherwise the transaction will not proceed

[23:45] <1077> I only have the card and the pin and the dob that's it

[23:46] <378> ahhhhhh

[23:46] <378> you want to offer me some cashout

[23:46] <378> LOL

[23:46] <1077> I try to find another guy who can do the same things as my former guy

[23:46] <1077> I want you to hack a bank account then put some cash on my card and I will cash it out

[23:47] <1077> that's it

[23:47] <1077> so can you still do it

[23:47] <378> well we would have to spam

[23:47] <378> and that is more preparation

[23:47] <378> you need to hack a website

[23:47] <1077> I know

[23:47] <378> you need to host a page

[23:48] <378> I think I have one in backup

[23:48] <378> give me two seconds to check

[23:48] <1077> 2k if you can do it I give you 500$

[23:48] <1077> per card

[23:48] <1077> that works

[23:48] <378> r you crazy

[23:48] <378> its 50 50

[23:48] <1077> well that's it

[23:48] <1077> lol

[23:48] <1077> 500/500

[23:48] <378> then you have 500 for the cost of the card

[23:48] <378> lol

[23:48] <378> your funny man

[23:48] <1077> because of the card owner I give him 1000$

[23:48] <1077> and I cashout 2k

[23:48] <1077> max

[23:49] <378> we can cashout

[23:49] <378> more than 2000 man

[23:49] <378> we can use the card

[23:49] <378> 2 3weeks

[23:49] <1077> before he realizes ?

[23:49] <1077> you think ?

[23:49] <378> yes

[23:49] <378> I am sure of it

[23:49] <378> you find a 10k account

[23:49] <378> you think you take just 5k$

[23:49] <378> but the account has to be activated [for online transfers]

[23:49] <378> its more difficult

[23:50] <1077> look my guy before I gave him the card and the dob and he came back the following day with cash

[23:50] <378> you need to call the bank to activate the accounts

[23:50] <1077> i know

[23:50] <378> and to start this

[23:50] <378> I need to do some work

[23:50] <378> I don't have spamming lists anymore

[23:50] <378> I don't have a spammer either

[23:50] <1077> damn

[23:51] <1077> so . . . what does it mean you can't do it ?

[23:51] <378> hey fatso you think I don't have a life and I spend my time defrauding banks

[23:51] <1077> well 2k you'd be rich hehe

[23:51] <378> it means I need some more stuff before I become operational

In this conversation, N1077, who has heard of N378's hacking reputation, offers to allow him to take the place of a previous technically savvy co-offender, whose fate is unknown, in initiating money transfers to bank accounts whose owners have sold him their debit cards. Although the owners pretend to be the victims of this fraud, they receive a share of the profits from N1077. N378's role is to hack into other bank customers' accounts (the real victims in this case) in order to initiate intra-bank transfers to the debit cards held by N1077. However, what initially seems simple to N1077 never happens and the discussion carries on for a few more days without any tangible outcome, as N378 always finds a technical pretext not to follow up on N1077's offers. This conversation took place at a time when N378 could have used the money to pay outstanding traffic fines and recover his seized car. What prevented him from exploiting the stolen debit card numbers was not some form of higher hacker ethic but a lack of familiarity with common fraud schemes, as can be seen in the following log excerpt:

[23:35] <378> hey man
[23:35] <378> have you ever fiddled with cc [credit cards]
[23:35] <378> because I just coded a new sniffer for my worm [a computer program that intercepts data and passwords between computers]
[23:35] <378> and I tested it
[23:35] <378> and it looks crazy
[23:35] <378> 125ko
[23:35] <378>.txt [refers to text files]
[23:35] <378> all cc
[23:35] <378> all fucken fresh
[23:35] <378> what the fuck do I do with that
[23:35] <378> I just know [name of his local credit union]
[23:35] <378> and not very well
[23:36] <852> weird I thought that cc required SSL encryption [a protocol to protect information when it travels on the internet]
[23:36] <852> well . . . cc are touchy . . . you need to find some kind of abandoned place where you can have things delivered . . .
[23:36] <852> a drop site
[23:36] <852> or else, you'll be caught instantly
[23:36] <852> and you need to avoid surveillance cameras that could film who is picking up the stuff . . .
[23:36] <852> it's shit as far as I am concerned
[23:37] <852> I would trade them on carding sites against whatever

[23:37] <852> You're more likely to end up in jail than anywhere else with these
[23:37] <852> or else, you can use anon proxy [an anonymous proxy to mask one's identity when surfing the internet] to create legit shells . . . or xxx websites access
[23:37] <852> that kind of shit
[23:38] <378> yep
[23:38] <378> but a shell is no better
[23:38] <378> you must not use your real IP [Internet Protocol address, a unique identifier assigned to each machine connected to the internet]
[23:38] <378> but I know something
[23:38] <378> my chum works in a store
[23:38] <378> he says you need cc
[23:38] <378> and the expiry date
[23:38] <378> and he can get a lot of stuff out
[23:38] <378> I will check it out
[23:38] <378> I have like
[23:38] <378> of lot of cc
[23:38] <378> and it increases every day
[23:38] <378> my sniffer has gone wild
[23:38] <378> check it out

In this conversation, N378, the technical mentor, turns to an outsider for advice on monetization strategies. Indeed, a keyword search through N378's entire logs reveals only one successful cash conversion, which was a fairly modest achievement, as can be seen in the following discussion with another network member.

[18:27] <378> fatso I was in a bind in Quebec City
[18:27] <378> the day before yesterday
[18:27] <378> really in deep shit
[18:27] <134> why
[18:27] <378> I carded a motel
[18:27] <378> some pizza
[18:27] <378> red wine
[18:27] <378> smokes
[18:27] <378> LOOOOl
[18:27] <378> can't imagine how easy it was
[18:27] <134> loll

[18:27] <378> no need for cvv [card verification value, an anti-fraud security feature] nothing

[18:28] <378> #carte exp: [expiration date] name of cardholder that's it

[18:28] <378> and pizza was the easiest

[18:28] <378> are you hungry?

[18:28] <134> lol

Being a skilled hacker does not equate with being a skilled fraudster, and controlling a large botnet that can harvest thousands of credit card numbers does not automatically make someone rich without some significant additional skills and a willingness to take some risks in the physical world. Despite his technical mastery, N378 experienced regular financial difficulties, as he made clear in the first excerpt in this section, and it is perhaps not surprising that his highest profile DDoS attack was in retaliation against the servers of the bailiff who seized his car. None of this network's other members seemed to have developed strong monetization skills and the largest proven gain discussed among them included the sale by N1 of a thousand bots to an undisclosed buyer for $300. The lack of monetary sophistication shown by this network can also be seen in their preferred method of payment, which involved direct bank transfers to their accounts, which were with the same bank that was the main target for their phishing campaigns. While there are a few skeptics (Herley & Florêncio, 2009; Anderson et al., 2012), most of the limited literature on hackers assumes that large botnets automatically generate matching revenues, but, as shown here, such a positive correlation cannot always be inferred. When technical and monetization skills reside in different parts of—or even outside—the network, social skills must be mobilized in order to establish a connection.

Social Skills

In their research on identity thieves, Copes and Vieraitis (2008: 100) define social skills

as the "ability to manipulate the social situation through verbal and non verbal communication." In the online context, manipulation takes place primarily through technical means and social skills therefore play a less central role in offender–victim interactions. They are, however, crucial in the search for suitable co-offenders who possess the required technical or monetization expertise, since traditional meeting opportunities such as residential proximity, leisure activities, or prison (Tremblay, 1993) are not as abundant for cybercriminals. The required social skills include the ability to establish and maintain productive interpersonal ties through computer-mediated communications with trustworthy accomplices they have never met in person, who must not only possess the needed qualifications but also refrain from defecting from established relationships. Social skills are as much a matter of quantity as of quality: a large number of contacts with a broad range of diversified skills is obviously one of the principal outcomes of social skills, but these contacts must also be available on short notice with minimal negotiation (in order to lower transaction costs) and must be sufficiently reliable to avoid malfeasance, mistakes, or failures (Tilly, 2005: 6). The ability to generate and cultivate trust among co-offenders is thus a strong qualitative indicator of one's social skills.

Valued graphs are well suited to measuring the varying strength or intensity of interpersonal relationships (Freeman, Borgatti, & White, 1991: 144–145; Wasserman & Faust, 1994: 140) and identifying prominent actors who seem to exhibit stronger social skills than their counterparts. In our sample, each conversation was coded as one interaction; Table 11.1 shows the number of interactions by each hacker with other network members and each actor's percentage of interactions within the overall network during the two years that preceded his arrest. N1 appears to be the most active member in this network, as he accounts for more than one third of

Table 11.1 Degree and flow betweenness centrality measures for the hacker network

	Degree centrality		Flow betweenness centrality	
	Degree	Share†	FlowBet (rank)	nFlowBet
1	85.000	0.376	32.401 (1)	45.001
378	50.000	0.221	8.160 (3)	11.333
516	24.000	0.106	9.219 (2)	12.805
134	20.000	0.088	2.551 (5)	3.543
564	18.000	0.080	1.267 (6)	1.759
286	13.000	0.058	8.140 (4)	11.306
142	8.000	0.035	0.120 (8)	0.167
121	6.000	0.027	0.000 (9)	0.000
841	2.000	0.009	0.936 (7)	1.300
737	0.000	0.000	0.000 (10)	0.000

Notes

For valued data, non-normalized values are used (Borgatti et al., 2002).

† The share is the centrality measure of the actor divided by the sum of all the actor centralities in the network.

intra-network interactions (37.6%), while N378, who has already been mentioned as the most technically competent hacker, comes second with 22.1% of exchanges.

Using a second type of centrality measure that does not focus exclusively on direct ties but also takes into account the brokerage role of a node—its capacity to relay information between two nodes—shows that N378's social skills remain lower than might be expected, as N1 has the highest flow betweenness centrality of all his counterparts, and two other players (N516 and N286) have higher or similar scores to N378. However, despite being by far the most central actor in this network, according to the investigator's records, N1 controlled only about 47,000 bots,[4] far behind N378 (290,000 bots), N121 (122,000 bots), or N516 (77,000 bots). This disconnect between social and technical activities may, to a certain extent, reflect a protective strategy designed by N378 in order to insulate himself from asymmetrical demands from less competent hackers who could never reciprocate his assistance. In this particular kind of network, it is important to recognize that social leaders (such as N1) can be distinct from technical leaders (such as N378) or even business leaders (none in this case)

and that attempts to disrupt the network will have slightly different outcomes depending on the type of leadership that is targeted.

So far, the main metric used to derive a ranking of the most central actors in this network has been the number of discussions. But social skills are as much about quality as about quantity, a feature that is hard to measure without conducting a content analysis of the conversations. Figure 11.1 uses the centrality measures computed above to represent the hacker network: the more frequent the interactions, the thicker the line used to visualize each tie. Figure 11.1 suggests that the two most significant relationships are the N378–N1 and the N1–N516 dyads, but examination of the content of these discussions clearly indicates that these partnerships did not always run smoothly and could very easily turn sour.

Therefore, in the following section, I complement the traditional social network analysis indicators of centrality and brokerage with a qualitative approach that seeks to determine what conversations were actually about. In this particular case, frequency of contacts is a poor measure of relationship strength, as conflicts between individuals present patterns of intense communication that look very similar to privileged connections.

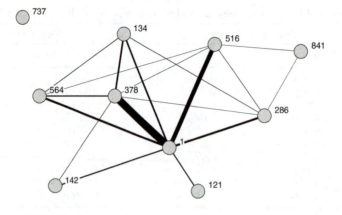

Figure 11.1 Valued ties within the hacker network

Note
Thicker lines depict more frequent interactions.

DISTRUST AND HOSTILITY AMONG NETWORK MEMBERS

In order to determine the levels of trust that linked the members of this network, each conversation in the dataset was coded using the qualitative software QDA Miner. Additional data provided by the investigative team, such as the profiles of arrested hackers prepared for the local detectives who conducted the first interview, were also taken into consideration. The goal of this exercise was to determine, for each pair of hackers, the quality of their relationship at two different periods: the years 2006 and 2007. The qualitative analysis uncovered three main types of links: high-trust relationships, which involved unconditional cooperation between members on various projects and even a level of personal intimacy; low-trust relationships, characterized by systematic cost–benefit analysis in order to determine for each demand the amount of assistance to be provided; and hostile relationships, where insults, threats, and frequent attacks were the main modes of interaction.

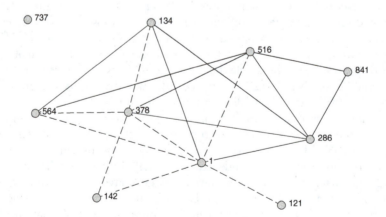

Figure 11.2 Trust levels between network members in 2006

Note
Solid lines indicate higher trust.

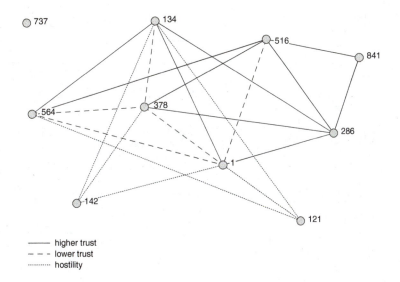

Figure 11.3 Trust levels between network members in 2007

It is possible to visualize the evolution of these ties over time by representing each relationship according to its level of trust, with solid lines indicating high-trust ties, broken lines reflecting low-trust ties, and dotted lines indicating hostility. Comparing Figures 11.2 and 11.3 makes it easy to locate resilient alliances or decaying partnerships, but it is difficult to assess how each hacker handles the three types of relationships and establish which individuals have more collaborative—or con-flictual—tendencies. Table 11.2 attempts to provide a more comprehensive overview of this network's stocks of individual and collective social capital and liabilities by showing the distribution of high-trust, low-trust, and hostile relationships for each hacker for the years 2006 and 2007. Arrows in the right-hand column indicate the upward, downward, or lateral evolution of these relationships.

The bottom line of the table suggests that the proportion of high- and low-trust relationships decreased significantly from the first to the second year, with hostile relationships between several members representing one third of interactions at the time of arrest. In absolute terms, high-trust rela-

tionships remained constant but the relative value of these relationships for the network as a whole was diluted by an increase in the number of hostile interactions. From 2006 to 2007, this network, which started as a high-trust environment, morphed into a web of distrust. In the following paragraphs, I examine the causes of this shift and its consequences for cooperation by analyzing each type of relationship.

High-Trust Ties and Cooperation

As discussed previously, network members displayed diverse levels of technical expertise. Hacker networks are principally involved in knowledge transfer, with the most talented members imparting knowledge, either explic-itly or implied, to newcomers or apprentices deemed worthy of it. More rarely, members of a hacker network will conduct a joint oper-ation, coordinating their activities to attack a target or pooling their resources for a specific task, such as testing the effectiveness of a newly coded program (Holt, 2009).

In this particular network, members who trusted each other exchanged information

Table 11.2 Evolution of the distribution of high-trust, low-trust, and hostile relationships for network members

	2006			2007		
	Hostile (N)	Low trust (N)	High trust (N)	Hostile (N)	Low trust (N)	High trust (N)
121	0.0000	1.0000 (1)	0.0000	1.0000 (3) ↑	0.0000 ↓	0.0000
142	0.0000	1.0000 (2)	0.0000	1.0000 (3) ↑	0.0000 ↓	0.0000
841	0.0000	0.0000	1.0000 (2)	0.0000	0.0000	1.0000 (2) →
737	0.0000	0.0000	0.0000	0.0000	0.0000	0.0000
1	0.0000	0.7143 (5)	0.2857 (2)	0.2857 (2) ↑	0.4286 (3) ↓	0.2857 (2) →
286	0.0000	0.0000	1.0000 (5)	0.0000	0.0000	1.0000 (5) →
378	0.0000	0.6667 (4)	0.3333 (2)	0.1667 (1) ↑	0.5000) (3) ↓	0.3333 (2) →
134	0.0000	0.2500 (1)	0.7500 (3)	0.3333 (2) ↑	0.1667 (1) ↓	0.5000 (3) ↓
516	0.0000	0.2000 (1)	0.8000 (4)	0.0000	0.2000 (1) →	0.8000 (4) →
564	0.0000	0.5000 (2)	0.5000 (2)	0.2000 (1) ↑	0.4000 (1) →	0.4000 (2) →
Network	0.0000	0.4444 (16)	0.5556 (20)	0.2857 (12) ↑	0.2381 (10) ↓	0.4762 (20) ↓

on how to obtain, modify, and operate certain malicious applications, collaborated in order to solve technical problems (such as the instability of the bots they were using), shared pieces of code they had written, let others access their servers by sharing their login and passwords, or warned each other about behavior that might attract the attention of governmental authorities. For example, N378 warned another network member against scanning IPs in range 140, which is largely allocated to military computers and is used by the US Defense Information Systems Agency and Fort Bragg, the home of the US Army Special Operations forces. N378 advised his apprentice to confine himself to more benign ranges such as 128, 129, and 130, which belong to educational institutions. In another instance, with an irony that

seemed to escape both protagonists, N516 asked N378 which would be the most effective anti-virus solution on the market to protect his mother's laptop. Here is N378's response, which he promised would make the computer "un-hackable":

[21:51] <378> what is the os [operating system]
[21:52] <516> p4 centrino
[21:52] <516> win xp
[21:52] <378> xp ?
[21:52] <378> k
[21:52] <516> yeah
[21:52] <516> like 1.76 ghz
[21:52] <516> 1 gb ram
[21:52] <378> you install her sygate for xp pro
[21:52] <516> yeah

[21:52] <378> as a firewall
[21:52] <516> sygate that's what I thought
[21:52] <378> you fetch adware ligit
[21:53] <378> a small anti virus
[21:53] <378> nothing too heavy
[21:53] <378> that only does the essential
[21:53] <378> like panda platinum
[21:54] <516> fuck it
[21:54] <378> with the permanent protection file
[21:54] <516> this is shit
[21:54] <516> lol
[21:54] <378> nah not that bad
[21:54] <378> mine yes
[21:54] <378> bcse it's old
[21:54] <516> ok
[21:54] <378> but they are not listed anywhere panda
[21:54] <516> ok
[21:54] <378> because
[21:54] <378> with these three tools
[21:54] <378> she cannot get hacked man
[21:55] <378> you have iptables firewall
[21:55] <378> a registry blocker
[21:55] <378> a permanent protection file
[21:55] <516> ok
[21:55] <378> a small antivirus that does the job and that is not annoying when it finds a virus
[21:55] <516> ok good
[21:55] <516> thx:)

Not all discussions were task-oriented and high-trust ties also implied that the long and dry technical exchanges would be interspersed with discussions of personal issues: frayed relationships with girlfriends or family members, lack or loss of employment, financial difficulties, weekend plans, and drug use were discussed between certain pairs of hackers and broke the monotony of computer programming and botnet management. These personal confidences were probably instrumental in creating rapport and reinforcing social ties between people who had never met in person, and whose social costs for defecting would therefore have been very low, if not null.

Low-Trust Relationships and Contingent Cooperation

High-trust relationships never comprised more than 56% of network ties and the two dyads with the most frequent interactions (N1–N378 and N1–N516; see Figure 11.1) were characterized by limited levels of trust from the start. In low-trust relationships, hackers exchanged information and shared resources only up to a certain threshold, beyond which cooperation was suspended or withdrawn. This more closely controlled flow of information and resources was generally the result of either the disparaging attitude displayed by more technically skilled hackers toward less qualified members of their entourage or a specific incident that led one hacker to question the reliability of another network member.

For example, N378, the master hacker and unofficial mentor in this network, explained to N834 (an outsider who said he earned more than $10,000 a month through credit card fraud) why he limited his collaboration with other network members:

[06:47] <378> I don't want to help anyone
[06:47] <378> for bots
[06:47] <378> each time I help someone
[06:47] <378> my worms stop working
[06:47] <378> since I stopped helping people
[06:47] <378> my worms are on fire
[06:47] <378> all those I help leech my codes
[06:47] <378> and leak it everywhere
[06:48] <834> don't worry, I am not like that
[06:48] <834> you know me better
[06:48] <378> so, I am fucking tired that everything I do is leeched but that I am considered as a fucking noob [an inexperienced person who has no will to learn in hacker jargon]
[06:48] <834> agree
[06:48] <834> accept the dcc send [an IRC code that allows users to send and receive files]

[06:48] <378> but everyone comes to see me when it's about bots
[06:48] <834> hehe your not noobs man
[06:48] <834> you're wiser than me
[06:48] <834> I can't even code a fucking bot
[06:48] <378> msn
[06:48] <378> well its tough man
[06:49] <378> I have been at it for years practicing coding worms
[06:49] <378> just doing that all the time
[06:49] <378> collect sources for bot packers and whatever
[06:49] <378> meanwhile I collect all kind of stuff

In this discussion, N378 describes how asymmetrical he feels his interactions with other hackers are: while he is being asked a lot of technical questions and even to share his proprietary malicious applications, he gets very little (not even the respect he believes he is due) from those interactions. This attitude reflects a very individualistic approach to hacking: far from seeing himself as a group leader, his mind-set is more that of a crafts-man—his skills have been acquired through trial and error and personal sacrifice and as a result should not be made available to people who are not ready to invest the same amount of time and effort. This lack of trust not only limited the network's technical effectiveness but also restricted its monetization oppor-tunities. In a follow-up discussion between N378 and N834, the former explains that he does not trust money transfer services such as Western Union, which are very popular with internet fraudsters (Moore, Clayton, & Anderson, 2009), and prefers face-to-face cash exchanges. This type of attitude was unlikely to facilitate the integration of the network with international fraud rings that operate at the transnational level (McCusker, 2007) and rely on virtual currencies and money transfer services to pay their associ-ates and repatriate criminal proceeds.

A second source of low-trust interactions results from specific instances of malfeasance,

mistakes, or failures (Tilly, 2005). In the fol-lowing excerpt, N378 denies N1's request to share some bots, justifying his decision by an operational mistake made a few years earlier that has never been forgotten:

[12:37] <1> do you think you would be able to download me some bots to help me out and I will help you back when you want
[12:38] <378> no lol
[12:38] <378> I gave you some a while back
[12:38] <1> you took them back
[12:38] <378> you did not keep them
[12:38] <1> it was 2 years ago
[12:38] <378> nah never
[12:38] <378> I gave them to you
[12:38] <378> you did not know how to keep them
[12:38] <378> it was 5 years ago
[12:38] <1> my exe [executable file] was detectable and not packed [compressed with a specific application in order to hide the file's true content] then
[12:39] <378> I have the same bots
[12:39] <378> and you're wrong they were packed
[12:39] <378> you had mew11
[12:39] <378> lo
[12:39] <1> no I had the small aspack [an executable file compression software]
[12:39] <1> it was not very good
[12:39] <1> and now they are packed and undetectable
[12:40] <1> I did not know anything then now I know better and I know how to keep them

In the end, N1 did not sway N378. A sub-sequent discussion about N1's alleged preda-tory behavior did not do anything to allay N378's distrust of N1's motives:

[15:59] <378> he man
[15:59] <378> did you steal N519's bots by any chance
[16:01] <1> nah I told you I removed all mines
[16:01] <1> I give up that shit

[16:02] <378> dude he says that when he logged on his server

[16:02] <378> he had 79 bots left

[16:02] <378> and that you left just after

[16:02] <1> I know he told me the same

[16:02] <1> and I told him I crashed as well

[16:02] <378> in any case man

[16:03] <378> a couple of people told me you were after their bots

[16:03] <1> I will not touch anything why don't he fixes his bots

[16:03] <1> and even if I am after their bots all bots are mine N121 and N519 would never had any bots without my help

[16:03] <378> last thing

[16:04] <1> but anyway I don't give a shit I gave up for good

[16:04] <378> when you accuse someone

[16:04] <378> make sure

[16:04] <378> you can prove what you say

[16:04] <1> anyway I am going to the beach

[16:04] <378> I have broad shoulders but there are limits to what I will tolerate

These low-trust interactions do not paralyze the network as superficial or low-level forms of cooperation can still take place, but the higher transaction costs they create certainly curtail its effectiveness. A lot of pleading and cajoling is required to overcome the underlying distrust, and the constant reassurance that must be provided to certain members does not always guarantee a positive outcome. Another consequence of the limited supply of trust within this network is reluctance to engage jointly in riskier (but potentially more rewarding) projects, as new initiatives are met with suspicion and skepticism—not the best way to foster innovation. The constraints and instability imposed by the high proportion of low-trust interactions among some of the network's most central members can culminate in the quick deterioration of relationships. Hackers are then entirely or partially excluded from the network and as a result must dedicate an inordinate amount of time to conflict management.

FRIEND TO FOE: THE ENEMY WITHIN

Toward the end of the second year, N121 and N142, who had been on the periphery of the network during the previous year, were locked into hostile relationships with the rest of the network and seemed to have exhausted the limited trust that had been extended to them. They were not, however, completely disconnected from the network, as they remained technically able to repeatedly attack their former allies' machines and servers. The same sequence led to these outbreaks of hostility. Both N121 and N142 had initially collaborated on a limited basis with N1, while N378 had imparted some of his knowledge to N142. But after a year of low-trust interactions, accusations were voiced about the careless handling of shared resources that had been lost to the group, and insults about selfishness and lack of support from the more experienced hackers became more common. It was not long before the technical and social leaders lost their patience and decided to make an example of N121 and N142, using their powerful botnets to launch repeated attacks against them. N121 and N142 refused to be intimidated and retaliated. The escalation of this conflict culminated with N1 and N142 receiving death threats on the phone.

This rapid decay of trust leading to the exclusion of some network members is not a marginal trend, as by the end of the second year more than 28% of the network's relationships can be classified as hostile. Such a sharp increase (from 0% the first year) is produced by the deterioration of low-trust partnerships and the spread of disputes to hackers who were not involved in the original arguments. By contrast, high-trust relationships demonstrated their resilience, as none of them suffered any deterioration during the reference period. However, in less than 24 months, this network, which had not (yet) been exposed to police action and was free to operate unrestrained, spontaneously became unstable and lost some of its effectiveness. This self-created fragmentation made the network dysfunctional and significant resources had to be diverted from hacking projects and allocated to minimize the fallout from these incidents.

This situation is radically different from the Caviar drug importation network studied by Morselli and Petit (2007), which remained operational despite the erosion of trust caused by recurring seizures of hashish and cocaine consignments. Faced with signs of mistrust between network members following one of the first police disruptions, that network leader tried to remain cool-headed in a telephone intercept with an associate:

> I'm trying to put things back on the road. I'm trying to save all this aggravation because, if it's gonna come to that, it's gonna be a mess and it's the last thing I want for you and for everybody, I just wanna fix this up diplomatically.
> (Morselli, 2009: 95)

By comparison, diplomatic skills were in very short supply in the hacker network under study, where random acts of aggression were often observed, fueled by a potent mixture of boredom and touchiness. In the following excerpt, N378 and N564, who share a low-trust relationship, discuss potential targets for N378's bots, which are online but idle.

[15:03] < 378> do you have someone
[15:03] <378> to flood [an attack that consists in sending data faster than the receiver can process, which causes the target to disconnect from the network]
[15:03] <378> I have 900 proxy
[15:03] <378> online
[15:03] <378> lol
[15:03] <564> no
[15:03] <564> but . . . don't flood [name of third hacker]
[15:03] <564> he'll be crazy hahaha
[15:03] <564> I'll find you someone to flood

[15:03] <564> fuck
[15:03] <564> [name of a fourth hacker] is not online
[15:03] <564> it stinks
[15:03] <378> lol
[15:03] <564> lol
[15:03] <378> wait
[15:03] <378> until he sees it
[15:03] <378> I flooded him
[15:03] <378> with 60 bot
[15:04] <378> now I have 800

When N564 attempts to clarify the reasons behind this attack, the answer he receives is laced with veiled threats. While attempting to deflect the planned assault against the third hacker, he keeps looking for a suitable alternative target.

[15:09] <564> why do you flood him exactly?
[15:09] <378> its a request
[15:10] <564> who from?
[15:10] <378> hahaha
[15:10] <378> you just saw me
[15:10] <378> on the chan
[15:10] <378> shut up
[15:10] <378> or I flood you
[15:10] <378> :P
[15:10] <564> yeah
[15:10] <564> i know
[15:10] <564> hahaha
[15:10] <378> hahah
[15:10] <378> nah i mess around
[15:10] <378> but man
[15:10] <378> I have 800 prox
[15:10] <378> online
[15:10] <564> take it easy
[15:10] <378> do you have someone
[15:10] <564> stop flooding him
[15:10] <378> that i hate
[15:10] <564> he's gonna eat crap

The lack of maturity displayed by network members,[5] combined with the availability of powerful tools that can be used for malicious actions, explains to a certain extent why already fragile low-trust relationships easily descended into open conflict. But the volatility of these ties can also be ascribed to structural features of the internet: the capacity to shed one's online identity at will and adopt new nicknames when a reputation is damaged, the unlimited pool of potential co-offenders who can be met online on dedicated underground forums and IRC channels, and the limited opportunities imposed by geographical distances and anonymity on the use of physical coercion as a compliance and control mechanism all contribute to lowering the costs of malfeasance and betrayal and to exacerbating distrust, a latent attitude among delinquents (Tremblay, 1993: 25). In that context, we should not be surprised to see such a high rate of infighting among network members.

CONCLUSION

Neither super-empowered technicians (Ohm, 2008) nor socially inept teenagers, malicious hackers face practical challenges that are very familiar to more traditional offenders. Finding suitable and reliable associates with a broad range of complementary skills is a time-consuming quest that often has inconsistent outcomes. Although technical skills have been the main focus of most empirical and theoretical studies on hackers—along with the complex issue of what motivates them (Taylor, 1999; Schell et al., 2002; Rogers, 2006)—I hope to have made a persuasive argument for the need to conduct more empirical studies on the equally important monetization and social skills.

Malware monetization strategies are being researched by computer scientists, using concepts borrowed from the economists' toolbox (Moore et al., 2009), but we still need to understand what constraints are at work, how opportunities are structured, and how decisions are made from a hacker's perspective (Reuter, 1983). The hacker network discussed here, for example, was never able to acquire monetization skills, despite the precarious financial situation of one of its leaders and his control of significant computer resources.

The social capital that flows through such technology-mediated criminal networks also deserves much closer scrutiny. The scientific literature has, in my view, overestimated the ability and willingness of hackers to collaborate (Taylor, 1999: 62; Schell et al., 2002; Holt, 2009), assuming that the convergence of the global proliferation of available communication platforms, the semi-anonymity afforded by these technologies, and the jurisdictional boundaries constraining law enforcement agencies have eliminated the barriers that traditionally constrained illicit markets. However, far from creating a frictionless social environment for malicious hackers, these digital tools have a darker side that, under certain conditions, hinders collaboration and fosters distrust.

As online or seized data become increasingly available to researchers and computational social science methods allow them to process and analyze massive amounts of data (Lazer et al., 2009, and, for the methodological and ethical limitations of this approach, see Boyd & Crawford, 2011), unique opportunities to study the social organization of malicious hackers open up. The data presented in this chapter suggest, for example, that a hacker network that controls large botnets and does not use them for fraudulent (or political) purposes will be tempted to turn this unused firepower against some of its close associates or even those in its own network, just because doing so seems amusing and has few consequences.

The small size of this network and its highly localized nature obviously prohibit any claim of representativeness, but recent in-depth journalistic investigations of much more sophisticated and profitable hacker groups have uncovered similar patterns of distrust, hostility, and betrayal (Poulsen, 2011; McCoy et al., 2012: 3; Olson, 2012). Reports of these features, which are familiar to those who study more traditional types of criminal organizations (Von Lampe & Johansen, 2004) or those who approach hackers from a psychological perspective (Schell et al., 2002), highlight the paucity of empirical research on hackers and reveal the need for criminology, sociology, and related disciplines to develop a more nuanced understanding of the social organization of malicious hackers. A core question to consider would be how skills and trust flow between such individuals when they are under external constraints such as law enforcement targeting, peer competition, and general market changes (Leeson & Coyne, 2005). The criminal career repertoire of offenders who straddle the line between street and online crime also promises to be a fascinating avenue of research. Such knowledge is important and is needed to offset the current public discourse on cybersecurity, which is too often characterized by hysterical statements about looming risks and presents hackers as a prodigious threat that requires extraordinary regulatory powers and the use of intrusive surveillance tools to preserve the internet from an impending state of anarchy. As seen in this chapter, malicious hackers are not exclusively beneficiaries of the chaos they create online—they can also easily fall victim to it, just like their street-offending counterparts.

NOTES

1. The author would like to acknowledge the invaluable help of the Sûreté du Québec, without which this research would not have been possible. Errors in the interpretation of the data remain his own.
2. Such as *War Games* (1983), *Sneakers* (1992), *Hackers* (1995), *The Net* (1995), *Swordfish* (2001), *Live Free or Die Hard* (2007), and, more recently, *The Girl with the Dragon Tattoo* (2011).
3. These keywords were chosen to capture the most frequent terms associated with botnet, DDoS, carding, and fraud activities.
4. The number of compromised IP addresses is usually about half the recorded signatures, as hackers tend to experiment and to infect the same computers with different bots. For a more detailed discussion of the impact of differing botnet measurement methodologies on the assessment of the problem, see Abu Rajab, Zarfoss, Monrose, & Terzis (2007).
5. For example, one hacker, upon entering the courtroom where he would have to convey his plea to the judge, raised his handcuffed hands as if he had just won a sport competition and smiled at press photographers.

REFERENCES

Abu Rajab, Moheeb, Jay Zarfoss, Fabian Monrose, & Andreas Terzis (2006). A multifaceted approach to understanding the botnet phenomenon. *Proceedings of the 6th ACM SIGCOMM Conference on Internet Measurement* (pp. 41–52). Rio de Janeiro: ACM.

Abu Rajab, Moheeb, Jay Zarfoss, Fabian Monrose, & Andreas Terzis (2007). My botnet is bigger than yours (maybe, better than yours): why size estimates remain challenging. *Proceedings of the First Conference on First Workshop on Hot Topics in Understanding Botnets* (pp. 1–8). New York: ACM.

Anderson, Ross, Chris Barton, Rainer Böhme, Richard Clayton, Michel J.G. Van Eeten, Michael Levi, Tyler Moore, & Stefan Savage (2012). Measuring the cost of cybercrime. *11th Annual Workshop on the Economics of Information Security*, June 25–26. Berlin: DIW Berlin.

Bächer, Paul, Thorsten Holz, Markus Kötter, & Georg Wicherski (2008). *Know Your Enemy: Tracking Botnets—Using Honeynets to Learn More About Bots*. Seattle: The Honeynet Project. Available at www.honeynet.org/book/export/html/50 (last accessed July 25, 2012).

Barford, Paul & Vinod Yegneswaran (2007). An inside look at botnets. In Mihai Christodorescu, Somesh Jha, Douglas Maughan, Dawn Song, & Cliff Wang (eds.), *Malware Detection* (pp. 171–191). New York: Springer Verlag.

Borgatti, Steve, Martin Everett, & Lin Freeman (2002). *Ucinet for Windows: Software for Social Network Analysis*. Harvard, MA: Analytic Technologies.

Boyd, Danah & Kate Crawford (2011). Six provocations for big data. *A Decade in Internet Time: Symposium on the Dynamics of the Internet and Society*, September 21–24. Oxford: Oxford University.

Calce, Michael & Craig Silverman (2008). *Mafiaboy: How I Cracked the Internet and Why It Is Still Broken*. Toronto: Viking Canada.

Coleman, Gabriella & Alex Golub (2008). Hacker practice: Moral genre and the cultural articulation of liberalism. *Anthropological Theory* 8(3), 255–277.

Copes, Heith & Lynne Vieraitis (2008). Stealing identities: The risks, rewards and strategies of identity theft. In Megan McNally & Graham Newman (eds.), *Perspectives on Identity Theft* (pp. 87–110). New York: Criminal Justice Press.

Danchev, Dancho (2010). Study finds the average price for renting a botnet. *ZDNet*, May 26. Available at www.zdnet.com/blog/security/study-finds-the-average-price-for-renting-a-botnet/6528 (last accessed July 22, 2012).

Décary-Hétu, David & Benoit Dupont (2012). The social network of hackers. *Global Crime* 13(3), 160–175.

Franklin, Jason, Vern Paxson, Adrian Perrig, & Stefan Savage (2007). An inquiry into the nature and causes of the wealth of internet miscreants. *14th Conference of the ACM on Computer and Communications Security*, October 29–November 2. Alexandria, VA: ACM.

Freeman, Linton, Stephen Borgatti, & Douglas White (1991). Centrality in valued graphs: A measure of betweenness based on network flow. *Social Networks* 13(2), 141–154.

Gilman, Nils (2009). Hacking goes pro. *Engineering and Technology* 4(3), 26–29.

Grabosky, Peter (2007). Editor's introduction to special issue on transnational cybercrime. *Crime, Law and Social Change* 46(4–5), 185–187.

Gu, Guofei, Roberto Perdisci, Junjie Zhang, & Wenkee Lee (2008). BotMiner: Clustering analysis of network traffic for protocol- and structure-independent botnet detection. *Proceedings of the 17th Conference on Security Symposium* (pp. 139–154). San Jose, CA: USENIX Association.

Herley, Cormac & Dinei Florêncio (2008). A profitless endeavor: Phishing as tragedy of the commons. *Proceedings of the 2008 Workshop on New Security Paradigms* (pp. 59–70). ACM: New York.

Herley, Cormac & Dinei Florêncio (2009). Nobody sells gold for the price of silver: Dishonesty, uncertainty and the underground economy. *8th Workshop on the Economics of Security*, June 24–25. London: University College London.

Hobbs, Dick (1995). *Bad Business: Professional Crime in Modern Britain*. Oxford: Oxford University Press.

Hollinger, Richard (1991). Hackers: Computer heroes or electronic highwaymen? *Computers & Society* 21(1), 6–17.

Holt, Thomas (2009). Lone hacks or groups cracks: Examining the social organization of computer hackers. In Frank Schmalleger & Michael Pittaro (eds.), *Crimes of the Internet* (pp. 336–355). Upper Saddle River, NJ: Pearson.

Jordan, Tim & Paul Taylor (2008). A sociology of hackers. *The Sociological Review* 46(4), 757–780.

Krebs, Brian (2011). Rent-a-bot networks tied to TDSS botnet. *Krebs on Security*, September 6. Available at http://krebsonsecurity.com/2011/09/rent-a-bot-networks-tied-to-tdss-botnet (last accessed July 22, 2012).

Lazer, David, Alex Pentland, Lara Adamic, Sinan Aral, Albert-Lázló Barabási, Devon Brewer, Nicholas Christakis, Noshir Contractor, James Fowler, Myron Gutmann, Tony Jebara, Gary King, Michael Macy, Deb Roy, & Marshall Van Alstyne (2009). Computational social science. *Science* 323(5915), 721–723.

Leeson, Peter & Christopher Coyne (2005). The economics of computer hacking, *Journal of Law, Economics and Policy* 1(2), 511–532.

Lemos, Robert (2010). Rise of the point-and-click botnet. *Technology Review* February 23. Available at www.technologyreview.com/news/417657/rise-of-the-point-and-click-botnet (last accessed July 25, 2012).

Leyden, John (2011). Bargain-basement botnet kit—yours for just €5. *The Register*, September 22. Available at www.theregister.co.uk/2011/09/22/aldi_bot/ (last accessed July 22, 2012).

McCoy, Damon, Andreas Pitsillidis, Grant Jordan, Nicholas Weaver, Christian Kreibich, Brian Krebs, Geoffrey Voelker, Stefan Savage, & Kirill Levchenko (2012). PharmaLeaks: Understanding the business of online pharmaceutical affiliate programs. *21st USENIX Security Symposium*, August 8–10. Bellevue, WA: USENIX.

McCusker, Rob (2007). Transnational organised cyber crime: Distinguishing threat from reality. *Crime, Law and Social Change* 46(4–5), 257–273.

Meyer, Gordon (1989). *The Social Organization of the Computer Underground*. A thesis submitted to the Graduate School in partial fulfillment of the requirements for the degree Master of Arts, Criminology, Northern Illinois University, DeKalb, IL.

Mitnick, Kevin & William Simon (2011). *Ghost in the Wires: My Adventures as the World's Most Wanted Hacker*. New York: Little, Brown & Company.

Moore, Tyler, Richard Clayton, & Ross Anderson (2009). The economics of online crime. *The Journal of Economic Perspectives* 23(3), 3–20.

Morselli, Carlo (2009). *Inside Criminal Networks*. New York: Springer.

Morselli, Carlo & Katia Petit (2007). Law-enforcement disruption of a drug importation network. *Global Crime* 8(2), 109–130.

Motoyama, Marti, Damon McCoy, Kirill Levchenko, Stefan Savage, & Geoffrey Voelker (2011). An analysis of underground forums. *Proceedings of the 2011 ACM SIGCOMM Conference on Internet Measurement* (pp. 71–80). New York: ACM.

Newman, Graeme & Ronald Clarke (2003). *Superhighway Robbery: Preventing E-commerce Crime*. Cullompton: Willan.

Ohm, Paul (2008). The myth of the superuser: Fear, risk and harm online. *UC Davis Law Review* 41(4), 1327–1402.

Ollmann, Gunter (2008). Hacking as a service. *Computer Fraud & Security*, 2008(12), 12–15.

Olson, Parmy (2012). *We Are Anonymous: Inside the Hacker World of LulzSec, Anonymous, and the Global Cyber Insurgency*. New York: Little, Brown & Company.

Perlroth, Nicole (2012). Widespread virus proves Macs are no longer safe from hackers. *New York Times Bits Blog*. Available at http://bits.blogs.nytimes.com/2012/04/06/widespread-computer-virus-indicates-mac-users-no-longer-safe/ (last accessed July 4, 2012).

Poulsen, Kevin (2011). *Kingpin: How One Hacker Took Over the Billion-dollar Cybercrime Underground*. New York: Crown Publishers.

Reuter, Peter (1983). *Disorganized Crime: The Economics of the Visible Hand*. Cambridge, MA: MIT Press.

Rogers, Marcus (2006). A two-dimensional circumplex approach to the development of a hacker taxonomy. *Digital Investigation* 3(2), 97–102.

Schell, Bernadette, John Dodge, & Steve Moutsatsos (2002). *The Hacking of America: Who's Doing It, Why and How*. Westport, CT: Quorum Books.

Shover, Neal (1996). *Great Pretenders: Pursuits and Careers of Persistent Thieves*. Boulder, CO: Westview Press.

Stevens, Kevin & Don Jackson (2010). *ZeuS Banking Trojan Report*. Atlanta, GA: Secureworks.

Stone-Gross, Brett, Marco Cova, Lorenzo Cavallaro, Bob Gilbert, Martin Szydlowski, Richard Kemmerer, Chris Kruegel, & Giovanni Vigna (2009). Your botnet is my botnet: Analysis of a botnet takeover. In Somesh Jha & Angelos D. Keromytis (eds.), *Proceedings of the 16th ACM Conference on Computer and Communication Security* (pp. 635–647). New York: ACM.

Taylor, Paul (1999). *Hackers: Crime in the Digital Sublime*. London: Routledge.

Tilly, Charles (2005). *Trust and Rule*. Cambridge: Cambridge University Press.

Tremblay, Pierre (1993). Searching for suitable co-offenders. In Ronald Clarke & Marcus Felson (eds.), *Routine Activity and Rational Choice* (pp. 17–36). New Brunswick, NJ: Transaction Publishers.

Turgeman-Goldschmidt, Orly (2009). The rhetoric of hackers' neutralizations. In Frank Schmalleger & Michael Pittaro (eds.), *Crimes of the Internet* (pp. 317–335). Upper Saddle River, NJ: Pearson.

Von Lampe, Klaus & Per Ole Johansen (2004). Organized crime and trust: On the conceptualization and empirical relevance of trust in the context of criminal networks. *Global Crime* 6(2), 159–184.

Wasserman, Stanley & Katherine Faust (1994). *Social Network Analysis: Methods and Applications*. Cambridge: Cambridge University Press.

Werry, Christopher (1996). Linguistic and interactional features of Internet Relay Chat. In Susan Herring (ed.), *Computer-mediated*

Communication: Linguistic, Social and Cross-cultural Perspectives (pp. 47–63). Philadelphia, PA: John Benjamins Publishing Company.

Wright, Richard & Scott Decker (1997). *Armed Robbers in Action*. Boston, MA: Northeastern University Press.

Yar, Majid (2005). Computer hacking: Just another case of juvenile delinquency? *The Howard Journal* 44(4), 387–399.

Young, Randall, Lixuan Zhang, & Victor Prybutok (2007). Hacking into the mind of hackers. *Information Systems Management* 24(4), 281–287.

Zarfoss, Jay (2007). *A Scalable Architecture for Persistent Botnet Tracking*. A thesis submitted in conformity with the requirements for the degree of Master of Science in Engineering, Johns Hopkins University, Baltimore, MD.

CHAPTER 12

Information Exchange Paths in IRC Hacking Chat Rooms

David Décary-Hétu

Criminals who wanted to socialize with like-minded individuals used to visit the local taverns where they could drink beers and learn a trick or two about their criminal trade. In the digital age, web pages, forums, and online chat rooms have replaced local taverns. Cybercriminals can now find detailed online tutorials that teach them anything they could ever need on denial of service attacks, software piracy, and credentials hijacking. Forums and chat rooms provide an environment where hackers can meet and casually discuss their problems and look for mentors or co-delinquents. These web 2.0 "taverns" are where social interactions are now happening and have proven to be a rich environment for academic research.

The aim of this chapter will therefore be to understand how hackers in the computer underground interact with each other and build their own personal networks. Information can be shared either by posting it publicly on forums, websites, and blogs or by socializing with others through online communications. This chapter will focus on the latter and examine not what information is exchanged but how it is exchanged. In order to do so, we will look at the personal social networks of hackers and build two partial correlation models that explain how individuals can maximize the amount and diversity of information they gather. Mentoring and social learning theory will be used as the theoretical framework of this study.

COMPUTER (IN)SECURITY

Movies have a funny way of presenting hackers. In many cases (see *Hackers*, 1995; *The Net*, 1995; or *The Matrix*, 1999), it seems that rapidly punching keys on a keyboard magically grants you access to whole computer systems. This illusion has been fed by many mediated "hacks" where the hacker has merely guessed the password of a Hollywood star or used commercial phone-number spoofing services to gain access to voicemails (Sullivan, 2005). The reality, unfortunately for hackers and tabloid editors, is much more complex.

There is no disputing that corporations and individuals should be concerned with computer and network security, especially since the advent of broadband internet at the beginning of the 2000s. Two new emergent trends in the criminal underground have drawn their attention particularly (Potlapally, 2011). First, while many attacks used to be the product of fame-driven hackers with modest skills, new threats now come from "well-funded criminal organizations or [. . .] sophisticated organizations with access to significant resources and talent" (Potlapally, 2011: 93). This increases the chances of success of attacks while reducing the rates of detection by law enforcement agencies. Second, hackers are now targeting victims at a much lower level than the software layer, meaning that their malicious software can run even after an operating system is erased and restored. This is done by forcing the computer to first run the malicious software and then launch the operating system, giving the ultimate control of the system to the malicious software. By taking over the devices on which operating systems and applications run, hackers can more much easily bypass security systems and take advantage of them.

To meet these constantly evolving threats, network administrators have adopted a number of techniques (Ahmad & Habib, 2010). The first one is to securely encrypt all confidential data. Using commercial and open-source software, administrators can hide their most treasured information in encryption that would require centuries of cracking by large amounts of supercomputers. The second is intrusion detection systems (IDS). These programs monitor networks for suspect or unusual behavior and warn the security officers when such a behavior is detected. These systems have become incredibly complex and can be configured to detect changes in established connections, login/logoff timestamps, and the amount of bandwidth used by a user. Lastly, almost every system connected to the internet is now protected by a firewall, a virtual bouncer who controls who and what comes in and out of the network. The first firewalls used blacklists where all behaviors were allowed by default and where the administrators blocked suspicious activities manually. Today, modern firewalls use whitelists, where all behaviors are blocked unless they are expressly authorized.

If these technologies keep on evolving and becoming more complex, it is largely due to the attackers' ability to compromise targets. To hone their skills, hackers can easily access detailed online tutorials on how to hack computers. A simple query on Google with the phrase "how to hack" returned more than 97 million documents. While most of these results are probably useless, a dedicated individual will likely find all the needed information to improve his skills or even get started

in the hacking field through some of these websites.

Hackers can also use resources that are geared toward the legitimate security industry. Websites such as The Academy Pro (www. theacademypro.com) produce high-quality tutorials on how to configure and use defensive and offensive security software. These videos are intended for an audience of penetration testers and security professionals but provide in-depth insight into how software packages work and how to exploit them.

While these online sources do and can provide helpful tips to hackers, some papers, such as Morselli, Tremblay, and McCarthy (2006), have shown that social interactions are of the utmost importance in the underworld. Their paper describes how a mentor in the criminal underworld can reduce the cost associated with a criminal career as well as increase illegitimate gains. Rogers (2000) also addressed the question of social capital and claimed that: "the area of learning theory may have the best chance at providing an understanding of hacking" (Rogers, 2000: 17). He analyzed theoretical concepts to determine how they applied to the problem of hacking and concluded that Akers' social learning theory, although not a perfect fit, was the best theory available. An extension of Sutherland's differential association (1939), Akers' theory can be summarized in the following four propositions (Rogers, 2010), which stipulate that people are more likely to commit crimes when they:

- Differentially associate with other criminals;
- Receive more reinforcement from their illegal actions than for their legal actions;
- Are more exposed to deviant definitions and individuals than normal ones; and
- Learn that committing crimes is normal and accepted.

These propositions revolve around three main concepts: differential association, differential reinforcement, and definitions. Differential association originates from Sutherland's (1939) work and stresses the impact of close relationships between individuals. Different social groups influence people at each stage of their life. Family is most influential at an early age, followed by school and peers at adolescence, and by neighbors and mass media later in life. The differential association varies in strength depending on the frequency, the duration, the time of first contact, and the significance of the relationship. Differential association is therefore a distant cousin of peer pressure: as effective but with a much lower profile. Differential reinforcement refers to the reinforcement of past behavior. The probability that an individual will commit a crime depends on the positive or negative consequences of that act in the past. Once a criminal behavior has been reinforced, it is said to be incredibly difficult to change. Finally, definitions are any and all attitudes or perceptions that tend to indicate whether a behavior is right or wrong. General definitions are largely adopted values, such as religion, that are usually socially accepted. Specific definitions refer to opinions regarding a certain type of behavior. This explains how an individual can believe in high moral values but still commit a specific type of crime. Definitions that are favorable toward criminal behavior can be categorized in two types: positive definitions and neutralizing definitions. Positive definitions are those that consider certain types of criminal behavior as acceptable, whereas neutralizing definitions find that specific crimes are acceptable but only under a certain set of circumstances (e.g., stealing to feed a family).

The social learning theory has been validated through empirical work in many settings. Akers, Krohn, Lanza-Kaduce, and Radosevich (1979) conducted a study on high-school students and found that a significant portion of their criminal behavior could be explained by social learning theory. Skinner and Fream (1997) and others (Denning, 1998; Parker, 1998) also tested the validity of the social learning theory in the context of computer crime and found similar, although weaker, relationships between the propositions of social learning theory and criminal behavior.

Social learning theory is, at its core, a theory of flows and exchanges. Individuals interact with others and through that process learn techniques, values, and information. In the case of Akers' (1979) students, this was done in face-to-face meetings. In the case of modern hackers, these interactions are quite different. As Rogers (2010) notes, hackers do not meet face to face. They instead use computer-mediated communications like online chat rooms, online forums, emails, and instant messaging to stay connected. Although many channels are available to them, it appears that hackers are particularly fond of one in particular: IRC. The Internet Relay Chat (IRC) was invented by Jarkko Oikarinen in 1988 and is a synchronous group instant messaging application that allows users (clients) to connect to chat rooms on IRC servers and to exchange messages and files with each other (Reid, 1991).

Figure 12.1 shows an example of an IRC client connected to the *casual* and *Paris* chat rooms on the EuropeNet server. There are hundreds of IRC servers all over the world, each sporting their own list of chat rooms. As shown in Figure 12.1, all messages are public by default and are posted in the middle column of the client software. Users can exchange private messages and those cannot be seen by anyone else. Both humans and computer programs can co-exist on IRC. Known as *bots*, computer programs can mimic the human behavior and provide certain services to other users. A bot can be programmed, for example, to ban from a chat room the users who curse too much. Such bots can be used to monitor chat rooms, a feature we will be revisiting later in this chapter.

It has been known for years that hackers gather and socialize in IRC chat rooms

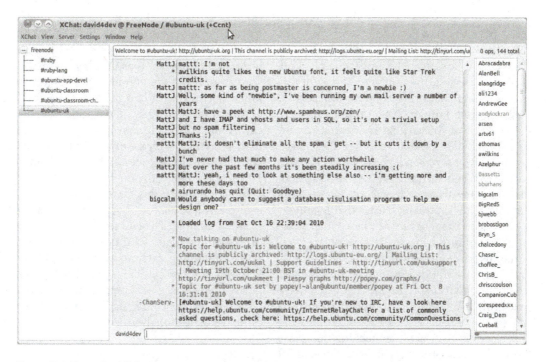

Figure 12.1 Example of IRC software

(Bratus, 2007). As a consequence, security researchers, journalists, and law enforcement agencies constantly monitor the shadier parts of IRC to gather intelligence on hackers. Although only the public messages can be accessed, the data captured in this fashion provide incredible insights into how hackers socialize and exchange information.

Hackers' social networks play an important role in their learning of new techniques and values. Morselli et al. (2006) and Rogers (2000) both highlight the importance of personal relationships in the transfer of human and cultural capital, such as specialized skills and rational justifications. By understanding how knowledge and perceptions flow amongst hackers, we hope to increase the security of computer networks. Monitoring online channels could become, we believe, an early warning system for upcoming threats. By looking at the network features of hacking chat rooms in IRC, this study aims to understand the structure of the hackers' personal networks, particularly those that are the most involved in the criminal underground. Since IRC is a nexus of interactions for hackers, much of the mentoring and information sharing should happen through its chat rooms. By looking at the flow of information inside them, it will be possible to understand how hackers develop their skills and their network of contacts. This better understanding of these deviant individuals will enable us to build better prevention programs and stop the flow of information and its negative impact on society.

DATA

To understand how hackers exchange information, we focused on one of the most bustling environments for hackers, the Internet Relay Chat (IRC). A North-American law enforcement agency which has been monitoring IRC channels over the past few years agreed to share some of the data it has gathered over the past few years with us. This chapter is based on this data the police collected from a single IRC server. Table 12.1 provides the descriptive characteristics of this sample data. It covers a 30-month period, ranging from January 2009 to June 2011.

The number of hacking chat rooms monitored each month fluctuated over this period with a low of seven and a peak of 15. The size of the data collected was massive as more than 16 million events were registered. These events could be public messages, users that login/logout, or users that change their nickname. Making sense of such a massive dataset of interconnections proved to be very problematic at first. In order to simplify our analyses, we decided to focus only on specific messages that were explicitly related to the world of hacking. To do so, we created a list of 79 discriminating keywords to extract the hacking messages from the mass of data. The list contained 79 words in order to cover a large scope of criminality (e.g., warez, botnet, ddos).

Two million messages contained at least one of the 79 aforementioned keywords. They unfortunately included a great deal of duplicates as the monitored chat rooms were often filled with bots that spammed visitors with the same message over and over again. These messages were mostly used to advertise illegal goods and services for sale. To set apart the real users from the bots, we

calculated the number of messages posted by each nickname and divided it by the number of distinct messages posted by that nickname in our database. This provided us with an index of the uniqueness of their messages. Anyone who had messages that were unique less than 90% of the time was discarded and categorized as a bot. This left us with a sample which only included people who posted original messages 9 times out of 10. While some individuals may have been eliminated during this classification process, it also ensured that all bots were eliminated from the sample. The end result was a sample of 262 individuals, who posted 1,618 messages containing each at least one keyword between January 2009 and June 2011. While fairly limited, the resulting dataset is still large enough to provide significant and interesting statistical analysis.

METHODOLOGY

As this chapter focuses on information exchange paths between individuals, we began by looking at the relationships between these 262 individuals and their contacts in IRC chat rooms. Doing so proved challenging as our dataset only included public chat room records where many individuals participated simultaneously in public discussions. Identifying precisely the flow of discussions as well as the individuals who were present when the messages were posted was unfortunately not possible with the dataset provided to us by the law enforcement agency. We therefore had to resort to a less-than-perfect solution but one that allowed us to build the social map of each hacker in our sample. We decided on a methodology which provided a good approximation of each individual's social network that could be done automatically and without the need for costly content analysis.

In order to do so, we grouped all messages in blocks of 20 units around each message containing a keyword. We then considered that all individuals who had posted a message

Table 12.1 Characteristics of study sample

Length of monitoring	30 months (January 2009–June 2011)
Number of chat rooms monitored (monthly)	7–15
Number of events	16,978,269
Number of relevant messages	2,232,729
Number of unique relevant messages	1,618
Number of hackers	262
Number of people in social network of hackers	356
Number of ties (reciprocal)	6,168

within that window of 20 messages were in a relation of some sort and we built an undirected relational matrix around these ties. Our decision to group messages in blocks of 20 was not random. We analyzed a sample of messages and determined that conversations were usually fairly short and that the 10 messages before and after a message containing a keyword were almost always linked to the same discussion. Occasionally, there would be concurrent discussions in public chat rooms but this was not the norm by far. Using this methodology, it is possible that our relational matrix included ties that did not exist or left out ties from people who were merely watching and not participating in the conversations. In the first case, our sample analysis shows that the signal-to-noise ratio was very high and that the added ties did not have a significant impact on our dataset as they were few and far between. As for the second limit, our dataset did not allow us to include in our analysis the individuals reading but not participating in the conversations. These individuals did profit from the information exchange but did so discreetly and additional research design will need to be developed to monitor these individuals as well. This study will therefore only focus on individuals who actively participated in chat room discussions.

Social network analysis (SNA) can work with either directed or undirected matrices. Directed matrices are used when the direction of a tie can be determined (e.g., who visited who, who called who). In the case of public discussions, it is often difficult to determine the intended recipient or recipients of a message. People tend to shout messages and wait for an answer from any of the members present at the time. Rather than guess the direction of messages and ties in this network, we opted to build an undirected matrix where all ties are reciprocal. Our analysis will take into account this research design when determining the impact and structure of the personal networks of hackers.

A relational matrix representing each of the 262 hackers' social graph was built using the aforementioned blocks of conversations. We found a total of 356 individuals who were tied to (spoke with) the 262 IRC users who had posted at least once a message containing a keyword. These 356 individuals never used one of the 79 keywords but were involved in conversations where that keyword was used. The sample for this study therefore includes 262 IRC hackers and their 356 contacts.

Figure 12.2 displays the structure of the ties between the hackers and their social graph. It is clear by looking at this figure that most

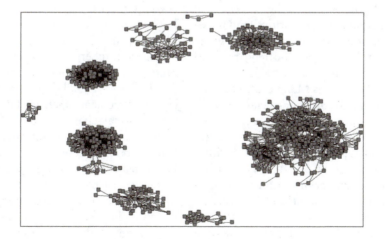

Figure 12.2 Structure of ties in hacking chat rooms

users did not visit more than one chat room. Most clusters are made from the messages of a single chat room and there is very little overlap between them, even though all chat rooms were centered on the hacking underground.

Given the structure of the network, we decided to focus on the ego or personal networks of individuals rather than look at the structure as a whole. The IRC data at our disposal did not include one unique network but nine separate networks that were linked by their origin on the Internet Relay Chat. Furthermore, as we intended to focus on the individual features of hacker networks rather than their structure, an approach focusing on the individual networks appeared as the most sensible.

Studying personal networks is known in the social network field as ego network analysis (Wasserman & Faust, 1994). The term *ego* refers to the individual at the center of a network and the term *alters* refers to the people linked to the ego. Although this method has been used in many social science studies (Kalmijn & Vermunt, 2007; Degenne & Lebeaux, 2005; Stefanone & Jang, 2008), it has yet to be adopted widely in criminology. Analysis of ego networks in the context of criminal networks is few and far between. Malm, Bichler, and Nash (2011) studied the co-offending of criminal organizations in Canada. In this research, they determined that certain types of organizations tend to co-offend more often with other groups, while others tend to choose their co-offenders based on their membership to the same group.

Past research, such as Malm et al.'s (2011), has focused mainly on four social network metrics: centrality, betweenness, composition, and density. Centrality is frequently used to assess the prominence of actors within a network (Wasserman & Faust, 1994: 172). It indicates the number of incoming and outgoing contacts and accounts for the direction of direct ties around each node (in directed networks). The pattern of ties originating from or sent to a network member is usually a reliable indicator of this person's prestige or status (Wasserman & Faust, 1994: 174) as it helps distinguish people with sought-after expertise. Betweenness measures the extent to which a node mediates between other nodes by its position along the geodesics (the shortest path between two nodes) within the network, thus providing useful additional information on the structure of a network. The more often a node is located along the geodesics, the higher its betweenness centrality, making it a broker within the network. The position of broker has been associated with the notion of power in networks (Prell, Hubacek, & Reed, 2008; Morselli, 2009; Toral, Martinez-Torres, & Barrero, 2010) since these individuals control the flow of information between the different actors. They can decide whether to allow messages to pass through, modify the information, or simply ignore it. Composition is a measure of the heterogeneity of the network (Malm et al., 2011). It measures whether individuals associate with others that share common characteristics (e.g., if boys talk more to boys than girls). Finally, density measures the number of actual ties compared to the number of possible ties (Wasserman & Faust, 1994). This metric gives a sense of the implication of individuals in a network; the denser the network, the more involved its participants are.

The first part of our analysis builds on Malm et al.'s (2011) work and focuses on a limited number of social network metrics: centrality, betweenness, density, and longest distance. The dataset provided by the law enforcement agency did not contain any personal characteristics of the hackers so it was not possible unfortunately to run composition analyses on our research data. We instead focused on the longest distance, a measure of the number of steps any node needs to reach any other node in the ego network. For each of these four social network metrics, the quartiles are presented in the first part of our analyses to generate a general understanding of the structure of each hacker's social network.

In the second part of our analysis, we will present a partial correlation, which is a normal correlation that takes into account the number of nodes in each personal network. Differences in sizes may have tainted our results otherwise. Six variables (centrality, density, betweenness, two-step reach, number of keywords, and number of conversations) will be included in two models which aim to understand how hackers build their social network to maximize their flow of information. In the first model, the correlation measures the relation between the number of different keywords used by each hacker and the five other variables. This is intended a as proxy of the diversity of topics discussed by each hacker. In the second model, the correlation measures the relation between the number of conversations of each hacker and the five other variables. This is also a proxy but for the bandwidth of information directed to and from each hacker. Rather than use longest distance, we instead opted to integrate the notion of two-step reach, which measures the number of nodes which can be reached within two ties in a given ego network. This provides a better understanding of the importance of weak ties or friends of friends in the context of information flows.

RESULTS

Table 12.2 presents a summary of the social network metrics for the ego networks of hackers who visited hacking chat rooms.

In our sample, hackers are connected to a limited number of alters in general (Minimum = 1; Maximum = 65). Twenty-five percent of egos are tied to four alters or fewer, and 75% of egos are connected to 12 alters or fewer. Since each conversation we flagged included a potential of 21 individuals (10 messages before and after, plus the ego), a median of seven connections is fairly low. That being said, there is still much variation in the sample population.

As for betweenness, the normalized version of the metric was used to eliminate the impact of the variations in the number of nodes in each ego network. Our results show that most hackers are very poor brokers. With half of our sample displaying a betweenness of 0.00, the number of ties between alters that transit through the egos is very low. Some egos are more essential than others. The last 25% of our sample has a betweenness score that varies between 9.86 and 100.00.

Given the limited size of most ego networks, it is not surprising to see that more than half of our sample displays density scores of 100. Once again, a select few hackers have different network configurations with lower densities than the others. Such high density in general means that the ego networks are close-knit groups where every actor knows one another. However, the undirected nature of our matrix increases the density of the ego networks.

Finally, with half the sample showing a longest distance of one, most ego networks are once again homogenous entities with low centrality and high density. The maximum

Table 12.2 Quartiles of social network metrics

	Centrality	Betweenness	Density	Longest Distance
Min	1	0.00	0	0
25th	4	0.00	55	1
50th	7	0.00	100	1
75th	12	9.86	100	2
Max	65	100.00	100	6

Note
N = 262

number of steps needed to reach any node on the largest ego network is six, a special number in social network analysis (Watts, 2004). Our data suggest this particular number still applies, even in the case of chat rooms.

Table 12.3 presents the partial correlation models between the number of unique keywords and the number of conversations. Correlations are all statistically significant except for the number of conversations and two-step reach.

The number of keywords is moderately and negatively correlated with the number of ties and the density (−0.352 and −0.274, respectively). This could be the result of the structural holes effect (Burt, 2010). It is thought that close-knit networks have access to more redundant data since all the actors in the network know each other and talk about the same subjects. It could be the case that these smaller and denser networks are experts in a limited range of subjects and thus only mentioned a limited number of our keywords. Betweenness and two-step reach are moderately and poorly, but positively, correlated to the number of keywords (0.369 and 0.102, respectively). As mentioned before, those with greater betweenness usually display more structural holes in their networks and can access more diverse sources of information. They can then expand their knowledge on a variety of subjects. This increased number of alters is reflected in the two-step reach metric, which is correlated positively to the number of keywords. It shows once again that having access to a greater number of nodes (directly or indirectly) increases the available knowledge base.

The number of conversations is negatively and poorly correlated to the number of ties and density. Individuals with a greater number of ties have fewer conversations. As we have mentioned before, the conversations in hacking chat rooms seem to be concentrated amongst tight and small networks. It is therefore normal to see that larger ego networks show lower levels of conversations. It is surprising though that the density is negatively correlated with the number of conversations. This could be explained by the fact that we are only monitoring the public messages on IRC chat rooms and not the complete communication channels between the individuals. Some of the conversations amongst individuals could be conducted over private messages or instant messaging. It could also be that certain smaller units would rather move their discussions to more private settings rather than discuss publicly. The number of conversation is positively correlated to the betweenness. With a greater level of communication, the chances that a node will sit in the middle of a dyad is higher and it is thus normal to see these two figures positively correlated, though we might have expected a slightly higher correlation between these two metrics.

Table 12.3 Partial correlation of diversity of interests and involvement in hacking chat rooms

	Number of keywords	Number of conversations
Centrality	−0.352**	−0.140**
Density	−0.274**	−0.113**
Betweenness	0.369**	0.169**
Two-step reach	0.102**	n.s.
Number of keywords	—	0.819**
Number of conversations	0.819**	—

Note
N = 618
** statistically significant
n.s. not significant

CONCLUSION

The aim of this chapter was to understand the structure of personal networks of hackers who are involved in criminal activities. The first part of our analysis demonstrated that most individuals only had a limited number of contacts in their social graph. This enables them to build stronger relations with other IRC users from whom they may be learning the hacking skills they need. This configuration supports Rogers' (2000) supposition that social learning theory could very well apply to the world of hacking. Intimate relationships are needed for differential association and differential reinforcement to occur. With small ego network structures, the winning conditions are met for differential association and differential reinforcement to happen and for mentor relationships to form.

The betweenness metric was also very interesting as it demonstrated that direct ties were more important than indirect ties. This increases once again the bonds between the players and increases the chances of mentoring and association with other criminals. This preference for direct ties could be a consequence of the IRC setting. Each user can contact any other user when they want, lowering the barrier of contacts. This could also be the consequence of the low level of trust in the hacking community. As individuals are unable to ascertain the true identity of their counterpart, they should prefer direct contacts to limit their exposure to law enforcement agencies.

Density and longest distance also confirm the previous statements as density is mostly high and longest distance is mostly low. Both settings are fit for the transfer of differential association and differential reinforcement as well as for mentoring relationships to form. This network structure indicates that the hackers are more inclined to participate in small communities rather than large ones. In these small circles, every member knows everyone else. In this context, there should be a higher level of trust amongst its members. This should stimulate the involvement and differential reinforcement in the hacking culture and community. This should also generally raise the security levels of these communities. Any outsider wishing to join these small communities will have to demonstrate that they are worth other people's time and that they too belong with them. This significantly raises the difficulty that law enforcement agencies and academic researchers will face when trying to get a deeper understanding of these hacking communities, and they will need to invest time and resources to build credible online personas which can gain access to these small circles. Public discussions may be accessible to any and all but the real data will undoubtedly come from private messages and private chat rooms for which personal contacts are needed. However, these close-knit groups may be at times the very weakness that police forces need. For example, Sabu, a leader of the Anonymous hacking movement, was arrested and served as an undercover agent for the Federal Bureau of Investigation for months (Cluley, 2012). This allowed direct access and monitoring of the criminal underground by the FBI, who took advantage of the network structure of the Anonymous community.

The partial correlations further enhance our understanding of the criminal underground by evaluating the ego network structure of the individuals based on the bandwidth and the diversity of information they have access to. Both concepts of bandwidth and diversity are highly correlated at 0.819. Individuals who manage to position themselves at the nexus of information flows have access to more information and information that is more varied. These individuals would make ideal investigation targets and they would be able to inform us on what is happening in the hacking underground and to show us how one should position himself in the network. These individuals may also be good mentors as their developed network of information could enhance their recognition and power amongst hackers.

Both correlation models are very similar. The number of keywords and the number of conversations are both correlated with centrality, density, and betweenness. However, only the number of keywords is associated with the two-step reach. In both cases, the strongest correlation is with betweenness followed by centrality, density, and two-step reach. Our models show that access to large amounts of diversified information is correlated to a small network that is not dense where the ego is playing a role of broker. The ego also benefits from friends of friends, as demonstrated by the two-step reach. In this context, hackers who would like to improve their hacking skills should decide carefully with whom they associate (centrality). The number of contacts is not what matters; it is who these contacts are—a recurrent theme in criminological research on social networks (Coles, 2001). Hackers should also work to limit the ties between his contacts as this reduces his importance in his ego network (Burt, 2010). Structural holes or holes between clusters of friends provide opportunities for egos who can capitalize on the needs of his contacts. In this context, structural holes provide the ego with more information and information that is more diversified. This reinforces the role of brokers in criminal networks as measured by the betweenness measure. Brokers control the flow of information in networks as other people use them to transit information. In the case of IRC hackers, brokers have access to more information—this increases the chances of them improving their hacking skills.

Mentors and social learning theory are both supported by these partial correlation models. The ego network structure described in the discussion is ideal for the appearance of mentors, who can use differential association, reinforcement, and definitions to recruit and teach new pupils. Individuals with access

to more information and more diversified information would make ideal mentors as they could share their strategic positioning in the network as well as the information they have access to with their protégés. Such individuals would be at the center of information flows and would undoubtedly be recognized in the hacking community as more efficient in their craft. While most hackers have ego networks that are compatible with mentors and social learning theory, a select few have network structures that match those of mentors, who can use their influence to teach the hacking tricks to the next generation of criminals. Using social network analysis, these individuals can be targeted in order to break the cycle and limit the upcoming threats coming from the computer underground. The network of hackers presented in this chapter therefore represents a fertile ground for mentors and hackers to meet and thrive, ensuring them more illegitimate gains and lower risks of detection.

Monitoring IRC channels has proven very effective at providing an understanding of the hacking community. There are, however, many technical and ethical challenges that need to be addressed. As mentioned before, the information available in IRC chat rooms is limited as many conversations happen in private (and password-protected) channels or in private messages. These cannot be monitored and skew the real nature of hacking networks. Furthermore, monitoring IRC means dealing with millions of messages and events, which can be time consuming to analyze. This chapter offers a simple yet effective way of dealing with this problem, but more complex solutions may be necessary to provide a better picture of the criminal underground. Future research may try to group messages by their timestamp to give a better representation of the network. Some chat rooms may have been silent for hours before someone posted a new message and simply grouping messages in blocks does not take this fact into account. By grouping messages in blocks of two or five minutes, one would limit the risk of creating ties where there are now. Researchers should also study carefully the login and logoff events in each chat room as they would indicate whether individuals were reading the messages even though they were not participating actively in the conversations. This would involve building a computer algorithm that would create an overview of each hacker's activity—where he was and when. Although difficult, this process is not insurmountable.

New ethical guidelines will also need to be developed for this new research environment. In this chapter, all IRC server names, chat room names, and nicknames were obfuscated in order to protect their anonymity and that of the law enforcement agency that provided us with the data. Such techniques should be the norm in social research. While this limits the duplication of studies, it provides enough information to evaluate the strength of studies and to test the hypotheses in other chat rooms. It also ensures that hackers do not feel muffled by too many researchers, who may all try to monitor their chat rooms at the same time. By using discrete bots to monitor the chat rooms, we ensure that we are not disturbing the ecosystem as hackers may very well move elsewhere once they realize that their private chat rooms are infested with researchers and law enforcement agencies.

Studies on IRC individuals are by no means new. Computer professionals have been using them for years but with their own technical angle. This chapter brings a practical framework that can be harnessed to better understand the social interactions of hackers online. This hybrid study, which combines the most up-to-date technical tools with tested criminological theories, offers a new take on the problem of hackers, and one that we hope will be picked up and replicated amongst more datasets in the upcoming years.

REFERENCES

Ahmad, N. & M.K. Habib. (2010). Analysis of network security threats and vulnerabilities by development and implementation of a security network monitoring solution. Masters thesis at the School of Electrical Engineering of the Blekinge Institute Of Technology, Sweden.

Akers, R.L., M.D. Krohn, L. Lanza-Kaduce, & M. Radosevich. (1979). Social learning and deviant behavior: A specific test of a general theory. *American Sociological Review* 44(4), 636–655.

Bratus, S. (2007). Hacker curriculum: How hackers learn networking. *IEEE Distributed Systems Online* 8(10), 2.

Burt, R.S. (2010). Structural holes in virtual worlds. *Working Paper*. University Of Chicago Booth School of Business, Chicago, IL.

Cluley, G. (2012). LulzSec leader Sabu betrayed Anonymous hackers, reports claim. *Naked Security*. Retrieved June 12, 2012 from http://nakedsecurity.sophos.com/2012/03/06/sabu-lulzsec-betrayed-anonymous-hackers/.

Coles, N. (2001). It's not what you know—it's who you know that counts: Analyzing serious crime groups as social networks. *British Journal of Criminology* 41 (4), 580–594.

Degenne, A. & M. Lebeaux. (2004). The dynamics of personal networks at the time of entry into adult life. *Social Networks* 27, 337–358.

Denning, D. (1998). *Information Warfare and Security*. Boston, MA: Addison-Wesley.

Kalmijn, M. & J. Vermunt. (2007). Homogeneity of social networks by age and marital status: A multilevel analysis of ego-centered networks. *Social Networks* 29, 25–43.

Malm, A., G. Bichler, & R. Nash. (2011). Co-offending between criminal enterprise groups. *Global Crime* 12(2), 112–128.

Morselli, C. (2009). Law-enforcement disruption of a drug-importation network. *Studies of Organized Crime* 8, 1–17.

Morselli, C., P. Tremblay, & B. McCarthy. (2006). Mentors And criminal achievement. *Criminology* 44(1), 17–43.

Parker, D. (1998). *Fighting Computer Crime: A New Framework for Protecting Information*. New York: John Wiley & Sons.

Potlapally, N. (2011). Hardware security in practice: Challenges and opportunities. IEEE International Symposium on Hardware-Oriented Security and Trust. San Diego, USA.

Prell, C., K. Hubacek, & M. Reed. (2008). Who's in the network? *Systemic Practice and Action Research* 21, 443–458.

Reid, E. (1991). *Electropolis: Communication and Community on Internet Chat Relay*. Masters at University of Melbourne, Australia.

Rogers, M. (2000). Psychological theories of crime and hacking. *Telematic Journal of Clinical Criminology*. Retrieved March 6, 2012 from www.dvara.net/HK/theory_crime_hacking.pdf.

Rogers, M. (2010). The psyche of cybercriminals: A psycho-social perspective. In S. Ghosh & E. Turrini (eds.), *Cybercrimes: A Multidisciplinary Analysis* (pp. 217–235). New York: Springer.

Skinner, W.F. & A.M. Fream (1997). A social learning theory analysis of computer crime among college students. *Journal of Research in Crime and Delinquency* 34(4), 495–518.

Stefanone, M.A. & C. Jang. (2008). Writing for friends and family: The interpersonal nature of blogs. *Journal of Computer-Mediated Communication* 13, 123–140.

Sullivan, B. (2005). Cell phone voicemail easily hacked. *MSNBC*.com. Retrieved August 12, 2011 from www.msnbc.msn.com/id/7046776/ns/technology_and_science-wireless/t/cell-phone-voicemail-easily-hacked/.

Sutherland, E.H. (1939). *Principles of Criminology*. Philadelphia, PA: Lippincott.

Toral, S., M.R. Martinez-Torres, & F. Barrero. (2010). Analysis Of virtual communities supporting OSS projects using social network analysis. *Information & Software Technology* 52(3), 296–303.

Wasserman, S. & K. Faust. (1994). *Social Network Analysis: Methods and Applications*. Cambridge, UK: Cambridge University Press.

Watts, D. (2004). *Six Degrees: The Science of a Connected Age*. New York: W.W. Norton & Company.

CHAPTER 13

Usenet Newsgroups, Child Pornography, and the Role of Participants

Francis Fortin[1]

The phenomenon of pedophile networks is not new: child pornography networks existed long before the internet was available to the public (Lanning, 1984; Burgess, 1984; Burgess & Hartman, 1987; Lanning & Burgess, 1989; Tate, 1992), but became increasingly important with the expansion of information technologies in the mid-1990s. According to Hanson and Scott (1996), research on this phenomenon, because of the organized and collaborative aspect of this type of illegal activity, necessitates a comprehensive study of the network's internal characteristics. However, perhaps because those who use child pornography are often described as isolated, less socially skilled (Corriveau & Fortin, 2011), and unable to openly discuss their deviance, there are few studies that specifically address the question of how communities devoted to child pornography are structured.

Virtual space has become important to cyberpedophiles and Usenet newsgroups play an important role in exchanging child pornography (Taylor, Quayle, & Holland, 2001). Sources suggest that somewhere between 2,800 and 5,000 newsgroups are available to tech-savvy internet users in search of child pornography (Wortley & Smallbone, 2006; Sellier, 2003; Taylor et al., 2001; Carr, 2001).[2] It is impossible to accurately assess the number of these newsgroups and, by extension, the number of pictures distributed daily, but researchers agree that newsgroups are a haven for those seeking such content.

This chapter looks at the diversity and complexity of the prevailing social dynamics in child pornography-related newsgroups. The following hypothesis is tested: Usenet newsgroups related to child pornography are structured networks, with different roles for those who produce, distribute, and view child pornography. The presence of different roles within the virtual community encourages the emergence of a pedophile subculture and a social hierarchy among its members. As in any network, deviant or not, active participation allows child pornographers or consumers of child pornography to be appreciated, understood, and acknowledged by their peers. Members also provide a set of safety rules to help others avoid capture by law enforcement. Child pornographers and those who seek out child pornography join and become integrated into a deviant subculture through a process of exchange and peer learning, which in turn reinforces their deviance in fantasizing about children.

THE INTERNET AND SOCIAL INTERACTION

According to Becker (1985), deviance is learned as the result of a social process. While society is involved in determining what counts as deviant, the essential aspects of deviance are determined in cooperation between participants in particular deviant behaviors. Such cooperation allows participants to share a common understanding of a behavior considered deviant by society and, when shared among peers, the behavior comes to be seen by them as legitimate. Becker (1985) argues that members of organized deviant groups have one obvious thing in common—their deviance—which gives them the feeling of sharing a common destiny, of being in the same boat. Mutual awareness of a common destiny leads to the progressive development of a subculture in which group members share a set of ideas about the social world and how to adapt to it. They develop a set of routines based on those views (Becker, 1985).

An individual who actively participates in a deviant group confirms and legitimizes his deviant identity through the realization that he is no longer alone. The greater the number of people involved in the group, the more legitimacy the subculture provides for the so-called deviant. Membership in a deviant group (network) is always marked by learning and by internalizing positive reinforcement from peers. As Becker (1985) notes, "in extreme cases, [individuals] develop historical, legal and psychological justifications, complicated by their deviant activity." There is support for this view from research into child pornography networks. Durkin and Bryant (1999) state that child pornography downloaders are able to legitimize their activity by reading and integrating content from the large number of "legitimizing stories" available on the internet. This identification technique is also widely used by child pornographers to exonerate themselves or to avoid blame. For example, some justify their behavior by claiming that they do it because they love children. Others argue that the attraction toward children is acceptable because homosexual relationships were socially acceptable in ancient Greece.

With this in mind, Becker (1985) explains that, by integrating into an organized deviant group (or network), an individual learns to carry out deviant activities with a minimum of trouble because others in the group have faced the same problems and have developed solutions. A transfer of knowledge occurs between the deviant and the beginner, perpetuating the deviant subculture and ensuring the group's sustainability. Becker (1985) argues that the deviant who enters an organized deviant group is more likely to continue in his deviancy. He has learned how to avoid difficulties and at the same time has acquired a system of justifications that encourage him to persevere.

McAndrew (1999) argues that a criminal network forms when a criminal activity has some complexity and requires specialized skills. According to him, it is inevitable that tasks within the group be specialized and that participants share roles. As a corollary, a certain formal or informal hierarchy develops between group members. At the top is a minority of participants whom everyone knows and recognizes. At the bottom are those who are new to the group's internal operations. The new participants depend on a few insiders to learn the rules and skills required to gain recognition from more experienced peers. These insiders have the respect of most group members, given the important role they play within the community. Typically, their level of expertise makes them almost "essential" to the security and proper functioning of the network. They have the gratitude of other members because they can help their fellow members with technology, they have already taken risks to keep the group running smoothly, and they interact frequently in the community. McAndrew (1999) believes that deviant networks have a number of advantages for participants, such as facilitating the sharing of innovative methods for committing certain crimes and simplifying the identification of potential targets, as well as allowing an exchange of information on police activities.

The notion of a pedophile subculture has been studied during the last decade.

According to Jenkins (2001), there is a subculture of child pornography, which is held together by shared beliefs and concepts. Aside from sharing techniques to avoid being caught by law enforcement, the group provides justification for "child love" in order to help individuals appreciate and understand the pedophile culture. These results are consistent with those found by other researchers. Recent findings suggest that such communities reinforce the belief that sexual offenses involving children are surrounded by love and consent (Holt, Blevins, & Burkert, 2010) and can even be seen as "consensual romantic relationships" (O'Halloran & Quayle, 2010). By studying five web-based forums "run by and for pedophiles," Holt et al. (2010) found that relationships were shaped by four normative orders: marginalization (the relationship between pedophiles and the larger society), sexuality (the forums are used to talk freely about sexuality with people with similar views), law (legal definitions of pedophilia, criminal cases involving pedophiles), and security (how to avoid getting caught and related subjects). These four concepts[3] set the boundaries to the subculture. Finally, Prichard, Watters, & Spiranovic (2011) looked at queries about child pornography on the Bittorent network. Their research focused on the potential normalization of child pornography among internet subcultures and how we should address this problem.

This chapter looks at the subculture related to child pornography with respect to the behavior and the role that different participants play within the group. The next section considers how Usenet differs from other internet services in terms of anonymity and general use.

Usenet Groups as a "Safe" Place?

In reviewing research on child pornography, it became evident that Usenet newsgroups constitute one of the largest sources of child pornography available in cyberspace (Taylor et al., 2001). Researchers have also found Usenet newsgroups useful for observing other types of criminal or deviant activities, such as online interaction between pedophiles (Durkin & Bryant, 1999), adult pornographers (Mehta, 2001), and writers of pornographic stories (Harmon & Boeringer, 1997), raising the question of why Usenet is attractive as a venue for exchanging illegal material.

To understand the interest in Usenet for sharing illegal content, we must examine the origins of this network, which is one of the oldest trading systems in the virtual world. Usenet came into existence in 1979, before the popularization of the internet. It was developed by two graduate students from Duke University and the University of North Carolina as a network that allowed users to exchange quantities of information too large for mailboxes (Gakenback, 1998; Sohier, 1998). Designed to facilitate exchanges of text between scholars, the network structure slowly adapted to allow the exchange of larger files, such as videos or images. Even today, some servers restrict users to 5,000 lines of text. To solve this problem, Usenet users exchange large files through segmentation, which involves dividing a large file into several smaller messages (binary files), which users reconstitute if they want to have the file. Usenet now permits thousands of internet users to exchange all types of information (pictures, videos, sound, etc.) through a multitude of newsgroups hosted on servers located around the world.[4]

Usenet is a decentralized system, which may be the attraction for those wishing to share illegal content. All information circulates through thousands of computers via various news servers across cyberspace, which makes it difficult to track the origin of the content. It is easy to hide an IP address and easier to conceal the participant's identity (Wortley & Smallbone, 2006), which minimizes the chance of being convicted of a crime. Furthermore, visitors to these groups leave very few traces, making detection more difficult for law enforcement. The architecture differs from that of websites, which have a client/server connection and where the system can only work if it knows the IP address.

DATA SOURCES AND METHODOLOGY

In order to understand the nature and functioning of online child pornography networks, researchers followed three groups[5] identified as import vectors of illegal material in a joint study of child pornography conducted by Justice Canada and the Quebec Provincial Police in 2004 for a period of 45 days, analyzing social interactions[6] within the group. This time period was sufficient to provide information on different exchanges and group mechanisms without disproportionately increasing the quantity of content to be analyzed. More than 24,000 messages were collected from the other two. These posts were subsequently classified in a database, which was analyzed through a spreadsheet. This database, more than 10 gigabytes, contained all available information, including the author of the item, IP address (if available), the size of the message sent, subject, nature of content (textual or binary), presence of attachments, and the date and time the message was sent. We also used information collected by Google regarding Google Groups newsgroups: their history, nature of content, number of exchanges, and percentage of content/text. Even if our main goal was to investigate text messages, an overview of the content convinced researchers that what was being distributed in the three groups was child pornography and would be considered as such even in countries with less stringent laws.

Text-only messages—more than 2,800—were analyzed within a qualitative framework. Each group's messages were read and categorized by theme by three researchers. Initially each researcher's task, without consultation with other team members, was to analyze one newsgroup to determine the themes discussed

by users. Categories from all three researchers were then pooled and compared. We found that there were overlaps in almost all categories. After validating the categories, all messages sent during the review period were grouped in the validated categories. We then designed a pyramid that illustrates different roles played by participants in the groups (see Figure 13.1).

It should be noted that anyone wishing to conduct a study on child pornography in Canada faces some legal constraints as Canada's Criminal Code, Article 163.1 (4.1), prohibits any person from knowingly accessing child pornography. However, in the context of this study, researchers would obviously require access to child pornography. Article 163 (3) of the Criminal Code, which deals with the defense of public good, was held to be applicable to the research protocol, following the interpretation of the Supreme Court of Canada in *R. v. Sharpe* that "the various defences provided by law (that is to say, the artistic merit, educational, scientific or medical and public good) should be interpreted liberally so as to protect freedom of expression and possession for socially redeeming purposes." Access was granted provided research took place under controlled conditions and was limited to data collection. To ensure compliance with the legal guidelines, this study was conducted under the supervision of the cybercrime unit of the Sûreté du Québec (Quebec provincial police).

GROUP OVERVIEW: MORE THAN JUST A NETWORK FOR SHARING IMAGES?

The data collected show that participants in the three groups sent more messages containing images than those containing only text. It is important to note, however, that these results do not account for all consumers of child pornography through a particular Usenet group or for discussion group participants who viewed or downloaded content without sending messages. The data consist of messages sent by active group participants and thus a user who only looked at messages and downloaded images would leave no trace and would not be represented in our data. Table 13.1[7] shows that more than 85% of messages posted on newsgroups were images or binary files (fragments of videos), the majority of which showed children aged eight to 16 years of age.[8] The number of posts in our data significantly increased by the inclusion of videos as, in order to transfer the material, the distributor must separate the video into hundreds of small chunks of files. The sender must break the file into multiple sections to send to the server and the chunks must be "reconstructed" by downloading all the fragments. Each chunk counts as a new post.

Analysis of textual communications between child pornography consumers highlights the importance of conversations for these individuals, as most send only text messages and not images. In the groups under study, 85% of all participants had written at least one text-only message, compared to 15% who sent at least one image or video. This finding suggests two things. First, the majority of participants in child pornography discussion groups have very little new content to share with others. Second, they rely heavily on a minority of participants to obtain new content. This observation supports the COPINE project findings that there is a limited amount of newly acquired child pornography available and that most material available on the Net is old images or digitized video (Taylor et al., 2001).

Group A, whose name made subtle allusions to children but without being explicit, was the most active, with an average of 347 posts (both images and text messages) per day. According to Google,[9] the group was known to have a high level of participation. It was started in November 1992, but the level of participation soared in 1998 (Google Groups, 2006). With few exceptions, the group maintained this high level at least until the time of the study, with 1,356 different authors submitting messages during the period. Overall, Group A had the highest number of posts (15,648), which included photos (42.7%) and binary files (45.7%).[10] However, only 129 of the participants—9.5% of all active participants—were responsible for this content. The remaining participants (1,227) sent text only. Because of the high volume of messages sent in this group (an average of 40.3 text messages every day), this group was the most active of our groups and might be seen as a continual provider of child pornography-related resources: discussions, comments, and, of course, child pornography images.

Group "B" appeared in April 1994 and had a much less explicit name, which did not clearly indicate the group's interests. This group, with 6,407 posts, is less significant than Group A in terms of participation, with less than half the number of postings. Google considers the group to be a low-participation group, as binary messages are not included when calculating participation rates. However, with an average of 142 messages sent daily, this group is still interesting. Like Group A, its focus is mainly on exchange of image content, with 88.1% of messages containing images or binaries, compared to 11.9% with text only. We counted 327 different authors in this group, with a similar pattern to Group A: 58 participants sent all image content (images or binary files), while most participants (269 or 82.3%) had sent at least one text-only message. With a less evocative name, the group seems to be a little more restricted than Group A. Participants were also more likely to engage in in-depth discussions than the other two groups.

The last group had the most evocative name. There are no participation statistics available through Google, probably because the name of the group contained words prohibited by company policy. During the 45-day study period, Group C sent 2,375

Table 13.1 Overview of content distributed in the three study groups

Content	Group A				Group B				Group C				Total			
	N in group	%	N of senders	% senders	N in group	%	N of senders	% senders	N in group	%	N of senders	% senders	N in three groups	%	N of senders	% senders
Text only	1,817	11.6	1,227	90.5	763	11.9	269	82.3	302	12.7	141	58.3	2,882	11.8	1,637	85.0
Attachment	6,683	42.7	129	9.5	642	10.0	58	17.7	2,073	87.3	101	41.7	9,398	38.5	288	15.0
Binary	7,148	45.7			5,002	78.1			0	0.0			12,150	49.7		
Total	15,648	100.0	1,356	100.0	6,407	100.0	327	100.0	2,375	100.0	242	100.0	24,430	100.0	1,925	100.0

messages, with an average of 52.8 per day. This group had the lowest participation of the three study groups. It was not used for sending binary files, but in 87.3% of cases, image content was sent as a file attachment. There were 239 different participants in Group C; 141 participants sent texts only, while 101 sent images. This group has almost equal text/content proportions but with less participation; some groups are simply more popular than others. While spam messages were present but limited in other groups, Group C had a high volume of messages promoting other websites or web rings. Spam messages are usually sent by different senders, which may account for the higher ratio of text senders to content senders in this group. Analysis also showed that discussions—"conversations" between members of the newsgroup— were important for this group. Most participants sent text-only messages rather than images: 82.4% of all participants sent at least one text message, while only 23.9% sent an attachment or binary file. Again, only a small proportion of participants sent images, even if images are involved in nearly 87% of all messages posted.

Our data suggest that a minority of active participants in child pornography newsgroups distribute the vast majority of illegal content available in these groups. Two participants were responsible for distributing 72% of all available images in newsgroup B; four participants were responsible for posting 51.7% of all images of child pornography in newsgroup A. In Group C, 14 individuals were responsible for sending 50.2% of all images. These small groups of individuals are referred to as "powerposters" and they frequently play an important role in the group.

A VIRTUAL COMMUNITY: THE ESTABLISHMENT OF A SUBCULTURE?

Is there a pedophile subculture in Usenet newsgroups? To answer this question, it is necessary to determine whether such groups form new communities with a particular subculture. Qualitative analysis of thousands of text exchanges between users seems to support this hypothesis as many of the messages clearly illustrate that users see themselves as part of a community, a "small company" on the margins of society. One participant wrote: "For many of us, this is our social life. We can discuss our feelings here and feel a part of something without fear of being condemned by society for our feelings and beliefs."

The idea of community is also found in responses to hostile message. A regular poster answered an "outsider" by using terms such as "we" and "they" to talk about the members and outsiders:

> There is *no* place that is safe for anyone, in this newsgroup, or anywhere else in real life. There is always a possibility that we will be attacked at any time, anywhere, by anyone who wants to.
> They give us hate, we express love. Who do you think will have the most pleasant experience? :-) . . .
> I still care about *all* of us, more than is possible for me to express.

Another user reinforces the idea of a well-developed virtual community, stating that he would only exchange information with people he "knows": "From now on, I'm only replying to messages posted by nicks I recognize from this community." In other words, you must prove your commitment in order to join this child pornography-related network. These comments reinforce the perception that there is an "us," active and complaisant users of child pornography as well as pedophiles, boy-lovers, girl-lovers, or whatever other terms are used in the self-definition of such individuals. There is also a "them," which can be non-pedophiles or society as a whole, which is likely to condemn the group.

This difference is also present in philosophical discussions on pedophilia and on the legitimate nature of the group. The form of legitimization/rationalization that takes place in pedophile communities has already been addressed (see Durkin & Bryant, 1999). The perception that pedophiles have of themselves has altered society's definition to a point where they see it as legitimate to define themselves as adults with a "romantic interest" in children (Durkin & Bryant, 1999). Even if there is still work to do in order to understand how cognitive distortions are linked to sexual agression, it has been suggested that they are a central characteristic of sex offenders against children (Howitt & Sheldon, 2007). It can be assumed that such distortions can be observed in discussions in newsgroups as well. While the analysis of cognitive distortions is beyond the scope of this chapter, we have observed such discourse in conversations between active users or when they are answering comments from outsiders. Examples are provided in the next section.

It was also observed that users have often communicated with each other for several years, with some exchanges being repeated. Discourse analysis shows that many users are so familiar with each other that they know if someone attempts to appropriate another member's pseudonym. Newcomers must prove their "good will" to join the group, often by exchanging child pornography. This certifies that: a) they are not law enforcement officers, and b) they are truly interested in joining the community. In light of the many precautions taken by users, it is obvious that members are fully aware of the illegal nature of their activities and recognize that they must organize and protect each other if they want to continue sharing material. For example, a user says:

> I understand where you are coming from, BUT you are just as guilty as anybody in this group just for viewing these articles. Why are you looking in this group in the first place? Obviously, you have viewed the files and know what is posted in this particular group. Yes it is well known one of our best friends has been arrested, intended as well as you know the rest of us that it is illegal to view as well as post these kinds of articles. If anon feels threatened and feels that he cannot trust anyone here, he will move on to post in other areas elsewhere.

Analysis of message exchanges between active participants shows that they are characterized, implicitly or explicitly, by a sense of community and recognition that the group shares ideas and beliefs. Some participants do not hesitate (especially when expressing their point of view when attacked by an outsider) to answer and defend what are known as the group's ideas. The presence of "old time virtual friends" probably reinforces the sense of community that some users feel. We saw comments such as "it's been a while since we heard from you" or messages indicating that a user is happy to see someone has come back to the group. The analysis of different roles in the next section also supports the importance of a particular subculture, showing that participants undertake different roles in order to reach the group's objective.

DISTRIBUTION OF ROLES

Our systematic coding of messages by categories suggests that some participants play recurring roles. These groups are relatively informal and socially hierarchical only in some respects as they are mainly places for collaboration among peers, and social relations are more cooperative than hierarchical. However, this does not exclude the possibility that a participant may have different roles in the community. Three types of participants emerged from our study: posters (content distributors), active participants, and passive participants.[11]

The pyramid in Figure 13.1 shows that the highest levels contain the fewest participants. That is where we find the most highly valued and admired participants. We were able to distinguish three subtypes of image and video

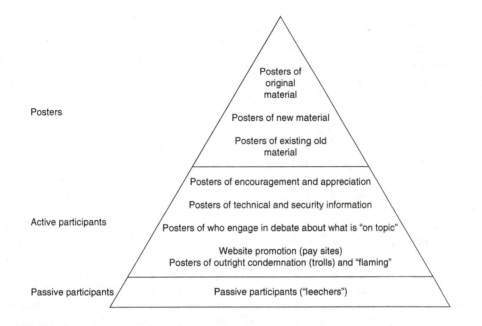

Figure 13.1 Roles in newsgroups under study

providers in the posters category. First, some content providers posted original, never-seen content. In these rare cases, posters suggested that they were the ones who had produced these images. Some tech-savvy participants searched on the internet for new content and supplied the group with links, images, and videos. Others posted material from old magazines or posted images that were easier to find. Images occasionally drew reactions from the community, with positive reaction directly proportional to the content's exclusivity. The most grateful reactions were toward a producer who claimed that he had had access to a victim. Participants sometimes asked questions to test the poster's veracity, but most were grateful and enthusiastic. The three types of posters were mainly of the type referred to as "powerposters" in the previous section. As we have seen, a small number of participants are responsible for a large quantity of shared content.

Posters also need to feel validated. Some said that they were tired of distributing child pornography or even exhausted from insults regarding their difference and deviance. For example, one participant wrote that he wanted to die following insults from another user. To cheer him up, other "colleagues" sent him messages:

Keep up the good work!

George, you are a beautiful person. I've seen your many posts you have written over time. I can see that you are a very caring man. I know of no one who would want you to die, except this Troll that caused you to post this. He wants everyone to die.

YOU are important to us. Many of us care about you and wish we could help you feel better. This in itself may not make you feel better, but we can hope.

Active participants tend to be well integrated into the group subculture, interacting extensively with other community members. Some actively participate in many discussions; others may ask for help—for example, when unable to download or restore a message from a "colleague." Sometimes, these amateurs request specific photos or videos to complete their collection. At first glance, it would seem that these participants play a minor role in maintaining the group, since their participation in the distribution of child pornography in the newsgroups is negligible or even nonexistent. However, analysis of discursive exchange between users reveals the special place they hold in the maintenance and reproduction of the group subculture. Their active participation in discussions contributes significantly to the dynamism of the group. They often express a desire to obtain the recognition of their peers by moving up in the hierarchy (by finding exclusive content, for example).

Many users who were not sending content provided support and encouragement to other posters and their encouraging and appreciative posts seemed to provide other posters with energy. After they received photos of interest to them, they thanked the other posters and encouraged them to continue:

Thank you again D4gotten1 for all these wonderful pics you are sharing.
Thanks for the classics.
This movie is one of the best i ever seen:) Please post the rest of it.
Please post it.
PLEASE POST.
OH MY . . . YOU CAN SEND HERE NORMAL FILES . . . PLEASE DO THAT.
Come on. Join the crowd and enjoy the pictures.

Some community members flatter the egos of others, either by congratulating them or by encouraging them to remain active in the group. Such messages are essentially expressions of gratitude or admiration for content that a member provided or for the central role that he occupies within the virtual community. Some common examples:

Many thanks you for your creations. You are an absolutely awesome poster. **I just want to pay tribute to your creativeness** here.
You just crack me up . . . I don't think you know just how big you are. Hey note that! I did

test you, remember? **I hope I can stay around long enough to watch you grow up.** It's going to be a amazing experience for all of us.

I like your post and I hope you will continue to post, here or elsewhere, this kind of pictures because I like them. Thanks a lot again for sharing.

Thanks for your constant efforts in sharing these wonderful pictures. I appreciated them fully (as well as your dedication at sharing them).

(Bold and capitalization as in the original messages)

Most users believe they deserve more recognition from their peers. Well-known members of the virtual community have little difficulty posting messages that are thinly veiled attempts to draw compliments and occasionally remind everyone of their importance within the group. Others are more modest in their attempts. As one of them said: "This does not mean that I'm a know-it-all and that I'm trying to boost the ego that isn't in play here? There are a great many things that I know very little about." Another went further, writing that:

Some people are angry with me for not saying what they wish me to say, even though they could have said these things for themselves. They may have placed too high a value on what I say. I have only one voice, just as everyone else does. I have no more or less value than anyone else. If my words have significance, it's the words, not me. It's the message, and not the messenger, that is important.

Groups must also keep up to date on technical details to work properly. "Technical experts" are seen as essential to the survival of the virtual community because they provide help and explanations to new members. They outline the basics of security needed to avoid arrest or provide help with technical problems. This type of relationship generally involves insiders who have specific expertise with new technologies, particularly in Usenet. Technical experts provide participants with two main types of technical assistance. First, such experts provide basic tips for protecting the user's identity. Thus, a user will explain to the whole community:

The only posters who got busted were those who made incredibly stupid mistakes. – Posting original material with your entire face in it. – Posting original material with personal identifiers in it (your car, watch, ring, identifying tattoo, scar, etc.) – Posting original material with location identifiers in it (e.g., newspaper, hotel, landmark, street signs, t-shirt of local sports team, locally produced soda or beer, workplace logo, etc.) – Posting ANYTHING with your true IP address or ISP name showing in your headers.

The truth is that newsgroup posters who use common sense and basic security precautions can, and have, gone on posting for years without incident.

It is also quite common for newcomers to seek advice from other members about how to avoid police detection. Community members are fully aware of the illegality of their actions and are more than willing to help keep each other "safe." A classic response to this type of query is:

You keep your IP address out of your headers by changing which news providers you use. The news server supplied by your ISP will usually include your IP address with every post. You can subscribe to a news provider that doesn't include your IP address, or you may even find a free news provider that masks that information.

Safety advice tends to be very accurate, educational, and easy for novices to use. For example, Nick1 will tell Nick2 exactly which software he needs, how much it costs, and how and where he can get it: "You can try a 3.95$ U$ FOR LIFE (yes, for life) with XXX. XXX will hide your IP address and by changing provider, you should also change your nick name because it is related to your past post."

Viewing or downloading the child pornography posted on the newsgroup requires some technical skills. Thus, messages like this are common: "Can anyone can help me with viewing images slip?" Sometimes the response from the technical expert is very short—"Splitting the movie will make it easier." Sometimes the response is more elaborate, and even didactic. For example:

Some posting programs automatically separate the text in a post from the file attachment, making an unnecessary multipart post. The settings that cause it can often be adjusted to remove this problem.

Depending on the original post, your newsreader can sometimes combine duplicated (caused by the poster or server error) posts into what looks like one multipart post. If this is a file you are downloading, your newsreader will probably download it correctly, and not give you duplicate files. How your newsreader presents the newsgroup downloaded header list to you, depends on it's settings, and what it understands of the subject line of each header. Each different newsreader looks at the subject line differently, and can get confused by unusual entries in them, or even the order in which the information is written. A good example is Invisible's newsreader's incompatibility with how yEnc files are posted by an older version of PowerPost, which creates a subject that his newsreader doesn't recognize as describing a yEnc post. Of course, there may be other difficulties as well.

Examples of technical assistance and shared safety tips between community members are common and consistent with Taylor's (2001) findings on newsgroups, which show that this form of technical assistance is vital in maintaining social relationships between users. Moreover, and as expected, the "technical advisors" enjoy high status within the online community and receive numerous posts expressing gratitude: "Thanks for your help" or "Thanks for your support." These messages are, in some ways, the other side of the relationship.

The technical and security posters have the role of posting messages warning the community of external threats, particularly the possible presence of police within the group. These warnings are not very frequent but are worth mentioning. Some are addressed to the entire community:

> This site is closely monitored by Interpol! They who used their credit card for membership or "donations" can expect a visit by (or an invitation from) law enforcement officers soon. This is also true for all who took part in any activities linked to these pages through MSN or Yahoo. Don't even think about checking out this site without hiding your IP because if you do, your name will feature on "the list"!
>
> This message probably did not originate from the above address. It was automatically remailed by one or more anonymous mail services. You should NEVER trust ANY address on Usenet ANYWAYS: use PGP!! Get information about complaints from URL below.
>
> You are charting into dangerous waters, or should I say You are driving on a dangerous highway.
>
> It's probably an FBI agent.

Researchers have extensively studied the discourse in cyberpedophile rings (Corriveau & Fortin, 2011; Durkin & Bryant, 1999). Participants seem to need to communicate their feelings and thoughts about the newsgroup topic. Some include discussions about pedophilia:

> From my unique perspective as a boy that LOVED SEX (starting in earnest when I was about 9 or 10 – the occasion of my first ass fucking by a 15 yo boy), I would have absolutely been willing to have sex with a man. I actually tried to initiate such one time but I was, to my dismay, rebuffed.

Most of the time, however, the values expressed toward pedophilia seem to be related to the content being shared. The use of smileys or comments about children that like what they are doing are relatively common. In this example, participants were talking about a prepubescent child depicted in a series of pictures shared in the group: "It seems unlikely that he was hurting the boys since no one had a clue about it. To them, it was probably just fun." Another participant defines on his own terms the concept of consent: "I want a donut. Chocolate. Sugar glazed. Do I deserve it? The donut wouldn't think so. Is that going to stop me? :-)."

For participants who were unsure about the purpose of the group, a powerposter states clearly that people are here for the love of boys and to keep messages "in topic": "We are here in these newsgroups for a reason; to share our love of boys. That's it. Everything else is extra. The subjects of politics and religion will divide us."

Because newsgroups are public and accessible to all, intruders can enter the group to post provocative and insulting messages. This phenomenon is not limited to child pornography forums. Kayany (1998) has found, by studying four mainstream Usenet forums, that "The number of flames directed at those who do not share socio-political, religious, or cultural affiliations are significantly greater than the number directed to those within the group." On the internet, such users are referred to as "trolls." A troll is someone who posts inflammatory, extraneous, or off-topic messages in an online group like a forum, a chat room, or a blog, with the intent of provoking readers and evoking an emotional response. Obviously, a community of pedophiles who share and discuss photos can provoke emotional reactions, as seen in these examples.

> If you choose to post any more illegal material in this group, YOU will be reported. You then can join your friend homeanon for the next thirty years. You have been warned. WWW.
>
> Just what the world needs. Another fucking pedo.
>
> All you fucking deserve is a bullet in your empty head. I understand you have become quiet the big shop in the little boy diddler groups.

Go fuck yourself, Y-Nut. Not everyone who fucking trolls your little child abuser groups is me.

The responses to trolls or to outsiders can also be emotional:

What a fool ass hypocrit. Too complicated for U????

Wrong group Asshole!

Lookin, Has anyone ever told you how much of a fucking retard you are!!?? PLONK!!!!! Kill file time!!

What is it with you assholes in here. You know what is posted in this group and therefore if you have a problem with it, don't download.

Finally, at the bottom of the pyramid are "passive participants." These users only surf into groups to take advantage of new images being distributed but do not participate directly in the subculture of the group. They are passive because they download materials but do not interact with other community members. They are virtually invisible. These "lurkers" are part of the unknown aspects of this virtual world. It is impossible to determine the precise number of passive users as the extent of participation in a newsgroup is measured by messages. Thus, an unknown number of people may have consulted the group without being counted as participants. According to Rafaeli, Ravid, and Soroka (2012), research suggests that lurkers may still get a sense of community by watching people talk and becoming comfortable with the people involved and the content of discussions.[12] In the groups under study, one member, who calls himself a lurker, decided to begin to participate and asked for technical help, writing:

I have recently bought some new Boy Nudist Movies in germany in dvd format and I want to know how i can put them on my computer into mpeg format so i can share them. Can someone please tell me what program i need to do this an how i go about doing it. i really enjoy the posts here and appreciate all the movies you guys post for us lurkers.

Another indicates that he is well-aware of the presence of lurkers:

Consider what is posted of Boy David and Man complete I choose not to complete it do to do to I can stand all the bigot that post in here i see noone else posting a damn thing and I made a truthfull posting about this from [poster] and then I get attacked for it so for now I will be a lurker.

Some posts contain pressure to share or simply reinforce the negative image of those who are invisible participants.

CONCLUSION

Our findings suggest that users of child pornography in Usenet newsgroups interact with each other and form their own community. In this sense, the social learning theory of a subculture of deviance (Becker, 1985) applies to our study. Reviewing discussions in newsgroups provides evidence that, for some participants, such virtual places are comfortable and are perceived as a real community, which enables members of the group to feel that they are not alone in having what the rest of society perceives as a shameful passion. The newsgroup is a place to hang out, to discuss, and to get fresh content.

The group demonstrates an "us and them" dichotomy and there are common beliefs about the content and the legitimacy of the group. Active participants visit the site and send messages regularly. These individuals develop relationships through online messages and friendships may be created, as well as hostile relationships. There is also an invisible crowd of participants who look at text and download content. The analysis of different roles and the way the group works also supports the hypothesis of the emergence of a subculture. We have found that more computer-literate users are willing to guide novices by showing them how to avoid police detection, how to remain relatively anonymous in the virtual community, and how to participate more actively in exchanging new material. It was also clear that participants are aware of the risks they face. Mutual aid, both moral and technical, is important within the group, which is why we chose to refer to roles rather than the hierarchy that predominates in traditional criminal organizations, for example. Being able to get pictures through the group and being taught to avoid getting caught provides a sense of support for those demonstrating a sexual interest in children. The "us and them" dichotomy then becomes even more established.

This study demonstrates that distribution of child pornography in Usenet newsgroups takes place in the context of some form of mutual assistance between individuals, which encourages participants to specialize in performing certain tasks. While the specialization of tasks is not as formal and specific as in traditional organized crime, for example, it does exist and is helpful in distributing and sharing child pornography.

Sharing material plays a predominant role for participants, allowing them to advance up the levels of the informal social hierarchy by increasing their credibility within the community. Members of the subculture are eager to praise themselves, to encourage each other, and to justify their deviance. We observed a great deal of encouragement given to people who share new content. A few of these, the powerposters, receive many messages of admiration and congratulation. Our quantitative analysis suggests that it is these individuals who are feeding the group with high levels of postings containing images and videos.

It is important to remember that behind every picture there is a child who has been abused. Given this, admiration for powerposters may have a consequence that is even worse than the already illegal activity of dissemination of child pornography—it might lead individuals to produce child pornography to gain recognition from the group. While our study provided no empirical evidence that such an effect is present, it is reasonable to expect that such a social context will have an impact on those who participate. While it would be difficult to conclude that this motivation is present for a majority of posters, it is possible that at least some are encouraged to engage in a more systematic quest for material. Research is needed to determine how this motivation may affect the acting-out process.

Finally, this study, like those of other researchers, shows how newsgroups are used by those interested in child pornography to carry out their activities with impunity. While services like email or websites leave traces, Usenet users can participate in illegal communities with a very low chance of being caught if they take the advice of other users. Technical research should be encouraged to find ways to mitigate or cope with the dissemination of child pornography through such sites.

NOTES

1. The author would like to thank Patrice Corriveau, Cynthia Giguère, Gareth Samson, and police officers from the Sureté du Québec for their help and technological infrastructure support.
2. O'Connell, a member of the COPINE project, estimated that 0.07% of 40,000 discussion groups deal specifically with child pornography (Chautard, 1999).
3. The groups involved differed from the groups in the present study as no images were shared in the web forums.
4. It should be noted that messages on Usenet are asynchronous and are not sent in real time. There is a variable time lapse between the question and the answer.
5. One of the newsgroups in the original study was unsuited to analysis because it contained only encrypted messages and was unreadable.
6. The period of data collection took place between March 18, 2004 and May 1, 2004. For obvious reasons related to the illegality of these newsgroups, any information that could trace these newsgroups will not be mentioned in this article.
7. For ethical considerations, the names of the study groups were changed.
8. Some pictures showed young adults, despite being titled "teens."
9. Google keeps usage statistics for some newsgroups on the Google Groups website.

10. Note that, even if the sender sent a comment with the photo, the message was still classified under the category of image content. Messages in response to a message with a picture were categorized as text messages.

11. The participants sometimes refer to passive participants as "leechers." In computing, and particularly on the internet, a *leech* or *leecher* is one who takes advantage, usually deliberately, of others' information or effort but does not offer anything in return.

12. See Rafaeli et al. (2012: 3) for the reasons newsgroup users lurk.

REFERENCES

Becker, H.S. (1985). *Outsiders: Études de sociologie de la deviance*. Paris: Métaillé.

Burgess, A.W. with M.L. Clark (ed.) (1984). *Child Pornography and Sex Rings*. Massachusetts, Toronto: Lexington Books.

Burgess, A.W. & C.R. Hartman (1987). Child abuse aspects of child pornography. *Psychiatric Annals* 17(4), 248–253.

Carr, J. (2001). La pornographie enfantine. *2e Congrès mondial contre l'exploitation sexuelle des enfants à des fins commerciales*. Yokohama, 17–20 décembre 2001.

Chautard, C. (1999). Internet et pédophilie. *Le Courrier de l'UNESCO*, September.

Corriveau, P. & F. Fortin (2011). *Cyberpédophiles et autres prédateurs virtuels*. Montréal: VLB éditeur.

Durkin, K.F. & C.D. Bryant (1999). Propagandising pederasty: A thematic analysis of the online exculpatory accounts of unrepentant pedophiles. *Deviant Behavior* 20, 103–127.

Gakenback, J. (1998). *Psychology of the Internet: Intrapersonal, Interpersonal, and Transpersonal Implications*. London: Academic Press.

Google Groups. (2006). *Google Groups*. Group search. Google. Retrieved July 18, 2006 from http://groups.google.com.

Hanson, R.K. & H. Scott (1996). Social networks of sexual offenders. *Psychology, Crime and Law* 2, 249–258.

Harmon, D. & S.B. Boeringer (1997). A content analysis of Internet-accessible written pornographic depictions. *Electronic Journal of Sociology* 3(1).

Howitt, D. & K. Sheldon (2007). The role of cognitive distortions in paedophilic offending: Internet and contact offenders compared. *Psychology, Crime & Law* 13(5), 469–486. doi:10.1080/10683160601060564

Jenkins, P. (2001). *Beyond Tolerance: Child Pornography Online*. New York: New York University Press.

Kayany, J.M. (1998). Contexts of uninhibited online behavior: Flaming in social newsgroups on usenet. *Journal of the American Society for Information Science* 49(12), 1135–1141.

Lanning, K.V. (1984). Collectors. In A.W. Burgess with M.L. Clark (ed.), *Child Pornography and Sex Rings* (pp. 83–109). Lexington, MA: Lexington Books.

Lanning, K.V. & A.W. Burgess (1989). Child pornography and sex rings. In D. Zillman & J. Bryant (eds.), *Pornography: Research Advances & Policy Considerations* (pp. 235–258). Hillsdale, NJ: Lawrence Erlbaum.

McAndrew D. (1999). The structural analysis of criminal networks. In D. Canter & L. Alison (eds.), *The Social Psychology of Crime: Groups, Teams, and Networks* (pp. 53–94), Offender Profiling Series. Aldershot: Dartmouth.

Mehta, Michael D. (2001). Pornography in Usenet: A study of 9,800 randomly selected images. *CyberPsychology & Behavior* 4(6), 695–703. doi:10.1089/109493101753376641

O'Halloran, E. & E. Quayle (2010). A content analysis of a "boy love" support forum: Revisiting Durkin and Bryant. *Journal of Sexual Aggression* 16(1), 71–85. doi:10.1080/13552600903395319

Prichard, J., P.A. Watters, & C. Spiranovic (2011). Internet subcultures and pathways to the use of child pornography. *Computer Law & Security Review* 27(6), 585–600. doi:10.1016/j.clsr.2011.09.009

Sellier, H. (2003). *Innocence-en-danger.com. Internet: le paradis des pedophiles*. Paris: Éditions Plon.

Sohier, D.J. (1998). *Internet: le guide de l'internaute 1998*. Montréal: Éditions Logiques.

Tate T. (1992). The child pornography industry: International trade in child sexual abuse. In C. Itzen (ed.)., *Pornography: Women, Violence and Civil Liberties*. Oxford: Oxford University Press.

Taylor, M. (2001). *La pédopornographie, Internet et les infractions*. Ministère de la Justice—Division de la recherche et de la statistique du ministère de la Justice du Canada (2001)—congrès transfrontalier—la frontière canada-états-unis: une réalité changeante séance sur Internet et la pédopornographie. Congress report, October 22, 2000, Vancouver, Canada.

Taylor, M., E. Quayle, & G. Holland (2001). La pornographie infantile, l'Internet et les compor-tements délinquants. *ISUMA, The Canadian Journal of Policy Research* 2(2), 1–12.

Wortley R. & S. Smallbone (2006). *Child Por-nography on the Internet. Problem-Oriented Guides for Police*. Washington, DC: US Depart-ment of Justice.

PART IV

*E*conomic Crime Networks

CHAPTER 14

Pushing the Ponzi

The Rise and Fall of a Network Fraud

Aili Malm, Andrea Schoepfer, Gisela Bichler, and Neil Boyd[1]

In 1920, Charles Ponzi was the talk of Boston. His business, The Security Exchange Company, was taking in more than $1 million a week from investors. He had guaranteed them an astonishing rate of return—50% interest on their principal in 45 days. The wealth was generated through an international reply postal coupon, a device for facilitating international business. Ponzi told his investors that he could buy a postal coupon in Spain for one cent and cash it in America for six one-cent stamps. It was all legal and lauded by many as a brilliant plan.

Ponzi's scheme seemed to work. Early investors achieved the promised rate of return on their money and, as a result, investments grew exponentially. However, Ponzi was simply using the money from new investors to pay himself and pay off earlier obligations; he had simply adapted the long-standing pyramid scheme—a variation that is now termed a "Ponzi" scheme. The Boston Post questioned Ponzi's business after a few months—who, after all, would buy the millions of dollars of stamps that Ponzi was said to be collecting? In response to increasing media criticism, Ponzi allowed an auditor to examine his books, and his abrupt decline began. The newspaper learned that Ponzi had previous convictions for forgery and smuggling and had spent time in prison in both Canada and the United States; his books quickly revealed his latest deception. He was convicted of fraud and sent to jail for

14 years, leaving thousands of Americans in financial ruin (Zuckoff, 2005).

Since 1920, there have been several "Ponzi schemes" in the United States and Canada. The most notorious of recent cases involves Bernard Madoff, who was convicted in the US of the largest investor fraud ever committed by a single person. Over 23 years, he managed to defraud investors of between $10 billion and $17 billion. While not all schemes have the notoriety of the original Ponzi fraud or the scope of Madoff's deception, each scheme leaves a trail of victimized investors behind.

Research on fraud victimization largely focuses on victim characteristics (see, for example: Anderson, 2004; Schoepfer & Piquero, 2009; Shichor, Sechrest, & Doocy, 2000; Titus, Heinzelman, & Boyle, 1995; Van Wyk & Benson, 1997; Van Wyk & Mason, 2001), neglecting how the fraud spreads over time (Baker & Faulkner, 2003, 2004; Comet, 2011). Clearly, social networks play an integral role in the growth of the fraud—many early investors become unwitting brokers and spokespersons for the frauds by drawing in friends, family, and co-workers with news about their initial returns (Fairfax, 2002).

While pre-existing social networks are seen to protect investors from financial loss by imposing certain social sanctions on the seller (e.g., Baker & Faulkner, 2004), the risk of losing face can lead investors/brokers to keep initial suspicions quiet. This will delay the spread of concern or skepticism about the scheme. Ironically, these positive and negative aspects of social capital can co-exist in the same organizations and phenomena (Portes & Sensenbrenner, 1993; Vaughan, 1999). This chapter applies social network analysis to a unique case study—the Eron Mortgage fraud—in an effort to better understand the bright side and dark side of social networks.

ERON MORTGAGE FRAUD

The Eron Mortgage corporation was started by two principals, Frank Biller and Brian Slobogian, in January 1993 and operated through October 1997 in British Columbia, Canada. This fraud, like that of Charles Ponzi and Bernard Madoff, was a Ponzi scheme based on a pyramid structure where early investors buy into the scheme based on the promise of high returns, and the influx of new investor capital is used to pay off early investors with false profit (Baker & Faulkner, 2003, 2004; Comet, 2011). The two Eron principals, and several employees, brokered syndicated mortgages where funds for single mortgages (for properties in Canada and the United States) were raised from many investors. Investors were supposed to receive interest, but instead received promissory notes or had their money moved to another mortgage without their consent or knowledge (British Columbia Securities Commission, 2004). In fact, much of the principal raised from new investors was going to pay existing investors.

Eron attracted investors through marketing that incorporated seminars, television and newspaper advertisements, and bulk mailings (British Columbia Securities Commission, 2004). As will be explained later in the chapter, social networks of investors and the staff of Eron also funded the Ponzi scheme. Despite the fact that annual market returns in the mid-1990s for guaranteed investments were around 6%, Eron guaranteed a return of 18–24% on its mortgages. Therefore, while the returns were guaranteed, they were certainly out of step with the prevailing market. Additionally, while the value of British Columbia real estate was continuously climbing in the five years preceding the scheme,[2] this climb could not be defined as a bubble in the same sense as the American real estate bubble of the late 1990s and 2000s. This incongruous return raised the risk and uncertainty of investing in Eron and most likely impelled investors to use their social networks to inform their decision to invest (Baker & Faulkner, 2003, 2004; Comet, 2011).

It is not completely clear whether this fraud started off as a legitimate business—what Clinard would term an intermediate fraud—or whether it was a pre-planned fraud from the beginning (Baker & Faulkner, 2003, 2004; Clinard, 1984). The British Columbia Securities Commission (BCSC) report concludes that the company began as a fraud, but they do not have indisputable proof (British Columbia Securities Commission, 1999).[3] Regardless, the investigation revealed that, early on, the executives of Eron knew the company was going to fail and they were intent on maximizing their profits before the scheme collapsed. Investors were defrauded out of about $240 million.

The contagious spread of a Ponzi scheme is not likely to rely on a single person or small group of people infecting a large number of people over time, but rather on a large number of infectors and impersonal methods (Baker & Faulkner, 2003). The next section reviews research on how a fraud is spread, and the factors that lead to investor discontent and skepticism.

Contagious Investments

In their study on stock purchasers, Shiller and Pound (1989) found that most bought stock on the recommendation of their trusted friends. Personal influence among investors is equivalent to the diffusion mechanism of *contagion* (Rogers, 2003; Valente, 1995). Such personal messages, while increasing in the first half of the process then declining as time goes on, are more influential than mass media throughout the entire process (Bowers, 1938; Rogers, 2003). An important stage in the diffusion process is the critical mass tipping point (inflection point) that occurs between the 5 and 20% levels of adoption (Rogers, 2003). After this point, the diffusion becomes self-sustaining and little promotion of the innovation is needed.

Two mediums, instrumental to the spread of a fraud—mass media and personal contact—interact to generate a distinctive adoption curve.[4] Research that examines the adoption of *legitimate* innovations finds that the mass media has a strong, concentrated effect in the early stages but that this impersonal mechanism remains relatively high throughout the diffusion process (Bass, 1969). Personal influence among investors exhibits a *contagion* effect, increasing in the first half of the process then declining as time goes on. The net impact of personal mechanisms is more influential than mass media throughout the entire process (Rogers, 2003; Valente, 1995). Thus, adoption activity creates a logistic (S-shaped) curve with the critical mass tipping point (Rogers, 2003). If adopters are dissatisfied with the innovation, the logistic curve will show a much slower rate of adoption or it will reach a plateau and then decline with more widespread dissatisfaction (Rogers, 2003).

The patterns found for the diffusion of legitimate investment activity are not replicated with illegitimate investments. Each fraud will contain conflicting forces—a leading edge spreading widely through networks and sparked by impersonal outreach mechanisms, with several seeds of discontent smoldering in the rear. Thus, it is likely that the original spread of investment activity would exhibit some aspects of an s-curve with varying importance of personal and impersonal "infection" mechanisms. Then, as the initial investors grow wise to the problems, they should initiate the unraveling of the pyramid.

Baker and Faulkner's (2003) study of an intermediate fraud (a business that starts out legitimate and becomes fraudulent) provides some indication of how these conflicting forces will affect the spread of frauds. These authors did not find a logistic curve; rather, they found a linear growth pattern. From interviews, they discovered that only 29% of investors learned about the investment opportunities from other investors. When the investor-based recruitment proved inadequate (many investors kept the opportunity secret), they relied on impersonal methods of recruitment, which proved just as successful. This reluctance of investors to spread the word did not lead to the emergence of a contagious diffusion effect driven by social networks (Baker & Faulkner, 2003). It follows that comparing adoption rates by mechanisms of introduction could identify possible investment fraud cases.

Social ties will also influence other aspects of investment activity. Beneficial information about the company will circulate better when more individuals within an investor network are known to each other (network closure) (Burt, 1992; Coleman, 1990). DiMaggio and Louch suggest that pre-existing ties with a principal or employee of a company introduces "obligations and sanctions external to the transaction" (1998: 625). Since the initial investors will be drawn from the principals' social network, the early adopters are more apt to see some return on their investment (thus lose less capital) and direct associations with the company brokers will increase an investor's likelihood of remaining in the scheme. Ponzi schemes can take advantage of these tendencies.

In their study of fraudulent oil investments, Baker and Faulkner (2004) show that the probability of investment loss depends on the investor's connection to the fraudulent company and whether the investor conducted due diligence. Specifically, investors with pre-existing social ties to the principals or employees of the company were less likely to lose their capital, even when this group did not conduct due diligence in researching the investment. Interestingly, Baker and Faulkner (2004) found that, once the company's practices turned fraudulent, social ties to the company increased their protective capacity.

AIMS OF THE CURRENT STUDY

The intent of this study is to incrementally advance our understanding of financial fraud by investigating the spread and unraveling of a Ponzi scheme by examining aspects of investor social networks. Using data from a survey of over 500 investors in the Eron Mortgage fraud, this study seeks to answer two research questions: 1) do mechanisms of exposure to an innovation (personal and impersonal) affect the diffusion of a fraud and 2) what influences the development and spread of skepticism about a fraudulent company?

DATA SOURCE AND METHODOLOGY

The data used in this study are from a survey administered to investors following the public collapse of the Eron Mortgage scheme. The list of investors was originally drawn from a database of approximately 2,800 names obtained from the Eron Lender's Committee and the British Columbia Securities Commission (BCSC). Duplicate names, incomplete addresses, and corporate addresses which did not refer to an identifiable individual were removed, leaving 2,285 unique names and addresses of Eron investors.

Investor surveys are likely to have generated credible data. To help develop questions for the survey and clarify potential recall issues (since seven years had passed since the end of the fraud), three focus groups were held with Eron investors who held substantial knowledge of the fraud.[5] These individuals were identified from the list with the help of the Eron Lender's Group and the BCSC. Par-

ticipants in the focus groups stated that, since the majority of the investors lost a substantial amount of money, and they were interviewed by the BCSC and police several times over the past seven years, their memories regarding the fraud were clear. Through an examination of archival and interview data, Baker and Faulkner (2004) also show that age, salience, and stress do not appear significantly associated with the accuracy of recalling fraud events. Thus, this group of victims should provide reasonably accurate information.

The survey was administered in two waves. The pilot survey was mailed to 520 randomly selected Eron investors in December of 2004. During the second phase of the survey, 1,765 surveys were mailed out between February and March 2005. Of the 2,285 surveys mailed, 438 (19%) were returned undeliverable and 559 investors responded. The total pool of survey respondents represents 30% of the investors. The current study uses a subset of 367 respondents who answered questions regarding their social network.

The survey questions were designed to obtain from respondents a summary of their age, education, gender, income, net worth, process of involvement in Eron (including personal and impersonal methods of introduction), extent of loss, perceptions of responsibility for the fraud, personal consequences from the fraud, and possibilities for future prevention of securities fraud.

Network Construction

A directional network was generated using information gleaned from a portion of the responses to the following question: "*How did you first hear of Eron Mortgage? (check all that apply)*"

- Through an Eron Principal [list name(s)]
- Through an Eron Mortgage Broker [list name(s)]
- Through an independent mortgage broker [list name(s)]

- Through family or friend(s) [list name(s)]
- Through a business associate [list name(s)]
- Through a hockey connection [list name(s)]
- Through an Eron seminar
- Newspaper advertisement
- Newspaper article or column
- Mail solicitation
- Television advertisement
- Other (specify)

Respondents were permitted to check individuals and impersonal mechanisms (i.e., newspaper advertisement, mail solicitation). Of those who responded, 367 answered this question with enough detail to be retained for the current study. On average, each investor named an average of 1.6 sources, including both individuals and impersonal mechanisms (with a standard deviation of 0.8, a minimum of one source and a maximum of four).

To build the network, each investor (considered the ego) is linked to the person or people (in the event of multiple nominations) that introduced them to the scheme (classed as alters). In order to test how both personal and impersonal mechanisms of exposure affect the development and spread of a fraud,

it was necessary to retain the respondents who were introduced to the fraud solely through impersonal sources. These respondents were included in the network as isolates (nodes unconnected to any other node), because while they did answer the network generator question, they were not introduced to the fraud by any individual.

The network includes 54 components, 59 isolates (respondents who nominated only impersonal sources), 437 nodes (investors and sources) and 345 ties (shown in Figure 14.1; isolates not shown). The main component (largest connected component) contains 239 nodes and 259 ties. Of the 376 individuals who answered the network generator question, 112 egos (30%) are unconnected to the main component and, therefore, unconnected to the Eron Mortgage principals.

Independent Variables

Path Distance to Eron Principals

To measure each investor's social closeness to the Eron principals, a path length variable was created. This variable counts the number of paths (ties) it takes to reach either of the two principals in the fraud. All Eron brokers

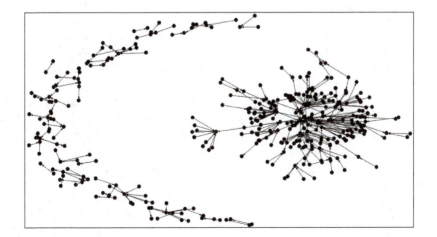

Figure 14.1 Personal investor network sociogram

were coded as being one path length from the principals, since they were responsible for all hiring. The number of paths needed to reach either of the principals in the main component ranged from a minimum of one to a maximum of four. Individuals not included in the principal component (including isolates) were given a path length of five, even though they are technically unconnected to the principals.[6]

Infection Mechanisms

Due to the possibility of naming several infection mechanisms, a set of dichotomous variables (1 = yes, 0 = no) was generated to capture information about the initial exposure to the fraud. The first variable measures whether the investor was infected through personal methods (Eron principal, Eron broker, independent mortgage broker, friends/family, business associate, and/or hockey connection). The second infection variable measures impersonal methods (Eron seminar, newspaper, mail, and/or television). Table 14.1 presents the percentages for each of these variables.

Initial Investment Activity

The number of investors per year was used to examine the diffusion process. Investors were asked, "In which year did you first become involved in a project or property of Eron Mortgage?" The year of first investment was also used as an independent variable in the multivariate models.

Control Variables

A number of control variables were included in order to check the influence of other correlates. The first control variable measures whether the respondent self-identified as a "sophisticated investor." Sophisticated investors, as defined by British Columbia securities legislation, must have at least $1 million in financial assets, independent of real estate, or an annual individual income of at least

Table 14.1 Independent variables

Variables	Percent
Mode of Infection	
Personal*	
Yes	83
No	17
Impersonal**	
Yes	70
No	30
Path Distance to Principals	
1	10
2	40
3	10
4	10
5 (unconnected)	30
Year Adopted	
1992	3
1993	3
1994	11
1995	15
1996	32
1997	36

Notes
N = 367
* "Personal" includes: Eron broker, independent broker, family or friends, business associates, financial advisor
** "Impersonal" includes: Eron seminar, newspaper ad, newspaper article or column, mail solicitation, TV ad, public events

$200,000. Langevoort (1996) contends that sophisticated investors are different from regular investors in that they truly understand the risks, and they know what questions to ask and what signs to look for, yet they may still make risky investments. Sophisticated investors understand that risk and return operate together; above-average return typically comes with above-average risk. Including the self-identified sophisticated investors controls for those investors who should have been knowledgeable enough to realize the risk versus those who invested without requisite knowledge.

Two demographic variables were also used as controls: gender and age at time of first investment, measured in years. Table 14.2 describes these variables.

Table 14.2 Control variables

Variables	Percent
Sophisticated Investor	
Yes	17
No	83
Gender	
Male	61
Female	39
Age at Time of Initial Investment*	
Less than 45	28
45–54	28
55–64	28
65+	16

Notes
N = 367

Dependent Variables: Presence and Onset of Skepticism

One of the initial reactions victims display is a reluctance to advertise their victimization (or suspected victimization); people tend to be embarrassed that they were defrauded and this might be exacerbated if they are responsible for spreading the victimization to their family and friends. Due to this reluctance, concern and skepticism about an investment is unlikely to spread quickly through investor networks; however, little is known about this phenomenon. To help understand 1) how skepticism spreads through a network, and 2) the impact of social network variables on investor skepticism, information was solicited about when each investor first attempted to withdraw their investments due to concern about the legitimacy of the company. Two questions were posed to investors: 1) "Did you ever try to pull any of your money out of Eron before the collapse in October 1997?"[7] and 2) "Approximately how many months before the collapse did you first try to pull your money out?" These questions provide the dependent variables for both of the models tested in this study.

Model 1 uses the simple presence of investor skepticism as the dependent variable.

This variable was coded as 1 = investor tried to pull money out of Eron and 0 = investor never tried to pull money out of Eron. Among the networked investors who answered this question (N = 356), 125 (35%) tried to pull money out before the collapse of Eron.

Model 2 uses a dichotomous indicator of skepticism onset, where 1 = tried to pull money out prior to public announcement of BCSC investigation (four months from Eron collapse) and 0 = tried to pull money out after public announcement. Among the networked investors who answered the skepticism onset question (N = 107), 35% pulled their money out prior to the public announcement of BCSC's formal investigation. The average length of time was about four months (median three months) with a standard deviation of 3.1 months, where initial withdrawal attempts ranged from a low of less than a month to a maximum of 24 months.

RESULTS

Diffusion of Adaptation

The first objective of this chapter is to look at overall growth of the fraud among investors. Specifically, this article is interested in how mechanisms of exposure to an innovation (personal and impersonal) affect the diffusion process of a fraud. Contagious diffusion follows a logistic curve (s-curve), spreading slowly at the beginning, rapidly spreading once it hits a "tipping point," and then evening out. Figure 14.2 compares a typical diffusion curve found among legitimate investment activity in new opportunities (14.2a) with investment activity in the Eron Mortgage fraud (14.2b).

Investment activity does not follow a typical smooth s-curve. Investment activity spread rather slowly in the first two years (1992 to 1994), before investment interest began leveling off. The second inflection point (occurring around 1995) leading up to the drastic increase in investors may be

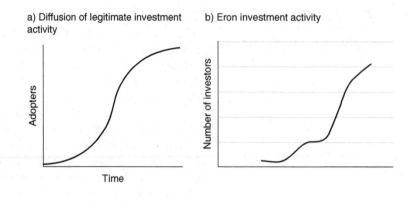

Figure 14.2 Spread of investment activity

indicative of the start of, or better management of, the control fraud. As the rate of adoption in the early years was slow, failure of the company was inevitable (as seen by the leveling out of investors in 1994), and the principals of Eron may have used these cues to enhance the control fraud to maximize profits before the inevitable collapse of the organization.

In the diffusion of legitimate ideas/innovations, once the critical mass tipping point (inflection point) is achieved, the diffusion becomes self-sustaining and little promotion of the innovation is needed. The critical mass tipping point occurs at 5% to 20% adoption. The critical mass tipping point in Eron investments occurred between 1993 (5%) and 1995 (25%). Investments were not self-sustaining at this point. In fact, investments had leveled off by 1994.

Parsing the investment activity by mechanism of infection provides a window into how personal infection differs from impersonal infection. It is apparent that, early in the fraud, all methods were used to recruit new investors. By the final year prior to collapse, Eron employees were recriting fewer investors compared to friends and media (Figure 14.3).

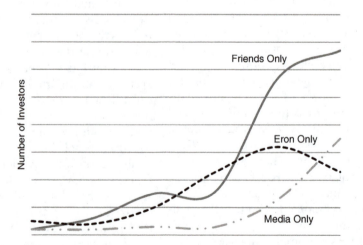

Figure 14.3 Eron investment activity by mechanism of infection

Diffusion and Factors Affecting Investor Skepticism

The second, and primary, objective of this chapter is to look at how investor skepticism about a company affects the growth of the fraud. Specifically, the researchers are interested in how mechanisms of exposure to an innovation affect the unraveling and eventual failure of the fraud. In Figure 14.4, the x axis is reversed to illustrate how many months before the collapse the investors became skeptical of the investment and tried to pull their money out. Starting in January 1996, the Financial Institutions Commission (FICOM) began its investigation of Eron and, in January 1997, FICOM and BCSC investigations intensified (BCSC, 1999). Finally, in July 1997, the investigations were widely publicized. Figure 14.4 indicates that these events seem to be associated with increasing skepticism and attempts to withdraw investments.

Two binary logistic models were used to better understand how Ponzi schemes unravel and how the publication of formal investigations affects investor confidence.[8] The first model shows that two variables have a significant impact on investor skepticism as measured by whether the individual ever tried to pull money out of Eron (see Table 14.3): path length to Eron principals and self-identification of being a sophisticated investor. Specifically, the model shows that the closer the investor was to being introduced to the fraud by one of the principals, the more likely they were to become concerned about the fraud. Interestingly, despite the insignificant correlation between skepticism and self-identification of sophisticated investor, the model also shows that a self-identification of sophisticated investor significantly increases the likelihood of the investor becoming skeptical of the fraud.

The second model shows that two variables influenced whether investors attempted to pull their investment prior to publication of formal investigations (see Table 14.3): path length to Eron principals and year of initial investment. Specifically, the model shows that the closer the investor was to being introduced to the fraud by one of the principals, the more likely they were to attempt to pull money out of Eron prior to the investigations being publicized. The model also shows that the longer investors were involved with Eron, the more likely they were to attempt to withdraw their investment prior to the investigation publication.

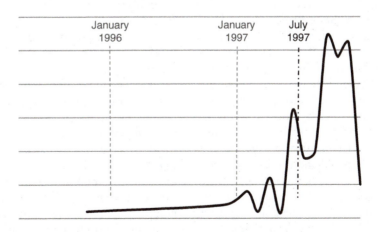

Figure 14.4 Number of investors who tried to pull their money out before the collapse

Table 14.3 Binary logit coefficients

	Model 1: Ever Tried to Pull Investment	Model 2: Tried to Pull Investment Prior to Publicized Investigations
Independent Variables		
Infection Mechanisms		
Personal Infection	0.428	0.220
Impersonal Infection	0.017	−1.010
Path Length to Eron Principals	−0.489**	0.349*
Contagious Diffusion		
Year Invested	−0.124	−0.374*
Controls		
Sophisticated Investor	0.881*	0.093
Gender	0.207	0.308
Age at Initial Investment	0.195	0.067
Constant	0.276	−0.609
Nagelkerke R^2	0.192	0.182
N	316	94

Notes
No. of observations is less than 367 for Model 1 and 107 for Model 2 due to listwise deletion of cases with missing data on one or more variables
*$p < 0.05$, **$p < 0.01$

CONCLUSION

In 2000, Frank Biller and Brian Slobogian were convicted of Canada's largest Ponzi scheme, the Eron mortgage fraud. Similar to Ponzi's postal reply coupon, the high returns on investments promoted by Eron Mortgage—real estate developments in Canada and the United States—seemed plausible to investors at the time. Like Charles Ponzi and Bernard Madoff, the principals of Eron Mortgage did not actually carry out much of the plans that they enthusiastically described to their willing contributors, though their businesses were widely praised by media commentators. In all three cases, after questions were raised about their businesses, their books were examined and frauds discovered. In all three cases, it was too late for the victims; the businesses had crashed, their money was gone, and little could be done to retrieve it. Since these frauds have devastating effects on their victims, this research sought to

advance our understanding by investigating the social diffusion of investment activity and the possible protective effects of social networks.

The results show that contagious diffusion was, in fact, present in the Eron Mortgage fraud. Investors, particularly toward the end of Eron's tenure, referred the company to their friends, family, and associates. This was not the case in Baker and Faulkner's case study (2003, 2004), where investors rarely made referrals, even at the request of company employees. There are two potential explanations as to why this fraud spread through contagious diffusion, contrary to Baker and Faulkner's case study (2003, 2004).[9] First, the Eron principals were instrumental in spreading the fraud. Their involvement increased trust among potential investors; therefore, investors were more willing to recruit for the company. Second, the company was able to maintain a professional public image. They conducted seminars, produced media campaigns, had a professional office space, and released detailed information on the investments. They also hired several brokers who assisted in recruiting, but were apparently not "in the know" about the fraud. The ability of the principals to create such a trustworthy reputation, even amongst employees, is perhaps the key factor that sets this fraud apart from the Baker and Faulkner (2003, 2004) example. This demonstrates the "dark side" of social networks in the spread of a financial fraud. The second research question reveals "the bright side."

Why does close social proximity to the principals increase the likelihood of investor skepticism? Diffusion theory suggests that network closure increases the speed and efficiency of information circulation (Burt, 1992; Coleman, 1990). It follows that, if the principals of the company were behaving suspiciously—selling off property, acting out of character—investors closer to the principals would be more likely to hear of such suspicious behavior. For example, when asked why he became suspicious of the fraud, one of the investors said, "My sister was one of the brokers (for Eron). About four months before the collapse, she stopped getting paychecks. That was a big red flag." Another possible reason lies in the diffusion sub-theory surrounding stability of rumors. Rumors change in content, consistency, and accuracy over time (Fine, 2007). Simply put, diffusion of a rumor resembles a children's game of telephone where information is whispered through a chain of individuals. The information reported at the end is significantly different from the original. While research results do not show information distortion on such a dramatic level, communication has been shown to get distorted the more people it needs to travel through to arrive at a source (Mason, Jones, & Goldstone, 2008). The information is more likely to get distorted or prematurely stopped if the individuals between origination and destination points are reluctant to share the original

content. This reluctance could be particularly relevant in the case of fraud victims. Baker and Faulkner (2003) reported three possible reasons for investor reluctance: 1) not wanting to spread information about a risky venture, 2) the feeling that investment activity is a personal matter not to be discussed with personal networks, and 3) keeping information about earnings to oneself. This theoretical position is supported by the finding that the closer the investor was to being introduced to the fraud by one of the principals, the more likely they were to attempt to pull their money out prior to the investigations being publicized.

Another explanation for close social proximity to the principals increasing the likelihood of investor skepticism might hinge on the type of fraud we are dealing with. Recall that Baker and Faulkner (2004) studied a company that started out legitimately and then turned fraudulent (intermediate fraud). Their finding that pre-existing social ties with company employees reduced capital loss was attributed to illegal preferential treatment in the ex post allocation of proceeds to investors with ties to the company. This is not supported in the current study. Available evidence points to Eron being a fraud from the very beginning. It is unlikely that the principals would have introduced their close friends and associates to a fraudulent venture, as was the case in Baker and Faulkner (2004). This is supported by the relatively low rate of respondents who are one path length from either principal (10%). Alternatively, the survey response rate of investors who were socially close to either principal might have been significantly lower than the general survey response rate.

An unexpected result in this project centered on the finding that sophisticated investors were more likely to become skeptical of the fraud, but not more likely to try to pull their investment prior to publication of problems. Sophisticated investors are those who are knowledgeable enough to know what to look for, what questions to ask, and what should look suspicious, yet they are also the ones who are the more likely to take risks (Langevoort, 1996). Under the idea of "loss framing," these investors have an increased willingness to accept risk, even when they sense the serious possibility of relative loss (Langevoort, 1996; Thaler & Johnson, 1990). Sophisticated investors invest their money in risky ventures for fear of missing out on an opportunity (Weisburd, Wheeler, Waring, & Bode, 1991), a need to maintain the status quo, or a need to bolster social comparisons (Langevoort, 1996). The prevalence of self-identified sophisticated investors in the sample (17%) gives credence to the idea that the investment opportunities may have looked legitimate to the most educated of investors, yet it also signifies that the investment opportunity may also have appeared risky from the beginning. It is not surprising that the findings suggest that the more sophisticated/knowledgeable investors became skeptical of the scheme than those who were less knowledgeable with investments. Again, these investors knew what to look for and what types of questions to ask, and they could arguably have also known when a risky venture became too risky. The paradox of this finding is the more educated the investor, the more likely they are to take risks, but they are also more likely to identify problems.

There are three primary limitations in this research. First, the sample of 376 respondents who answered the network generator question might not be representative of the population of 2,285 investors. The research team was able to conduct reliability assessments comparing the two groups on age, gender, and amount invested. Based on these three variables, the sample does not look significantly different from the population. Second, the networks examined here are incomplete and contain fuzzy boundaries. Factors contributing to this problem include the fact that only approximately 15% of the

investors answered the network question. Additionally, investors who had a personal relationship with the Eron principals might be less likely to respond to the survey due to their reluctance to discuss the case. Unfortunately, this limitation impacts all attempts at studying criminal acts (Morselli & Roy, 2008; Xu & Chen, 2008). Third, as previously mentioned, the decision to code unconnected investors with a path distance of five presents unique challenges when inserting the variable into a multiple regression. This type of methodological challenge, however, presents avenues for future research.

This study offers a rare glimpse into the social network dynamics of a Ponzi scheme. Supporting and extending the findings of Baker and Faulkner (2003, 2004), we found that financial frauds spread socially through a mechanism of contagious diffusion and that an investor's social network could serve a protective function. Specifically, the closer an investor was to being introduced to the scheme by a principal, the more likely they were to become skeptical of the fraud once it began to unravel. These findings provide evidence for the protective features of social ties in pre-planned frauds; such protection was previously believed to only occur in frauds that started out legitimately (Baker & Faulkner, 2004). Thus, the Eron case study shows that sellers committing fraud may unwittingly inform their close social network that something is *not quite right*, whether it is their intention or not.

NOTES

1. The authors would like to acknowledge the British Columbia Security Commission (BCSC) for their assistance and support of this research. The opinions and positions expressed by the authors are theirs alone and do not necessarily reflect the opinions and positions of the BCSC.
2. According to British Columbia Real Estate Board statistics, in the five years preceding the scheme (1988–1992), the average price of a single-family dwelling increased approximately 25%; however, during the scheme (1993–1997), prices remained relatively flat.

3. Within the financial crime literature, the actions taken by Eron principles would suggest that this was a control fraud (Black, 2005). Control frauds are accounting schemes where profits are overstated and loses are hidden. This is especially applicable to Ponzi schemes in which the seemingly legitimate company is used to defraud investors (Black, 2005). Firms that deal in "assets that have no readily ascertainable market value, e.g., large, unique real estate projects" (Black, 2005: 3) are attractive to those intent on running a control fraud. This is exactly what the Eron principals did. What is interesting about control frauds is that failure of the firm is inevitable; the control fraud simply delays this failure, allowing the executives/owners more time to loot the company (Black, 2005).

4. A fraud could be considered a new idea, or innovation, and since the "newness" of the idea is what separates diffusion from other forms of communication (Rogers, 2003), diffusion theory is applicable to the study of fraud (Baker & Faulkner, 2003). Inherent in this newness is a certain degree of risk or uncertainty about the innovation, which is especially relevant in the current study regarding investment fraud.

5. Cohen and Faulkner (1989) suggest that several factors might impede the ability of a respondent to accurately recall events of victimization—stress, age, and other factors.

6. The issue of disconnected components in studying path length is contentious (Steen, MacAulay, & Kastelle, 2010). Technically, the path length for unconnected nodes is infinite, but this does not allow for the inclusion of unconnected nodes in path length (small world) analyses. A common solution is to exclude unconnected components and only analyze the principal component (Chen & Guan, 2010), but this does not suffice for the current study. Only using the largest component would exaggerate the direct influence of the fraud principals and exclude individuals who were introduced through impersonal sources. The authors decided to use the largest path length, five, to represent unconnected nodes for the purpose of the multivariate models; however, this designation is a pragmatic one. The rationale is based on the assumption that people infected indirectly or directly through impersonal means still need to make formal contact with a broker or a principal in the end to close the deal.

7. A subsequent question asked investors, "What caused you to try to pull your money out of Eron?" In response to this, 93% answered, "concerns with investment."

8. No substantial problems of multicollinearity were revealed; the highest intercorrelation was 0.603 (dummy variables for personal mode of infection and impersonal mode of infection), which is below the standard 0.700 benchmark for exclusion set by Tabachnik and Fidell (1989; see Appendix A).

9. For a complete discussion, refer to Nash, Bouchard and Malm (forthcoming).

REFERENCES

Anderson, K. (2004). *Consumer Fraud in the United States: An FTC Survey*. Washington, DC: Bureau of Economics and Consumer Protection.

Baker, W. & R. Faulkner (2003). Diffusion of fraud: Intermediate economic crime and investor dynamics. *Criminology* 41(4), 1173–1206.

Baker, W. & R. Faulkner (2004). Social networks and loss of capital. *Social Networks* 26, 91–111.

Bass, F. (1969). A new product growth model for consumer durables. *Management Science* 13(5), 215–227.

Black, W. (2005). Control fraud as an explanation for white-collar crime waves: The case of the savings and loan debacle. *Crime, Law, and Social Change* 43, 1–29.

Bowers, R. (1938). Differential intensity of intra-societal diffusion. *American Sociological Review* 2, 826–836.

British Columbia Securities Commission (1999). Policy Documents: Eron Mortgage Corporation. Available at: www.bcsc.bc.ca/comdoc.nsf/allbyunid/141cc62c7db8fc39882568e9005eb079?opendocument.

British Columbia Securities Commission (2004). Securities Commission finds that Eron investors were defrauded. Available at: www.bcsc.bc.ca/release.aspx?id=892.

Burt, R.S. (1992). *Structural Holes*. Cambridge, MA: Harvard University Press.

Chen, Z. & J. Guan (2010). The impact of small world on innovation: An empirical study of 16 countries. *Journal of Infometrics* 4, 97–106.

Clinard, M.B. (1984). The phantom capitalists: The organization and control of long-term fraud. *British Journal of Sociology* 35, 141–143.

Cohen, G. & D. Faulkner (1989). Age differences in source forgetting: Effects on reality monitoring and eyewitness testimony. *Psychology and Aging* 4, 1–20.

Coleman, J.S. (1990). *Foundations of Social Theory*. Cambridge, MA: Harvard University Press.

Comet, C. (2011). Anatomy of a fraud: Trust and social networks. *Bulletin of Sociological Methodology* 110, 45–57.

DiMaggio, P. & H. Louch (1998). Socially transmitted consumer transactions: For what kinds of purchases do people most often use networks? *American Sociological Review* 63, 619–637.

Fairfax, L. (2002). With friends like these: Toward a more efficacious response to affinity-based security and investment fraud. *Georgia Law Review* 63, 63–119.

Fine, G. (2007). Rumor, trust, and civil society: Memory and cultures of judgment. *Diogenes* 213, 5–18.

Langevoort, D. (1996). Selling hope, selling risk: Some lessons for law from behavioral economics about stockbrokers and their sophisticated customers. *California Law Review* 83(3), 627–701.

Mason, W., A. Jones, & R. Goldstone (2008). Propagation of innovations in networked groups. *Journal of Experimental Psychology* 137(3), 422–433.

Morselli, C. & J. Roy (2008). Brokerage qualifications in ringing operations. *Criminology* 46, 71–98.

Nash, R., M. Bouchard, & A. Malm (forthcoming). Investing in people: The role of social networks in the diffusion of a large-scale fraud. *Social Networks*.

Portes, A. & J. Sensenbrenner (1993). Embeddedness and immigration: Notes on the social determinants of economic action. *American Journal of Sociology* 98, 1320–1351.

Rogers, E. (2003). *Diffusion of Innovations* (5th ed.).New York: The Free Press.

Schoepfer, A. & N. Piquero (2009). Studying the correlates of fraud victimization and reporting. *Journal of Criminal Justice* 37, 209–215.

Shichor, D., D. Sechrest, & J. Doocy (2000). Victims of investment fraud. In H. Pontell & D. Shichor (eds.), *Contemporary Issues in Crime and Criminal Justice: Essays in Honor of Gilbert Geis* (pp. 87–96). Upper Saddle River, NJ: Prentice Hall.

Shiller, R. & J. Pound 1989). Survey evidence of diffusion of interest and information among investors. *Journal of Economic Behavior* 12, 47–66.

Steen, John, S. MacAulay, & T. Kastelle (2010). A review and critique of the small worlds hypothesis: The best network structure for innovation? Conference paper presented at Opening up Innovation Conference. Available at www2.druid.dk/conferences/viewpaper.php?id=501744&cf=43.

Tabachnik, B. & L. Fidell (1989). *Using Multivariate Statistics*. New York: HarperCollins.

Thaler, R. & R. Johnson (1990). Gambling with the house money and trying to break even: The effects of prior outcomes on risky choice. *Management Science* 36(6), 643–660.

Titus, R., F. Heinzelman, & J. Boyle (1995). Victimization of persons by fraud. *Crime and Delinquency* 41, 54–72.

Valente, T.W. (1995). *Network Models of the Diffusion of Innovations*. Cresskill, NJ: Hampton Press, Inc.

Van Wyk, J. & M. Benson (1997). Fraud victimization: Risky business or just bad luck? *American Journal of Criminal Justice* 21, 163–179.

Van Wyk, J. & K. Mason (2001). Investigating vulnerability and reporting behavior for consumer fraud victimization. *Journal of Contemporary Criminal Justice* 17, 328–345.

Vaughan, D. (1999). The dark side of organizations: mistake, misconduct, and disaster. *Annual Review of Sociology* 25, 271–305.

Weisburd, D., S. Wheeler, E. Waring, & N. Bode (1991). *Crimes of the Middle Classes*. New Haven, CT: Yale University Press.

Xu, J. & H. Chen (2008). The topology of dark networks. *Communications of the ACM* 51, 58–65.

Zuckoff, M. (2005). *Ponzi: The Man and his Legendary Scheme*. Boston, MA: Random House.

CHAPTER 15

Breakdown of Brokerage

Crisis and Collapse in the Watergate Conspiracy

Robert R. Faulkner and Eric Cheney

This chapter provides empirical evidence supporting the hypothesis that those who occupy mediating positions between blocs in political conspiracies face a relative broker penalty. When we say that doing bridging work entails a "brokerage penalty," we mean that those in these positions are, on average, targets of suspicion, enmity, and hostility. While working at the crossroads of the secret working groups, they invite invective behavior and are fingered by their co-conspirators. When we say that action that bridges between subgroups entails a "brokerage premium," we mean that those who occupy these intermediate positions between subgroups—as representatives and/or gatekeepers, for example—have access to unique resources and information that make them influential players in a system. We operationalize these concepts and test the brokerage penalty hypothesis in a statistical model by ascertaining whether there is a negative effect of brokerage in Watergate in which conspirators are supposed to represent their bloc.

We make this contribution by examining the sociological significance of the break-in at the Democratic National Committee headquarters at the Watergate complex on June 17, 1972, which was ultimately revealed to be part of a conspiracy of wiretapping, spying, campaign sabotage, secret funds, interference with investigations, and cover-up reaching to the top of the Nixon Administration.

While Watergate represents the most major case of presidential corruption in American twentieth century history and is perhaps the paradigmatic case of political corruption, little is understood about how such a well-organized political machine like the Nixon Administration collapsed after having earlier successfully withstood constant and enormous pressure and adversity to persevere. Serious scholarship has yet to adequately explain how the Watergate conspiracy collapsed in terms of its own inner workings. Instead explanations have tended to unfortunately rest on superficial "black box" explanations. Examples of black box explanations of Watergate's collapse can be found in what we call "the media did it" thesis and rational choice and game theories of defection.

The general public and some in the media tend to echo a taken-for-granted hypothesis that media coverage "brought down" Watergate. However, scholars of American journalism and of Watergate itself have dismissed the "media brought down Watergate" thesis as mythology because the media thesis fails to withstand a close scrutiny of the historical record that clearly shows that "leaks" from within the conspirators' social circle led to Watergate's collapse (see Feldstein, 2004; Kutler, 1990). We agree that "leaks" are what brought down Watergate, but we maintain that explanations about the reasons for the sources of the leaks are still vaguely understood at best. The Watergate literature's current explanations about specific conspirators who "leaked" are idiographic rather than nomothetic. We seek a more general, structural explanation of "who" leaked than is currently available in the Watergate literature.

Like the "media brought it down" hypothesis, game theorists and rational choice theorists also offer black box explanations of the collapse of the Watergate conspiracy. Game theorists and rational choice theorists offer explanations of conspiracy breakdown as part of a strategic game among the conspirators seeking to maneuver against their co-conspirators and trade information with state authorities in exchange for more lenient punishment. In short, conspirators defect and testify against the conspiracy and against their co-conspirators in deals with government prosecutors. These theories do not identify which specific actors operate internal to the conspiracy defected, but instead offer a theory of how some generalized "rational actor" defects. These theories tell us about rational actors as generalized agents that go into the black box as rational actors and somehow come out defectors.

Our structural model is, we believe, a vast improvement over rational choice and game theory models theorizing that all conspiracies are prone to defection due to each conspirator's self-interest. Such models and theories are nonspecific in terms of which particular actors defect from political conspiracies because they assume all conspirators are the same in terms of roles and social position. By modeling roles and social position, structural sociology goes beyond black box explanations and gains the important insight about which specific social actors defect.

Our essay is organized as follows. First, we briefly describe the historical case of the Watergate scandal and its collapse. Second, we conceptualize brokerage and defection and develop a theory of the social organization of political conspiracy and the stresses and strains faced by brokers. We then test hypotheses related to the breakdown of brokerage using standard network analytics and statistical techniques. We conclude with a reflection on how a study of illegal organization is similar and different compared to overt, legal social organization. Specifically, we conclude by discussing how political conspiracies highlight the penalties that can accrue to brokers under specific conditions.

WATERGATE

Early morning June 17, 1972, five men were caught burglarizing the national headquarters of the Democratic Party at the Watergate Hotel. Evidence immediately suggested connections to the White House and the Committee to Re-Elect the President (or CRP, pronounced like creep). One of the burglars—James McCord—was on the payroll of CRP. Two other burglars were found with address books that had White House personnel and White House phone numbers listed in them.

The burglary was part of a wider plan within the Nixon Administration to place loyal Nixonites at the heads of the government agencies that dealt with surveillance. Then loyal Nixonites in agencies like the Central Intelligence Agency (hereafter CIA), the Federal Bureau of Investigation (hereafter FBI), the Internal Revenue Service (hereafter IRS), and so forth, would use the tools of government to damage political opponents, securing Nixon's successor as the next President. The Nixon Administration referred to this plan as "the Perpetual Presidency." Watergate was thus part of what is called "big-time corruption" in white-collar crime studies. Watergate was much more than a burglary.

The unit that carried out illegal covert activity was known as "the plumbers" because they were initially set up to stop "leaks" of classified government information to the press. One of the plumbers, G. Gordon Liddy, put together a plan to conduct illegal espionage against political opponents. Liddy drew up plans to bug the

Democratic National Headquarters at the Watergate Hotel and was authorized $250,000 to finance the operation.

In January 1973, the burglars were found guilty. Judge John J. Sirica sentenced the burglars on March 23, 1973. Initial sentences by Judge Sirica were harsh. Sirica gave burglars Bernard Barker, Frank Sturgis, Virgilio Gonzalez, and Eugenio Martinez 40-year prison sentences. E. Howard Hunt received a 35-year prison term. McCord feared prison and wrote a letter to Judge Sirica saying that "higher ups" in the White House were involved in the burglary, that the burglars were not the only conspirators, and that the burglary was not a CIA operation.

The United States Senate Watergate Investigative Committee asked James Butterfield if he was aware of any listening devices in the White House; he answered in the affirmative. The committee then subpoenaed the tapes Nixon had kept of conversations held in his office. Nixon originally refused to turn the tapes over, but the US Supreme Court ruled that he must.

When the committee listened to the tapes, they heard a conversation in a meeting on June 23, 1972 between President Nixon and Chief of Staff H.R. Haldeman in which Nixon and Haldeman conspired to order the CIA to tell the FBI to stop investigating the Watergate case because it would jeopardize CIA covert operations. This taped conversation between Haldeman and Nixon is the so-called "smoking gun" of Watergate—the President and his Chief of Staff were caught on tape plotting to use government agencies to illegally halt a criminal investigation.

As impeachment proceedings went forward, Republican leaders in the Senate told Nixon there were enough votes against him to remove him from office if he stood trial in the Senate. To preempt his impeachment, Nixon resigned the Office of the Presidency. Nixon resigned on August 9, 1974. President Ford pardoned Nixon on September 8, 1974.

The Social Organization of Political Conspiracy

Our structural model and theory of the social organization of the Watergate corruption depicts political conspiracies as a web of co-conspirators organized into a cadre and a set of clandestine cabals. Through this cadre/cabal organization, conspirators attempt to corrupt the official government.

A cadre is a highly manipulable skeleton organization of trained agents; it is sustained by political combat and is linked to a mass movement, as its members become leaders of wider groups in the community (Selznick, 1952). The cadre is engaged in the continuous pursuit of power by illegal means. In the case of Washington politics, the cadre's goal is the perpetual presidency. The White House's palace guard, aides, functionaries, allies, and friends promote, defend, and extend state capacity through overreaching, unacceptable, and often criminal means. They reach into government agencies, bureaus, and departments, along with campaign groups, lobbyists, corporate contributors, and other legal organizations involved in national politics.

In the Nixon White House, it is known that Nixon, John Ehrlichman, and H. Robert Haldeman, for example, formed part of the inner circle of the Administration—they formed the core of the Nixon Administration, what we are calling the cadre. Ehrlichman and Haldeman were sometimes referred to as "the Berlin Wall" and "the Dobermans" in reference to both their German surnames and the designed social barrier between them and the President. Haldeman and Ehrlichman erected the barrier and they acquired and maintained a power to exclude others as a result of using their exercise of domination. Other White House officials like Charles Colson or John N. Mitchell, for example, also formed part of the core cadre of Nixon's White House.

A cabal (Burns, 1955) is an organizational subunit or team that is part of the overall organization of the cadre. A cabal is a clandestine team assembled to carry out political sabotage, espionage, and other illegal activity. An example of a cabal would be the plumbers, whose members included H. Howard Hunt and G. Gordon Liddy. The Watergate conspiracy was organized around cabals assembled for illegal espionage, diversion of campaign funds, unethical campaign "dirty tricks," and the burglary itself.

Differentiation into cabals provides the conspiracy with effective coordination and heightened, but not perfect, secrecy from detection. Differentiating the conspirators into blocs of actors with appropriate talents forms the cabals required for specific illegal tactics and strategies. For example, by grouping former agents from the FBI and CIA with others of similar expertise in espionage together on the plumbers' unit, the cadre created an effective bloc of actors to carry out illegal espionage. Similarly, by grouping campaign fundraisers, financial managers, and professional accountants together, the cabal for procurement of illegal campaign funds, authorization and disbursement of those funds, and structuring the money trail through conduits was created.

Differentiation of conspirators into cabals not only facilitates coordinated action, it also facilitates secrecy. By creating the cabals to do the "dirty work," the core members of the cadre are only indirectly associated with illegal activity—it is the cabal members themselves, not the core cadre, who directly engage in wiretapping, espionage, and political sabotage.

The cadre/cabal conspirators do not operate in a social vacuum; individuals who are not part of the conspiracy constantly surround them. Conspirators regularly interact with the overt government and its agents. We call this circle of overt, legitimate actors that the conspirators operate within "the periphery." The periphery actors form an important environment of the conspiracy. Some periphery actors are targets of the conspiracy's strategies and tactics meant to illegally

manipulate the covert, official government. An example of a target located on the periphery of the conspiracy is the FBI director that the Nixon White House illegally manipulated to impede the Watergate investigation under the ruse of the FBI possibly exposing CIA covert operations if the FBI continued its investigation. Other periphery actors are simply obstacles for the conspirators; they are people from whom the conspirators must endeavor to keep the conspiracy secret. An example of such a periphery actor in the Watergate scandal would be Dr. Henry Kissinger. Kissinger was the Secretary of State, and was never indicted nor even accused by anyone of any serious merit of being involved in the Watergate corruption. Yet Kissinger interacted regularly with the cadre, including some of the cadre who were indicted and convicted as part of the conspiracy. In either case, whether the actor is an actual target or an innocent by-stander from whom the conspiracy must be kept secret, we refer to actors that interact with the conspirators, but who are not part of the conspiracy, as the periphery. Of particular interest here are those illegitimate, illegal, and covert practices that may be deemed corrupt; for behaviors to be deemed corrupt, a larger audience, beyond those involved, must view the action as inappropriate by some standard.

The above conceptualization of the social organization leads us to our first hypothesis:

Hypothesis 1: *Data on political conspiracies will show structurally similar blocs of actors that resemble cabals, a core cadre, and a peripheral set of actors.*

BROKERAGE AND MEDIATION

Political conspiracies rely on brokers between individuals and mediators between groups to integrate the cabals with each other and cabals with the cadre. A mediator is a social actor who brokers the relations of otherwise disconnected social groups of blocs of similar actors. In our definition, a social actor is not limited to an individual, but could also be a legitimate organization, cabal, or clique or the cadre. In the Watergate study, the mediators are actors that connect the core cadre with the cabals, and connect the cabals with other cabals. A broker is an actor who connects otherwise disconnected actors (Burt, 1976, 1992; Galaskiewicz, 1979; Marsden, 1982; Gould & Fernandez, 1989; Fernandez & Gould, 1994; Rider, 2009). Through brokerage and mediation, the differentiated cabals are integrated into a cohesive conspiracy designed to illegally manipulate the political order and official government.

Mediation is designed to facilitate inter-network communication between cadre and the cabal through the use of brokers. We focus on two types of brokers: gatekeepers and representatives (Gould & Fernandez, 1989; Fernandez & Gould, 1994).

Gatekeepers occupy a middle position and their work is to: a) buffer the core cadre or their own cabal from the demands on time and energy from outside personnel, b) shield top-level core cadre personnel or their own cabal members from outsiders, and c) filter communications, deciding what stays outside and is not let into the core cadre or their own cabal.

Representatives are the counterpart to the gatekeepers; they too occupy a middle position and their work is to: a) channel communications and demands from cadre to the cabal or cabal to cabal, b) shield cabal personnel from the inner workings of the cadre or other cabals, and c) color the communications from the cadre to the cabal or from cabal to cabal, making communications simpler, more concise, and more understandable from the viewpoint of the core cadre or their cabal, and hence easier to execute. As representatives of the core cadre or their own cabal, they mediate from inside the core cadre or their cabal to the outside; they decide what flows from the inside to the outside. The representatives achieve the following goal: bro-

kering relationships between the core cadre and the cabals or between their cabal and other cabals. Specialized roles enacted into positions go between the core cadre and the cabals, and the cabals themselves. Representatives have the capacity to withhold and control information between the cadre and the cabals and to shield the top members of the core cadre from cabal activities and information from the outside so the core cadre can have deniability.

The conspirators themselves were well aware of their mediating and brokering roles. John Dean describes his critical position as "linchpin" (Dean, 1977: 120–121), running communications between the White House cadre and the leadership of Committee to Re-elect the President, with its finance and campaign division of labor (see also Kutler, 1990: 239–241). In an interview some 30 years later, John Dean himself said his job was to work with personalities, and that he was the "glue trying to hold this together" (Corporation for Public Broadcasting, 2003). The historical record describes the mediating role of conspirators aptly as well. For example, "Dean acted as go-between between Haldeman-Ehrlichman and Mitchell-LaRue" (Woodward & Bernstein, 1974: 319).

Broker Penalty and Defection

Most sociological studies document the positive returns to brokers due to the social capital advantages of brokerage (see Burt, 2002, for a review). However, no theory exists highlighting the limitations, stresses, strains, and negative consequences that might accrue to brokers under certain social conditions. The historical record of Watergate suggests that, when actors deal with a powerful and at times punitive cadre, brokerage may be a dangerous social position. Brokerage and mediation can be a liability in some social contexts.

Network analysis has recently looked at how actors brokering within groups strengthen "localism" or loyalty to a local community rather than a national network (Hillmann, 2008). As Hillman notes, "the political danger of playing this position lies in brokers may become victims of the perception that they lack commitment to one block or subgroup and therefore cannot be trusted by either side" (Hillmann, 2008: 295). A case in point: Howard Hunt's request that the cadre "take care of" the burglars' families financially—which is a custom for CIA agents apprehended for spying in foreign countries. The Nixon White House perceived Hunt's request as nothing but blackmail.

The mediating position is also a source of strain for the mediators due to the often contradictory demands to serve both the cadre and the cabal while being expected to be a guise for each of these blocs simultaneously. An apt example of broker stress occurred in the containment stage of the conspiracy when the core cadre needed more "hush money" for the burglars. The money raisers at CRP were asked once again to ask political supporters for more money. The money raisers at CRP saw themselves abused by the cadre and were also embarrassed when trying to explain to the corporate donors why they needed more money and what it was being used for. The brokers became stressed under the interaction with donors as they were exposed to unsavory tactics and the clandestine conduit and money trails. These tactics exacerbate the unrest in the conspiracy. The consequence was a backlash among Hugh Sloan, Jeb Magruder, Fred LaRue, Robert Mardian, and other administrators and conduits for the illegal use of campaign funds and resources.

Brokers and mediators can be used as pawns to manipulate the cabals at the mediators' expense. Brokers and mediators can be used as symbolic buffers and decoys sacrificed for the cadre as the core cadre seals itself off from external exposure to wrongdoing or political controversies. John Dean, a broker by all accounts, was aware of being a

scapegoat for the cadre during the conspiracy's containment phase, and that is one of his reasons for defecting and offering testimony to the Senate investigative committee. Another example: Howard Hunt, a representative mediating between the core cadre and burglary cabal, after talking to Colson and knowing that Colson taped the call and had it transcribed, wrote: "I hung up feeling that the White House had not only thrown us to the wolves but bated us so that we would be a more tasty treat" (Hunt, 2007: 262).

Brokers are typecast, negatively, as "too cagey," which is an accusation of their becoming not only highly active, but also having a tendency to place their own self-interests ahead of the interests of the cabal. Dean spoke about the dangers of the broker role in his autobiography, where he describes using the counsel's office as a platform for exerting cadre influence into bureaus and agencies. "We asked to be designated the official White House liaison office for all the regulatory agencies. We added a lot of clearance functions, legal functions, legal power, and perquisite" (Dean, 1977: 145).

As the conspiracy enters its containment stage, it is the brokers that are likely to be cut from communication lines with the core cadre, as the core cadre attempts to seal its self off from the cabals. In Watergate, the core cadre called their sealing actions "circling the wagons." The unintended consequence of circling the wagons is the alienation and resentment from the cabal members who once relied on the broker to relay information about their relations with the cadre. With communication lines cut, cabal members struggle to make sense of what is going on, and their frustration grows into suspicion of the broker and the core cadre. A case in point: The burglars were not relieved when LaRue delivered a considerable amount of "hush money." Instead they interpreted the money to be "just enough" to keep them quiet until after the election—later, after the election, they thought, they would be "thrown to the wolves." A chorus of "commitments not honored" by the White House began in the burglar unit as they sat at trial, and then at sentencing.

As cabal/cadre relations strain in the crisis stage of the conspiracy, brokers may defect, and go over to the "other side," cooperating with prosecutors and investigators, implicating their co-conspirators in illegal and criminal action, and betraying others by revealing team secrets of the cadre. Most dangerously for the cadre, they may not only point fingers but also reveal the web of connections within the conspiracy, the conduits, brokers, money routes, couriers, payouts, payoffs, and policies for the accumulation of power.

Hypothesis 2: *Data on political conspiracies will show conspirators structurally located between other conspirators and groups of conspirators to be vulnerable to defection and legal penalties.*

DATA

We heed Gould's call for the use of network methods in historical research (Gould, 2003, 1991). Numerous books have been written by historians, journalists, and the principals themselves about Watergate, especially about the intrigues that marked Richard Nixon's White House staff and operations (Colson, 1976; Dean, 1977, 1982; Haldeman, 1978, 1994; Ehrlichman, 1982; Safire, 1975). In every historian's description of this Administration, in every journalist's depiction of the break-in and cover up, and in biographies of Nixon, there is a more or less explicit account of the coalitions, cabals, and alliances as well as the loyalties and betrayals (Black, 2007; Kutler, 1990; Perlstein, 2008, Summers, 2000; Sussman, 1974; White, 1975; Woodward & Bernstein, 1974). Fortunately for scholars of the minutiae of critical interaction and events among the participants, there are also extensive transcriptions of taped conversations between the White House principals Nixon,

Dean, Colson, Ehrlichman, Gray, Haldeman, Peterson, and others (Kutler, 1997).

There are numerous accounts written on or about the legal and illegal activities of conspirators working at the Committee to Re-Elect the President (Magruder, 1974, 1978; Rosen, 2008; Stans, 1985; Ulasewicz & McKeever, 1990), the burglar and wire-tapping cabal and the illegal work of Hunt, Liddy, McCord, and the so-called Five Cubans (Hunt, 1974, 2007; Liddy, 1996), including details about the multiple break-ins, illegal "dirty money" campaign funds, dirty tricks pulled on the Democratic candidates, plus the tactics of containment and cover-up (Lukas, 1976; McCarthy, 1978; Adler, 1976; Sussman, 1974; Weissman, 1974). The Senate Select Committee also provided documentation of both legal and illegal campaign activities (United States Congress, 1973). And Mark Felt at the Federal Bureau of Investigation was of continuing fascination for Watergate investigators and historians in his role as Woodward's confidant (Felt & De Toledano, 1979; Felt & O'Connor, 2006; Garment, 2001; Hougan, 1984; Woodward, 2005).

Background to the Watergate scandal and the Nixon years can be found in a number of sources (Abrahamsen, 1977; Alexander, 1988; Emery, 1994; Fremon, 1998; Gray, 2008; Lukas, 1976; McCarthy, 1978; Olson, 2003; Sirica, 1979; White, 1975; Woodward & Bernstein, 1974). As we carefully read and watched each of these historical narratives and artifacts, we made careful notes of who did what with whom. Notes were made with a structured code sheet. From these structured notes, we constructed a number of sociomatrices of Watergate action. Our data scores high on reliability. The two researchers agreed in nearly all cases and, where disagreements occurred, rereading the multiple sources and independently recoding positions and their actors resolved them. This internal consistency between the coders meets the standards of high reliability. Moreover, we believe our coding to meet the criterion of face validity because almost all of the claims of the conspirators about who did what with whom were also cited by another Watergate co-conspirator or a journalist covering Watergate.

Sociomatrices

For this research article, we coded two sociomatrices, which we refer to as:

- The Working Web of Watergate Action; and
- The Sociomatrix of Who Testified Against Whom at Trial.

The first sociomatrix—the Working Web of Watergate Action—was constructed by simply putting a "1" in the sociomatrix if the two corresponding co-conspirators worked together on illegal espionage, on sabotage, or as covert money conduits. If the two conspirators did not work together on illegal activities, then we entered a "0" in the sociomatrix at the point where the column and row of the two conspirators intersect. This first sociomatrix essentially maps out who worked with whom in the illegal action of Watergate.

The second sociomatrix—the Sociomatrix of Who Testified Against Whom at Trial—was constructed by putting a "1" in the sociomatrix if the conspirator in the row of the matrix testified against the conspirator found in the column of the matrix. If the conspirator in the row of the matrix did not testify against the conspirator in the column of the matrix, then a "0" was entered in the sociomatrix at the point where the column and row of the two conspirators intersect. This matrix is a key map of one important part of conspiracy defection.

The Sociomatrix of Who Testified Against Whom at Trial reflects much more than prosecutor strategies and tactics at trial. Legal strategies and tactics are structurally coupled

with the actual information available about wrongdoing, which is in turn structurally coupled to conspirators' positions in the illegal networks of Watergate action. Prosecutors do not have a case without testimony about wrongdoing and therefore their courtroom strategies are structurally coupled with information about wrongdoing. Brokers are in a structural position both to observe other conspirators and to be observed, which in turn yields information for brokers to trade with prosecutors as testimony against their co-conspirators as well as yielding testimony from other conspirators that prosecutors can use against them. Brokerage position, observation of wrongdoing, and testimony are thus intrinsic to the prosecutor's trial strategy and therefore the Sociomatrix of Who Testified Against Whom at Trial is driven by social position in networks. Graphs of the sociomatrices are reported below (Figures 15.1 and 15.2).

The Working Web

Figure 15.1 graphs the social relations of the Working Web of Watergate Action. The conspirator's name is placed in a blocked label, and a line running between two conspirators indicates that they worked together on illegal activity.

Who Testified Against Whom at Trial

Figure 15.2 graphs the social relations of who testified against whom at trial. The graph shows the conspirator's name placed in a blocked label. The lines are directed, as indicated with an arrow, signifying that the conspirator with the arrow pointing away testified against the conspirator the arrow points toward.

MEASURES

A number of the hypotheses can be investigated by simply examining the graphs in

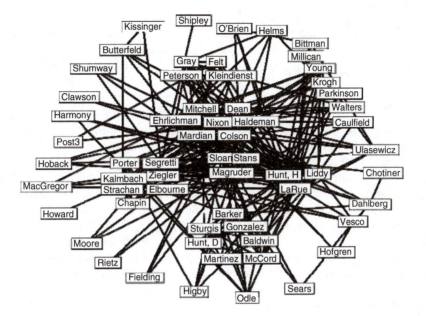

Figure 15.1 The Working Web of Watergate Action

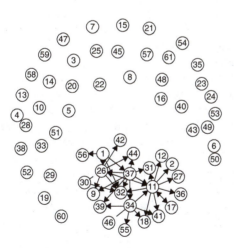

Actor Identities

1.	Baldwin	32.	Liddy
2.	Barker	33.	MacGregor
3.	Bittman	34.	Magruder
4.	Butterfield	35.	Mardian
5.	Caulfield	36.	Martinez
6.	Chapin	37.	McCord
7.	Chotiner	38.	Millican
8.	Clawson	39.	Mitchell
9.	Colson	40.	Moore
10.	Dahlberg	41.	Nixon
11.	Dean	42.	O'Brien
12.	Ehrlichman	43.	Odle
13.	Elbourne	44.	Parkinson
14.	Felt	45.	Peterson
15.	Fielding	46.	Porter
16.	Gonzalez	47.	"Post3"
17.	Gray	48.	Rietz
18.	Haldeman	49.	Sears
19.	Harmony	50.	Segretti
20.	Helms	51.	Shipley
21.	Hoback	52.	Shumway
22.	Higby	53.	Sloan
23.	Hofgren	54.	Stans
24.	Howard	55.	Strachan
25.	Hunt, D	56.	Sturgis
26.	Hunt, H	57.	Ulasewicz
27.	Kalmbach	58.	Vesco
28.	Kissinger	59.	Walters
29.	Kleindienst	60.	Young
30.	Krogh	61.	Ziegler
31.	LaRue		

Figure 15.2 Who Testified Against Whom at Trial

Figures 15.1 and 15.2 with the hypothesis in mind. Looking at what predicts the variance of a dependent variable will pursue other hypotheses.

Dependent Variables

We use a number of dependent variables and sociometric measures to investigate the above hypotheses. Defection forms an important dependent variable for this study. We define defection as an act that symbolizes, communicates, and carries out an actor's breaking from the organizational goals of the conspiracy.

Defection plays a crucial role in the breakdown of political conspiracies. We measure two types of defection. We simply refer to the types of defection as primary and secondary defection. We define primary and secondary defection below.

Primary defection is an act of defection that breaks off commitment to the goals of the conspiracy through a variety of means, but the means of breaking off from the conspiracy fall short of a direct report to external regulators, prosecutors, judges, grand juries, and/or Senate investigative committees. Primary defection can involve purposeful shirking. Primary defection can involve the following defection strategies:

- Defection by complaint: The conspirator secretly complains to outsiders;
- Defection by opportunism: The conspirator secretly misappropriates valuable resources;
- Defection by exit: The conspirator voluntarily and publicly relinquishes his or her role in the organization;
- Defection by extortion: The conspirator threatens to reveal organizational or team secrets to external regulators, prosecutors, judges, grand juries, and/or Senate investigative committees;
- Defection by sabotage: The conspirator undermines the work of the conspiracy by supplying subordinates, superiors, and peers with inaccurate, incomplete, and untimely or stale information;
- Defection by covert alliance: The conspirator secretly allies with one or more elements of the opposition, or rival factions outside the conspiracy, without the consent or control of the secret organization.

Secondary defection is an act of defection that breaks off participation in the goals of the conspiracy by means of testifying to prosecutors, grand juries, judges, or special investigative committees. In a nutshell, secondary defection involves subversion and rebellion or resistance. Examples of secondary defection include:

- James McCord's public testimony during the Watergate Senate hearings;
- Jeb Magruder's public testimony against John N. Mitchell and John Ehrlichman;
- John Dean's public, televised testimony implicating President Nixon, his chiefs of staff, aides, and others involved in the conspiracy.

As we read the Watergate material discussed in the data section, we coded the conspirators as carrying out either primary or secondary defection. If a conspirator was a primary defector, the conspirator was coded with a 1 on the primary defection variable; otherwise, they were coded with a 0. Similarly, if a conspirator was a secondary defector, the conspirator was coded with a 1 on the secondary defection variable; otherwise, they were coded with a 0.

An additional two dependent variables are derived from the matrix of who testified against whom at trial. The row sums of this matrix count the number of times a conspirator testified against other conspirators. The column sums of this matrix count the number of times a conspirator was testified against by other conspirators.

Finally, length of sentencing at trial and verdict at court form our final dependent variables. We measure the length of "time served" for each conspirator in months. We measure guilt at trial through an indicator variable, where 1 is guilty and 0 is not guilty.

Independent Variables

We used the standard network measure of betweenness centrality to measure the extent to which a conspirator connected other actors—or lay between two actors—in the sociomatrix of the Web of Watergate Action (see Wasserman & Faust, 1994).

We not only measure the brokerage between individual conspirators, but we also measure the mediation of groups by individual conspirators. The key groups in the conspiracy are the espionage cabals, the political sabotage cabals, the core cadre, and so on. We coded each conspirator according to whether they played a mediating role between these groups.

First, we coded each conspirator in terms of whether they played a gatekeeper role mediating their cabal or core cadre members with other cabals. A gatekeeper serves to buffer contact from those outside the core cadre. The clearest examples of gatekeepers are perhaps H.R. Haldeman and John Ehrlichman. Haldeman and Ehrlichman were famous for keeping outsiders away from the President; they were nicknamed "the Berlin Wall" for doing just that. "Chuck" Colson is another example of a gatekeeper because Colson assisted the Berlin Wall, keeping Hunt away from the White House once Hunt's role in the burglary was revealed. Hunt, in turn, had played the role of gatekeeper prior to the burglary arrests by keeping the burglar unit away from contact with the core cadre. Sloan, Magruder, and Chapin are other examples of gatekeepers since they each played a role in keeping campaign workers at CRP from directly communicating with the cadre. For each conspirator, we considered all their relations with the other cabals and core cadre. If the conspirator played a gatekeeper role, we scored the conspirator with a 1 for the variable and 0 otherwise.

Next, we coded each conspirator in terms of whether they played a representative role mediating their cabal or core cadre members with other cabals. A representative serves to actively contact those outside their core cadre or cabal. An example of a representative would be E. Howard Hunt. Hunt made the case for the burglars to the core cadre, explaining to the cadre that they needed cash assistance for their families while they served prison time. John Dean also serves as an example of a representative—it was Dean who made the cadre's case to Deputy Director of Intelligence Vernon Walters that the CIA should instruct the FBI to back off investigating Watergate. For each conspirator, we considered all their relations with the other cabals and core cadre. If the conspirator played a representative role, we scored the conspirator with a 1 for the variable and 0 otherwise.

Some conspirators were coded as both representative and gatekeeper because representative and gatekeeper are not mutually exclusive roles. For example, as mentioned above, Howard Hunt at an early phase of the conspiracy, prior to the burglars' arrest, played a gatekeeper role, keeping the burglar unit away from contact with the core cadre. Hunt was also a representative. When Hunt and the burglars stood trial, it was Hunt who represented the burglars' case for financial assistance for the burglars' families as they served prison time.

METHODS

Our hypotheses are tested using historical sociology to uncover the patterns of interaction in the Watergate scandal, standard sociomatrix measures, blockmodeling, logistic regression, and quadratic assignment procedure (QAP) analysis.

Blockmodeling

We do not assume social structure. We instead empirically investigate social structure by recovery of the naturally occurring social networks of blocs via biographical and autobiographic writings. The autobiographic and bibliographical information provides rich data of who did what with whom in the Watergate corruption. Virtually all of the information of who did what with whom for the major events of Watergate corruption is cross-validated by these sources. Distilling the social architecture of who did what with whom is greatly facilitated by blockmodeling (Arabie, Boorman, & Levitt, 1978; Bearman, 1993; Faulkner, 1983; White, Boorman, & Breiger, 1976; Winship, 1988).

Blockmodeling is a multivariate statistical technique that identifies actors who have common patterns of interaction with other actors. Blockmodeling uses a clustering algorithm to group conspirators together *based on their relations with other conspirators.* Conspirators who share similar relations—those who worked with similar others—are clustered together into similar groups. The visual depiction of these clusters enables the social researcher to discover the social structure of conspiracy, rather than to assume it.

Regression Modeling

Logistic regression modeling is suitable for dichotomous dependent variables. We model the probability of a conspirator defecting as we have defined both primary and secondary defection. We also use a logistic regression to predict guilt or innocence of the conspirators at trial, whether a conspirator testified against co-conspirators, or whether other conspirators testified against a conspirator.

QAP Analysis

Quadratic assignment procedure analysis is a bootstrap method that measures the level of association of two sociomatrices. Of particular interest is to see if the finger pointing at trial matrices is related to the other sociomatrices of Watergate relations and action. QAP analysis takes two matrices in question and uses an empirical sampling distribution to estimate their association. Mechanically speaking, the interpretation of the procedure is something like interpreting a correlation coefficient and then assessing the probability of the coefficient using a p-value (see Krackhardt, 1987, for a discussion of quadratic assignment procedure).

RESULTS

Hypothesis 1 predicts that data on political conspiracies will show conspirators to be socially organized into distinct teams of clandestine activity. Figure 15.1 clearly shows this. In Figure 15.1, we organized the nodes or actors according to the results of the cluster analysis—a standard procedure of blockmodeling. We used the Ward clustering algorithm for these data. Figure 15.1 shows five structurally equivalent groups—which is equivalent to the role structure of the conspiracy. Figure 15.1 shows the core cadre of Nixon, Haldeman, Ehrlichman, Mitchell, Colson, and Dean. Next, Figure 15.1 shows how the blockmodeling grouped together Felt, Peterson, and Kleindienst. This group represents the agents of government bureaus that the core cadre attempted to manipulate in the cover-up and as part of the plans of the perpetual presidency. Another structurally equivalent group is seen among the conspirators Kalmbach, Porter, Segretti, Strachan, Ziegler, Chapin, and Elbourne. These conspirators formed the political campaign group, with many drifting into unethical and sometimes illegal "dirty tricks." The blockmodeling also groups together Magruder, Sloan, and Stans. This group formed the finance group of the official White House and participated as covert money conduits for the cabals and cadre. The burglars themselves are seen in the group labeled Gonzalez, McCord, Barker, Baldwin, Hunt (Dorothy), Sturgis, and Martinez—this is the burglar team as caught in the Watergate, plus Dorothy Hunt, who was a conduit of "hush money" for the burglars. Another group consists of Hunt (Howard), LaRue, and Liddy—these are the organization leaders of "the plumbers" and the organizers of the burglary team. The cluster analysis grouped together a number of peripheral actors; we organized these conspirators as a group circling the true conspirators in Figure 15.1.

Figure 15.1 shows that the conspirators organized themselves into structurally distinct clandestine teams or cabals. Figure 15.1 also shows a core cadre and a periphery of actors that the conspirators regularly interacted with. Figure 15.1 is also consistent with the historical record of the conspiracy. Hypothesis 1 states cabals, a periphery, and a core cadre would organize the conspiracy, which is clearly supported by these data.

Hypothesis 2 states that conspirators who are mediators or are high in betweenness centrality will be likely to defect. A number of regression models offer support for this hypothesis. We also conducted a QAP analysis that showed that the Sociomatrix of the Web of Watergate Action is correlated with the Sociomatrix of Who Testified Against Whom at trial with a coefficient of 0.183, with a probability of this coefficient being due to sampling chance of $p \leq 0.001$.

We model the effects of the independent variables measuring types of mediation—betweenness centrality, gatekeeper, and representative—on the probability of defection, guilt at court, and jail time served separately because the independent variables are highly correlated or co-linear since they are derived from an inter-related network or relations. We note that the models reported in the tables are independently estimated bivariate models.

Table 15.1 reports the results of a set of separate logistic regression models using betweenness centrality to predict a number of important conspiracy outcomes. Row 1 models the probability that a conspirator testified against another co-conspirator at trial and shows a positive coefficient significant at the 0.05 significance level, implying that as betweenness centrality increases, the probability that a given conspirator testifies against another co-conspirator increases as well, which is consistent with Hypothesis 2. Row 2 models the probability that a conspirator was testified against—was the object of testimony—by another co-conspirator at trial and shows a positive coefficient significant at the 0.001 level, implying that as betweenness centrality increases, the probability that a given conspirator is testified against by another co-conspirator increases as well, which is consistent with Hypothesis 2. Row 3 models the probability that a conspirator engaged in primary, or Type I, defection and shows that the coefficient is not significant at the 0.1 level. Row 4 models the probability that a conspirator engaged in secondary, or Type II, defection and reports a positive coefficient significant at the 0.05 level, implying that as betweenness centrality increases, the probability that a given conspirator engages in Type II defection increases as well, which is consistent with Hypothesis 2. Row 5 models the probability that a conspirator was found guilty in court and reports a positive coefficient significant at the 0.001 level, implying that as betweenness centrality increases, the probability that a given conspirator was found guilty increases as well, which is consistent with Hypothesis 2.

Table 15.2 reports the results of a set of separate logistic regression models using gatekeeper position between the cabals and cadre to predict a number of important conspiracy outcomes. Row 1 models the probability that a conspirator testified against another co-conspirator at trial and shows a positive coefficient significant at the 0.01 level, implying that gatekeeper position increases the probability that a given conspirator

Table 15.1 Logistic regression estimates of betweenness centrality predicting conspiracy outcomes

Dependent Variable	Estimate	Std. Error	z value
(1) Probability of Testifying Against Co-conspirators	0.0124*	0.0059	2.12
(2) Probability of Being Testified Against	0.0260***	0.0076	3.42
(3) Probability of Type I Defection	0.0060	0.0053	1.13
(4) Probability of Type II Defection	0.0127*	0.0059	2.16
(5) Probability of Guilt in Court	0.0235***	0.0070	3.35

Notes

*$p = 0.05$; **$p = 0.01$; ***$p = 0.001$

testifies against another co-conspirator, which is consistent with Hypothesis 2. Row 2 models the probability that a conspirator was testified against—was the object of testimony—by another co-conspirator at trial and shows a positive coefficient significant at the 0.001 level, implying that gatekeeper position increases the probability that a conspirator is testified against by another co-conspirator, which is consistent with Hypothesis 2. Row 3 models the probability that a conspirator engaged in primary, or Type I, defection and reports a positive coefficient significant at the 0.05 level, implying that gatekeeper position increases the probability that a given conspirator engages in Type I defection, which is consistent with Hypothesis 2. Row 4 models the probability that a conspirator engaged in secondary, or Type II, defection and reports a positive coefficient significant at the 0.05 level, implying that gatekeeper position increases the prob-

ability that a given conspirator engages in Type II defection, which is consistent with Hypothesis 2. Row 5 models the probability that a conspirator was found guilty in court and reports a positive coefficient significant at the 0.001 level, implying that gatekeeper position increases the probability that a given conspirator was found guilty, which is consistent with Hypothesis 2.

Table 15.3 reports the results of a set of separate logistic regression models using representative position between the cabals and cadre to predict a number of important conspiracy outcomes. Row 1 models the probability that a conspirator testified against another co-conspirator at trial and shows a positive coefficient significant at the 0.05 level, implying that representative position increases the probability that a given conspirator testifies against another co-conspirator, which is consistent with Hypothesis 2. Row 2 models the probability that a conspirator

Table 15.2 Logistic regression estimates of gatekeeper status predicting conspiracy outcomes

Dependent Variable	Estimate	Std. Error	z value
(1) Probability of Testifying Against Co-conspirators	3.5329**	1.299	3.13
(2) Probability of Being Testified Against	2.4849***	0.6872	3.62
(3) Probability of Type I Defection	1.3610*	0.6775	2.01
(4) Probability of Type II Defection	3.5329**	1.1299	3.13
(5) Probability of Guilt in Court	2.9978***	0.7499	4.00

Notes

*$p = 0.05$; **$p = 0.01$; ***$p = 0.001$

was testified against—was the object of testimony—by another co-conspirator at trial and shows a positive coefficient significant at the 0.01 level, implying that representative position increases the probability that a conspirator is testified against by another co-conspirator, which is consistent with Hypothesis 2. Row 3 models the probability that a conspirator engaged in primary, or Type I, defection and reports a positive coefficient significant at the 0.1 level, implying that representative position increases the probability that a given conspirator engages in Type I defection, which is consistent with Hypothesis 2. Row 4 models the probability that a conspirator engaged in secondary, or Type II, defection and reports a positive coefficient, consistent with Hypothesis 2, but the coefficient is not significant. Row 5 models the probability that a conspirator was found guilty in court and reports a positive coefficient consistent with Hypothesis 2, but the coefficient is not significant.

Table 15.4 reports the results of a set of separate ordinary least squares regression models using betweenness centrality and then gatekeeper and representative position between the cabals and cadre to predict the length of prison time served for those Watergate conspirators found guilty in court. Row 1 models betweenness centrality predicting length of sentence served and reports a positive coefficient significant at the 0.05 level, implying that as betweenness centrality increases, so too does the length of sentence served, which is consistent with Hypothesis 2. Row 2 models gatekeeper status predicting the length of time served and reports a coefficient of 4.5417, which can be interpreted to mean that, among the conspirators that served time, gatekeepers on average served an additional 4.5417 more months in prison, but the coefficient is not significant. Row 3 models gatekeeper status predicting the length of time served and reports a coefficient of 8.8297, which can be interpreted to mean that, among the conspirators that served time, gatekeepers on average served an additional 8.8 more months in prison, but the coefficient is not significant.

Table 15.3 Logistic regression estimates of representative status predicting conspiracy outcomes

Dependent Variable	Estimate	Std. Error	z value
(1) Probability of Testifying Against Co-conspirators	1.5870*	0.7961	1.99
(2) Probability of Being Testified Against	1.9095**	0.6872	2.78
(3) Probability of Type I Defection	1.2977	0.7016	1.85
(4) Probability of Type II Defection	0.9478	0.8103	1.17
(5) Probability of Guilt in Court	1.0415	0.6406	1.63

Notes
*$p = 0.05$; **$p = 0.01$; ***$p = 0.001$

Table 15.4 Regression estimates of brokerage and mediation predicting prison time served

Dependent Variable	Estimate	Std. Error	t value
(1) Betweenness Centrality	0.0878*	0.0341	2.57
(2) Gatekeeper Status	4.5417	5.5395	0.82
(3) Representative Status	8.8297	5.4082	1.63

Notes
*$p = 0.05$; **$p = 0.01$; ***$p = 0.001$

DISCUSSION

The empirical findings of the QAP analysis show that the matrix of working conspiracy relations—the matrix of who worked with whom to carry out the Watergate corruption—is significantly related to who testified against whom in the trials of Watergate.

The empirical findings show that betweenness centrality is related to Type II defection and testifying against other conspirators at trial. Betweenness centrality also increases the risk of being testified against at trial, as well as increasing the probability of being found guilty at trial and the length of sentence.

The empirical findings also show that gatekeeper status between the cabals, and the cabals and core cadre, is related to both Type I and Type II defection, testifying against other conspirators at trial, and being testified against by other conspirators at trial. Gatekeeper status also increases the probability of a Watergate conspirator being found guilty at trial.

The empirical findings further show that representative status between the cabals, and the cabals and core cadre is related to testifying against other conspirators at trial, and to being testified against by other conspirators at trial.

The results of our regressions show that brokerage had penalties for conspirators and the conspiracy, but a close reading of the historical record shows that, in the earlier phases of the Watergate corruption, brokerage had a premium for the conspiracy. In the early stages of the conspiracy, brokerage and mediation enabled the conspirators to carry out many of the plans of the perpetual presidency in secrecy and in coordinated action. Brokerage and mediation enable the political conspiracy to be differentiated into cabals that were simultaneously integrated into a web of conspiracies directed by a core cadre. Mediation and brokerage allowed Watergate to be organized as many conspiracies, organized by one cadre pursuing the per-petual presidency. Mediation and brokerage allowed flexibility in the Watergate conspiracy. Brokers and mediators delivered "hush money" to keep conspirators from testifying against the cadre. Brokers and conspirators assembled illegal spy operations, keeping the core cadre distant from such activity, while providing an organized means to communicate the results back to the cadre. Brokers and mediators laundered money. And brokers and mediators sabotaged the political campaigns of Nixon's enemies. But in the end, it was the brokers and mediators who defected. There is both a premium and a penalty to brokerage.

There are two mechanisms that we believe help explain the dynamics of brokerage in terms of whether brokerage is a premium or a penalty for the conspirators and the conspiracy. The first contingency is the status of the cadre's authority over the cabals—do the cabals perceive the cadre as acting with authority or acting in terms of sheer power? The status of authority varies by stages in the conspiracy—which can be called the normal "working stage" and the "crisis stage." The second contingency shaping whether brokerage is a premium or a penalty is whether brokerage is horizontal or vertical.

When the brokers perceive the core cadre as holding legitimate authority, the brokers follow the scripts assigned to them by the cadre, which is seen to be the "glue" holding the conspiracy together. In the normal, routine working stage of a conspiracy, brokerage operates as it should: it coordinates cabals with the cadre and keeps the cadre at enough distance from the illegal activity to maintain secrecy. However, when brokers begin to question the authority of the cadre, the conspiracy enters a crisis stage and the cadre is vulnerable to broker defection because brokers can use their structural position to their advantage as a strategic premium. In fact, in Watergate, the core cadre was extremely sensitive about their being perceived as legitimate and developed their own argot to communicate concerns that their authority had lost its hold over the conspirators. For example, the core cadre frequently used the phrase "off the reservation" to communicate concerns about a wayward conspirator. And the cadre's concerns were justified.

Being set up as scapegoats, and worries about being "thrown to the wolves," ruined the perception of the cadre holding legitimate authority once held by the cabals and the brokers themselves. In the end, the cadre learned that the brokerage position gave brokers the structural resources to act autonomously through defection. Brokers were in the thick of the conspiracy and had a lot to offer prosecutors in plea deals when the Watergate ship began to sink. There is no greater profound statement of autonomy than defecting from the cadre, and brokers asserted their autonomy and brokerage premium by defecting. The brokers used their structural position of betweenness to turn the tables on the cadre—from the cabal/cadre crossroads they placed the cadre in the prosecutor's crosshairs. When authority vanished from the brokers' perceptions of the cadre, the brokers used their structural autonomy due to their betweenness to play the cadre off against the legal system. This "playing one side against the other" was possible because they were in the middle of the Watergate action and had witnessed the inner workings of the conspiracy—they had information to trade in plea bargains. Ironically, what was a premium for the brokers was a penalty for the core cadre's conspiracy because, as each broker cut deals with prosecutors, the conspiracy moved quickly to collapse.

A second contingency that explains whether there is a brokerage premium or a brokerage penalty hinges on whether the brokerage is vertical or horizontal. Much of the network literature on brokerage studies voluntary action settings, like markets, where the absence of a clear organizational hierarchy means the brokerage is tying together actors or mediating groups horizontally. In horizontal brokerage, the broker as ego is assumed to be in strategic control of the social action at the brokerage position. In contrast, for political/authority relations, brokerage may more often be characterized as vertical brokerage. In political conspiracies, brokers are connecting actors and mediating groups that have clear hierarchical responsibilities and expectations. For example, the plumbers were subordinate to the core cadre. The plumbers could ask for resources and offer advice and input about budget needs and strategic plans, but the final say about what plans were to be carried through rested with the core cadre. While the plumbers were subordinate to the core cadre, the burglars were in turn subordinate to the plumbers. An example at the actor level: Dean, Magruder, Sloan, and Porter, and other brokers, generally speaking, did not carry out their own self-direction but were following directions from Ehrlichman, Haldeman, Mitchell, or some other core cadre member. These brokers may have been the authors of some minor acts of their brokerage role, but clear directions communicated by the core cadre to each individual broker tightly scripted the main contours of their brokerage actions. Until they defected, these brokers were instructed to bring together the cabals, and they were not instructed, nor given the choice, to play one cabal off against the other to gain their individual self-interest. Political conspiracies thus operate under vertical brokerage.

The breakdown of vertical brokerage is in turn related to a collapse of cadre authority because vertical brokerage requires a sense of trust among the cabal members that the cadre and the brokers that serve it will not betray the cabals. Because the normal operations of the broker in the political conspiracy are best characterized as vertical brokerage, the conspiracy normally operates under the assumption that the broker is in service to the core cadre. Thus vertical brokerage works in the normal working stage of the conspiracy when the cabals still perceive the authority of the cadre as legitimate. However, in the crisis phase of the conspiracy, vertical brokerage leads to suspicions among the cabals that the broker has betrayed or may betray the cabal in favor of the core cadre. Brokers as liaisons and representatives for a cabal may be perceived as beholden to the leadership cadre. As such, they will be distrusted by their own group and penalized by its members. Brokers as representatives for the cadre may be perceived as deploying heavy-handed tactics as they reach into a cabal to direct its operations and personnel. As such, they will become hated by the leadership of the affected cabal and penalized by them. Power begets resistance. Thus, during the crisis stage of the conspiracy, the collapse of the cabals' perception of authority in the cadre furthers the breakdown of trust in the cadre—a trust the brokers need so that their communications between the cabals and the cadre are interpreted in friendly, cooperative terms, rather than with suspicion and doubt. In the crisis stage, the distrust is not limited to cabals distrusting the core cadre, but the distrust begins to reverberate from all sides as the core cadre comes to distrust the cabals as well.

In the crisis stage, mutual distrust sets in between the blocs. Brokers as gatekeepers for a cabal may be perceived as distorting information for their own self-interest or as altering communication they receive from another subgroup (i.e., another cabal or from the leadership cadre). As such, they will be suspected of disloyalty to their own group and penalized by its members. During the crisis stage, the mutual distrust is channeled from cabals and cadre toward the broker mediation positions due to the structural organization of the conspiracy. Distrust, enmity, and hostile action overload at the brokerage and mediation positions. It was this structural stress that led to the breakdown of brokerage.

CONCLUSION

The dominant way of thinking about political conspiracies in social science is to view the entire system from the top down as if there were only a single group—or bloc, or leadership cadre—dictating and regulating everything. The Watergate conspiracy did have a single leadership group lead by all the President's men; but, by contrast, there were individual blocs or cabals involved in different tasks, struggling among themselves and with the White House for extended periods, trying to find methods and tactics that would insulate the core and stockpile resources (Thompson, 1967) for their political espionage and sabotage conspiracy.

The dominant way (as portrayed in Woodward and Bernstein's book *All The President's Men*) is overly simplified. It is essentially a one-level representation of a multileveled world. The perverse view is that the WoodSteins (as Woodward and Bernstein were referred to by their colleagues at the Washington Post) and political/economic analysts see only the cadre or "the government" as the key actor. They ignore the dense networks, their complex organization of differentiation and mediating roles integrating the cabals, and the "struggles," as we have noted above, and then the solution is the cadre-imposed solution, as if they are the all-controlling actors who manage and control everything. Yes, the cadre did try to control the crisis in the conspiracy, but the cadre's solution and its policy of "containment" backfired—the cadre's solution exacerbated the situation. The result was mutual antagonism and disaster in the long run. Individuals in the blocs tried to cope with various problems, and that included the mediators or brokers between the blocs. Our network analysis draws attention to the compound constituency or numerous blocs with delegated work (burglary, wiretapping, campaign sabotage, money procurement, money transfers, etc.). They faced internal divisions, dyadic discontent, and troubles with communication across to other blocs.

Economists' game theory models and sociologists working within rational actor assumptions predict that political conspiracies succumb to defection as state authorities detect wrongdoing and threaten punishment. Although strategic action is part of the defection process, we contend that game theory and rational actor assumptions and analysis do not offer a model predicting which specific actors defect in political conspiracies. We argue that the assertion of the economist's abstract, deductive, game theoretic framework is distinct from understanding the conditions that foster or suppress the collapse of conspiracies.

We have depicted the game theory approach as a black box explanation in which a generalized rational actor goes into the box and somehow comes out a defector. In the classic prisoner's dilemma game, the police do not have enough information to convict the prisoners. The game is then designed so that, if both testify against each other, each prisoner receives three months in prison. If one prisoner testifies against the other, and the other prisoner does not, the betrayer goes free but the silent prisoner receives a one-year prison sentence. If both prisoners remain silent, then they each receive a one-month sentence (see Poundstone, 1992, for an overview of the prisoner's dilemma). As analytically interesting as game theory is, it remains highly artificial, in our view, because it is too abstract and too far removed from social reality. Specifically, the game theory approach offers no conceptualization of the variation in roles and social positions among the conspirators and, perhaps even worse, has no explanation about why some conspirators defect while others do not.

Thus, the game-based approach provides limited insight into why a specific individual in a conspiracy is involved in defecting. Thus, the deductive and abstract game theoretic approach ignores the ways in which people

are empirically connected to one another in and through dyads and blocs and how those connections influence the propensity for defection. We have shown how structural sociology overcomes these limitations and have shown that structural sociology predicts which specific individuals are likely to defect in political conspiracies. We show that those occupying in-between positions in a social network are exceptionally prone to defection and increase the likelihood of one person testifying against another at trial.

Our structural model and theory of the social organization of the Watergate corruption depicts political conspiracies as a web of co-conspirators organized into a cadre and a set of clandestine cabals. Through this cadre/cabal organization, conspirators attempt to corrupt the official government. To coordinate the cabals and to maintain the secrecy of the illegal actions, the cadre creates various social roles for the conspirators that govern the flow of communication between the cadre and the cabals. Expectations and responsibilities of who reports to whom are communicated from the cadre to specific conspirators and constitutes the role assignment of broker. The role of broker is related to structural positioning between social groups—i.e., between the cabals and the cadre, and between the cabals themselves.

Network analysis of the Watergate scandal identifies a new dilemma of inter-mediation in conspiracies and the liabilities of the liaison. In terms of contributing to the coordination and secrecy of the conspiracy, brokerage plays a positive role for the social organization of conspiracy. However, from the perspective of cadre discipline and control, the individual autonomy that brokerage creates also constitutes the opportunities for brokers to break ranks and exploit the conspiracy for their own individual benefit. Moreover, brokers face an enormous amount of pressure and structural strain as their positioning between two or more groups often leaves brokers facing incompatible and contradictory demands. Thus it is the structural position of the broker that predicts defection from the conspiracy. The irony of brokerage is that, in political conspiracies, it facilitates the positive group contributions of coordination and secrecy while it simultaneously creates individual stress and individual autonomy that leads to broker defection and conspiracy collapse.

Brokerage can be either a premium or a penalty for conspiracy organization and for its conspirators; these crucial outcomes of brokerage depend on two conspiracy contingencies. We have identified the contingencies of vertical brokerage and conspiracy stages, which consist of periods of normal operations under perceived cadre authority, and a crisis stage of dysfunctional distrust in the cadre and the resulting devastating breakdown of brokerage. In the normal working stage of the conspiracy, brokered communications are met with confidence and, under this situation, brokerage works to keep the cadre and cabals coordinated, while simultaneously keeping the cadre at a secretly safe distance from the illegal work of the cabals. Brokers are a small subset of highly resourceful and interested members. This is why they are critical and enjoy a broker premium initially because they make things work. This explains why successful collective action tends to emerge initially in response to the crisis in Watergate. The tactics backfire and brokers become the targets of typecasting, suspicion, and enmity. However, as the conspiracy enters a crisis stage due to an erosion of perceived cadre authority, the confidence in the cadre required for brokered cadre–cabal communication breaks down, resulting in structural stress and strain at the brokerage position. The cabals' distrust, suspicion, and sense of betrayal toward the cadre are not evenly distributed; they are focused and overloaded at the brokerage positions. Brokers feel the hostility and hear the invective from all sides. They are in the crosshairs, as evidenced by their being testified against at

trial and their own reflective biographies in which they write about their awareness of being set up by the cadre. In the crisis stage, the brokers' loyalty to the cadre busts under the structurally focused stress and strain of the conspiracy and they defect in devastating numbers. It is this breakdown in brokerage that explains the collapse of the conspiracy.

The brokerage penalty is likely to increase during periods of crisis in a conspiracy for two reasons: 1) Crises increase the level of interest in the outcomes, and 2) crises provide a nodal point for the responses needed to implement the tactics, such as penetration of agencies, insulation of the core, and stockpiling cash. This need for decisive and immediate reaction to threats throws the spotlight on the conspiracy's liaisons, linchpins, go-betweens, and conduits. It concentrates organizing efforts on those individuals whose potential contributions are the largest. Initially the broker premium for coordination and timing results in bold, dramatic, and effervescent mobilizations of action; however, this initial enthusiasm and payoff can turn into a trap as tactics fail, demoralization sets in, and "the pinstripe atmosphere" of Watergate turns into everyone "looking out for themselves."

REFERENCES

Abrahamsen, David (1977). *Nixon vs. Nixon: An Emotional Tragedy*. New York: Farrar, Straus, and Giroux.

Adler, Renata (1976). Searching for the real Nixon scandal. *Atlantic Monthly*, December, 12–20.

Alexander, Jeffrey C. (1988). Culture and political crisis: "Watergate" and Durkheimian sociology. In Jeffrey C. Alexander (ed.), *Durkheimian Sociology: Cultural Studies* (pp. 187–223). Cambridge: The Press Syndicate of the University of Cambridge.

Arabie, Phipps, Scott Boorman, & Paul Levitt (1978). Constructing blockmodels: How and why. *Journal of Mathematical Psychology* 17, 21–63.

Bearman, Peter S. (1993). *Relations into Rhetorics:*

Local Elite Social Structure in Norfolk, England, 1540–1640. New Brunswick, NJ: Rutgers University Press.

Black, Conrad (2007). *Richard M. Nixon: A Life in Full*. New York: PublicAffairs.

Burns, Thomas (1955). The reference of conduct in small groups: Cliques and cabals in occupational milieu. *Human Relations* 8, 467–486.

Burt, Ronald. S. (1976). Position in networks. *Social Forces* 55, 93–122.

Burt, Ronald. S. (1992). *Structural Holes: The Social Structure of Competition*. Cambridge, MA: Harvard University Press.

Burt, Ronald. S. (2002). The social capital of structural holes. In M. Guillen, R. Collins, P. England, & M. Meyer (eds.), *New Directions in Economic Sociology* (pp. 148–190). New York: Russell Sage Foundation.

Colson, Charles W. (1976). *Born Again*. Adam, MI: Chosen Books.

Corporation for Public Broadcasting (2003). *Watergate Plus 30: Shadow of History*. PBS Home Video.

Dean , John W. III (1977). *Blind Ambition*, Pocket Book edition. London: Simon and Schuster.

Dean, John W. III (1982). *Lost Honor*. Los Angeles: Stratford Press.

Emery, Fred (1994). *Watergate: The Corruption of American Politics and the Fall of Richard Nixon*. New York: Crown Publishers.

Ehrlichman, John D. (1982). *Witness to Power: The Nixon Years*. New York: Simon & Schuster.

Faulkner, Robert R. (1983). *Music on Demand*. New Brunswick, NJ: Transaction Books.

Feldstein, Edward J. (2004). Watergate revisited. *American Journalism Review*, August/September. Available at www.ajr.org/article_printable. asp?id=3735.

Felt, Mark & J. O'Connor (2006). *A G-Man's Life: The FBI, Being "Deep Throat," and the Struggle for Honor in Washington*. Cambridge, MA: PublicAffairs.

Felt, Mark & Ralph De Toledano (1979). *The FBI Pyramid From the Inside*. New York: Putnam.

Fernandez, Roberto M. & Robert V. Gould (1994). A dilemma of state power: Brokerage and influence in the National Health Policy domain. *American Journal of Sociology* 99, 1455–1491.

Fremon, David K. (1998). *The Watergate Scandal in American History*. Springfield, NJ: Enslow Publishing Incorporated.

Galaskiewicz, J. (1979). *Exchange Networks and Community Politics*. Beverly Hills, CA: Sage.

Garment, Leonard (2001). *In Search of Deep Throat: The Greatest Political Mystery of Our Time*. New York: Basic Books.

Gould, Roger V. (1991). Multiple networks and mobilization in the Paris Commune, 1897. *American Sociological Review* 56, 716–729.

Gould, Roger V. (2003). Uses of network tools in comparative historical research. In James Mahoney & Dietrich Rueschemeyer (eds.), *Comparative Historical Analysis in the Social Sciences* (pp. 241–269). Cambridge: Cambridge University Press.

Gould, Roger V. & Roberto M. Fernandez (1989). Structures of mediation: A formal approach to brokerage in transaction networks. *Sociological Methodology* 19: 89–126.

Gray, Patrick L. III (2008). *In Nixon's Web: A Year in the Crosshairs of Watergate*. New York: Times Books.

Haldeman, H.R. (1978). *The Ends of Power*. New York: Times Books.

Haldeman, H.R. (1994). *The Haldeman Diaries: Inside the Nixon White House*. New York: Putnam.

Hillmann, Henning (2008). Localism and the limits of political brokerage: Evidence from revolutionary Vermont. *American Journal of Sociology* 114, 287–331.

Hougan, Jim (1984). *Secret Agenda: Watergate, Deep Throat, and the CIA*. New York: Random House.

Hunt, Howard E. (1974). *Undercover: Memoirs of an American Secret Agent*. Toronto: Berkley Publishing Corporation, distributed by Putnam.

Hunt, Howard E. (2007). *American Spy: My Secret History in the CIA, Watergate and Beyond*. New York: Wiley.

Krackhardt, David (1987). QAP partialing as a test of significance. *Social Networks* 9, 171–186.

Kutler, Stanley I. (1990). *The Wars of Watergate: The Last Crisis of Richard Nixon*. New York: W.W. Norton & Company.

Kutler, Stanley I. (ed.). (1997). *Abuse of Power: The New Nixon Tapes*. New York: Touchstone Books.

Liddy, G. Gordon (1996). *Will: The Autobiography*

of *G. Gordon Liddy* (Rep Sub ed.). New York: St. Martin's Press.

Lukas, J. Anthony (1976). *Nightmare: The Underside of the Nixon Years.* New York: Viking.

Magruder, Jeb Stuart (1974). *An American Life: One Man's Road to Watergate.* New York: Atheneum.

Magruder, Jeb Stuart (1978). *From Power to Peace.* Waco, TX: Word Books.

Marsden, Peter V. (1982). Brokerage behavior in restricted exchange networks. In P.V. Marsden & N. Lin (eds.), *Social Structure and Network Analysis* (pp. 201–219). Beverly Hills: Sage.

McCarthy, Mary (1978). *Mask of State: Watergate Portraits.* San Diego, CA: Harvest Books.

Olson, Keith W. (2003). *Watergate: The Presidential Scandal That Shook America.* St Lawrence, KS: University Press of Kansas.

Perlstein, Rick (2008). *Nixonland: The Rise of A President and The Fracturing of America.* New York: Scribner, Simon & Schuster, Inc.

Poundstone, William (1992). *Prisoner's Dilemma.* New York: Doubleday.

Rider, Christopher (2009). Constraints on the control benefits of brokerage: A study of placement agents in U.S. venture capital fundraising. *Administrative Science Quarterly 54,* 575–601.

Rosen, James (2008). *The Strong Man: John Mitchell and The Secrets of Watergate.* New York: Doubleday.

Safire, William (1975). *Before the Fall: An Inside View of the Pre-Watergate White House.* Garden City, NY: Doubleday.

Selznick, Philip (1952). *The Organizational Weapon: A Study of Bolshevik Strategy and Tactics.* Santa Monica, CA: The Rand Corporation.

Sirica, John J. (1979). *To Set the Record Straight: The Break-In, the Tapes, the Conspirators, and the Pardon.* New York: W.W. Norton & Company.

Stans, Maurice H. (1985). *The Terrors of Justice:*

The Untold Side of Watergate. Washington, DC: Regnery Publishing.

Summers, Anthony (2000). *The Arrogance of Power: The Secret World of Richard Nixon.* New York: Viking.

Sussman, Barry (1974). *The Great Cover-Up: Nixon and the Scandal of Watergate.* New York: Thomas Y. Crowell.

Thompson, J.D. (1967). *Organizations in Action: Social Science Bases of Administrative Theory.* New York: McGraw-Hill.

Ulasewicz, Tony & Stuart A. McKeever (1990). *The President's Private Eye: The Journey of Detective Tony U. from N.Y.P.D. to the Nixon White House.* Westport, CT: Macsam Pub Co.

United States Congress, Senate Select Committee on Presidential Campaign Activities (1973). *Presidential Campaign Activities of 1972, Senate Resolution 60; Watergate and Related Activities.* Washington, DC: Government Printing Office.

Wasserman, Stanley & Katherine Faust (1994). *Social Network Analysis. Methods and Applications.* Cambridge, UK: Cambridge University Press.

Weissman, Steve (1974). *Big Brother and the Holding Company: The World Behind Watergate.* Palo Alto, CA: Ramparts Press.

White, Harrison C., Scott A. Boorman, & Ronald L. Breiger (1976). Social structure from multiple networks. 1. Blockmodels of roles and positions. *American Journal of Sociology 81,* 730–780.

White, Theodore (1975). *Breach of Faith: The Fall of Richard Nixon.* New York: Scribner.

Winship, Christopher (1988). Thoughts about roles and relations: an old document revisited. *Social Networks 10,* 209–231.

Woodward, Bob (2005). *The Secret Man: The Story of Watergate's Deep Throat.* New York: Simon & Schuster.

Woodward, Bob & Carl Bernstein (1974). *All The President's Men.* New York: Simon & Schuster.

PART V

*E*xtremist Networks

CHAPTER 16

Terrorist Network Adaptation to a Changing Environment

Sean F. Everton and Dan Cunningham

Dark networks—that is, covert and illegal networks (Raab & Milward, 2003)—evolve over time. They undergo changes caused by both endogenous and exogenous factors, such as the attempt by network leaders to recruit talented members to plan and carry out attacks or their reaction to operations by hostile authorities. Changes can be gradual and/or rapid and can affect the way in which a network behaves and its ability to launch successful attacks. Indeed, the study and use of the term "dark networks" has grown dramatically in recent years, as has the application of social network analysis (SNA) to explore and understand the phenomenon. However, most social network analyses of dark networks have tended to use data that merely provide snap-shots at single points in time. Seldom have they drawn on longitudinal data that capture how networks change and adapt over time, making it impossible to explore how important changes in network structure affect a host of related issues, such as network resiliency, network structure and performance, and measuring the effectiveness of counter-terrorism strategies.

Nevertheless, a few scholars, building on the insights of research on bright networks, have begun applying longitudinal modeling techniques to dark networks. These studies have examined the issues mentioned above, but most have not fully accounted for the interaction between them. This chapter contributes to this growing body of research by fusing the related issues of network adaptability, the relationship between network structure and performance, and strategies for targeting dark networks. We draw on social network analysis to examine a unique longitudinal dataset, namely, the Noordin Top terrorist network, combining descriptive analysis and multivariate regression statistical models. Our analyses allow us to draw tentative conclusions with regards to various theories about how terrorist networks adapt to a hostile environment. For example, recent research suggests that, all else being equal, successful terrorist groups tend to become increasingly dense and adopt a more decentralized form of organization. Such adaptation not only provides greater security but also improves effectiveness. Adaptation can create new vulnerabilities, however. Terrorist groups that become too dense or fail to decentralize can become vulnerable to a well-connected member's capture or elimination.

This chapter begins with two overviews: one regarding the analysis of longitudinal dark network data; the other regarding network resiliency and effectiveness. The next section examines the topographical metrics we use to explore Noordin Top's network structure over time. Our analysis does not draw on all network topographical metrics but instead focuses on three commonly used sets of metrics. This section is followed by a brief discussion of the network data used in this chapter. In particular, we focus on what we call

Noordin's trust and operational networks, although future analyses may want to consider others (e.g., communication and financial networks). Next, we conduct an exploratory analysis that examines how our topographical metrics of interest vary across time. Then, we expand this analysis by regressing these measures on a handful of variables that we believe lead dark networks to adapt and change. We conclude with a reflection on our results as well as offer suggestions for future research.

THE LONGITUDINAL ANALYSIS OF DARK NETWORKS

Historically, longitudinal network data have been difficult to come by, and the methods for examining them underdeveloped. As a case in point, Wasserman and Faust's classic text on social network analysis makes little mention of longitudinal networks. Only in the final chapter does it note the importance of developing good and easy-to-use methods for examining longitudinal network data (Wasserman & Faust, 1994: 730–731). In recent years, this situation has begun to change. Longitudinal network data and their analysis are becoming more common. Many analyses have been largely descriptive in nature, but they are increasingly becoming more sophisticated, employing model-based approaches that seek to identify the underlying mechanisms of network change (Breiger, Carley, & Pattison, 2003; de Nooy, 2011; Doreian & Stockman, 1997; McCulloh & Carley, 2011; Snijders, 2005; Snijders, Bunt, & Steglich, 2010; Steglich, Snijders, & Pearson, 2010). Using these methods, analysts have analyzed a variety of types of networks (Doreian & Stockman, 1997), such as friendship (Leenders, 1996) and communication ties (Kossinets & Watts, 2006). This is not meant to suggest that descriptive analyses of longitudinal network data are of no value. Indeed, we employ them in this chapter to initially explore our data. Rather, it is merely to point out that the development of these

new models allows analysts to supplement descriptive approaches with more sophisticated approaches.[1]

To date, the majority of longitudinal analyses have focused on the application of models to "bright" or "light" networks. Only a handful of scholars have applied them to the longitudinal study of dark networks. Most notably, Carley and her colleagues (Carley, 2001–2011, 2003; Carley, Lee, & Krackhardt, 2002) have contributed significantly to the field through modeling dynamic dark networks and the development of the meta-matrix approach. Xu, Hu, and Chen's (2009) interesting analysis of the Global Salafi Jihad (GSJ) network and its survival suggests that the network experienced three distinct phases over time, including an emerging, maturing, and disintegration phase. They also found that the GSJ network gradually evolved into a scale-free topology (Barabási, 2002; Barabási & Albert, 1999; Barabási & Bonabeau, 2003). Building on Kossinets and Watts (2006), Hu, Kaza, and Chen (2009) applied a Cox survival analysis on a co-offending network for identifying facilitators of cyclic and focal closure. They found that acquaintances and shared vehicle affiliations serve as key link facilitators, while homophily in age, race, and gender were not significant predictors of either type of closure. McCulloh and Carley (2011) recently took a unique approach by applying social network change detection (SNCD) techniques to a number of longitudinal networks, including the al-Qaeda communication network from 1988 to 2004. SNCD allows real-time analysis and alerts analysts whether and when a statistically significant change occurs in the network so that they can focus on specific times and examine the potential causes for the change.

THE RESILIENCY AND EFFECTIVENESS OF DARK NETWORKS

An additional set of scholars has examined the factors contributing to network resiliency

(Bakker, Raab, & Milward, 2011), which is essentially a dynamic perspective to the study of dark networks since they must continuously withstand and adapt to various levels of external pressure in order to survive. Some influential studies have accounted for the relationship between resilience and scale-free networks (Barabási & Bonabeau, 2003; Sageman, 2004; Xu et al., 2009), and network survival and decentralized network structures (Arquilla & Ronfeldt, 2001; Bakker et al., 2011; Milward & Raab, 2006; Raab & Milward, 2003). Tsvetovat and Carley's (2005) simulated attacks on a cellular terrorist network suggest that covert networks rebound from shocks primarily through activating latent resources. Milward and Raab's (2006) insightful work argues that dark networks are resilient to the extent that they can balance differentiation and integration (i.e., the capacity to act and persist) in the face of mounting pressure. Furthermore, a dark network's ability to operate and respond to shocks is largely contingent upon the group's motivations and resources, such as money, access to technology, and territory. Building upon this research, Bakker et al. (2011) examine how the operational activity of a series of dark networks reacted and adapted to external shocks and, in so doing, identify additional factors that contribute to the resiliency of dark networks. For instance, they note that, to be successful, dark networks must maintain and replace nodes and ties at a rate faster than they are destroyed. They also argue that legitimacy (both internal and external) is a crucial factor for network survival, particularly for grievance-based dark networks. Finally, they identify a number of network characteristics, such as the degree to which a network is decentralized, that they believe contribute to dark network resiliency.

Some scholars have gone beyond examining the factors contributing to network survival and have explored the relationship between structural characteristics of dark networks and their ability to effectively launch attacks. For example, Rodriguez's (2005) examination of the Madrid terrorist network concluded that "weak" ties (Granovetter, 1973, 1983) were crucial not only to its security and adaptability but also to its operational success. Most studies also appear to conclude (or assume) that dark networks must balance operational capacity with network security but do so in the environmental contexts in which they operate, some of which are more hostile than others (Bakker et al., 2011; Bienenstock & Bonacich, 2003; Enders & Su, 2007; Kenney, 2007; Lindelauf, Borm, & Hamers 2009; Milward & Raab, 2006). However, it is often difficult for dark networks to reach or maintain an optimal balance. For instance, while some research suggests that network density is positively related to a network's command and control capability, it may also render the network more vulnerable to rapid deterioration in the event of a well-connected member's capture (Granovetter, 1973, 1983; Koschade, 2006; US Army, 2007). On the other hand, Helfstein and Wright's (2011) recent analysis of six successful attack networks found that neither operational security type (OPSEC) nor scale-free structures are associated with network success (as measured by casualties). They also concluded that network characteristics such as density had no causal relationship with success (i.e., casualties), although they did find that the networks became increasingly dense and cohesive over time, particularly as they entered an operation's execution phase.

Multiple authors have also suggested strategies for disrupting and destabilizing dark networks. Marc Sageman (2003, 2004), for instance, discovered that the GSJ shares the characteristics of scale-free networks, which have been found to be relatively immune to random failures but vulnerable to targeted attacks on well-connected actors known as hubs (Barabási, 2002; Barabási & Albert, 1999; Barabási, Albert, & Jeong, 1999;

Barabási & Bonabeau, 2003). Building upon this analysis, Xu et al. (2009) used Sageman's data to compare simulated and actual node removal strategies from 1993 to 2003. They found that actual counter-attacks launched against the GSJ were largely ineffective in disrupting the network, while simulated attacks targeting hubs were relatively successful. Other scholars have also contributed significantly to the study of destabilizing dark networks through simulated counter-attacks (Carley, 2006; Carley et al., 2002; Tsvetovat & Carley, 2005), proposing alternative actor-centric strategies, including targeting actors with critical skills (Klerks, 2001), identifying key brokers for removal (Morselli & Roy, 2008), and by developing new and useful algorithms for identifying key actors for the purposes of diffusing something (i.e., information) or fragmenting a network (Borgatti, 2006). More recently, Roberts and Everton (2011) have considered a variety of kinetic and non-kinetic strategies and proposed that counter-terrorism strategies should be context driven rather than using SNA metrics to drive particular strategies. The available literature using SNA for targeting dark networks, however, has yet to account for changes in strategies across time and what those changes mean for a dark network's structure and consequently its ability to operate. Similar to static analyses of dark networks, longitudinal studies, including those focusing on network resilience and the relationship between structure and attacks, will often suggest ways to disrupt the networks. Nevertheless, it appears that the available social network literature does not fully account for the interaction between dark network evolution, structure and performance, and strategies for disrupting them across time.

NETWORK TOPOGRAPHY

In this chapter, we combine descriptive and multivariate regression analysis in order to tease out how a particular dark network, the Noordin Top terrorist network, adapted and changed from 2001 to 2010 in reaction to endogenous and exogenous factors. Before turning to this analysis, however, we need to first briefly discuss the various topographical measures we will use to track these changes. While there are a number available, we focus on three of the more common ones: density, centralization, and fragmentation. Density measures capture a network's inner connectedness. As we will see, the traditional measure of density is unhelpful when analyzing networks that vary in size; consequently, we use an alternative measure of connectedness, average degree, which is not sensitive to network size (de Nooy, Mrvar, & Batagelj, 2011; Scott, 2000). Centralization metrics estimate the degree to which a network revolves around different centers of power. As those familiar will social network analysis know, however, there are a variety of centrality metrics. In this chapter, we focus on two—degree and betweenness centrality—although subsequent analysis may want to consider analyzing dark networks with other or additional measures. Finally, fragmentation algorithms, which are somewhat similar to density algorithms, calculate the proportion of network members who are unconnected (either directly or indirectly) to one another. The traditional measure is simply the proportion. An alternative measure weights this proportion by how close (in terms of path distance) each actor is, on average, to all other actors in the network. We utilize both of these in this analysis. It is to a discussion of these metrics that we now turn.

Density and Average Degree

In what is now considered a classic study, Mark Granovetter (1973, 1974) discovered that, when it came to finding jobs, people were far more likely to use personal contacts than they were other means, such as formal means[2] or directly applying for their job.[3]

Moreover, of those who found their jobs through personal contacts, most were weak (i.e., acquaintances) rather than strong ties (i.e., close friends). Granovetter concluded that this was because not only do we tend to have more weak ties than strong ties (because weak ties demand less of our time), but also our weak ties are more likely to form the bridges that tie densely knit clusters of people together. In fact, if it were not for these weak ties, Granovetter argues, these clusters would not be connected at all. Thus, whatever is to be diffused (e.g., information, influence, and other types of resources), it will reach a greater number of people when it passes through weak ties rather than strong ones. Because of this, actors with few weak ties are more likely to be "confined to the provincial news and views of their close friends" (Granovetter, 1983: 202). Granovetter did not argue that strong ties are of no value, however. He noted that, while weak ties provide individuals with access to information and resources beyond those available in their immediate social circles, strong ties are more likely to be sources of support in times of uncertainty. Others have noted this as well (see e.g., Krackhardt, 1992).

> There is a mountain of research showing that people with strong ties are happier and even healthier because in such networks members provide one another with strong emotional and material support in times of grief or trouble and someone with whom to share life's joys and triumphs.
>
> (Stark, 2007: 37)

This suggests that people's networks differ in terms of their mix of weak and strong ties. They range from local (i.e., provincial) ones, consisting primarily of strong, redundant ties, to worldly (i.e., cosmopolitan) ones, consisting of numerous weak ties and few strong ties (Stark, 2007: 37–38). It also suggests that people's networks should ideally consist of a mix of weak and strong ties. Their networks should be neither too provincial nor too cosmopolitan but rather should land somewhere between the two extremes, not necessarily at the arithmetic mean, but rather at a "golden mean" of sorts (Aristotle, 1998: 36–43). That a mix of the two is ideal has been captured by a number of studies. For example, Pescosolido and Georgianna's (1989) study of suicide found that the density of actors' social networks has a curvilinear (or inverted U) relationship to suicide. Individuals whose social networks are very sparse (i.e., cosmopolitan) or very dense (i.e., provincial) are far more likely to commit suicide than are those whose networks lie between the two extremes. Similarly, in his study of the New York apparel industry and Broadway musicals, Uzzi (1996, 2008; Uzzi & Spiro, 2005) found that a mix of weak and strong ties proved beneficial to the long-term survival and success. More precisely, he discovered that, like Pescosolido and Georgianna, a U-shaped association exists between the degree of embeddedness (i.e., its density) and the probability of an apparel firm's failure or a Broadway musical's critical and financial success.

What these studies suggest is that, in order to be successful, dark networks can be neither too provincial nor too cosmopolitan. What constitutes a particular dark network's optimum balance will likely vary depending on the environment in which it operates (e.g., the IRA can operate more openly in Ireland than al-Qaeda can in the United States). However, because the survival of dark networks depends largely on them recruiting members whom they can trust (Berman, 2009; Tilly, 2004, 2005), they tend to recruit through strong (rather than weak) ties, and networks formed primarily by strong ties become increasingly dense as ties form between previously unlinked actors (Granovetter, 1973; Holland & Leinhardt, 1971; Rapoport, 1953a, b; Rapoport & Horvath, 1961). Thus, we should expect that dark networks will, on the whole, be denser than will light networks, recognizing that it can become too dense and consequently limit its effectiveness.

Formally, network density is defined as the total number of ties in a network divided by the total possible number of ties. Networks with no ties have a density of 0.0 (or 0%), while networks where all possible ties between actors exist have a density of 1.0 (or 100%). As noted above, this formal measure of density is inversely related to network size because the number of possible ties increases exponentially as actors join the network, while the number of ties that each actor can maintain tends to be limited. Thus, following the lead of other social network analysts (de Nooy, Mrvar & Batagelj, 2011; Scott, 2000), we use average degree centrality, which is simply the average number of ties that each actor in the network has, in order to measure how "dense" a network is.

Degree and Betweenness Centralization

Another well-developed body of research has explored how the extent to which an organization is hierarchically structured impacts its performance (see e.g., Nohria & Eccles, 1992; Podolny & Page, 1998; Powell, 1985, 1990; Powell & Smith-Doerr, 1994). This literature typically identifies two ideal types of organizational form: networks and hierarchies. The former are seen as decentralized, informal, and/or organic, while the latter are seen as centralized, formal and/or bureaucratic (see e.g., Burns & Stalker, 1961; Powell, 1990; Ronfeldt & Arquilla, 2001). While this distinction is useful in some contexts (see e.g., Arquilla & Ronfeldt, 2001; Castells, 1996; Podolny & Page, 1998; Powell & Smith-Doerr, 1994; Ronfeldt & Arquilla, 2001), among social network analysts, all organizations are networks, regardless of whether they are hierarchical or decentralized. Thus, it is better to think of these two ideal types as poles on either end of a continuum, running from highly decentralized networks one end to highly centralized networks on the other.

Current research suggests that, much like the provincial–cosmopolitan dimension, an optimal level of centralization appears to exist. For example, Rodney Stark (1987, 1996), in his analysis of why some new religious movements succeed, identified centralized authority as an important factor but noted that too much centralization can be a bad thing and that successful religious movements, such as the Mormon (LDS) Church, balance centralized authority structures with decentralized ones (Stark, 2005: 125). Like the provincial–cosmopolitan dimension, the optimal level almost certainly varies depending on environmental context (Tucker, 2008). Because decentralized networks tend to be better suited for solving non-routine, complex, and/or rapidly changing problems or challenges because of their adaptability (Saxenian, 1994, 1996), it is likely that successful dark networks will gravitate toward the decentralized end of the continuum (Arquilla & Ronfeldt, 2001; Ronfeldt & Arquilla, 2001). Even here, though, dark networks that are too decentralized may find it difficult to mobilize resources, leading them to underperform and suggesting, once again, that analysts need to take into account this dimension of a network when crafting strategies to disrupt it.

Social network analysis uses the variation in actor centrality to calculate the level of centralization in a network (Wasserman & Faust, 1994). More variation yields higher network centralization scores; less variation yields lower scores. The standard centralization score (Freeman, 1979) estimates variation by comparing each actor's centrality score to the score of the most central actor in the network. With this measure, the larger the centralization index, the more likely it is that a single actor is central (Wasserman & Faust, 1994: 176). An alternative measure recommended by Coleman (1964), Hoivik and Gleditsch (1975), and Snijders (1981) is the variance of actor centrality. That is, it compares each actor's centrality to average centrality (rather than the highest centrality score). In this case, the larger the centralization index, the more likely that a group of actors (rather than a single actor) are central. Because keeping the analysis in the original unit of measure is generally desirable (Everton, 2012; Hamilton, 1996), the standard deviation, rather than variance, is probably a better metric to use. We use both the standard and alternative centralization measures in our analysis below. Finally, because network centralization scores are based on the measure of centrality used to calculate them (e.g., degree, betweenness, and closeness), we need to interpret them appropriately. For example, degree centrality counts the number of ties each individual actor has; thus, degree centralization measures the extent to which one or a handful of actors possess numerous ties while other actors do not. By contrast, betweenness centrality estimates the extent to which actors lie between other actors and are in a position to broker the flow of resources; thus, betweenness centralization is probably best interpreted as indicating the level to which one or a handful of actors are in a position of brokerage.[4]

Fragmentation

Network fragmentation, as its name implies, measures a network's cohesiveness (or lack thereof). It is equal to the proportion of all pairs of actors that cannot either directly or indirectly reach one another. In addition to this "traditional" approach to calculating network fragmentation, an alternative measures takes into account the (path) distance between actors. Network fragmentation metrics could prove useful for understanding how a network has changed over time as well as in the crafting of strategies. For instance, if analysts were seeking to determine the degree to which different scenarios will fragment a particular network, they could estimate before and after measures of fragmentation. In fact, one social network analysis package, UCINET (Borgatti, Everett & Freeman, 2011), reports a series of scores for each actor in the network that indicates the degree

of network fragmentation, the degree of distance-weighted network fragmentation, the change in network fragmentation, the change in distance-weighted network fragmentation, the percent of change in fragmentation, and the percent of change in distance-weighted fragmentation if a particular actor is removed from the network. In our analysis below, we use both the standard and distance-weighted fragmentation measures.

DATA

We use longitudinal network data on the Noordin Top terrorist network to explore the relationships between dark network structure, resilience, and counter-terrorism strategies. Until his death in September 2009, Top was Indonesia's most wanted terrorist and thought to be the mastermind behind a series of terrorist attacks in Indonesia from 2003 to 2005 (i.e., the 2003 Marriott bombing, the 2004 Australian Embassy attack, and the October 2005 Bali bombing). At one time, Noordin was an active member of the terrorist group Jemaah Islamiyah (JI) and may have participated in the first Bali bombings in 2002. Evidence suggests that, not too long after the first Bali bombing, Noordin began to break away from JI and form his own terrorist network. Sought by a host of authorities, he was placed on the FBI's Seeking Information—War on Terrorism List in 2006. Noordin and his associates carried out simultaneous bombings three years later against the Ritz-Carlton and Marriott hotels in August 2009, which subsequently led to stepped-up police operations and his eventual demise. Not long after Noordin was killed, his network essentially fell apart. To analyze Noordin's network, we utilize the relational data drawn from two International Crisis Group (ICG) reports (2006, 2009). We supplement these data with open source literature in order to generate time codes by month from January 2001 through August 2011, which allows us to account for when actors entered the network and if and when individuals were arrested or killed.

The two ICG reports on Noordin contain rich one-mode and two-mode data on a variety of relations and affiliations (friendship, kinship, meetings, etc.) along with significant attribute data (education, group membership, physical status, etc.). From these, we constructed three networks from several sub-networks, each containing 237 individuals. Specifically, we created a *trust network* that is an aggregation of one-mode classmate, friendship, kinship, and soulmate subnetworks. We constructed a second network, what we call Noordin's *operational network*, from four one-mode networks that were derived from corresponding two-mode networks, namely logistics, meetings, operations, and training events. We then created a *combined* network that is simply the aggregation of the *trust* and *operational* networks in order to obtain a better overall picture of the Noordin Top network. Finally, we assigned time codes to each actor in the network that indicated when they entered and left Noordin's trust, operational, and combined networks. In assigning these time codes, we assumed that ties between actors were constant over time. That is, if two actors were coded as friends at one point in time, we assumed they remained friends throughout their mutual presence in the networks. The one exception to this concerns the meetings subnetwork, where, building on the work of Krebs (2001), we assumed that a meeting tie did not form until the meeting took place (unless, of course, a tie was previously formed along another relation, such as friendship or kinship). We recognize the potential limitations of these assumptions and how they may affect the estimation of the various topographic metrics we utilize in this chapter. Nevertheless, we believe that the approach taken here is reasonable and valid.[5]

As noted above, we use both descriptive statistics and multivariate regression analysis to explain the variation in several key

topographical characteristics of Noordin's network. We begin with our descriptive analysis of the network, visually graphing the change in the topographical metrics outlined above. We then turn to a multivariate analysis of these same metrics along with two others that are discussed below. It is to the descriptive analysis that we now turn.

EXPLORATORY DESCRIPTIVE ANALYSIS

Figures 16.1 through 16.3 graphically present results of our analysis of the Noordin Top trust, operational, and combined networks. Specifically, the figures graph the average degree, centralization,[6] and fragmentation for each of the three networks. The vertical lines in each of the graphs indicate key points in the life cycle of Noordin's network. Moving from left to right, they indicate the first Bali bombings (October 2002), the Marriott Hotel bombing (August 2003), the Australian Embassy bombing (July 2004), the second Bali bombings (October 2005), the Jakarta Hotel bombings (July 2009), and the death of Noordin and other key operatives (September 2009). Because the combined network is a combination of the trust and operational networks, for the most part, we limit our comments to the trust and operational networks.

Trust Network

Several observations are in order concerning the trust network. One is that it displays less variability than does the operational network and combined networks. Average degree begins at a relatively low level. However, shortly after the first Bali bombing in October 2002 and as Noordin began to pull away from JI, the network becomes increasingly connected, perhaps reflecting security concerns. There is a small drop just before and after the JW Marriott bombing in August 2003. This trend is followed by a sharp increase through the Australian

Embassy bombing in July 2004 and up to the second Bali bombings in October 2005. Then it slowly decreases for the next four years while the network was apparently on the run and relatively inactive. The July 2009 bombings of the Ritz Carlton and JW Marriott hotels mark the beginning of the end of Noordin's network. Two months later, Indonesian authorities killed Noordin and other key operatives, and its average degree drops precipitously shortly thereafter.

A similar pattern is observable in the trust network's level of centralization. In terms of both degree and betweenness centralization, we see a steady increase from the first Bali bombing up until the Australian Embassy bombing. The increase in betweenness centralization is more dramatic, suggesting that the network became increasingly reliant on a handful of individuals for the brokerage of resources. This could reflect the fact that, as Noordin pulled farther away from JI, he was forced to recruit from a variety of sources and use individuals who could broker between him and leaders of other insurgent groups (International Crisis Group, 2006). What is somewhat surprising, however, is the increase in the degree centralization of Noordin's trust network. As noted earlier, in rapidly changing environments, decentralized networks are typically more effective than centralized ones, and we expected to discover that Noordin's network became more decentralized over time. However, this could be an exception that proves the rule because the increasing centralization of Noordin's network may help explain why it fell apart after the removal of a handful of leaders in September 2009. As Bakker et al. (2011) have found, centralized networks are less resilient to exogenous shocks (e.g., the removal of central nodes).[7]

The variation in the trust network's fragmentation levels tell a similar story (although in reverse) to the average degree story. Both measures indicate that the network became less fragmented (i.e., more cohesive) between

the first and second Bali bombings, stabilized in the four years between the 2005 Bali bombing and the 2009 Jakarta hotel bombings, and then broke apart after Noordin was killed. The distance-weighted fragmentation measure suggests that the change over time was not as dramatic as the more traditional measure indicates. This difference between

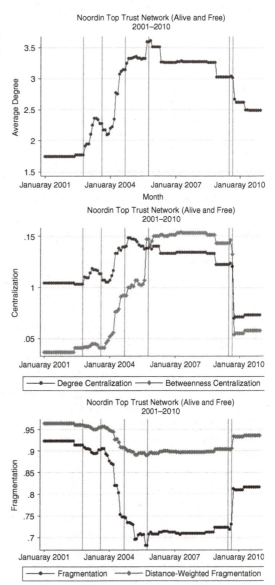

Figure 16.1 Noordin Top trust network (alive and free)

the two primarily reflects the fact that, while the proportion of unconnected pairs in Noordin's network decreased substantially from 2002 to 2005, so did the average (path) distance between network actors. This increase in average distance indicates the network was becoming more distributed over that period of time, and may reflect a decision by Noordin to spread his network out or that his network was growing in size during that time. It may, of course, reflect both.

Operational Network

The operational network reflects similar patterns to that of the trust network. Average degree remains constant from January 2001 until the Bali bombings in 2002. This is hardly surprising given Noordin's near absent role in the bombings, while this is also the same time when Noordin began to strike out on his own. The subsequent drop in average degree between the Bali bombings and the August 2003 attacks likely highlights the increase in counter-terrorism operations targeting the Bali perpetrators, which removed some highly dedicated and skilled terrorists, as well as putting significant pressure on others (e.g., Umar Patek, Dulmatin). This may have created a power vacuum within JI that Noordin leveraged to his own advantage. This trend reversed itself from August 2003 to September 2004, which might suggest that density is positively related to command and control. The sharp decrease following the Australian Embassy bombing in September 2004 could reflect effective counter-terrorism operations, but the network rebounded immediately prior to the second Bali bombing, suggesting that Noordin may have risked network security for operational success. Noordin's success, however, led to an increase in counter-terrorism operations that targeted the network; the drop in average degree following Bali II may indicate that these operations met with initial success, but they ultimately failed to prevent the July 2009 hotel bombings.

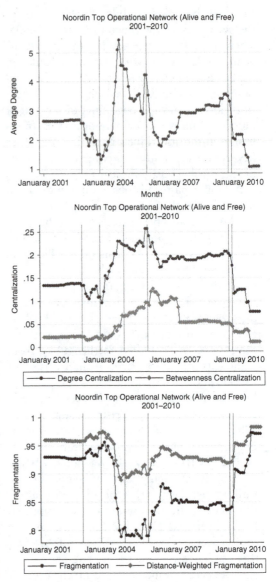

Figure 16.2 Noordin Top trust network (alive and free)

The trends in network centralization for the operations network are in many ways similar to the trust network. There is an overall increase in both degree and betweenness centralization from the first Bali bombings through the second. It probably indicates that Noordin increasingly relied on fewer and fewer actors (in particular, himself) for brokerage and resources. The increase in degree centralization is more pronounced in the operations network, which suggests that operations increasingly became largely in the hands of a few actors, particularly from the August 2003 attack through the second Bali bombing, as Noordin moved away from the formal JI structure. Finally, the comparison of this graph with that of the trust network suggests that Noordin relied more on those with whom he could trust rather than those with whom he had an operational tie.

The operation network's fragmentation scores indicate that the network became more cohesive from the August 2003 operation to the second Bali bombing, perhaps providing it with greater operational capability. However, the higher fragmentation scores in the immediate aftermath of the second Bali bombing highlight the largely successful counter-terrorism operations in degrading the network directly after the attack. This success appears to have been only temporary, however, as the network rebounded and began to stabilize in 2006. It remained fairly stable prior to the July 2009 attacks, but it almost completely disintegrates following Noordin's demise in September 2009. Although the combined network is an aggregation of the trust and operational networks, it more closely mirrors the operational network than it does the trust network. That said, the variation in average degree, centralization, and fragmentation closely follows what we see in the operational and trust networks.

MULTIVARIATE ANALYSIS

We now turn to our multivariate regression analysis of the three networks. Because our outcome variables are continuous, we utilized ordinary least squares (OLS) models to regress several outcome variables on a series of factors we believe could account for the variation observed in Figures 16.1 through 16.3.[8] The outcome variables include the topographical metrics presented in Figures 16.1 through 16.3, plus a "recruitment"

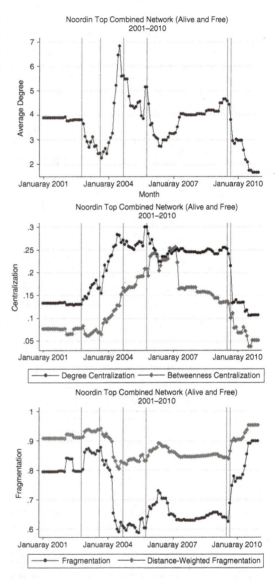

Figure 16.2 Noordin Top trust network (alive and free)

variable that attempts to capture the Noordin network's ability to recruit new members. The recruitment variable is measured by the growth or decline in the size of Noordin's network from one month to the next.

Explanatory variables included in our analysis seek to capture the effect of various exogenous factors on the topography of Noordin's network. These include three dummy variables that attempt to capture shifts in the strategic approaches used by Indonesian authorities: 1) the formation of *Detachment 88*, the Indonesian counter-terrorism squad, 2) the establishment of the *Jakarta Centre for Law Enforcement Cooperation*, and 3) the election of *Susilo Yudhoyono* to the Indonesian presidency. Detachment 88 was formed in July 2003 shortly after the first Bali bombings and is funded, equipped, and trained by the United States and Australia. A dummy variable is included that indicates the time Detachment 88 has been in operation. The Jakarta Centre for Law Enforcement Cooperation (JCLEC) was established in July 2004 under an agreement between the Australian and Indonesian governments. It is located in Semerang, Indonesia, and provides a range of training programs, seminars, and workshops with the goal of enhancing regional law enforcement capacity. A dummy variable is included that indicates the formation of the center and its continued existence. Finally, in October 2004, Susilo Yudhoyono, a retired Army general, became President of Indonesia; he was reelected in 2009. He ran on a platform to combat terrorist groups. Thus, a dummy variable is included in order to capture the effect, if any, of the policies he put into place to fulfill this pledge.

We have also included a dummy variable that indicates the *death of Noordin and his key operatives* and their subsequent "absence" from the network from September 2009 through the end of our analysis. An additional dummy variable included seeks to measure the effect of Noordin's ability to acquire surplus explosives from the 2000 Christmas Eve bombings in Indonesia. This *explosives* variable covers the time from which Noordin obtained the explosives in December 2002 to the time at which they were used for the network's first attack in August 2003. We also have added a series of *post-operation* dummy variables that capture the three-month period immediately following each of the five major operations:

Bali I, the JW Marriott Hotel bombing, the Australian Embassy bombing, Bali II, and the Jakarta Hotel bombings. In each of these periods, Indonesian authorities increased their efforts to kill or capture Noordin and his colleagues.

Finally, to control for the curvilinear effect that time appears to have on the various dependent variables (see Figures 16.1 through 16.3), independent variables that capture the passage of time are included in our models. Specifically, a *month* variable is included in order to model the initial effects of time, while a *month squared* variable is included in order to capture the apparent opposite effects of time.[9]

RESULTS

Tables 16.1 through 16.3 present the estimated coefficients for multivariate regression models that regresses various topographical measures on the explanatory variables.[10] Table 16.1 includes the results for the trust network, Table 16.2 includes the results for the operational network, and Table 16.3 includes the results for the combined network. Because there are three tables with each containing eight dependent variables and 12 independent variables, it is impossible to discuss all 288 coefficients. Thus, we concentrate on overall patterns and focus on coefficients that are both substantively and statistically significant (McCloskey, 1995; Ziliak & McCloskey, 2008).[11]

The tables contain many interesting findings. Most notably, the adjusted R^2 for the models that regress average degree, the four centralization measures, and the two fragmentation measures on the various independent variables are extremely high and indicate that our models largely account for the variation in most of our dependent variables. Adjusted R^2 scores above 0.20 warm the hearts of most social scientists, and the fact that they range from 0.63 and above should provide us with the confidence that our

Table 16.1 Multivariate regression results for Noordin Top trust network (alive and free)

| | Average Degree | Centralization | | | | Fragmentation | Distance Fragmentation | Recruitment |
| | | Degree | | Betweenness | | | | |
		Freeman	Std. Deviation	Freeman	Std. Deviation			
Intercept	-45.470***	-1.067***	-45.595***	-1.709***	-3,043.354***	4.970***	1.913***	-100.186
Month	0.173***	0.004***	0.185***	0.006***	11.199***	-0.015***	-0.004***	0.387
Month²	-0.000***	-0.000***	-0.000***	-0.000***	-0.010***	0.000***	0.000***	-0.000
Post Bali I (2002)	-0.110	-0.001	-0.083	-0.002	-3.780	0.004	0.000	0.032
Explosives	0.167+	0.004	0.462**	-0.007+	-11.460	0.007	-0.005**	-0.120
Post Marriott (2003)	-0.220+	-0.012*	-0.231	-0.013**	-25.856**	0.030*	0.010***	-2.785
Post Australian (2004)	-0.043	0.005*	0.156*	-0.050***	-107.645***	0.025***	0.006***	1.065
Post Bali II (2005)	0.185***	0.000	0.147*	-0.005*	-9.554*	0.001	-0.000	-2.030
Post Hotels (2009)	0.006	-0.003+	0.005	-0.007+	-10.372	0.002	0.001	-2.142***
Key Deaths	-0.336***	-0.046***	-0.423***	-0.085***	-106.680***	0.080***	0.028***	0.728
Detachment 88	0.277*	0.008	0.534**	0.007	20.550	-0.022+	-0.012***	3.482**
JCLEC	0.763***	0.021***	0.958***	0.029***	93.382***	-0.112***	-0.037***	-1.750
President Yudhoyono	0.199***	0.002	0.000	0.055***	109.566***	-0.035***	-0.012***	-0.694
Observations	119	118	118	112	112	119	114	119
AIC	-182.21	-946.65	-83.39	-872.73	808.32	-744.78	-1,075.34	474.97
BIC	-146.09	-910.63	-47.37	-837.39	843.66	-708.65	-1,039.77	511.10
Adjust R²	0.971	0.965	0.936	0.992	0.994	0.987	0.995	0.311

Note
Coefficients are unstandardized; bootstrap standard errors used to estimate significance; results from best fitting models based on AIC and BIC
+ p < 0.10; * p < 0.05; ** p < 0.01; *** p < 0.001 (two-tailed)

Table 16.2 Multivariate regression results for Noordin Top operational network (alive and free)

| | Average Degree | Centralization | | | | Fragmentation | Distance Fragmentation | Recruitment |
| | | Degree | | Betweenness | | | | |
		Freeman	Std. Deviation	Freeman	Std. Deviation			
Intercept	21.606	−2.399**	61.137	−3.043***	−2,510.846	2.883*	0.772	−84.065
Month	−0.711	0.009***	−0.207	0.012***	9.734***	−0.007+	0.000	0.314
Month²	0.000	−0.000**	0.000	−0.000***	−0.009***	0.000+	−0.000	−0.000
Post Bali I (2002)	0.253	−0.006	0.060	−0.004+	−3.674*	0.001	−0.003	−1.210
Explosives	−0.652***	−0.034***	−0.976***	−0.008**	−5.550	0.015+	0.002	−2.144+
Post Marriott (2003)	−0.686*	−0.030*	−0.856*	−0.008	−16.442*	0.033*	0.013**	−4.164**
Post Australian (2004)	1.409***	0.011+	1.647***	−0.025***	−25.612***	−0.032***	−0.022***	−0.783
Post Bali II (2005)	0.150	0.216**	0.150	0.023*	27.350***	−0.006	−0.002	−2.734
Post Hotels (2009)	0.165	−0.005	0.190	0.003	−0.904	−0.016*	−0.008*	−3.464+
Key Deaths	−1.560***	−0.075***	−2.741***	−0.001	−19.410***	0.062***	0.033***	−0.007
Detachment 88	−0.165	0.015	−0.792*	0.003	5.490	−0.015	−0.008	4.860**
JCLEC	2.399***	0.058***	3.606***	0.031***	42.274***	−0.114***	−0.063***	−4.616*
President Yudhoyono	−2.019***	−0.018*	−2.652***	0.036***	30.922***	−0.024*	0.020***	−0.219
Observations	119	118	118	120	120	119	114	118
AIC	179.71	−646.00	263.920	−711.82	900.19	−561.10	−711.95	549.92
BIC	215.84	−609.98	299.939	−675.59	936.43	−524.97	−676.38	585.94
Adjust R²	0.637	0.887	0.670	0.849	0.917	0.839	0.821	0.286

Note
Coefficients are unstandardized; bootstrap standard errors used to estimate significance; results from best fitting models based on AIC and BIC
+p < 0.10; * p < 0.05; ** p < 0.01; *** p < 0.001 (two-tailed)

Table 16.3 Multivariate regression results for Noordin Top combined network (alive and free)

	Average Degree	Centralization				Fragmentation	Distance Fragmentation	Recruitment
		Degree		Betweenness				
		Freeman	Std. Deviation	Freeman	Std. Deviation			
Intercept	39.395	-4.177**	79.312*	-6.044***	-4,197.947***	4.398*	0.701	-81.377
Month	-0.131	0.015**	-0.269*	0.024***	16.769***	-0.013+	0.001	0.305
Month^2	0.000	-0.000***	0.000*	-0.000***	-0.016***	0.000+	-0.000	0.000
Post Bali I (2002)	0.064	-0.011	0.174	0.000	3.131	0.002	-0.001	-1.202
Explosives	-0.857***	-0.008	-1.001***	-0.020**	-27.522***	0.079***	0.021***	-2.135+
Post Marriott (2003)	-0.754*	-0.023	-0.813	-0.016*	-35.802**	0.056+	0.014**	-4.169**
Post Australian (2004)	1.408***	0.014*	1.421***	-0.084***	-75.822***	-0.032**	-0.024***	-0.790
Post Bali II (2005)	0.073	0.020**	0.038	-0.007	11.410	0.026*	0.008	-2.734
Post Hotels (2009)	0.236	-0.004	0.145	0.007	6.038	-0.032	-0.016	-3.465+
Key Deaths	-1.956***	-0.104***	-3.108***	-0.018**	-38.207***	0.153***	0.073***	-0.014
Detachment 88	0.178	0.048**	-0.684*	0.027*	22.259	-0.024	-0.009	4.880**
JCLEC	2.543***	0.518***	3.353***	0.048***	59.747***	-0.149***	-0.086***	-4.609*
President Yudhoyono	-2.166***	-0.027*	-2.456***	0.071***	91.597***	0.030	0.029**	-0.211
Observations	119	118	118	112	112	119	114	118
AIC	199.80	-640.23	254.43	-588.01	934.54	-434.63	-632.94	549.93
BIC	235.93	-604.21	290.45	-552.67	969.88	-398.50	-597.37	585.95
Adjust R^2	0.662	0.922	0.713	0.925	0.943	0.855	0.861	0.286

Note
Coefficients are unstandardized; bootstrap standard errors used to estimate significance; results from best fitting models based on AIC and BIC
$^+ p < 0.10$; $^* p < 0.05$; $^{**} p < 0.01$; $^{***} p < 0.001$ (two-tailed)

models adequately explain the variability in our dependent variables. Our models are not quite as good at predicting Noordin's ability to recruit new members, although they do reasonably well, with R^2s ranging from 0.28 to 0.31.

Noordin's success in acquiring the left-over explosives in December 2002 is an early indicator of the network's operational motivations. We can see that the trust network became more cohesive and possibly more centralized (degree) during this period. This pattern is what we would expect given the explosives came from a trusted associate and Noordin's need to maintain a low profile with these newly acquired resources in the aftermath of the first Bali bombings. On the other hand, the acquisition of the explosives also appears to have caused the trust network to decentralize in terms of betweenness centralization. These trends highlight Noordin's initial practice of incorporating only a small number of actors whom he trusted and with whom he had established contacts; however, none of these trusted associates appear to have served as the network's sole broker at the time, which is probably because at the time the network consisted solely of JI members and had yet begun to reach out to other terrorist/insurgent organizations (International Crisis Group, 2006). Interestingly, the operational and combined network became less dense, less cohesive, and less centralized. One possible explanation is that many dedicated and well-connected terrorists who participated in the first Bali bombings were captured or killed in its aftermath. Many of these actors (e.g., Ali Ghufron) had pre-existing and sometimes operational relationships with Noordin associates. Consequently, their removal may be why the operational and combined networks initially became less dense, cohesive, and centralized, while at the same time creating a vacuum that Noordin eventually filled with the acquisition of the explosives.

As far as the post-operation periods, it appears that the three months immediately following the Marriott attack, all three networks became less centralized, which lends support to the commonly held view that, all else being equal, dark networks will decentralize in increasingly hostile environments. The three months after the Australian Embassy and the Bali II bombings tell somewhat different stories, however. After the Australian Embassy attack, all three networks became more centralized in terms of the degree but became less centralized in terms of the betweenness. These seemingly conflicting results suggest that, after the attack, Noordin and/or a few of his well-connected associates may have maintained a high level of control over each network while at the same time relying on more and more actors to serve as brokers. This later process may have begun prior to the attack as Noordin began exploring new recruitment avenues, such as reaching out to several new organizations and non-affiliated actors (International Crisis Group, 2006). It appears that, post-Bali II, counter-terrorism operations led to an increase in degree centralization and a decrease in betweenness centralization in the trust network, but a general increase in centralization in the operations and combined networks. This may reflect the mounting pressure placed by the Indonesian government on the network. We see similar results in terms of network fragmentation. While the trust network fragmented after both the Marriott and the Australian Embassy attacks, the operational and combined networks fragmented after the Marriott bombing but became more cohesive after the Embassy bombing.

The deaths of key individuals clearly had a deleterious effect on all three networks. They led to substantial decreases in its average degree, centralization, and cohesiveness (i.e., more fragmented). The network's structural characteristics prior to Noordin's death suggest that a few other actors possessed the majority of the command and control, which may have helped the network successfully mount attacks in July 2009 but ultimately made it extremely vulnerable, lending support, as we noted earlier, to the argument that decentralized networks are more resilient to exogenous shocks (Bakker et al., 2011). Thus, while the targeting of key individuals does not always cause dark networks to implode, it can when the network is highly centralized.

The results suggest that formation of Detachment 88 and the JCLEC contributed to Noordin's network becoming denser and more cohesive. Both seemingly caused the trust network to become more cohesive, and the JCLEC appears to have led to increases in the average degree and cohesiveness of the other two networks. It is hard to say whether this was good or bad for the network. It is what we expected, though, since, as we have discussed earlier, all else being equal, dark networks should be denser than light networks and become increasingly dense in hostile environments. Perhaps more interestingly, the formation of the two organizations apparently caused the trust, operational, and combined networks to become more centralized. Detachment 88 seems to have had this effect only on the trust and combined networks, while the JCLEC appears to have had it on all three. Interestingly, Detachment 88's formation appears to have boosted Noordin's recruitment efforts. As the coefficients for all three networks indicate, the effect is both positive and statistically significant. It is unclear why this was so, but it is possible that the presence of the US and Australian trained and funded counter-terrorist unit fed into anti-western sentiment. An alternative explanation is that Detachment 88's creation was simply a response to an already growing recruiting pool from which Noordin had the potential to exploit.

President Yudhoyono's election had some effect but not always in the expected magnitude or direction. In terms of the trust network, it led to an increase in average degree, betweenness centralization, and network cohesiveness. One possible explanation is

because the President's counter-terrorism policies specifically targeted Noordin; another, one that was noted previously, is that Noordin increasingly relied on a handful of trusted individuals to broker and reach out to other groups as his network moved farther away from JI and faced an increasing hostile environment. Interestingly, Yudhoyono's policies appear to have been among the factors that led Noordin's operational and combined networks to become less dense.

CONCLUSION

Strategic Implications

In considering what implications this analysis has for the disruption of networks, it is helpful to distinguish between two general approaches to countering dark networks: kinetic and non-kinetic (Roberts & Everton, 2011).[12] Kinetic approaches use coercive measures to eliminate or capture network members and their supporters (a bombs-and-bullets approach). By contrast, non-kinetic approaches employ neither bombs nor bullets but instead use non-coercive means. It includes activities such as the reconstruction of war-torn areas, the disruption of electronic fund transfer networks, information campaigns to win over the "hearts and minds" of local populations, and efforts at the rehabilitation and reintegration of dark network members into civil society.

Based on this study's results, one might conclude that decapitation strategies are effective at disrupting dark networks. Such a conclusion, however, would fail to take into account the fact that this strategy probably *only succeeded* because Noordin appears to have made the crucial strategic mistake of centering his network around a few key actors. If he had not, then his network would have been less vulnerable and alternative strategies may have proven more successful. In fact, one could argue that the establishment and gradual improvement of counter-terrorism organizations, such as Detachment 88 and the JCLEC, along with improved counter-terrorism training and targeting operations, appear to have been critical to creating the environment that caused Noordin to turn inward and place the future of his organization in the hands of a few people. Put differently, without the Indonesian authorities' non-kinetic approaches to disrupting Noordin's network, the killing of Noordin may have had less of an effect than it did. It is also helpful to keep in mind that, as Charles Tilly (2004, 2005) has noted, throughout history, covert networks (e.g., insurgencies, trade diasporas, clandestine religious groups, terrorist groups)[13] have segregated themselves from what they perceive to be hostile or predatory regimes. Tilly argues, however, that regimes, and in particular democratic ones, cannot survive without at least the partial integration of these networks back into civil society. Thus, while Indonesian authorities appear to have successfully put an end to Noordin's network, there is still work for them to do. Specifically, they need to pursue strategies that facilitate the reintegration of members of Noordin's network and other insurgent groups into Indonesian society. If they do not, there is a strong possibility that a new insurgency will raise its ugly head and pick up where Noordin left off.

To conclude: this chapter has sought to demonstrate the utility of analyzing longitudinal dark network data. It moved beyond previous research by examining the relationship between resilience, structure and performance, and strategies targeting dark networks. It has also sought to highlight the utility of alternative strategies targeting dark networks and the effect that non-kinetic strategies have on shaping these networks. Clearly, we have only begun to scrape the surface of what is possible in the examination of longitudinal networks. In the future, analysts will want to expand the approach taken here and employ other modeling techniques, such

as social network change detection (SNCD) (McCulloh & Carley, 2011) and stochastic actor-based models (Snijders, 2005; Snijders et al., 2010).

NOTES

1. Whether all of these new modeling techniques meet Wasserman and Faust's "easy-to-use" criterion is doubtful.

2. Formal means is where the job seekers used the services of impersonal intermediaries, such as advertisements, public and private employment agencies, interviews, and placements sponsored by universities or professional associations.

3. Direct application is where the job seekers went or wrote directly to a firm, did not use a formal or personal intermediary, and had not heard about a specific opening from a personal contact.

4. As one reviewer noted, network measures of centralization do not perfectly capture how hierarchical a network is. Krackhardt's (1994) measure of hierarchy is preferable but can only be estimated with a directed network, which we do not have here. Thus, the conclusions we draw concerning the factors lying behind the variation in the centralization of Noordin's network should be regarded with caution.

5. One could argue that we could have constructed our networks differently. This, of course, is true. However, that is true of any network analysis. What is ultimately important is to be explicit as to which networks have been used so that others may follow (and possibly disagree) with one's analysis (Roberts & Everton, 2011).

6. Here we only present graphs of the standard centralization measures because the correlation between them and the alternative measure is relatively high (correlation coefficients range from 0.53 to 0.85), making the presentation of both somewhat redundant. Both measures are used in the multivariate analysis below, however.

7. It is also consistent with the contention of Barabási and his colleagues (Barabási, 2002; Barabási & Albert, 1999; Barabási et al., 1999; Barabási & Bonabeau, 2003) that networks with a handful of well-connected nodes (i.e., hubs) are more vulnerable to targeted attacks than are those with few or none.

8. See notes 9 and 10, which address potential limitations of using OLS to estimate models using social network data.

9. In addition, Ramsey regression specification tests indicated the possibility of omitted variables from some of the models. This is typically rectified by including, with the independent variables, additional variables that are simply current variables raised to a specific power, as we have done here by including a month squared variable for the estimated models (Hamilton, 2009: 210).

10. We used a variety of regression diagnostic plots (e.g., residual vs. fitted plots, proportional leverage plots, leverage vs. squared residual plots) to identify potentially influential cases that, if removed, substantially changed our regression results. For each model, we then estimated a regression equation that included all cases and one that removed potentially influential cases. Then, using the Akaike information criterion (AIC) and Bayesian information criterion (BIC) measures of fit, we compared the models to one another. The results from the models having the best fit are presented in Tables 16.1 through 16.3.

11. Regression analysis of social network data differs from standard regression models in two important ways. One is that standard statistical models are designed to analyze random samples so that researchers can generalize their results to the population at large. Variables that are statistically significant are seen as being unlikely to have occurred by random chance and thus can be generalized to the population from which the sample was drawn. By contrast, social network analyses do not typically analyze samples of networks; instead they analyze (at least in theory) complete networks, so there is no need to generalize to the population at large. A second difference is that standard statistical models assume that observations are independent of one another, but social network analysis assumes that observations (i.e., actors) are tied to one another (i.e., they are not independent of one another) and that these interdependencies influence behavior. For these reasons, with social network data, we should not use standard approaches for estimating statistical significance. Instead, we turn to nonparametric approaches, such as bootstrapping, which entails the drawing of random samples from the original data hundreds or thousands of times in order to calculate a sampling distribution of statistics that can then be compared to the statistics generated by the observed (i.e., actual) network. If the observed statistics differ significantly from the randomly generated ones, we can conclude that the observed statistics could not have occurred by random chance and are "statistically significant." For this reason, we use bootstrap standard errors, using approximately 1,500 randomly drawn samples for each model, rather than traditional standard errors for estimating statistical significance.

12. There is no agreement in the literature on how to describe the alternative approaches to countering terrorism. Some authors use different characterizations—e.g., direct and indirect strategies (Arreguin-Toft, 2001, 2005; Fridovich & Krawchuck, 2007; Krawchuck, n.d.). Our preference is to focus on the behavior of the combatants and the level of the coercion involved in their strategies and hence we have chosen to use the terms "kinetic" and "non-kinetic."

13. Tilly defines trust networks as "ramified interpersonal connections, consisting mainly of strong ties, within which people set valued, consequential long-term resources and enterprises at risk to the malfeasance, mistakes, or failures of others" (Tilly, 2005: 41).

REFERENCES

Aristotle (1998). *The Nichomachean Ethics.* Translated by David Ross, J.L. Ackrill, & J.O. Urmson. Oxford and New York: Oxford University Press.

Arquilla, John & David Ronfeldt (2001). The advent of netwar (revisited). In John Arquilla & David Ronfeldt (eds.), *Networks and Netwars* (pp. 1–25). Santa Monica, CA: RAND.

Arreguin-Toft, Ivan (2001). How the weak win wars: A theory of asymmetric conflict. *International Security* 26(1), 93–128.

Arreguin-Toft, Ivan (2005). *How the Weak Win Wars: A Theory of Asymmetric Conflict.* Cambridge, UK: Cambridge University Press.

Bakker, René M., Jörg Raab, & H. Brinton Milward (2011). A preliminary theory of dark network resilience. *Journal of Policy Analysis and Management* 31(1), 33–62.

Barabási, Albert-László (2002). *Linked: The New Science of Networks.* Cambridge, MA: Perseus Publishing.

Barabási, Albert-László & Reka Albert (1999). Emergence of scaling in random networks. *Science* 286, 509–512.

Barabási, Albert-László, Reka Albert, & Hawoong Jeong (1999). Mean-field theory for scale-free random networks. *Physica A* 272, 173–187.

Barabási, Albert-László & Eric Bonabeau (2003). Scale-free networks. *Scientific American* 288(5), 60–69.

Berman, Eli (2009). *Radical, Religious, and Violent: The New Economics of Terrorism.* Cambridge, MA: The MIT Press.

Bienenstock, Elisa Jayne & Phillip Bonacich (2003). Balancing efficiency and vulnerablity in social networks. In Ron Breiger, Kathleen M. Carley, & Philippa Pattison (eds.), *Dynamic Social Network Modeling and Analysis: Workshop Summary and Papers* (pp. 253–264). Washington, DC: National Academy of Sciences/National Research Council: National Academies Press.

Borgatti, Stephen P. (2006). Identifying sets of key players in a social network. *Computational, Mathematical and Organizational Theory* 12, 21–34.

Borgatti, Stephen P. , Martin G. Everett, & Linton C. Freeman (2011). *UCINET for Windows: Software for Social Network Analysis*. Lexington, KY: Analytical Technologies.

Breiger, Ron, Kathleen M. Carley, & Philippa Pattison (eds.). (2003). *Dynamic Social Network Modeling and Analysis: Workshop Summary and Papers*. Washington, DC: National Academy of Sciences/National Research Council: National Academies Press.

Burns, Tom & G.M. Stalker. (1961). *The Management of Innovation*. London: Tavistock.

Carley, Kathleen M. (2001–2011). *Organizational Risk Analyzer (ORA)*. Pittsburgh, PA: Center for Computational Analysis of Social and Organizational Systems (CASOS): Carnegie Mellon University.

Carley, Kathleen M. (2003). Dynamic network analysis. In Ron Breiger, Kathleen Carley, & Philippa Pattison (eds.), *Dynamic Social Network Modeling and Analysis: Workshop Summary and Papers* (pp. 133–145). Washington, DC: National Academy of Sciences/National Research Council: National Academies Press.

Carley, Kathleen M. (2006). A dynamic network approach to the assessment of terrorist groups and the impact of alternative courses of action. *Visualizing Network Information Meeting Proceedings RTO-MP-IST-063*. Retrieved from www.vistg.net/documents/IST063_PreProceedings.pdf.

Carley, Kathleen M., Ju-Sung Lee, & David Krackhardt (2002). Destabilizing networks. *Connections* 24(3), 79–92.

Castells, Manuel (1996). *The Information Age: Economy, Society and Culture, Vol. I: The Rise of the Network Society*. Malden, MA: Blackwell Publishers.

Coleman, James S. (1964). *Introduction to Mathematical Sociology*. New York: Free Press.

de Nooy, Wouter (2011). Networks of action and events over time: A multilevel discrete-time event history model for longitudinal network data. *Social Networks* 33(1), 31–40.

de Nooy, Wouter, Andrej Mrvar, & Vladimir Batagelj (2011). *Exploratory Social Network Analysis with Pajek* (revised and expanded ed.). Cambridge, UK: Cambridge University Press.

Doreian, Patrick & F.N. Stockman (eds.). (1997). *Evolution of Social Networks*. Amsterdam: Gordon and Breach Publishers.

Enders, Walter & Xuejuan Su (2007). Rational terrorists and optimal network structure. *Journal of Conflict Resolution* 51(1), 33–57.

Everton, Sean F. (2012). *Disrupting Dark Networks*. Cambridge and New York: Cambridge University Press.

Freeman, Linton C. (1979). Centrality in social networks I: Conceptual clarification. *Social Networks* 1, 215–239.

Fridovich, David P. & Fred T. Krawchuck (2007). Special operations forces: Indirect approach. *Joint Forces Quarterly* 44(1), 24–27.

Granovetter, Mark (1973). The strength of weak ties. *American Journal of Sociology* 73(6), 1360–1380.

Granovetter, Mark (1974). *Getting a Job*. Cambridge, MA: Harvard University Press.

Granovetter, Mark (1983). The strength of weak ties: A network theory revisited. *Sociological Theory* 1, 201–233.

Hamilton, Lawrence C. (1996). *Data Analysis for Social Scientists*. Belmont, CA: Duxbury Press.

Hamilton, Lawrence C. (2009). *Statistics with Stata: Updated for Version 10*. Belmont, CA: Brooks/Cole.

Helfstein, Scott & Dominic Wright (2011). Covert or convenient? Evolution of terror attack networks. *Journal of Conflict Resolution* 55(5), 785–813.

Hoivik, T. & N.P. Gleditsch (1975). Structural parameters of graphs: A theoretical investigation. In H.M. Blalock (ed.), *Quantitative Sociology* (pp. 203–222). New York: Academic Press.

Holland, Paul W. & Samuel Leinhardt (1971). Transitivity of structural models of small groups. *Comparative Group Studies* 2, 107–124.

Hu, Daning, Siddharth Kaza, & Hsinchun Chen (2009). Identifying significant facilitators of dark network evolution. *Journal of the American Society for Information Science and Technology* 60(4), 655–665.

International Crisis Group (2006). *Terrorism in Indonesia: Noordin's Networks*. Brussels, Belgium: International Crisis Group.

International Crisis Group (2009). *Indonesia: Noordin Top's Support Base*. Brussels, Belgium: International Crisis Group.

Kenney, Michael (2007). *From Pablo to Osama: Trafficking and Terrorist Networks, Government Bureaucracies, and Competitive*

Adaptation. University Park: Pennsylvania State University Press.

Klerks, Peter (2001). The network paradigm applied to criminal organisations: Theoretical nitpicking or a relevant doctrine for investigators? Recent developments in the Netherlands. *Connections* 24(3), 53–65.

Koschade, Stuart (2006). A social network analysis of Jemaah Islamiyah: The applications to counterterrorism and intelligence. *Studies in Conflict & Terrorism* 29, 559–575.

Kossinets, Gueorgi & Duncan J. Watts (2006). Empirical analysis of an evolving social network. *Science* 311, 88–90.

Krackhardt, David (1992). The strength of strong ties: The importance of philos in organizations. In Nitin Nohria & Robert G. Eccles (eds.), *Networks and Organizations: Structure, Form and Action* (pp. 216–239). Boston: Harvard University Press.

Krackhardt, David (1994). Graph theoretical dimensions of informal organizations. In Kathleen M. Carley & Michael J. Prietula (eds.), *Computational Organization Theory* (pp. 89–111). Hillsdale, NJ: L. Erlbaum Associates.

Krawchuck, Fred T. (n.d.). Winning the Global War on Terrorism in the Pacific region: Special operations forces' indirect approach to success. Retrieved from http://igcc3.ucsd.edu/research/security/DACOR/presentations/krawchuk.pdf.

Krebs, Valdis (2001). Mapping networks of terrorist cells. *Connections* 24(3), 43–52.

Leenders, Roger Th. A.J. (1996). Evolution of friendship and best friendship choices. *Journal of Mathematical Sociology* 21(1–2), 133–148.

Lindelauf, Roy, Peter Borm, & Herbert Hamers (2009). Understanding terrorist network topologies and their resilience against distruption. *CentER Discussion Paper No. 85.*

McCloskey, Deirdre (1995). The insignificance of statistical significance. *Scientific American* April, 32–33.

McCulloh, Ian & Kathleen M. Carley (2011). Detecting change in longitudinal social networks. *Journal of Social Structure* 12(3). Retrieved from www.cmu.edu/joss/content/articles/volume12//McCullohCarley.pdf.

Milward, H. Brinton & Jörg Raab (2006). Dark networks as organizational problems: Elements of a theory. *International Public Management Journal* 9(3), 333–360.

Morselli, Carlo & Julie Roy (2008). Brokerage qualifications in ringing operations. *Criminology* 46(1), 71–98.

Nohria, Nitin & Robert G. Eccles (eds.). (1992). *Networks and Organizations: Structure, Form, and Action.* Boston: Harvard Business School Press.

Pescosolido, Bernice A. & Sharon Georgianna (1989). Durkheim, suicide, and religion: Toward a network theory of suicide. *American Sociological Review* 54(1), 33–48.

Podolny, Joel M. & Karen L. Page (1998). Network forms of organization. In *Annual Review of Sociology 1998* (pp. 57–76). Palo Alto, CA: Annual Reviews, Inc.

Powell, Walter W. (1985). Hybrid organizational arrangements: New form or transitional development. *California Management Review* 30(1), 67–87.

Powell, Walter W. (1990). Neither market nor hierarchy: Network forms of organization. In Barry M. Staw & L.L. Cummings (eds.), *Research in Organizational Behavior: An Annual Series of Analytical Essays and Critical Reviews* (pp. 295–336). Greenwhich, CT: JAI Press, Inc.

Powell, Walter W. & Laurel Smith-Doerr (1994). Networks and economic life. In Neil J. Smelser & Richard Swedberg (eds.), *The Handbook of Economic Sociology* (pp. 368–402). Princeton, NJ: Princeton University Press.

Raab, Jörg & H. Brinton Milward (2003). Dark networks as problems. *Journal of Public Administration Research and Theory* 13(4), 413–439.

Rapoport, Anatole (1953a). Spread of information through a population with socio-structural bias I: Assumption of transitivity. *Bulletin of Mathematical Biophysics* 15(4), 523–533.

Rapoport, Anatole (1953b). Spread of information through a population with socio-structural bias II: Various models with partial transitivity. *Bulletin of Mathematical Biophysics* 15(4), 535–546.

Rapoport, Anatole & W.J. Horvath (1961). A study of a large sociogram. *Behavioral Science* 6, 279–291.

Roberts, Nancy & Sean F. Everton (2011). Strategies for combating dark networks. *Journal of Social Structure* 12(2). Retrieved from www.cmu.edu/joss/content/articles/volume12//RobertsEverton.pdf.

Rodriguez, Jose A. (2005). The March 11th terrorist network: In its weakness lies its strength. *EPP-LEA Working Papers*. Retrieved from http://citeseerx.ist.psu.edu/viewdoc/summary?doi=10.1.1.98.4408.

Ronfeldt, David & John Arquilla (2001). What next for networks and netwars? In John Arquilla & David Ronfeldt (eds.), *Networks and Netwars* (pp. 311–361). Santa Monica, CA: RAND.

Sageman, Marc (2003). Statement to the National Commission on Terrorist Attacks upon the United States. Retrieved from www.9-11commission.gov/hearings/hearing3/witness_sageman.htm.

Sageman, Marc (2004). *Understanding Terror Networks*. Philadelphia, PA: University of Pennsylvania Press.

Saxenian, AnnaLee (1994). *Regional Advantage: Culture and Competition in Silicon Valley and Route 128*. Cambridge, MA: Harvard University Press.

Saxenian, AnnaLee (1996). Inside-out: Regional networks and industrial adaptation in Silicon Valley and Route 128. *Cityscape: A Journal of Policy Development and Research* 2(2), 41–60.

Scott, John (2000). *Social Network Analysis: A Handbook* (2nd ed.). Thousand Oaks, CA: Sage Publications.

Snijders, Tom A.B. (1981). The degree variance: An index of graph heterogeneity. *Social Networks* 3, 163–174.

Snijders, Tom A.B. (2005). Models for longitudinal network data. In Peter J. Carrington , John Scott, & Stanley Wasserman (eds.), *Models and Methods in Social Network Analysis* (pp. 215–247). New York: Cambridge University Press.

Snijders, Tom A.B., Gerhard G. van de Bunt, & Christian Steglich (2010). Introduction to stochastic actor-based models for network dynamics. *Social Networks* 32(1), 44–60.

Stark, Rodney (1987). How new religions succeed: A theoretical model. In David G. Bromley & Phillip E. Hammond (eds.), *The Future of New Religious Movements* (pp. 11–29). Macon Georgia: Mercer University Press.

Stark, Rodney (1996). Why religious movements succeed or fail: A revised general model. *Journal of Contemporary Religion* 11, 133–146.

Stark, Rodney (2005). *The Rise of Mormonism*. Edited by Reid L. Nielson. New York: Columbia University Press.

Stark, Rodney (2007). *Sociology* (10th ed.). Belmont, CA: Wadsworth Publishing Company.

Steglich, Christian, Tom A.B. Snijders, & Michael Pearson (2010). Dynamic networks and behavior: Separating selection from influence. *Sociological Methodology* 40(1), 329–393.

Tilly, Charles (2004). Trust and rule. *Theory and Society* 33, 1–30.

Tilly, Charles (2005). *Trust and Rule*. Cambridge and New York: Cambridge University Press.

Tsvetovat, Maksim & Kathleen M. Carley (2005). Structural knowledge and success of anti-terrorist activity: The downside of structural equivalence. *Journal of Social Structure* 6(2). Retrieved from www.cmu.edu/joss/content/articles/volume6/TsvetovatCarley/index.html.

Tucker, David (2008). Terrorism, networks and strategy: Why the conventional wisdom is wrong. *Homeland Security Affairs* 4(2), 1–18. Retrieved from www.hsaj.org.

US Army (2007). *U.S. Army/Marine Counterinsurgency Field Manual (FM 3-24)*. Old Saybrook, CT: Konecky & Konecky.

Uzzi, Brian (1996). The sources and consequences of embeddedness for the economic performance of organizations: The network effect. *American Sociological Review* 61(4), 674–698.

Uzzi, Brian (2008). A social network's changing statistical properties and the quality of human innovation. *Journal of Physics A: Mathematical and Theoretical* 41, 1–12.

Uzzi, Brian & Jarrett Spiro (2005). Collaboration and creativity: The small world problem. *American Journal of Sociology* 111(2), 447–504.

Wasserman, Stanley & Katherine Faust (1994). *Social Network Analysis: Methods and Applications*. Cambridge, UK: Cambridge University Press.

Xu, Jie, Daning Hu, & Hsinchun Chen (2009). The dynamics of terrorist networks: Understanding the survival mechanisms of global Salafi Jihad. *Journal of Homeland Security and Emergency Management* 6(1), Article 1.

Ziliak, Stephen T. & Deirdre N. McCloskey (2008). *The Cult of Statistical Significance*. Ann Arbor: The University of Michigan Press.

CHAPTER 17

Understanding Transnational Crime in Conflict-Affected Environments

The Democratic Republic of the Congo's Illicit Minerals Trading Network

Georgia Lysaght

Transnational crime (TNC) networks are difficult to chart due to their flat and flexible structures, which continually adapt to the changing external environment. Unlike traditional organized crime groups, these networks are often spatially protracted, organized around multiple non-linear hierarchies, and linked by weak ties. Elements of TNC networks inevitably intersect with conflict-affected environments, which typically feature a fragile state apparatus; weak rule of law; high levels of civilian-directed violence and underdevelopment; and an unstable security environment.[1] Such conditions render these regions particularly vulnerable to the most labor-intensive processes associated with TNC, or the "dirty end" of the supply chain—for example, the mining and transport of raw conflict minerals, opium poppy cultivation, and overland cocaine trafficking. The conflict landscape houses a complex set of relationships between actors who are involved in both militant and illicit activities. The lines between illicit and licit are further blurred when civilians who do not fit the "deviant" or "belligerent" character typically associated with traditional understandings of criminal activity are compelled or coerced to participate. In Afghanistan, for example, opium poppy is cultivated almost exclusively by peasant farmers, who sell their crops to local traders, who on-sell the product to larger-scale opium traf-

fickers, and later the product is turned into heroin. The environment offers a crude choice to cultivate this illicit crop or risk starvation, thus making the label of "criminal" difficult to stick and challenging the orthodox counter-narcotics strategies of national and international forces. The illicit minerals trading network centered around the conflict-affected environment of the Democratic Republic of the Congo (henceforth DRC), the topic of this chapter, is similarly complex.

Research approaches to the subject of violent protracted conflict in DRC and other areas of sub-Saharan Africa largely focus upon the relationships between the prominent state, sub-state and non-state actors; the role of the international community in its purported attempts to mitigate the conflict (Autesserre, 2010); and the phenomena of so-called ethnic conflict and intra-state war. Within this framework, the literature commonly seeks to identify a driver or set of drivers underpinning the conflict.[2] For example, Camm (2011) argues that longstanding tribal land ownership disputes weathered by colonization, decolonization, and then nationalization (under Mobutu) have clearly played an enduring role in eastern DRC's (and also Rwanda, Uganda, and Burundi's) instability. Quinn, on the other hand, focuses upon the political-economic framework of the region, and the legacy of post-colonial and post-cold war regional ethnic conflict in the era of a western pro-democracy agenda advanced in the developing world primarily by international financial institutions (Quinn, 2004). Gondola's historical account proposes an international politicization of DRC's vast mineral wealth and the employment of neo-colonial strategies by western government to ensure continued access. Implicit in this is the intentional erosion of DRC's domestic political system (Gondola, 2002). Nest (2011) also provides an exacting empirical account of the interests surrounding Congolese coltan (or tantalum), while Dunn (2003) and Braekman (2003) articulate in detail the violence employed by various DRC and Rwandan militant groups in their pursuit of eastern DRC minerals. As argued by Nest, it is clear that the DRC conflict is multifaceted,[3] as are its drivers, and while the contestation over resources cannot be understood as the sole cause of violence, it certainly may be considered a key element. Thus the objective of this chapter is to better understand the relational dynamics and organizational structure of the illicit trading networks involved in the extraction, trafficking, and sale of minerals originating within DRC. The research will identify the key drivers within this network who in turn may be considered in part responsible for the continued violence and instability throughout DRC and the region.

The research undertaken for this study identified a vast group of key actors, all of whom are key participants in DRC's illicit minerals trading network, including local and international criminals, civilians/private citizens, businesses/corporations, and military/militant components. A particularly striking element of this illicit network and its interface with DRC's ongoing conflict is the extreme levels of sexual and gendered violence perpetrated against the civilian population as a weapon of war and control. A reported 45,000 civilian deaths a month are the result of violent conflict over DRC's notorious "lawless mines" (Journeyman Pictures, 2005). Upon

further examination of the networks that both underpin and promote the continuance of DRC's illicit mineral trade, a group that had previously received only limited attention emerged as central to the study. This is particularly evident through the examination of profit motive, proportion of conflict minerals in DRC, and pre-financing relationships. Thus, the research demonstrates that a small group of international companies—termed the "foreign importers"—who purchase the vast majority of minerals exported outside of DRC play a much more prominent driving role in the network than originally understood. The evidence also prompts questions about the relationship of foreign importers with violence and conflict in the region.

DATA AND METHOD

The data for this study are cultivated from three key reports: a 2009 report by Global Witness, the 2008 Final Report of the Group of Experts (GOE) in the Democratic Republic of the Congo (United Nations, 2008), and the 2009 Final Report of the Group of Experts on the Democratic Republic of the Congo (United Nations, 2009). Morselli (2009: 44) notes that

> once the parameters of a setting are clearly established, it is often a challenge to assess the extent to which individuals interacting within those parameters are missing. Thus, what social network researchers refer to as a "whole network" is rarely whole to begin with.

Indeed, collecting evidence presents a unique set of obstacles for researchers when navigating the illicit. Most obviously, illicit activity rarely appears, or is rarely recorded accurately, in official documents such as police and government records. This may be an inability of the agencies themselves to compile a complete dataset or, in some cases, a reluctance to compile a complete data if vested interests are at work. Interviews too may not produce a complete picture as respondents may be reluctant to provide accurate information for fear of personal security, compromising interests, or exposing incompetence. Yet these challenges do not necessarily render the research invalid or not worthwhile. On the contrary, interesting trends and indicators may emerge from research that has not begun with a "whole of network" picture. While the key reports for this study are not insulated from the aforementioned pitfalls common to researching illicit activity, data were collected through extensive sets of comprehensive field interviews, field observations, audio and video recordings, and private and government documents. The data have been corroborated and triangulated in an effort to produce information of sound accuracy. Furthermore, the key documents are considered highly reliable by a number of NGOs, international organizations, and scholars and researchers not aligned with either organization. In fact, the Group of Experts Report has formed the basis of many subsequent analyses about conflict minerals trading in the DRC. Importantly, for this research, the content of these reports includes: the names of private individuals, groups, and businesses found to be involved in DRC's conflict minerals trade; the names of militant groups and militant individuals (including the Congolese army) found to be involved in the conflict minerals trade; and the relationship between these groups.

In order to formulate a picture of the transnational trading network for conflict minerals of DRC origin, information about trading relationships between actors was extrapolated from the key reports and tabulated. The actors were then assigned a coded category, as demonstrated in Table 17.1, based upon their role in the minerals trade. Each actor was assigned a number within the category to differentiate them from one another. For example, the hypothetical actors Prince's Precious Stones Co. and Minerals Trading Co.[4] were both categorized as Trading Houses (THs) and then assigned the respective codes TH1 and TH2.

Table 17.1 Actor categories

Code	Category
AM	Artisanal Miners
FI	Foreign Importers
IT	International Traders
LT	Local Traders
MC	Militant Components
TH	Trading Houses
TT	Transit Traders

Although not finite, the categories capture the main elements of the trading network (explained in more detail in the following section) that geographically originates inside the mines with the Artisanal Miners (AM) and concludes on the international market with the Foreign Importers (FIs). The AM category appears only once, as it was not possible to individually chart the estimated 750,000 to 2 million AMs and their relationships with other individual actors in the network. However, the disparity in estimated figures is extensive, and necessitates further empirical research. The FI category includes all the FIs, or end users for this study, which were reported to have trading relationships with actors selling illicit DRC minerals. International Traders (ITs) are foreign-registered companies that run trading houses or manage trading operations inside as well as outside of DRC. The ITs were often reported to be responsible for some trading inside DRC and in part for organizing mineral purchases by FIs. Local Traders (LTs) represent the small-scale DRC traders (both individuals and small companies) who trade minerals between one another and also in the local marketplaces. It is this category that is comprised of individuals who are considered negociants. Because porters often are acting on behalf of local traders, or double as local traders themselves, they are also classified as LTs. Rebel, militia, and elements of the Congolese army constitute the Militant Component (MC) category, hence the term "Militant" to represent state and non-state elements. The key reports did provide some specific information about the relationships between particular named military and militia personnel and LTs and THs. These individuals were not considered as separate components but were placed under the umbrella of their military or militia group. Transit Traders (TTs) represent a distinct element of the network. These are trading houses located across the border from DRC in neighboring Rwanda, Tanzania, and Burundi. TTs import minerals trafficked across the border and export them to FIs in an effort to distance them as commodities of conflict origin. Finally, THs are also referred to as comptoirs in the discussion below and are comprised of the reported trading houses (of which in total there are some 40, although not all appear in the key reports) in DRC. Figure 17.1 represents a crude illustration of each category's position in the supply chain.

While virtually all actors' names are freely available in all three (and other) key reports, the purpose of this research is not a name-and-shame exercise; hence the employment of a coded set of categorizations. Rather, the research presents an analysis of the illicit trading relationships between private and militant components based in a violent conflict environment. A binary network analysis was conducted with the statement "trades with" to map the relationships between actors and determine the trading network. Note that "trades with" refers to an inferred or explicitly stated trading relationship in the GOE and Global Witness documents. In some cases, a relationship could not be proven but the report authors found compelling evidence to support its existence. Centrality measures: a) confirm the pervasiveness of military components in the minerals trade, and b) indicate potential sources of external pressure through pre-financed supply chains. The network analysis was undertaken using UciNet and NetDraw software.

Time and network factors pose two potential limitations to the analysis. First, the availability of reliable information for mineral trading in DRC is restricted to the years 2007 to 2009. Thus, the scope of the chapter can only present an analysis specific to these years; however, it may be considered broadly representative of longer network patterns. Second, the chapter does not include the final-end consumers (such as electronics manufacturers) as part of its analysis. Reliable

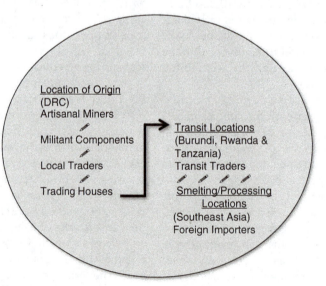

Figure 17.1 Example supply chain

data about trading relationships cannot be sourced at this point in time for this group and beyond. Therefore, the network presented in this chapter does not extend beyond the trade relationships of the FIs, who typically process the minerals before they are on-sold with minerals sourced from other countries to electronics (and other) manufacturers.

CONFLICT MINERALS AND LEGALITY

Deeming minerals illicit is a particularly difficult process because the actual commodity itself is not considered illegal. That is, commodities such as narcotics are necessarily recognized as illicit by virtue of their chemical composition, while to trade in minerals is not necessarily illegal. Yet widespread concern about the so-called blood diamond phenomenon, originating in Sierra Leone and Liberia, resulted in lobbying against the trade in conflict minerals by mainstream media, scholars, and NGOs. Thus, in recent years, the connection between illicitness and conflict minerals has gained international and national legal traction. In the United States, the Dodd-Frank Wall Street Reform and Consumer Protection Act was passed by Congress in July 2010. The Conflict Minerals section (1502) is a direct response to the extraction and trading of minerals originating in the DRC, a violent conflict environment. It contains a disclosure requirement for companies to undertake supply chain due diligence, and report to the Securities and Exchange Commission on whether their products contain conflict minerals. While the adequacy (or lack thereof) of Dodd-Frank 1502's requirements is widely debated, it nevertheless flags the United States' recognition that so-called "conflict minerals" are indeed illicit. Supported by the United Nations when it came into effect in 2000, the "Kimberley Process Certification Scheme" requires that rough diamonds sourced from non-conflict locations be certified before entering the international trading market. The intended outcome of these regulations is to create transparent supply chains that effectively prohibit consumer companies from purchasing conflict minerals. In turn, the sources are financially starved, which undermines the illicit network at its origin and provides an incentive for the creation of licit commodity networks in its place. Whilst noble, the complicating factors of conflict and poverty mean that a large percentage of the Congolese civilian population, an estimated 10 million people (Nest, 2011: 37), rely upon this trade for their livelihood—besides the artisanal miners and porters, a number of tributary enterprises have been set up around the mining sites, such as the sale of food and water to the miners and militants. While the debate about conflict mineral regulations is beyond the scope of this discussion, it is asserted here that minerals traded from the conflict zones of the DRC are considered illicit by the international community.

A HISTORY OF VIOLENT CONFLICT

DRC has one of the most turbulent histories of state-sponsored and civil violent conflict in the world, of which the details here are lacking and brief. In the mid-nineteenth century, the Congolese people were the target of Arab slave traders, and later King Leopold II's Forces Publique carried out incredible acts of violence against the population. In a contemporary context, the reign of dictator President Mobutu Sese Seko (1965–1997) inflicted large-scale violence and murders, while the so-called Congo Wars also resulted in an extreme civilian death toll. Bordering Uganda, Rwanda, Burundi, and the United Republic of Tanzania, Eastern Congo in particular remains a hotbed of political and "ethnic" tensions. Land and agricultural ownership has been continually contested by civilian groups and the Congolese state since the occupation of King Leopold's forces. In 1994, the Rwandan genocide sparked a mass exodus from the country across the border into Eastern Congo. Around

2 million Rwandan Tutsi and Hutu people fled in from the genocide and later from fear of the reprisals. DRC was subsequently host to a number of militia groups (originating from within DRC and also from bordering countries) who were opposed to a range of issues, including the authority of the central government, the ownership of land, and the control over resources—they waged conflict against the state, one another, and in particular, the civilian population. It is too simplistic to assert that the contemporary DRC conflict trajectory has shifted decidedly from a political one driven by greed for resources. The complexities underpinning a conflict of such scale, in terms of deaths and violence, and protraction, are beyond the scope of this study. Suffice to say here that the struggle for control over natural resources, in particular minerals, is a prominent feature of the conflict landscape.

The rise of the illicit minerals industry in DRC as a serious economy of scale may be marked from the beginning of the Second Congo War (also known as the Coltan War) in 1998. Officially, the war concluded in 2003; however, extreme violence and hostilities continue. Around 5.4 million people were killed as a result of conflict and associated poverty between 1998 and 2009. Sexual and gendered violence is the combatants' hallmark weapon of war, with groups from all sides, including the Forces démocratiques pour la liberation du Rwanda (FDLR, Democratic Forces of the Liberation of Rwanda) and the Congolese army (Forces armées de la République démocratique du Congo [FARDC, Armed Forces of the Democratic Republic of Congo]) carrying out systematic, wide-scale rapes. A research team from the International Food Policy Research Institute at Stony Brook University in New York and the World Bank found that around 1,152 women are raped in DRC every day (Adetunji, 2011). Complicit in such violence are the two strongest militant groups who control the vast cassiterite, coltan, wolframite, and gold deposits located

in the North and South Kivu areas of Eastern Congo: the FDLR and the Congolese army (the FARDC). The FDLR is a Rwandan Hutu militia group, the leaders of which allegedly played a central role in the 1994 Rwandan genocide. Fearing reprisals from the events of 1994, the FDLR crossed the border into the DRC and has remained a prominent group in the area. While the FARDC is stationed in eastern Congo to mitigate inter-militia hostilities, it plays a central role in the Congolese mining industry. Other militant groups active in the area include Congrès national pour la defence du people (CNDP), Patriotes resistants congolais (PARECO, Congolese Resistance Patriots), the Lord's Resistance Army (LRA, from Uganda), and other mai-mai.

DRC'S ILLICIT MINERAL NETWORK

Used in motherboards and other electronics, alloys, personal and industrial tools, ammunition, medical equipment, automobiles, and a host of other instruments, the level of DRC-originated minerals on the world market is significant. For example, Géraud de Ville (c. 2009) found that "an estimated 80% of the world's known coltan[5] supply is in Africa, and 80% of this is believed to be located in the DRC." This chapter does not focus on one particular mineral, rather it encompasses the four minerals traded in bulk out of DRC—that is, coltan, cassiterite, wolframite, and gold. Particularly because around 70% of DRC-sourced minerals are extracted and traded illicitly, the supply chain paths can vary considerably; however, with this is mind, a brief overview remains necessary. Typically, the mineral supply chain starts with extraction and moves through domestic tributaries, across the border, and then into the international market. Although AMs can purchase permits to extract the minerals, the arrangements vary from mine to mine. Various generals, commanders, and other militant personnel of rank often "own" a particular mine shaft. In these situations, AMs are met at the mine mouth by agents (many of whom work for militant components), who collect the minerals, allowing the miners to retain a small percentage as payment. At the mines, minerals (with the exception of gold) are loaded into 50 kg sacks and transported by porters out of the forest, where the mines are located, and onto transport, whether it be the planes at Walikale airstrip near Bisie mine, trucks, or cars. In areas where the MCs have been met with resistance by the local population, extreme violence, and in particular rape, is employed to coerce this labor force into working. Child labor is also commonplace on the mine sites. Between the mine and the point of export, minerals are sold and re-sold by as much as six times by a series of LTs (some individuals from the MC category also act as LTs and some LTs have a direct relationship with individuals from the MC category), some of whom are known as negociants, between each other or at small local markets, and then reach the main THs, or comptoirs, of Goma and Bukavu. This loosely describes the DRC supply network. Minerals are then generally smuggled across the border, mostly by ITs, into neighboring Burundi, Rwanda, and Tanzania, and sold onto FIs for processing. It is sometimes difficult to conclusively determine the operational location(s) of the FIs as they are often large and transnational in nature, with various subsidiaries, mother-houses, operations houses, managers, and shareholders all in different parts of the world.[6] In the processing and smelting houses, DRC minerals are mixed with minerals from other sources and then sold on to manufacturing companies, and then onto the retail market.

Based around the mines, the MCs (primarily FDLR and FARDC) form the virtual starting point of the supply network, which operates DRC's illicit mineral trade. On a day-to-day basis, these groups cooperate, even sharing roads, trucks, and planes to move the minerals that are extracted by the AM force. However, contestation over mine "ownership" is common and often involves fighting, resulting in wide-scale militant and civilian deaths. As previously stated, it is often assumed that these domestic networks are the driving forces that shape the conflict landscape in the vying for access to profits from export onto the international market. The comptoirs or THs in particular have been subject to scrutiny, as they represent the final resting place of minerals in DRC before they are trafficked to transit countries and/or released into international circulation. The comptoirs are a source of legitimacy for FIs wising to remain distanced from the illicitness of the industry and networks that control it. FIs have often claimed that, because the comptoirs that supply their minerals are legitimate businesses registered with the DRC government, they are assured that the product has originated from a conflict-free DRC mining site. The comptoirs themselves too claim that they do not knowingly source minerals from conflict areas. The aforementioned Global Witness Report wrote to a number of comptoirs to ask how they ensured their minerals were conflict-free and that they were not fueling violence: "Representatives of several comptoirs claimed that they could not know exactly where minerals came from, as it was not possible to distinguish minerals from different sites, and that minerals from different locations were often mixed together before reaching them" (Global Witness, 2009: 56). However, Global Witness also reported that the businesspeople managing these comptoirs "have extensive networks of contacts in the mining areas of both provinces and use local agents to visit the mining sites and trading centres" (Global Witness, 2009: 56). Furthermore, the Group of Experts Report (United Nations, 2008: 20) states that

many negociants have told the Group that comptoirs need to know where the product comes from, as the ore content carries from one area to the next. In addition, these buying houses are aware of the presence of armed groups, as their taxation often drives prices higher. In practice, many comptoirs work with preferred negociants who they know and trust, pre-financing their activities. These negociants have often developed close relationships with FDLR at mining sites.

While FIs are not necessarily looked upon favorably, they are often rendered peripheral in the greed and grievance style rhetoric framing debates around the drivers of conflict and criminal networks. They are considered benefactors, irresponsible ones at that, of a conflict and illicit activity from which they are removed. Often, FIs are profiled in the research as a group of self-interested actors that should "know better," and who indirectly provide capital to belligerent groups and thus by extension fuel violent conflict. Yet this appraisal ultimately displaces the FIs as end-users who sit outside the direct domestic trading and border smuggling networks. Such a position also allows FIs to maintain a moral and legal distance, and a marked lack of directness, from the illicitness of the minerals that they purchase. As stated previously, FIs tend to claim their purchases are legitimate as they are sourced from registered comptoirs, while others attribute responsibility to the Congolese government. In a communication with Global Witness, one FI argued that it was the "exclusive responsibility of the Congolese state" to ensure that all minerals exported outside the country were conflict-free, not the responsibility of the importer (Global Witness, 2009: 64). Yet a number of factors, discussed in the following section, strongly suggest that FIs, first, are acutely aware of the origin of the conflict minerals they import and, second, are more integrated into the illicit trading network as pivotal, not peripheral, actors than what has initially been understood.

TNC mappings involving natural resource extraction in conflict-affected environments have conventionally conceptualized both the greed of warring militant parties and vested domestic (and to an extent foreign) political interests as the key drivers underpinning the illicit minerals trading network (see, for example, Mantz, 2008). Private external companies and corporations are understood as beneficiaries of low-cost products who inadvertently at best, or inconsiderately at worst, fuel the conflict by providing capital and profits. However, network-based evidence suggests that TNC networks are not necessarily formed nor function in this way. For example, the position of West Africa as a transit region for cocaine trafficking over the last decade demonstrates that drivers outside the West Africa-located network (namely cocaine producers in Colombia and cocaine retailers in western Europe) play a pivotal role in driving the illicit supply chain. The implications for conflict and violence were understood by then UNODC-chief Maria Antonio Costa, who in 2009 stated that "West Africa is under attack, from within and especially from aboard" (United Nations Office on Drugs and Crime, 2009: 30). Other international agencies too are starting to recognize the levity of such activity and the influence that it may have upon protracted conflicts as external actors strive to keep the controllers of resources and land intact. Network analysis allows us to re-think the impacts of relationships between actors regardless of geographic distance or stage in the supply chain. Such a proposition reconfigures our understanding of this illicit trading network, the driving forces that shape it, and, by extension, the elements underpinning violent conflict in DRC. By no means are the MCs, negociants, and comptoirs benign actors manipulated into procuring conflict minerals for FIs; however, nor are the FIs insulated from the domestic network. The next section will consider profit motive, proportion of conflict minerals in DRC, and pre-financing relationships to further analyze the role of FIs in the network.

FIS: PERIPHERAL OR PIVOTAL TO THE NETWORK?

A profit motive may be utilized to determine in part those actors most invested in maintaining a particular supply chain. DRC minerals can often be purchased at a lower than market price because of the low costs associated with exploitative labor (or in some cases forced labor), cash transactions, and tax evasion of illicit minerals trading. Nest's (2011: 59) discussion on this topic underscores the high level of profits that actors outside of the DRC yield from the trade of DRC coltan, the vast majority of which is extracted and traded illegally. In terms of profit, the MCs only receive around 1% of the global profit from the trade and in fact domestic revenue only stands at around 12%. However, international minerals brokerage firms, processors, and capacitor manufacturers derive 14%, 27%, and 46%, respectively, accounting for 87% of profit in total (Nest, 2011). The seemingly inequitable ratio of labor to profit and the significance of vested interests outside the country of origin in this illicit trading network is not wholly unique to the DRC. "Producer" or "origin" zones for commodities that are illicitly traded on a transnational scale are commonly located in conflict-affected environments and in the developing world. For example, only $1 billion or 2% of the $50 billion annual profit derived from the trade of opium and heroin of Afghan origin is earned by the cultivators—the Afghan farmers. The small-time Afghan traffickers fare a little better, receiving around a 5% share of the $50 billion, while corrupt officials and other traffickers also retain a modest portion of the profits (United Nations Office on Drugs and Crime, 2010). However, large-scale illicit "retailers" in the consumption countries of the developed world retain the lion's share of the profit. While much important critical research has been conducted on the political and domestic economic relationships at play—between farmers, traffickers, the Taliban, the Afghan state, international counter-narcotics programs, and western state interests (see, for example, Felbab-Brown, 2009; Peters, 2010)—much less attention is afforded to the external commercial actors, specifically the heroin "retailers," as drivers of illicit trading and conflict. If profit proves an important indicator of vested interests, then ensuring conditions in the origin location are kept intact would also be of primary significance to the FIs in the cases of DRC, Afghanistan, and other conflict-affected environments that operate as "producer" or "origin" zones.

Second, FIs and TTs create distance from the network by claiming that minerals sourced from the DRC originate from non-conflict areas. This claim is disputed because, first, local traders often sell a mix of conflict and non-conflict minerals and, second, the overwhelming majority of DRC minerals originate from areas of conflict. Due to the absence of formal reporting on conflict-minerals in-country, as is typical of all illegally traded commodities, the precise accuracy of figures may be questioned; however, it may be concluded that the illicit minerals industry in DRC is indeed representative of an economy of scale. The United Nations Transnational Organized Crime Threat Assessment (United Nations Office on Drugs and Crime, 2010) estimates around $130 million worth of cassiterite is trafficked out of DRC every year. According to research conducted by a documentary team, this constitutes around 70% of total cassiterite mined and exported (Journeyman Pictures, 2005). Similar proportions exist for coltan, whilst reliable figures on wolframite are more difficult to obtain. However, the Group of Experts sourced a 2009 DRC Report estimating around "40 tonnes, or $1.24 billion of gold, is smuggled out of the Democratic Republic of the Congo each year" (United Nations, 2009: 32). The Group conducted further research and concluded that on the basis of that figure and other interviews, the Group estimates that armed groups, in particular, FDLR, may derive several million dollars of revenues each year from the trade, which therefore represents one of the most significant avenues of direct financing.

(United Nations, 2009: 72)

Figures 17.2 and 17.3 represent the trading data collected from the three key reports. MC1 and MC2 yielded the highest centrality scores, suggesting that most DRC minerals are sourced, or pass through, areas of conflict. ITs and THs also feature prominently, particularly those who were listed by the Group of Experts as being largely responsible for trading in conflict minerals. Large-scale FIs of DRC minerals, as is indicated in the centrality analyses, reflecting supply chains from AMs, to MCs, to LTs, to THs, to ITs, to TTs, to FIs, will unavoidably purchase from areas of conflict. Thus the argument by FIs that they are unaware of whether their purchases are from a conflict area or not must be met with

cynicism considering the proportional scale of such operations in DRC. Figure 17.2 also demonstrates that there are some variational instances of FIs purchasing directly from THs, bypassing ITs and TTs.

The profit motive and proportion of conflict minerals provide compelling evidence to suggest that FIs are readily aware of from where and under what conditions these DRC purchases are sourced. Yet actors from the FI category continue to insist upon a marked lack of direct connection to the domestic networks and, by extension, violence operating in DRC around these minerals. However, the Group of Experts collected evidence from field interviews that revealed "some of the foreign companies pre-finance their 'own' comptoirs [THs], in other words, acknowledging a chain of financing that flows from the foreign companies down to the FDLR-controlled mining pit" (United Nations, 2008: 20). Global Witness confirmed that this was also the case for pre-financing that started with foreign

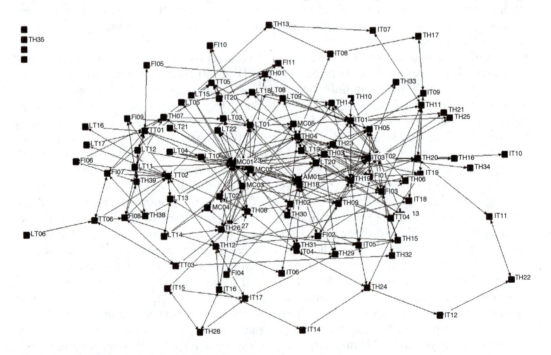

Figure 17.2 Centrality, DRC illicit minerals trading network

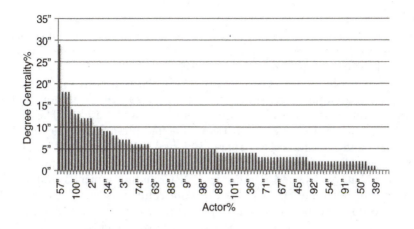

Figure 17.3 Degree centrality, DRC illicit minerals trading network

companies and flowed down to FARDC-controlled mining pits, asserting that "some of these foreign companies are also using suppliers who buy minerals produced by the FARDC" (Global Witness, 2009: 61). However, neither report went on to demonstrate potential pre-financed networks. By using one of the FIs named by the Group of Experts as a pre-financer as a start point, the data extracted and tabulated using the "trades with" relationship revealed the set of actors involved in one particular pre-financed network. While this does not draw upon specific pre-financing records (i.e., Actor A pre-finances Actor B), it demonstrates the relationship of a pre-financer with other actors in the illicit minerals supply network. In the sample in Figure 17.4,

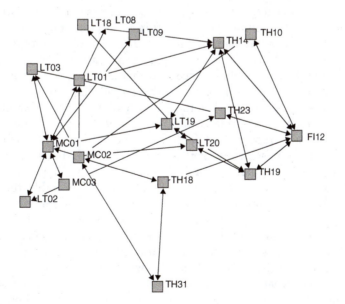

Figure 17.4 Potential FI-driven pre-financing network

FI12 (bold), a named pre-financier by the Group of Experts, demonstrates direct and indirect trading relationships across multiple stages of the supply chain. In this sense, the network is reconfigured as the FIs are placed not just as ignorant or opportunistic bystanders, but rather as key drivers of this illicit industry. It shows that, despite being located at the "end" of the supply chain, these actors remain very much central to the network and have a vested interest in keeping the arrangement intact. As stated in the previous section, this network can only be considered a potential network as it is based upon GOE and Global Witness documented trading relationships between 2007 and 2009. As businesses open and close, and relationships change, so too may the specific actors involved in this network.

CONCLUSION

Illicit minerals trading is comprised of a complex network with various sets of pressure points located within and external to the country in question, and at all stages of the supply chain. The sheer scale of death, violence, and profit associated with conflict minerals in the DRC necessitates a keen understanding of the actors implicated in this crisis. Network analysis facilitates a departure from identifying the significance of actors based upon their geographic centrality; instead, relational centrality is the primary indicator of an actor's role. Data extracted from the key reports provides important insights into the structure of the network and the relationship between militant, civilian, corporate domestic and foreign actors. Underpinned by a triumvirate of evidence regarding profit motive, proportion of conflict minerals in DRC, and pre-financing relationships, this chapter has argued that FIs play a far more significant role in DRC illicit minerals network than what has previously been understood. The data was employed to demonstrate the centrality of MCs in the

illicit trade of Congolese minerals and concluded that an overwhelming majority are of conflict origin. Therefore, on the basis of the scale of minerals purchased by FIs from the DRC, the argument made by FIs that minerals are sourced from non-conflict areas of DRC is highly fallible. The procurement of potential pre-financing networks reflects the pivotal role played by FIs, implicating this group in a highly integrated position with DRC conflict minerals trading and the violent conflict itself. Thus network analysis facilitates the process of redeploying actors that have remained conceptually peripheral, and connecting them directly to illicit trading and conflict.

Further research is required to drill down into the trading, and in particular pre-financing, networks to produce a more detailed understanding of what constitutes a very complex set of relationships. It is essential to understand those factors underpinning the illicit minerals trade in DRC as these factors also contribute significantly to conflict and violence in unstable environments. Hanneman's (2005) assertion that "ideally we will know about all of the relationships between each pair of actors in the population" is an aspiration most criminologists and researchers of the illicit agree is unobtainable. However, more primary research may be conducted so that as much as possible is known about the relationships between the actors. Further fieldwork interviews and the collection of official documents and company records would contribute to the existing knowledge base. This would serve to update the information in the key reports, which is for 2007 to 2009 only. Inevitably, the particular actors presented in this study may have changed, but it will be useful to observe whether or not the trading relationships between the actor categories have remained intact post-2009. It would also prove useful to collect further data on the concentration of miners in various areas. While the intent of this chapter is to present a broad canvas of an illicit minerals network, a more detailed analysis may be procured if a single mineral is considered in isolation. Each trading network associated with a single mineral type is accompanied with its own complex array of actors, participating in unique ways at each stage of the process. A network analysis solely of this area could also yield more specific results.

NOTES

1. These elements are not finite, rather they provide a loose descriptor of the key characteristics common to conflict-affected environments.
2. For contemporary literature on this subject that is not necessarily exclusive to Africa, see, for example, Collier and Hoeffler (2000); Kaldor (2006); Keen (2008); and Kalyvas (2006).
3. For a comprehensive account of the multifaceted elements of DRC's conflict and for a detailed analysis of the various theoretical approaches to this, see Turner (2007).
4. "Prince's Precious Stones Co." and "Minerals Trading Co." are fictitious entities and have been employed to explain part of the data and method process. At no point do the names of these entities appear in the key reports.
5. "Coltan" is more commonly known as tantalum on the world market. Coltan refers explicitly to tantalum sourced from DRC.
6. For examples of the various trading networks described, see de Ville (c. 2009); Nest (2011: 61); and United Nations (2009: Annex 52: 173).

REFERENCES

Adetunji, J. (2011). Forty-eight women raped in Congo every hour, study finds. *The Guardian*, 12 May.

Autesserre, S. (2010). *The Trouble with the Congo: Local Violence and the Failure of International Peacebuilding*. Cambridge: Cambridge University Press.

Braeckman, C. (2003). *Les Nouveaux Predateurs: Politique des Puissances en Afrique Centrale*. Paris: Fayard.

Camm, M. (2011). Conflict in Congo. *World Policy Journal* 28(4), 70–80.

Collier, P. & A. Hoeffler (2000). Greed and grievance in civil war. *Policy Research Working Paper 2355*, The World Bank Development Research Group.

de Ville, Géraud (c. 2009). An outline of trade flows of legally and illegally extracted mineral resources from fragile states: The case of coltan in the Kivus, DRC. Pathfinder Programme, Institute for Environmental Security.

Dunn, Kevin C. (2003). *Imagining the Congo: The International Relations of Identity*. New York: Palgrave Macmillan.

Felbab-Brown, V. (2009). *Shooting Up: Counterinsurgency and the War on Drugs*. Washington, DC: Brookings Institution Press.

Global Witness (2009). *Faced With Gun, What Can You Do? War and Militarisation of Mining in Eastern Congo*. London: Global Witness.

Gondola, Ch. Didier (2002). *The History of Congo*. Westport, CT: Greenwood Press.

Hanneman, R. (2005). Why formal methods? In Robert Hanneman & Mark Riddel (eds.), *Introduction to Social Network Methods* (Chapter 2). University of California, Riverside, CA (published in digital form at http://faculty.ucr.edu/~hanneman/).

Journeyman Pictures (2005). *Grand Theft Congo*, Ref 2705, www.journeyman.tv/18683/shortfilms/grand-theft-congo.html (accessed February 28, 2012).

Kaldor, M. (2006). *New and Old Wars: Organized Violence in a Global Era*. Cambridge: Polity Press.

Keen, D. (2008). *Complex Emergencies*. Cambridge: Polity Press.

Kalyvas, S. (2006). *The Logic of Violence in Civil War*. New York: Cambridge University Press.

Mantz, J.W. (2008). Improvisational economies: Coltan production in Eastern Congo. *Social Anthropology/Anthropologie Sociale* 16(1), 34–50.

Morselli, C. (2009). *Inside Criminal Networks*. New York: Springer.

Nest, M. (2011). *Coltan*. Cambridge: Polity Press.

Peters, G. (2010). *Seeds of Terror: How Drugs, Thugs, and Crime are Reshaping the Afghan War*. New York: Picador.

Quinn, J.J. (2004). Diffusion and escalation in the Great Lakes region: The Rwandan genocide, the rebellion in Zaire, and Mobutu's overthrow. In S.E. Lobell & P. Mauerci (eds.), *Ethnic Conflict and International Politics: Explaining Diffusion and Escalation* (pp. 111–131). Gordonsville, VA: Palgrave Macmillan.

Turner, T. (2007). *The Congo Wars: Conflict,*

Myth, and Reality. London and New York: Zed Books.

United Nations (2008). *Final Report of the Group of Experts on the Democratic Republic of the Congo*, S/2008/773.

United Nations (2009). *Final Report of the Group of Experts on the Democratic Republic of the Congo*, S.2009/603.

United Nations Office on Drugs and Crime (2009). *Transnational Trafficking and the Rule of Law in West Africa: A Threat Assessment*. Vienna: UNODC.

United Nations Office on Drugs and Crime (2010). *The Globalization of Crime: A Transnational Organized Crime Threat Assessment*. Vienna: UNODC.

Contributor Biographies

EDITOR

Carlo Morselli is a Professor at the École de criminologie, Université de Montréal and Deputy Director of the International Centre for Comparative Criminology. His research focuses on criminal networks and organized crime, with recent studies aimed specifically at illegal firearm markets, synthetic drug markets, collusion in the construction industry, and denunciation. In 2011, he was awarded the Outstanding Publication Award from the International Association for the Study of Organized Crime (IASOC) for his book *Inside Criminal Networks* (2009). He is also the author of *Contacts, Opportunities, and Criminal Enterprise* (2005) and a series of articles that have been published in *Criminology*; *Journal of Research in Crime and Delinquency*; *Critical Criminology*; *Crime, Law, and Social Change*; and *Social Networks*. Since 2011, he has served as the Editor-in-Chief for the journal *Global Crime*.

CONTRIBUTORS

Gisela Bichler is a Professor of Criminal Justice at California State University, San Bernardino and Director of the Center for Criminal Justice Research (CCJR). Her current research examines the structure of illicit networks associated with criminal enterprise groups, transnational illicit markets, terrorism, and corporate interlock. Recent publications have appeared in the *Journal of Research in Crime and Delinquency*, *Policing: An International Journal of Police Strategies and Management*, *Global Crime*, *Crime and Delinquency*, *Security Journal*, *Crime Patterns and Analysis*, and *Psychological Reports*.

Rémi Boivin is an Assistant Professor at the École de criminologie, Université de Montréal. His research interests include crime trends, crime analysis, drug trafficking, and police discretion.

Martin Bouchard is an Associate Professor of Criminology at Simon Fraser University and Associate Director Research of TSAS: The Canadian Network for Research on Terrorism, Security, and Society. His research focuses on the organization of illegal markets and the role of social networks in a variety of criminal phenomena connected to criminal careers and organized crime. His work has appeared in numerous prominent scientific journals in criminology, including *Journal of Quantitative Criminology*; *Journal of Research in Crime and Delinquency*; and *Justice Quarterly*. Dr. Bouchard is also the co-editor of two recent books focusing on criminal careers in illegal markets and organized crime (*Illegal Markets* *and the Economics of Organized Crime*, 2010; *World Wide Weed: Global Cannabis Cultivation and Its Control*, 2011).

Neil Boyd is an author and a Professor at Simon Fraser University, where he teaches courses related to law, crime, and criminal justice policy. He has worked on a wide variety of research projects and has written seven books for both national and international markets. His most recent book, *A Thousand Dreams,* is co-authored with former Vancouver mayor Senator Larry Campbell and Vancouver Sun writer Lori Culbert. It explores the social history and current realities of Vancouver's Downtown East Side, and was shortlisted for the Roderick Haig Brown Prize, the Donner Prize, and the Ryga Award. The fifth edition of his textbook, *Canadian Law,* was published by Thomson Nelson in 2010.

David A. Bright is a Lecturer in Criminology with the School of Social Sciences at the University of New South Wales, Australia. Prior to his current appointment, David was a Research Fellow at the National Drug and Alcohol Research Centre, where he worked on a number of research projects related to illicit drug policy. His current research interests include offender rehabilitation and treatment, offender recidivism, illicit drugs and crime, law enforcement effectiveness, criminal networks, and organized crime.

Francesco Calderoni is an Assistant Professor at the Faculty of Sociology at Università Cattolica del Sacro Cuore of Milan. He has also been a researcher at Transcrime since September 2005. His areas of interest are mafias, organized crime, illicit trade in tobacco products, organized crime legislation, and social network analysis. In 2010, he was awarded the Ambrosoli Prize by the Municipality of Milan for the best Ph.D. thesis, on the relationship among ethics, legality, and justice.

Peter J. Carrington is Professor of Sociology and Legal Studies at the University of Waterloo (Canada) and editor of *Canadian Journal of Criminology and Criminal Justice*. He is currently researching co-offending, criminal networks, and criminal careers. His work has recently been published in *Criminology, Canadian Journal of Criminology and Criminal Justice,* and *Criminal Justice Policy Review*. He is co-editor of *The SAGE Handbook of Social Network Analysis* (2011) and *Models and Methods in Social Network Analysis* (2005).

Eric Cheney is an Associate Professor of Sociology at Central Washington University. His research interests include social networks, economy and society, the sociology of deviance, and white-collar crime.

Dan Cunningham is a Research Associate in the Defense Analysis Department's CORE Lab at the Naval Postgraduate School in Monterey, where he also lectures on the visual analysis of dark networks. Dan earned his MA in International Policy Studies with a focus in Terrorism Studies at the Monterey Institute of International Studies in 2009. He has presented several papers on dark networks at conferences and is currently working on multiple publications.

David Décary-Hétu is a Ph.D. candidate at the School of Criminology of the University of Montreal. His Ph.D. dissertation focuses on the impact of new technologies on crime and the increasing importance of criminal reputation. He has published many papers on the subject of economic crimes, cybercrimes, and social network analysis, and has been invited to many international academic and non-academic conferences.

Benoit Dupont is the Director of the International Centre for Comparative Criminology at the Université de Montréal, where he also holds the Canada Research Chair in Security and Technology. He is the current President of the International Association of French Speaking Criminologists (2010–2014). His research focuses on two interconnected areas: 1) how security networks composed of public, private, and hybrid organizations exchange data, knowledge, and intelligence in order to deliver security to their constituents and to fight dark networks; 2) developing an empirical research program on the co-evolution of crime and technology, in order to understand how offenders adapt to and exploit new online tools to advance their objectives.

Sean Everton is an Assistant Professor at the Naval Postgraduate School and Co-Director of the Defense Analysis Department's CORE Lab. Prior to joining NPS in 2007, he was an Adjunct Professor at both Santa Clara University and Stanford University. Professor Everton earned his MA and Ph.D. in Sociology at Stanford University (2007) and wrote his doctoral thesis on the causes and consequences of status on the economic performance of venture capital firms. He has published articles in the areas of social network analysis, sociology of religion, economic sociology, and political sociology. He currently specializes in the use of social network analysis to track and disrupt dark networks and, in the fall of 2012, his monograph on using social network analysis to disrupt dark networks (*Disrupting Dark Networks*) was published by Cambridge University Press.

Robert R. Faulkner is a Professor of Sociology at the University of Massachusetts. He is the author of *"Do You Know…"? The Jazz Repertoire in Action*, with Howard S. Becker, and *Music on Demand: Composers and Careers in the Hollywood Film Industry*, a new edition by Transaction. He is also a jazz musician.

Francis Fortin works in the field of criminal investigations and intelligence. He is currently a Ph.D. candidate at the École de criminologie, Université de Montréal. His research focuses on cybercrime, criminal intelligence, data mining, and forensic analysis. He has published numerous scientific papers, including one book on cyberpedophiles (published by VLB) and another on cybercrime (published by PIP).

Richard Frank completed a Ph.D. in Computing Science at Simon Fraser University and is currently enrolled in the Ph.D. program in Criminology, also at SFU. Dr. Frank's main research interest is computational criminology—the application of computer solutions to model or solve crime problems. Cybercrime is another area where his two domains mix. Specifically, he is interested in hackers and security issues, such as online terrorism and warfare. Dr. Frank has recent publications at top-level data mining outlets, such as in Knowledge Discovery in Databases, and security conferences such as Intelligence and Security Informatics.

Andrea Giménez-Salinas Framis is a Lecturer in Criminology at the Universidad Autonoma de Madrid and Deputy Director of the Institute of Forensic Sciences and Security. She has been President of the Spanish Society of Criminological Research from 2010 to 2012. Her areas of interest are primarily in private and public security, terrorism financing, organized crime networks, and human trafficking.

Catherine Greenhill is a Senior Lecturer in the School of Mathematics and Statistics at the University of New South Wales. Her research is in the area of combinatorics, particularly graph theory. While most of her research has been purely theoretical, recently she has become interested in questions which arise from the study of real-world networks.

Natalia Iwanski is pursuing a Masters in Applied and Computational Mathematics at Simon Fraser University. Her main research interests include mathematical modeling, scientific computing, graph theory, and social network analysis. Her publications are in the areas of computational criminology, spatial crime analysis, and offender travel patterns.

Richard Konarski has been a member of the Royal Canadian Mounted Police (RCMP) since 1977. He has had a range of experience in Detachments throughout British Columbia, including RCMP's largest municipal Detachment in Surrey. He has worked in a variety of functions, including general duty policing, serious crime investigations, and polygraph. Richard is also a doctoral candidate at Simon Fraser University, writing his Ph.D. on risk assessment in domestic violence investigations. He has pursued integrating social network analysis into the day-to-day operations of policing. Richard is presently the Officer in Charge of the Mission RCMP Detachment.

Natalya Levenkova is a Ph.D. student in the School of Mathematics and Statistics at the University of New South Wales. Her research areas are graph theory and applications to contact and criminal networks.

Georgia Lysaght is a consultant in the fields of security, governance, and development and a former research fellow with the Centre for Transnational Crime Prevention, University of Wollongong. Her research has been primarily concerned with the implications of transnational crime for international peace operations in conflict-affected environments. Dr. Lysaght's current regions of interest include Afghanistan, West Africa, Central Africa, and Timor-Leste.

Aili Malm is an Associate Professor in the Department of Criminal Justice at California State University, Long Beach. Dr. Malm's research interests center on the intersection between policing and social policy. She is interested in both the assessment and evaluation of policing strategies and intelligence and integrating empirical evidence and theory to inform policy. In this capacity, her research makes use of social network analysis, spatial analysis, and textual analysis. Her peer-reviewed publications appear in *Journal of Research in Crime and Delinquency*, *Crime and Delinquency*, *Global Crime*, *Policy Science*, *Social Networks*, and others.

Jean Marie McGloin is an Associate Professor in the Department of Criminology and Criminal Justice at the University of Maryland. Her research interests include peer influence, co-offending, and offending specialization. Her recent work has appeared in *Criminology*, the *Journal of Research in Crime and Delinquency*, and *Justice Quarterly*.

Holly Nguyen is a doctoral student in the Department of Criminology and Criminal Justice at the University of Maryland. Her research interests include groups and crime, rewards from crime, and various aspects of illicit drug markets. Recent publications have appeared in *Criminology*, *Justice Quarterly*, and the *International Journal of Drug Policy*.

Andrew V. Papachristos is an Associate Professor in the Department of Sociology at Yale University. His research focuses on social networks, neighborhoods, street gangs, illegal gun markets, and interpersonal violence. Papachristos was awarded an NSF Early Career award to examine how violence spreads through high-risk social networks in four cities. His writing has appeared in *Foreign Policy, The American Journal of Sociology, The Annals of the American Academy of Social and Political Science, The American Journal of Public Health, The Journal of Urban Health, Criminology & Public Policy, Journal of Quantitative Criminology*, and several edited volumes and other peer-reviewed journals.

Andrea Schoepfer is an Assistant Professor at California State University, San Bernardino. She received her Ph.D. from the University of Florida in 2007. Her research interests include white-collar/corporate crime, criminological theory, and quantitative research methods.

Chris M. Smith is a Ph.D. candidate in the Department of Sociology at the University of Massachusetts Amherst. Her dissertation examines women in organized crime networks in Prohibition-era Chicago.

Sarah B. van Mastrigt is Associate Professor of Psychology and Behavioural Sciences at Aarhus University, Denmark. She received her Ph.D. from the Institute of Criminology at Cambridge University in 2008, where she carried out a large-scale study of co-offending patterns in England. Her core research interests concern co-offending, criminal networks, and psychological criminology. Her work has appeared in the *British Journal of Criminology, Justice Quarterly*, and a number of psychology journals.

Sheldon Zhang is Professor of Sociology at San Diego State University. His research interests include transnational organized crime, trafficking and smuggling of human beings, evaluation research, offender rehabilitation, and community reentry efforts. He has published and lectured extensively on these topics to both domestic and international audiences. He is the author/co-author of five books and edited volumes. His articles have appeared in journals such as *Criminology, British Journal of Criminology, Crime and Delinquency*, and *Research in Crime and Delinquency*.

Index

Note: The following abbreviations have been used – *f* = figure; *n* = note; *t* = table.

Custom Materials
DELIVER A MORE REWARDING EDUCATIONAL EXPERIENCE.

The Social Issues Collection

This unique collection features 250 readings plus 45 recently added readings for undergraduate teaching in sociology and other social science courses. The social issues collection includes selections from Joe Nevins, Sheldon Elkand-Olson, Val Jenness, Sarah Fenstermaker, Nikki Jones, France Winddance Twine, Scott McNall, Ananya Roy, Joel Best, Michael Apple, and more.

1 Go to the website at routledge.customgateway.com

2 Choose from almost 300 readings from Routledge & other publishers

3 Create your complete custom anthology